The Greatest of All The Prophets

Russell R. Standish   Colin D. Standish

Highwood Books
Narbethong, Victoria, Australia
2004

First published in Australia in 2004 by

Highwood Books
291 Maroondah Hwy
Narbethong
Vic 3778
Australia

Copyright © 2004 Russell R. Standish and Colin D. Standish

The National Library of Australia Cataloguing-in-Publication
Standish, Russell R.
    The greatest of all the prophets.

    Includes index.
    ISBN 9 20892494.

    1. White, Ellen G. (Ellen Gould), 1827-1915. 2.
    Seventh-Day Adventists - Doctrines. 3. Prophecy -
    Christianity. I. Standish, Colin D. II. Title.

Cover illustrator: Crystal Ward
Produced by Publishing Solutions Pty Ltd
Printed in the United States of America

This book is copyright. Apart from any fair dealing for the purposes of private study, research, criticism or review as permitted under the Copyright Act, no part may be reproduced by any process without the express written permission from the author.

Table of Contents

PART I
A Tragic History

Chapter
1. Who Was the Greatest Prophet? — 3
2. If One of Them — 6
3. The South Pacific Yet Again! — 10

PART II
Stratagems

4. February 2004 — 15
5. Stratagem I – Church Leaders Reassess Ellen White — 22
6. Stratagem II – Prophets Are Human — 30
7. Stratagem III – An Ellen White Reality Check — 44
8. Stratagem IV – Ellen White for Today — 49
9. Strategem V – Clear View — 62
10. Stratagem VI – Understanding the Gift — 72
11. Stratagem VII – Ministers' and Elders' Summits – Revelation, Inspiration and Ellen White — 77
12. Stratagem VIII – Editorial Comments on Letters — 94
13. Are Inspired Writings Sometimes Correct and Sometimes Incorrect? — 99

PART III
Conferences to Alter Faith

14. Conferences — 107
15. General Conference International Conferences — 113
16. The International Conference on Faith and Science, 2002 — 123
17. Did We Not Know? — 130

PART IV
Divine History

18. Sister White's Historical Selections — 137
19. Historical Accuracy — 145
20. Disparity Between the 1888 and 1911 *Great Controversy* Editions — 153
21. Administrators, Editors and Academics Evaluate the Spirit of Prophecy – The 1919 Bible Conference — 162
22. Doubts and More Doubts — 173
23. The Doubts Mount — 179
24. *The Great Controversy* Attacked — 188

Part V
The Health Message

25.	Sister White and Health	201
26.	Ticks and Crosses for God	208
27.	Self Abuse	220
28.	The Amalgamation of Man and Beast	226

Part VI
An Ineffective Ministry

29.	The Ministry and the Ellen White Reality Check	239
30.	The Current State of Our Ministry	249

Part VII
Was Sister White a Prophet?

31.	A Perceptive Woman	259
32.	A Turning Point in American History	266
33.	September 11	271
34.	Sister White's Twenty-First Century Prophecy	278
35.	Has Rome Changed?	288

Part VIII
The Remnant Church

36.	The Remnant	301
37.	The Sabbath and the Seal of God	310
38.	Sister White's Claims	316

Part IX
From Doubt to Trust

39.	Dispelling False Accusations	321
40.	Sister White's Health Practices	328
41.	If They Hear Not Moses	336
42.	Drifting Away From Bible Truth	343
43.	No Coherent Corpus of Belief	354
44.	The End Point	361
45.	Cities of Favor	371
46.	The T-Junction	378

Indexes

1.	Scriptural Index	391
2.	Spirit of Prophecy Index	396
3.	Index of Personalities	401
4.	Books Authored by Colin and Russell Standish	408

Part I
A Tragic History

1 Who Was the Greatest Prophet?

In 1979, Russell was itinerating in the north of Thailand with Dr. Dunbar Smith, the Medical Director of the Far Eastern Division. Russell was then the newly-appointed President of the Bangkok Adventist Hospital in the Thai capital city.

One of the great joys of denominational service was the camaraderie which existed between fellow-workers for God in the Mission Field. The same is true in self-supporting work. As we traveled together in the cause of our Lord we did not engage one another in small talk. Rather, the chief themes of our conversation were either "Discussion of the means to further pursue God's commission to spread His gospel to the billions of precious souls in Asia," or "The deeper matters of God's inspired Word, which He has graciously provided to us that we may find the path to heaven."

Dr. Smith was considerably senior in years to Russell. An American, he was an ordained minister who, following his ordination to the ministry, studied medicine. Russell's calling was in the reverse order. Although he did not possess the least anticipation in 1979 that he, too, would also have placed upon him the sacred responsibility of an ordained minister in addition to that of a medical missionary, however, on December 6, 1980, this transpired.

Prior to his appointment to the Far Eastern Division, Dr. Smith had held the same post in the Trans-African Division, which included the former British colonies in southern and eastern Africa.

The passage of time has dimmed Russell's memory of how the conversation between Dr. Smith and himself turned to the work of Sister Ellen White. But Russell will never forget the impact of a statement uttered by Dr. Smith. It was a thought which had never previously entered Russell's mind and which dominated his moments of contemplation for days ahead.

Dr. Smith proposed a conjecture. "Russ, I wonder if when we finally reach heaven we shall discover that Sister White was the greatest of all the prophets." Russell's thoughts did not match his response. He held Dr. Smith in too great respect to challenge this proposition. Yet in his mind many thoughts were traveling in rapid succession. These thoughts did not arise in neat articulation or well-crafted sentences. "Sister White greater than Jeremiah, Isaiah, Daniel? Surely not!" "What about John the Baptist?" "How can Dunbar even think this?" "Only God can judge this matter."

Yet, during the subsequent days, Dr. Smith's "outrageous" suggestion plagued Russell's thoughts. Russell emphatically concluded that neither Dr. Smith nor he himself, was appointed a judge in this matter. God alone declares such assessments. Russell well knew that there was not a single word of inspiration concerning Sister White which paralleled Christ's assessment of John the Baptist –

> For I say unto you, Among those that are born of women there is not a greater prophet than John the Baptist: (Luke 7:28).

> Verily I say unto you, Among them that are born of women there hath not risen a greater than John the Baptist: notwithstanding he that is least in the kingdom of heaven is greater than he. (Matthew 11:11).

Nevertheless, as Russell reviewed the work of Sister White during his contemplations, Dr. Smith's conjecture became less and less outrageous within his thoughts. God had raised up a prophet of the first magnitude in order to prepare the way for Christ's first advent. The thought entered Russell's mind, "Would God select a 'minor' prophet, in the last climactic days of the era of the Second Coming?" The mighty prophets of the antediluvian era, the exodus, the Babylonian destruction of Jerusalem, and the first advent of Christ, Noah, Moses, Jeremiah, and John the Baptist, respectively, certainly attested to the fact that in the critical eras of His church, God has raised prophets of mighty stature.

And now we are living in the most critical era of God's church in its history from Adam to the final conflict between Christ and Satan. It is little wonder that Sister White, the prophet of the end time, wrote twenty-five million words, likely to be considerably more than any other prophet. Her prophetic ministry covered seven decades, exceeding that of all other post-deluvian prophets except the apostle John and Daniel whose prophetic ministries also stretched for about seven decades. Her writings covered a vast array of spiritual themes, broader in their scope than even those of the prophet Moses. Nothing less was required in these final climactic days of earth's history, for, as never before, Satan, our adversary, is

> as a roaring lion ... seeking whom he may devour. (1 Peter 5:8).

Thus when God's prophetess of the last days comes under serious attack in the precious church of God, we believe it devolves upon us to rise up in her defense. Sister White is dead. She cannot defend herself. It showed little courage on the part of General Conference leaders to wait four years after Sister White's death before they launched into a decided denigration of her prophetic gift in 1919.

More years have passed – eighty-five, at the time of writing this manuscript – since that disgraceful denial of faith in 1919. In the South Pacific Division, at the present time, the spirit of rebellion against the inspired words of Sister White has reached unprecedented proportions.

One hundred and seven years ago, in 1897, also in Australia, false accusations were levelled against Sister White. In *Letter 98a*, Sister White wrote:

When man assails his fellow men, and presents in a ridiculous light those whom God has appointed to do work for Him, we would not be doing justice to the accusers, or to those who are misled by their accusations should we keep silent, leaving the people to think that their brethren and sisters, in whom they have had confidence, are no longer worthy of their love and fellowship.... And on every point the accusers should be called upon to bring their proof. Every charge should be carefully investigated; it should not be left in any uncertain way, the people should not be left to think that it may be or it may not be. The accusers should do all in their power to lift every sign of reproach that cannot be substantiated.... The people must not be left to believe a lie. They must be undeceived. The filthy garments with which the servant of God has been clothed must be removed.

(*Selected Messages*, Vol. 3, pp. 348, 349).

In this book we rise in response to this divine command.

2 If One of Them

Satan desired to destroy the ministry of John the Baptist. In Herod and his degraded and despicable de facto wife, Herodias, Satan found his allies to achieve his will.

But they did not bear this responsibility alone. Many civic leaders and likely some religious dignitaries in God's church of the First Advent shared the culpability.

When Salome, at the instigation of Herodias, her wicked mother, uttered the fearful words,

> ...I will that thou give me by and by in a charger the head of John the Baptist.
> (Mark 6:25)

not one of these leaders and members of God's church who were assembled at Herod's banquet offered a word of protest. Not one! All stood guilty of the murder of John the Baptist.

Notice Sister White's words. Please read them carefully:

> Herod was astonished and confounded. The riotous mirth ceased, and an ominous silence settled down upon the scene of revelry. The king was horror-stricken at the thought of taking the life of John. Yet his word was pledged, and he was unwilling to appear fickle or rash. The oath had been made in honor of his guests, and if one of them had offered a word against the fulfillment of his promise, he would gladly have spared the prophet. He gave them opportunity to speak in the prisoner's behalf. They had traveled long distances in order to hear the preaching of John, and they knew him to be a man without crime, and a servant of God. But though shocked at the girl's demand, they were too besotted to interpose a remonstrance. No voice was raised to save the life of Heaven's messenger. These men occupied high positions of trust in the nation, and upon them rested grave responsibilities; yet they had given themselves up to feasting and drunkenness until the senses were benumbed. Their heads were turned with the giddy scene of music and dancing, and conscience lay dormant. By their silence they pronounced the sentence of death upon the prophet of God to satisfy the revenge of an abandoned woman. (*Desire of Ages*, pp. 221, 222).

"If one of them"! Just one! One voice in that large crowd of men who "occupied high positions of trust in the nation," those men who "had travelled long distances in order to hear the preaching of John." Those men who well "knew him to be a man without crime, and a servant of God," those men who were "shocked by the girl's demand;" one voice alone was required to stay the execution of John, the prophet of the first advent, and sustain his godly witness.

We, as ordained ministers of the gospel, refuse to remain silent while God's last-day messenger, the prophet of the second advent, has her witness destroyed posthumously. We will raise our voices in her defense. We call upon every faithful layperson, every faithful pastor, every faithful church administrator, to rise up and do likewise, not because we have done so, but because God demands it. To remain silent in this era of crisis, is a sin of great magnitude.

> What astonishing deception and fearful blindness had, like a dark cloud, covered Israel! This blindness and apostasy had not closed about them suddenly; it had come upon them gradually as they had not heeded the word of reproof and warning which the Lord had sent to them because of their pride and their sins. And now, in this fearful crisis, in the presence of the idolatrous priests and the apostate king, they remained neutral. If God abhors one sin above another, of which His people are guilty, it is doing nothing in case of an emergency. Indifference and neutrality in a religious crisis is regarded of God as a grievous crime and equal to the very worst type of hostility against God.
> (*Testimonies for the Church*, Vol. 3, pp. 280, 281).

The last sentence of this passage is well known to many sincere Seventh-day Adventists. Less often is read the preceding words of the paragraph. Sister White is here referring to Elijah on Mount Carmel. We are informed that all Israel was present (1 Kings 18:19). This vast crowd clearly included the

> ...seven thousand in Israel, all the knees which have not bowed unto Baal....
> (1 Kings 19:18).

Yet when Elijah made his challenge to the people in the presence of King Ahab and the apostate prophets, the courage of these non-Baal worshipers apparently failed them for,

> ...the people answered him not a word. (1 Kings 18:21).

None, Elijah excepted, dared to raise his voice in defense of the faith, not one! Despite the fact that the passage quoted above from the Spirit of Prophecy refers to the spiritual crisis in Elijah's day, the title of the chapter clearly demonstrates that Sister White's focus is not upon God's church in the ninth century BC, but our church, for the title of the chapter is "The Laodicean Church." The message is for us.

Countless thousands of truth-believing Seventh-day Adventists in the 1950's, 1960's, 1970's and the 1980's, chose to remain silent when wolves determinedly attempted to demolish our faith by the inroads made by the New Theology into the body of doctrines delivered to the saints of God. The New Theology was promoted in our midst by College professors, church administrators and church pastors who deftly inserted it among us with subtle sophistries.

As at Herod's feast, when those who knew the holy credentials of John the Baptist remained silent, so did most Seventh-day Adventists, even daring to charge those who risked all and cared only for the integrity of God's truth, with being critical of the church. Such committed the fearful sin of neutrality and even hostility to God's truth, in a shameful crisis.

No position in the church organisation, or the local church, no fear of the destruction of reputation, no dread of ecclesiastical denunciation or ostracism, will stand as a valid excuse or will avail in the judgment. Remember,

> if one of them had offered a word against the fulfillment of his promise, he would gladly have spared the prophet.... Herod waited in vain to be released from his oath; (*Desire of Ages* pp. 221, 222).

In a church, one man, one woman who is filled with courage, can make a real difference. Just one! In AD.31 one man did stand alone in the midst of seventy and in so doing he saved the lives of the apostles Peter and John. His name was Gamaliel.

> So enraged were the Jews at these words that they decided to take the law into their own hands and without further trial, or without authority from the Roman officers, to put the prisoners to death. Already guilty of the blood of Christ, they were not eager to stain their hands with the blood of His disciples. But in the council there was one man who recognized the voice of God in the words spoken by the disciples. This was Gamaliel, a Pharisee of good reputation and a man of learning and high position. His clear intellect saw that the violent step contemplated by the priests would lead to terrible consequences. Before addressing those present, he requested that the prisoners be removed. He well knew the elements he had to deal with; he knew that the murderers of Christ would hesitate at nothing in order to carry out their purpose. He then spoke with great deliberation and calmness, saying: "Ye men of Israel, take heed to yourselves what ye intend to do as touching these men. For before these days rose up Theudas, boasting himself to be somebody; to whom a number of men, about four hundred, joined themselves: who was slain; and all, as many as obeyed him, were scattered, and brought to nought. After this man rose up Judas of Galilee in the days of the taxing, and drew away much people after him: he also perished; and all, even as many as obeyed him, were dispersed. And now I say unto you, Refrain from these men, and let them alone: for if this counsel or this work be of men, it will come to nought: but if it be of God, ye cannot overthrow it; lest haply ye be found even to fight against God." The priests saw the reasonableness of these views, and were obliged to agree with Gamaliel. (*Acts of the Apostles*, pp. 83, 84).

One man's voice had prevailed!

Notice that in the days of Elijah, God's church had gradually permitted itself to slide into apostasy. Faithful witnesses were ignored. Look at the words quoted above once more:

> This blindness and apostasy had not closed about them suddenly; It had come upon them gradually as they had not heeded the word of reproof and warning

which the Lord had sent to them because of their pride and their sins. And now, in this fearful crisis, in the presence of the idolatrous priests and the apostate king, they remained neutral. (*Testimonies for the Church*, Vol. 3, p. 281).

As a people in the twentieth century, we did not protest in support of our God-bestowed faith. We did not earnestly seek the Lord to preserve it. While a few pastors, administrators, theologians, evangelists and laymen, rose in its defense, they were marginalised by those who loved the sin-tolerant words of the New Theology. Others who still believed the truth, sat in cowardly silence lest they, too, be marginalized, covering their failure to defend the truth, by claiming loyalty to God's Church and an aim to keep the peace. Such conduct is disloyalty of the worst order. It is covert rebellion against God. It is sin of the greatest magnitude.

When gross apostasy entered the Christian Church in the fourth century, God had a faithful few who boldly and openly denounced the iniquity in the face of imprisonment, torture and death. These noble saints must be our example today.

To secure peace and unity they were ready to make any concession consistent with fidelity to God; but they felt that even peace would be too dearly purchased at the sacrifice of principle. If unity could be secured only by the compromise of truth and righteousness, then let there be difference, and even war.
(*Great Controversy*, p. 45).

3 The South Pacific Yet Again!

In March 1978 we were sitting in the office of the General Conference President, Elder Robert Pierson, in the old General Conference Headquarters in Takoma Park, Washington D.C. Also with us was Pastor Duncan Eva, Vice President of the General Conference.

We had sought to visit with Elder Pierson because of our deep concern over events in Australia, events which were destroying the Seventh-day Adventist faith. We knew Pastor Pierson to be a man of utmost fidelity to the truth. Colin at the time was President of Columbia Union College, also located in Takoma Park, about one mile from the General Conference Headquarters.

Colin knew Elder Pierson's deep burdens concerning the events which were causing fearful divisions in our church in Australia. Knowing that Colin received frequent communications through his homeland letters, letters which related the attempted doctrinal takeover which was transpiring there, Elder Pierson quite frequently enquired of Colin the latest information which he had gleaned from these communications.

Elder Pierson had known Pastor Eva, a South African, for a considerable period of time prior to his appointment as President of the General Conference, for Elder Pierson had been President of the Trans-African Division, a Division which no longer exists.

In a tone of frustration with the discord in Australia, Pastor Eva asked a pointed question, "What's wrong with you colonials in Australia?" His question referred to Australia's past as a composite of six former British colonies – New South Wales, Queensland, South Australia, Victoria, Tasmania and Western Australia. "Down there you are forever stirring up strife in the church."

Since Pastor Eva was born in South Africa, which too had been formed from former British colonies: Cape of Good Hope, Natal, Orange River Colony and Transvaal, Colin, in a less combative tone, replied, "Well, Elder, I perceive that you, too, are a colonial."

There has developed no small level of frustration in various parts of the world with the perception that the Seventh-day Adventist Church in Australia and New Zealand is a breeding ground for combative individuals who stir up trouble and spread it worldwide.

In 1978 we never dreamed that in later years we, too, as Australians, would be placed in this denominational stereotype by some opponents of truth. We pray to God that in the Day of Judgment we will never be burdened with this stereotype, when the Righteous Judge searches our hearts.

Yet we cannot deny that in our homeland, more apostasy has been promoted and accepted than in the great majority of nations upon earth. The New

Theology teachings reject the Sanctuary message; Christian character perfection; the fallen human nature of Christ; the gift of the Spirit of Prophecy. In its later manifestations, the New Theology teachings have blossomed into the rejection of the literal facts presented in Genesis, chapters one to eleven. Sabbath desecration has been adopted, as has the spirit of ecumenism: also a false identification of the antichrist, and other deviations from truth. The New Theology commenced in the 1880's with Elder Dudley Marvin Canright (1840-1919),. It was later to become the domain of Australians.

A second American, Elder Albion Fox Ballenger (1861-1921) forwarded the cause of the New Theology from 1905 until his mantle fell upon German pastor, Louis Richard Conradi (1856-1939). It was Pastor Conradi who convinced Pastor William Warde Fletcher (1879-1947) of his false doctrines when Pastor Fletcher was President of what is now termed the Southern Asia Division, and Pastor Conradi was Field Secretary of the General Conference. Thus, through Pastor Fletcher, Pastor Conradi was instrumental in bringing the views of the New Theology to Australia.

Upon his return to Australia in the late 1920's, Pastor Fletcher was appointed head of the Bible Department at the Australasian Missionary College (now Avondale College). He passed his error on to one of his pupils, Pastor Robert Greive, who used his post while President of the North New Zealand Conference to promote it in the 1950's. (See our book *The General Conference and Apostasy* for much greater detail).

Not one of these five men – Pastors Canright, Ballenger, Conradi, Fletcher, Greive – met with success in their attempts to insinuate these New Theology errors into God's church. But the sixth prominent proponent – yet another Australian, Dr. Desmond Ford – did succeed. We were fellow-students at the Australasian Missionary College with Dr. Ford in 1950, the year he graduated from the ministerial course.

Not only did Dr. Ford achieve that which his forerunners, Pastors Canright, Ballenger, Conradi, Fletcher and Greive failed to do, his theological transformation of the Seventh-day Adventist faith from truth to apostasy is now well entrenched at every level of the church, on all continents of the earth.

Later – aided by yet another Australian, Robert Brinsmead, whose influence also spread around the world – the New Theology found fertile soil for its rapid growth like weeds in a beautiful flower bed. Robert Brinsmead, who possessed undoubted intellectual skills which were utilized in order to destroy the faith, later formed a loose alliance with Dr. Ford. Robert Brinsmead even accepted the aid of an Australian Anglican Priest, Geoffrey Paxton, who wrote an exposé of Seventh-day Adventism entitled, *The Shaking of Adventism*. In this book Geoffrey Paxton cited Russell's name in less than complimentary terms, on no less than six occasions; and the book Dr. John Clifford and Russell had co-authored in 1976, *Conflicting Concepts of Righteousness by Faith in the Seventh-day Adventist Church, Australasian Division*, in eight such references.

Early in 2004, yet another concerted effort – to damage even further God's precious truth – was made in the South Pacific. This was initiated in the form of a five-pronged assault. Four days in the first week of February, 2004, the South Pacific Division held a

> summit at Avondale College which ran this past week, about the church's understanding and application of Ellen White's writings.
>
> (South Pacific *Record*, February 7, 2004).

A report in the *Record* 21 February, 2004 provided some details of the summit, held February 2-5.

The second assault came – also in the first week of February, 2004 – from a book which appeared on the bookshelves of the Adventist Book Centers around the South Pacific Division. This book, *Prophets are Human*, was promoted by a full page colored advertisement in the South Pacific *Record*, February 14, 2004. It was launched by Pastor Laurie Evans, South Pacific Division President, at the Summit on February 3, 2004.

Pastor Manners' editorial in the *Record* of February 7, 2004 entitled "An Ellen White Reality Check," was the third prong in the attack. Yes, once more the South Pacific had chosen to place itself in a position to destabilize and attempt to destroy "this treasure in earthen vessels" (2 Corinthians 4:7), the "glorious gospel of Christ," (2 Corinthians 4:4) which God in His great love for the Seventh-day Adventist Church, has entrusted to it and to none other.

In addition, the South Pacific *Record* of February 7, 14, 21, 28 included a series of four "conversations" between Pastor Bruce Manners, Editor of the South Pacific *Record*, and Dr. Arthur Patrick, retired credentialed ordained minister of the Seventh-day Adventist Church and a former Director of the Ellen G. White SDA Research Centre at Avondale College. These conversations were entitled "Ellen White for Today."

The fifth assault on the Spirit of Prophecy consisted of a series of seven monthly articles which appeared as an insert in the first issue of the South Pacific *Record* of each of the months of February to August, 2004. It was termed *ClearView – a Way of Seeing Prophecy*. The initial issue, published in the month of February, appeared in February 7, 2004.

The editor of *ClearView* was Pastor Paul Petersen, Field Secretary of the South Pacific Division. It was

> an initiative of the Biblical Research Committee of the South Pacific Division.
>
> (Page four of each *ClearView* edition).

These five initiatives all appeared in a period of six days, February 2-7, 2004. Later, three other allied initiatives were added in the first half of the year 2004. This was a well planned and orchestrated effort to decidedly take God's children from Scriptural truth to doctrines which, without dispute, defy plain words of inspiration.

PART II
Stratagems

February, 2004

At Avondale College from February 2-5, 2004, the South Pacific Division leadership called together

> More than 100 ministers, church educators and administrators
> (South Pacific *Record*, February 21, 2004)

in order

> to gain a better understanding of the role and ministry of Ellen White.
> (*Ibid*).

Three overseas denominational workers were invited in order

> to have expertise in three basic areas, biblical exegesis and theology [Dr. Jon Paulien, head of the New Testament faculty at Andrews University], history [Dr. Gary Land, Andrews University] and then an expert in relation to Ellen White and her writings [Dr. James Nix, Director of the Ellen G. White Estate at the General Conference]." (*Ibid*).

Dr. Paul Petersen, Field Secretary of the South Pacific Division declared at this meeting that,

> We have two extreme options with Ellen White ... one is to treat Ellen White as if she lived today: the other is to ignore her. Neither of those would be helpful for the church. (*Ibid*).

No doubt most people reading the first of these two cited options would find it to be expressed in obscure language. However, in simple terms Dr. Petersen was simply making the point that it is an extreme position to judge Sister White by the literary and factual standards of 2004, rather than those prevailing in the nineteenth and earliest years of the twentieth century.

Such a position has some merit, but it is also pregnant with danger. The great danger is that unpalatable statements in Sister White's writings are summarily dismissed on the grounds that she was simply regurgitating information which was believed by experts or society in her day, while today advanced knowledge has demonstrated her concepts to be not only antiquated but, in some cases, false. The question we would pose is, As the Holy Spirit guided Sister White's writings, was He dependent upon nineteenth century experts or contemporary general beliefs, or upon the infinite, inerrant knowledge of the Godhead? There has developed in our midst an altogether too human concept of Sister White's inspired writings.

Dr. Paulien was reported as declaring that he

> commended the high standard of scholarship demonstrated by members of Avondale's theology faculty, who presented at the summit. 'The Avondale guys have been particularly helpful, providing a good summary of the biblical material.... They've done an outstanding job and the church should be proud about the standard of work going on here. The people they pulled together and the quality of the presentations has been enlightening.' (Ibid).

Dr. Paulien's assessment is alarming. Although the papers presented have not yet been made available to the church membership, the theme of Dr. Graeme Bradford's book, *Prophets Are Human*, is published for all to read. Later, however, we will review one paper presented. Even more important is the fact that the theologians of Avondale College during 2002 were in the forefront of the move by Avondale College Church to have Dr. Desmond Ford returned to the pulpits of our churches in the South Pacific Division. No individual in the history of Seventh-day Adventism has destroyed faith in the Spirit of Prophecy, as manifested by Sister White, as has Dr. Ford.

Further, Avondale College hosted the Convention of the Institute of Study of Christianity in an Age of Science and Technology, July 18-20, 2003. This Institute is

> A vocal theistic evolutionary organization in Australia.... They spend much time attacking biblical creationism and creationists. In fact, one gets the feeling that they have more in common with skeptics than with Christians who disagree with them. (Dr. Jonathan Sarfati, http:/answersingenesis.org/3906,asp).

July 19 was a holy Sabbath day. What a day for God's people to host a theistic evolution conference which promoted a view of origins which comprehensively destroys the foundation of Sabbath-keeping! What really hurt was that the non-Seventh-day Adventist Creation organization, Answers in Genesis, on their website, AigNews@answersingenesis.com headed its article on the conference hosted at Avondale College, "With friends like these, who needs skeptics?" It hurt most because it was a fair question. Yet it is the professors from Avondale College whom Dr. Paulien chose to flatter.

It may be coincidental, yet not without significance, that one of the two non-presenters quoted in the report of the *Record*, February 21, 2004, was the lay pastor of the Wangaratta and Benalla Churches in the Victorian Conference. On Sabbath, October 25, 2003, the lay pastor, Robert Stankovic, had invited Colin Lockyer to preach the divine service in the Wangaratta Church. Mr. Lockyer was a former ordained, credentialed pastor of the Wangaratta and the Benalla Churches. He was trained under Dr. Ford, then chairman of the Theology Department at Avondale College.

Colin Lockyer lost confidence in the Seventh-day Adventist understanding of the prophecy of Daniel 8, especially in the early 1980's, resigned from the Seventh-day Adventist ministry and joined the ministry of the Presbyterian

Church. Russell recalls having a number of conversations with Colin Lockyer at Victorian Conference Camp Meetings in the late 1970's. He possessed then little faith in the writings of Sister White.

Colin Lockyer later became one of the subjects of a PhD thesis in the field of sociology presented by a candidate for that degree at Monash University, Melbourne – Australia's largest university. The subjects of that thesis, written by Dr. Harry Ballis, were the more-than-one-hundred-and-eighty ministers who left the ministry in Australia and New Zealand in the decade of the eighties, after the dismissal of Dr. Ford from denominational employment. Dr. Ford had taught the large majority of these pastors. Dr. Ballis, himself, was one of the number. Most departed from the faith, and many discarded their church membership. Though slower to do so, Dr. Ford voluntarily surrendered his church membership, held at Pacific Union College Church, in 2001.

At this Summit, on February 3, Dr. Graeme Bradford's book, *Prophets Are Human*, was launched by the President of the South Pacific Division, Pr. Laurie Evans. In the launch Pr. Evans stated that:

> It is a very readable book, which has been long overdue.... Graeme has long been one of those who have been committed to answering critics of the church. He has done the church a great service in writing this book.   (*Ibid*. p. 7).

Dr. Bradford is better known as a man who condemns faithful ministers who nobly stand by the principles of the faith. Pastor Austin Cooke was born in New Zealand in July, 1917. He was approaching his eighty-seventh birthday as we wrote this portion of this manuscript, one day after Russell and he presented faithful messages over the weekend of February 13-15, 2004, to God's people in the city of Adelaide, South Australia. Pr. Cooke, whose physical and mental state would be envied by many men thirty years his junior, had flown over one thousand miles from his home in Queensland. He presented five outstanding messages using PowerPoint, a skill he had recently mastered. The temperature was 112°F (44.3°C) on the Sabbath and 106°F (41°C) on Sunday. Not for a moment did he wilt under the heat, even though the defective air conditioning at the venue did little to reduce the room temperature. As will be documented later, in the past Dr. Bradford attempted to despoil the reputation of this warrior of the Lord. (See chapter entitled "Stratagem II – Prophets Are Human").

Dr. Bradford's book, *Prophets Are Human*, was promoted by a full-page colored advertisement in the South Pacific *Record* of February 14, 2004. A portion of the South Pacific President's Foreward, as we have cited, stated that:

> This book is long overdue.   (Dr. Bradford, *op.cit*. p.7).

These words were prominently displayed at the top of the advertisement. At its bottom edge, the following words appeared:

> This book proudly printed and published in Australia by Signs Publishing Company, Victoria.   (*Ibid*).

The Signs Publishing Company, situated in Warburton, Victoria, is our denominational publishing house in the South Pacific.

The Director of the Ellen G. White SDA Research Centre, Dr. Lester Devine, described the book as:

> ...a stimulating and provocative read for the intelligent Christian.
> (back cover of the book and also quoted in the *Record* advertisement).

Perhaps Dr. Devine was more accurate than he purposed.

Other accolades upon the book's back cover were written by the editor of the *Adventist Review*, Dr. William Johnsson; the Secretary of the South Pacific Division, Dr. Barry Oliver, who was a Professor of Theology at Avondale College prior to taking up his Division appointment, and Dr. Jon Paulien, Chairman of the New Testament Department, Andrews University.

In part these men wrote the following words in support of Dr. Bradford's book:

> Dr. Johnsson:
> Graeme Bradford is an honest seeker who writes honest answers to questions about Ellen White. (*Ibid*).

> Dr. Oliver:
> Graeme Bradford has my highest admiration...for his personal integrity and commitment to truth. (*Ibid*).

> Dr. Paulien:
> Bradford's book is must reading for anyone interested in Ellen White's inspiration. (*Ibid*).

Thus, in the minds of those unacquainted with the genuine issues at stake, this book bore the certified credentials, both of denominational leadership, and of theological opinion.

A large portion of the full-page advertisement depicted a cartoon, with Sister White, occupying approximately one-third of the page. Sister White was represented standing behind a pulpit, her feet astride, her right arm lowered with its fingers splayed and her left hand covering her mouth. The cartoonist had drawn an able representation of Sister White in a state of shock, and horror, in fear that the secrets of her written "errors" were now about to be revealed.

Apparently protests about this advertisement in the April edition of *The Remnant Herald* and by such other authors as Dr. Barry Harker, of Edessa International Ministry in Queensland, and no doubt others, bore fruit, for the Division President wrote a letter to the editor of the South Pacific *Record* in which he stated:

> In respect of the advertisement in the RECORD of February 14 and poster distributed to churches for the excellent book *Prophets Are Human*, I want to

express my appreciation to the Signs Publishing Company for producing a new poster advertising it.

It is important that we not appear to trivialise nor in any way denigrate the gift to the church, embodied in the ministry of Ellen White, that has been such a blessing to us as a people.

Thank you for recognising the need to give a positive message in this regard. This book *Prophets Are Human* has been written with this objective in mind, and I am glad that the promotion of it is reflective of this intent.

(South Pacific Record, May 1, 2004).

We can not recall a previous letter to the editor of the South Pacific Division *Record*, under the signature of a Division President. Of course our concerns on the entire issue of the Spirit of Prophecy were not allayed by Pastor Evans' comment that the book is an "excellent book," for it was not only the poster which trivialized and denigrated the Spirit of Prophecy but also the book which it advertised.

The new advertisement appeared in the *Record* of May 8, 2004 for the first time.

The advertisement also stated that:

> Ellen White wrote that some races are a mixture of man and beast[;] said she would be alive when Jesus returns.

It is true that on pages 13, 14 of his book, Dr. Bradford listed these two matters along with seven others, the three sentences written prior to this list of nine "mistakes" read:

> But now there are doubts. There are so many unanswered questions. The Internet site has listed them. (*Ibid*, p.13).

While these words are placed in the mouth of Dr. Bradford's fictional character, "Doug," what follows is a list of doubts which cry out for godly explanation, doubts which are designed to persist, unless the reader prayerfully searches these matters or is provided with solutions.

Incredibly, one may read every word in the book's fifty-six pages of actual text and yet discover no answers proffered except in the case of the "doubt" covering the charge that Sister White is a plagiarist. This is a most serious matter! It left the readers with the "doubts" fixed in their minds and unless those reading this book possessed a high level of diligence in discerning the difference between truth and error, they were condemned to wallow in a morass of doubt and dwindling confidence in the testimonies of Jesus Christ for these perilous last days.

Such a book should never have passed the scrutiny of the denominational book reading committee, much less received the accolades of leaders and theologians entrusted to further the pure faith of God.

Curiously Chapter 1 (pages 13-19), possessed neither footnote nor endnote. Thus the reader had to undertake his own research in order to locate the claimed "errors" in Sister White's writings, as cited by Dr. Bradford, and be able to read the context for himself. This is yet another serious failing of this book.

It may be superficially argued that no such documentation is present because *Prophets Are Human* is written in the style of a novel. Husband and wife Doug and Jean and Pastor Jared Downton and Dr. Harold Smithurst, the characters in the book, are all fictional figures. But this defense of the absence of documentation in Chapter 1 does not stand because all of the other four chapters possess documentation in their endnotes.

Two other matters are raised in the book and left without resolution. On occasions a book can achieve much more damage by what it omits than that which it declares. This is one book which may be so categorized.

The first matter is the references to the minutes of the 1919 General Conference Bible Conference. In the second last sentence of the book (p.89) is stated,

> Doug and Jean are left to ponder, *What could be in those minutes that are so important for us to read?* (Italics in original).

Some, ever seeking to defend the indefensible, may suggest that Dr. Bradford intended to write a sequel to this book. He may well do so, although he made no statement concerning such a prospect in his book. However, on June 19, 2004, Dr. Bradford did make a passing reference to a sequel. If this is in preparation, we would pray that such does not eventuate. Rather than defending the veracity of the Spirit of Prophecy, if written in the same vein, it will effectively undermine God's end-time testimonies for His people. Even if a second book were to be devoid of the manifold defects of the first book, what guarantee is there that all who read the first book would even peruse the second? Prior to its publication, some of those who read the first may well have left the faith or died and lost their eternal inheritance, while others would simply ignore it.

The second issue which is raised repeatedly, especially by Doug, is the question of why the information concerning Sister White's published "mistakes" was kept from the knowledge of the laity. We cite one such statement:

> But both [Doug and Jean] feel perturbed that this type of material [concerning Sister White's "errors"] has not always been available to them.
>
> (Dr. Bradford, pp. 67, 68).

This question too, is left unresolved and unchallenged in the book. (See chapter entitled, "Did We Not Know?") Dr. Bradford is guilty of a far graver issue – he has cited the doubts of Spirit of Prophecy skeptics without, in most cases, providing the clear evidences which nullify the charges leveled against Sister White's veracity.

There are valid and satisfying answers to all these questions, but few were provided in this book. Clearly Dr. Bradford and most of his advisers deemed it beneficial to their agendas to raise the doubts and leave them unresolved. This silence would lead the reader to the conclusion that no valid refutations of these false claims are possible. The reader of Dr. Bradford's book would do well to bear this matter in mind.

There is yet a graver concern than those already addressed. Repeatedly, in claiming to defend and excuse Sister White's purported "mistakes," these men assert that the Scriptural writers made similar "mistakes." Dr. Lester Devine could well be correct in his back cover endorsement of this book when he stated that it was a "provocative read for the intelligent Christian."

The matter which we ponder in sadness is how many "intelligent Christians" will draw the conclusion after reading this book that neither the Bible nor the Spirit of Prophecy offer reliable statements in their declarations concerning the plan of salvation. This book engenders no confidence in either Holy Writ or the Spirit of Prophecy as credible, safe guides to salvation.

5 Stratagem I – Church Leaders Reassess Ellen White

Under the heading "Church leaders reassess Ellen White," the South Pacific *Record*, February 21, 2004 reported:

> More than 100 ministers, church educators and administrators met at Avondale College, NSW [New South Wales], from February 2-5 to gain a better understanding of the role and ministry of Ellen White.

It is essential that we recognize that this Summit, as it was termed, was specifically convened, as the headline attests, by church leaders in the South Pacific Division. This meeting was not initiated by a few marginalized, discredited Seventh-day Adventists, nor was it planned by a discontented group of laypeople. The gathering was organized by the appointed leaders of our church.

The very headline of the *Record* report was itself a cause for apprehension – reassess Sister White? Was it the prerogative of church leaders to make judgment upon the prophetic guide so lovingly provided to our church by our God? Clearly the leaders believed it was. Many earnest Seventh-day Adventists would judge otherwise. We are now walking the road to Emmaus, the road of doubt, the rocky path of disbelief. Surely our Savior cries out to us today,

> O fools, and slow of heart to believe all that the prophets have spoken:
> (Luke 24:25).

And if we would only listen to Him our Redeemer would patiently walk with us, as He did with Cleopas and his companion while

> beginning at Moses and all the prophets, [He would] expound unto [us] in all the scriptures the things concerning himself. (Luke 24:27).

Today we may justifiably be described as "fools and slow of heart to believe all that the prophets have spoken." Our doubts, as a people, have extended from the prophet Sister White, back to the prophets John and Daniel and beyond to Moses, the prophet designated by Christ in this conversation. Their writings on salient truths have been largely discounted.

The purpose of the Summit was plainly set forth:

> To inform people of the challenges we have with Ellen White and the development we have in scholarship in Ellen White over the past few decades.
> (*Record*, op. cit., p. 5).

To date this stated aim has only partially been fulfilled. Requests made to the Avondale College Ellen G. White Research Centre and the South Pacific

Division have revealed that the academic papers presented at the Summit are not available for examination, although a few "neutral" papers may be at a later date.

It is only because of the open spirit of one presenter, Dr. Arthur Patrick, our contemporary at Avondale College in 1950, 1951, that we possess his paper. We are also aware of the presentations Dr. Don McMahon likely made, from Russell's personal attendance at one of his open presentations and the *Spectrum* report of the First International Conference on Ellen G. White and Seventh-day Adventist History held at Battle Creek, May 15-19, 2002. Dr. Don McMahon's research and conclusions have been evaluated in our chapter entitled *Ticks and Crosses*.

While we hold diametrically-opposed views on many issues of faith, to those held by Dr. Patrick, we still possess warm sentiments toward him on a personal level. We wrote these words before we learned of his present illness, to which he alluded in his answer to Pastor Manners in the article of February 28, 2004. But this must not be interpreted to mean that there is no passion in our defense of the faith once delivered to the saints. While Dr. Patrick presented his views in the current measured, didactic, academic style of theological writings, our presentations – while assiduously attempting to be fair to those whose views we oppose and to scrupulously research our data – may be termed emotive, for the defense of our faith and our love for and trust in God and His Word burns within our hearts. We are passionate both in this defense and in our desire to promote the preservation of truth.

We do not hide our pain in reading the presentation which Dr. Patrick read at the Summit. His paper was entitled *Ellen White and South Pacific Adventism: Retrospect and Prospect*. As Dr. Patrick well established, the diminution of Sister White's guiding messages in our church has been achieved through a series of hallmark conferences and discussion papers over the past eighty-five years. We list the more significant ones cited by Dr. Patrick.

1919	The General Conference Bible Conference.
1978	Conference examining Sister White's status in our church.
1982	The International Guidance Workshop, Washington D.C.
1999	The South Pacific Division Group Discussion paper, entitled *A Strategy for a Better Appreciation of the Ministry and Writings of Ellen G. White*, dated November, 1999.
2002	The First International Conference on Ellen G. White and Seventh-day Adventist History, Battle Creek.
2004	The South Pacific Summit, Avondale College.

Dr. Patrick identified three eras in the South Pacific Division in respect of the understanding of Sister White as the "messenger of the Lord," using the sub-headings:

I   Packaging the First 95 Years [1885-1980]
II The Effervescent Decade: The Eighties [1980's]
III The Evidence of Consensus: The Nineties [1990's]

Sub-heading III speaks volumes. It presents, in Dr. Patrick's view, a position in our church where:

> If *certitude* relating to Ellen White was the order of the day until the 1970's, and *controversy* characterised the 1980's, it can be argued that the Church began to exhibit a strong impulse toward *consensus* in the 1990's.
>
> (Dr. Patrick, *op. cit.*, p. 4 – italics in the original].

The contrasts between these three eras is evident. Thus if *certitude* characterized the era of 1885-1980 then manifestly *doubt* was the salient feature of the 1990's. And doubt there was aplenty!

Dr. Patrick traced the development of this *consensus* of doubt in the prophetic gift in this church to the mid-1980's, although it could be well traced back to the 1919 General Conference Bible Conference and even beyond to the rejection by leadership of the 1888 General Conference Session messages of Elders Alonzo T. Jones and Ellet J. Waggoner, messages which Sister White enthusiastically endorsed.

But since Dr. Patrick was focusing upon the South Pacific Division and the two earlier rejections of Sister White's prophetic counsels occurred in North America, his focus upon the later era was valid. Our experience, however, has been that the major destruction of the prophetic authority of Sister White in the South Pacific commenced at least a decade or two earlier as Dr. Desmond Ford used his post as Chairman of the Theology Department of Avondale College from the early 1960's-1977 to diminish the prophetic gift in our midst. Colin was Chairman of the Avondale College Department of Education throughout five of these years – 1965-1969.

In a footnote, Dr. Patrick referred to Dr. Ford's book, *Physicians of the Soul: Prophets Through the Ages,* Southern Publishing Company, 1980, in which Dr. Ford authored:

> One of the few book-length publications relating to biblical prophets and Ellen White by an Adventist press from the era… Dr. Ford, ever an omnivorous reader, became aware of most of the relevant issues within the decade of the 1960's, so his 1980 book benefited from years of careful Bible study and reflection.
>
> (Dr. Patrick, *op. cit.*, footnote, p. 4).

A most disturbing feature of Dr. Patrick's presentation at the Summit in February, 2004, was that he presented accolades for numbers of authors who have blighted the reputation of Sister White, while he diminished the work of faithful presenters of materials supporting Sister White's prophetic gift.

In the latter category Dr. Patrick demeaned the book, *Issues in Revelation and Inspiration,* Adventist Theological Society, Berrien Springs, 1992, Edited by Dr.

Frank Holbrook of the General Conference Biblical Research Institute and Dr. Leo van Dolson, Editor of the Adult Sabbath School Quarterly, by making what he believed to be a negative comparison with the book written by Dr. Alden Thompson, *Inspiration: Hard Questions, Honest Answers*, Review and Herald, Hagerstown, Maryland, 1991. Dr. Patrick correctly pointed out that,

> Whereas Thompson's volume was published by a denominational press, the ATS [Adventist Theological Society] volume was privately printed.
> (Dr. Patrick, *op. cit.*, p.5 – footnote).

We are living in a period when this comparison reflecting negatively upon the non-denominational publication may, indeed, be its recommendation.

The faithful defense of truth in two books, also published by a non-denominational press, received similar treatment. The two books cited were both written by Dr. Samuel Koranteng-Pipim and both published by Berean Books, Ann Arbor, Michigan. The books were, *Receiving the Word: How New Approaches to the Bible Impact Our Biblical Faith and Lifestyle*, (1996) and *Must We Be Silent? Issues Dividing Our Church*, (2001). Dr. Patrick added:

> Pipim's sponsorship as a guest speaker in the SPD [South Pacific Division] was without official authorisation of the Church, and his privately-printed volume *Receiving the Word* was distributed widely, often free of charge.

Contrary to Dr. Patrick's assertion, Dr. Koranteng-Pipim was indeed invited to Australia by the Church. Dr. Patrick implied the false concept that the church organization is THE church. The Seventh-day Adventist church existed before there was any corporate organization. That organization is the servant of the church, not its dictator. Some of the books published by our denominational presses today lead some of God's children to cast skeptical eyes over those books which are "approved", believing that such books may be tainted with error. The last book manuscript written by the faithful General Conference President, Elder Robert Pierson, was rejected by both the Pacific Press Publishing Association and the Review and Herald Publishing Association. Elder Pierson personally confided this matter to Colin not long before his death in 1989.

In contrast to his gentle demeaning of books faithful to the faith, Dr. Patrick awarded accolades to the works of men who have been in the forefront of attacking the faith. In his book, *The White Lie*, Walter Rea, a long-time Seventh-day Adventist minister, attempted to destroy Sister White as a prophet. Only in the day of judgment, if unrepented, will Walter Rea's full damage to God's beloved church be revealed. Despite this indisputable fact Dr. Patrick stated that,

> Another Adventist example is the experience of Walter Rea, who has done more than any other person to tabulate literary parallels between Ellen White's writings and those of other authors. For this endeavor the church owes Rea a great deal of

gratitude even though some of his language is intemperate and some of his interpretations may not be sustained by the evidence he offers.

(Dr. Patrick, *op. cit.*, p. 7 footnote).

Dr. Patrick's reservations at the conclusion of this footnote are appropriate. We were presented with one of Walter Rea's claimed parallels, by the White Estate. The non-Seventh-day Adventist author's work, although not devoid of some merit since he had visited Palestine in the nineteenth century, possessed far fewer insights into Christ's ministry and his presentation lacked the depth of that found in the "parallel" passage of *The Desire of Ages*. The only major parallel we could discern was that the articles followed a similar chronological sequence.

The state of some of our churches in the United States may be measured by a recent report which stated:

> Walter Rea ... now belongs to the Turlock Seventh-day Adventist Church and lives in Patterson, Ca[lifornia]. He was taken back by profession of faith and I understand teaches a S[abbath] S[chool] class.
> (E-mail from Brother Cecil Renfro, received June 6, 2004).

We stand perplexed by Dr. Patrick's claim that "the church owes Rea a great deal of gratitude." That such a thought was presented and entertained at this Summit is a sorry fact. We were also surprised to read that, among others, Dr. Ronald Numbers and Dr. Ron Graybill, together with Dr. Don McAdams were said to be,

> too often unappreciated or in various ways restricted, laid aside or condemned in the 1970's and 1980's. (Dr. Patrick, *op. cit.*, p.7).

Sufficient evidence is presented in the chapter entitled "Sister White and Health" to demonstrate how inappropriate these conclusions were in respect of Dr. Numbers', and, in the cases of Dr. Graybill's and Dr. McAdams' pursuit of "errors" in Sister White's *Great Controversy* account of the life of John Huss. (See chapter entitled "Historic Accuracy"). In doing so they revealed themselves to be men with a mission to destroy Sister White's credibility as a prophet of God, rather than to uphold her evident prophetic calling.

The paper Dr. Patrick presented at the Summit is something of a *tour de force* of Biblical scholars who have not distinguished themselves as proponents of the established Seventh-day Adventist faith. Names such as Harry Ballis (former pastor, Australia), Graeme Bradford (Avondale), Noel Clapham (Avondale), Rick Ferret (Queensland, Australia), Le Roy Froom (Andrews University and General Conference), Ron Graybill (former officer of the White Estate of the General Conference), Fritz Guy (former President of La Sierra University), Milton Hook (former church pastor, Australia), Fred Hoyt (La Sierra University), William Johnsson (Editor of the *Adventist Review*), Sakae Kubo (USA), George Knight (Andrews), Ronald Lawson (New York City University and former Kinship International liaison officer with the General Conference),

Don McAdams (former President of Southwestern Adventist College), Bruce Manners (Editor of the South Pacific *Record, Signs* and *The Edge*), Ronald Numbers (Professor of the History of Medicine and Science, University of Wisconsin), Walter Rea (former church pastor, California), Ray Roennfeldt (Avondale), Alden Thompson (Walla Walla College), Laurence Turner (Newbold College, England), Gilbert Valentine (Avondale), Robert Wolfgramme (Australia), Norman Young (Avondale College), and many others, are cited in a positive manner throughout Dr. Patrick's paper.

God's people have sought certainty in this present era of skepticism. These men, despite the fact that many are ordained credentialed pastors and in denominational employment, have set forth doubt before God's flock. This doubt – rather than building up God's church – has greatly weakened its fabric. Many have focused on the marginalization of the Spirit of Prophecy and, in some cases, Scripture, and have diverted the minds of many adherents from the mission of our church, the very purpose for which God raised it up. By way of illustration we cite extracts from letters written by two of these men.

> Bravo, RECORD and church administrators. You've taken Ellen White's advice and affirmed her fallibility in religious matters.... E. G. White apologists have been spin doctoring far too long.
> (Dr. Milton Hook, South Pacific *Record*, April 17, 2004).

> When we claim inerrancy for Mrs. White's writings or the Scriptures, we assume more than she does or that Scripture intended. Are the Bible and Ellen White's writings inerrant? No. Are they trustworthy? Yes. (Rick Ferret, *Ibid*).

We name these men with no purpose in mind to judge their characters. As with ourselves, God alone possesses that right. But it is our duty, as it is the duty of all, to evaluate the impact of each individual's contribution to God's church lest we seek error and eschew truth and righteousness.

We see the drift of the work of these men clearly expressed by an unnamed theologian in an email dated January 30, 2004. He stated:

> I guess what I'm pointing at is that for many the whole arena of authority has changed (and part of that is the result of cultural shifts). To ask the question in a different way: Why should I read Ellen White when she points me to read Scripture with the help of the Spirit and the community of Jesus?
> (Dr. Patrick, *op. cit.*, p. 15 – parenthesis in original).

The final paragraph of Dr. Patrick's presentation to the Summit well presents the current chaos and pluralism which is rampant in our midst, and which is even judged to be desirable by some. Satan is the author of chaos and pluralism. Christ is the author of unity based on the platform of truth. This paragraph deserves to be read with care as Dr. Patrick has ably expressed the condition of our church today in respect to the issue of the Spirit of Prophecy as a crucial tenet of our faith.

> A further consideration has reference to the pastoral care of congregations in which a plurality of ideas may be present. There are Adventist congregations in which reversionists worship with the belief that Ellen White's writings are inerrant in the autographs. In the same pew may sit members who are totally disillusioned in view of their experience with Ellen White and what they believe the Church has said about her, to the point they cannot hear her name or read her writings without an intense emotional reaction. In between are people that view biblical inspiration and the inspiration of Ellen White's writings in similar terms and are earnestly seeking to benefit from both while maintaining the Bible as their primary source of doctrinal authority. Also saying Amen to the same prayers on any given Sabbath may be people that affirm Ellen White's historical significance but see little contemporary relevance for her writings: other folk that sincerely believe the prophetic model the Church has fostered needs adjustment in terms of New Testament patterns rather than Old Testament prophetism: members who see Ellen White more as "seer" or "oracle" than a prophet as in the traditional Adventist interpretation, and so on. If the Church chooses to enforce a single view of Ellen White rather than nurture trustful relationships and a climate within which growth in understanding can develop, it will repeat the processes which have frequently resulted in *congregational reduction* rather than effective *church growth*. (Ibid, pp. 15, 16).

A like statement could be correctly asserted concerning almost every salient doctrine held by our people today. There is urgent need for leadership to stand back and evaluate whether the holding of these summits, conferences, workshops and strategic sessions is stabilizing the faith of our members or systematically destroying it; whether these meetings generate the unity of the flock or a devastating splintering of the body of Christ; whether they glorify God's truth or defame and ridicule it.

Large amounts of tithe money are often expended upon these gatherings. That sacred means possesses the purpose of the funding of the spread of the last and greatest message of God to fallen beings, messages presented by our God of love. Can leadership sit easily in their administrative chairs as this means is utilized to focus on the destruction of that privileged obligation entrusted to Seventh-day Adventists? Must church leaders continue to bear the responsibility of the shaking of the faith? Must they ever remain blind to the high and holy purpose of the offices they hold? Must these men, holding high posts in God's church fulfill the end-time prophecies concerning THE truth, the pure Seventh-day Adventist faith entrusted to our care?

> [3]For the time will come when they will not endure sound doctrine; but after their own lusts shall they heap to themselves teachers, having itching ears; [4]And they shall turn away their ears from the truth, and shall be turned unto fables. (2 Timothy 4:3, 4).

¹Now the Spirit speaketh expressly, that in the latter times some shall depart from the faith, giving heed to seducing spirits, and doctrines of devils; ²Speaking lies in hypocrisy; having their conscience seared with a hot iron; (1 Timothy 4:1, 2).

While the second of these texts primarily applies to the Roman Catholic Church (see verse 3), it also bears a secondary meaning for our church in apostasy today, as the first verse certifies. Providing advice to Seventh-day Adventist young people, Sister White confirms this application.

Those who waver now and are tempted to follow in the wake of apostates who have departed from the faith, "giving heed to seducing spirits, and doctrines of devils," will surely be found on the side of those who make void the law of God, unless they repent and plant their feet firmly upon the faith once delivered to the saints. (*Testimonies for the Church*, Vol. 5, p. 525).

We notice the emphasis on the adjective THE qualifying faith. It is pregnant with meaning for us today. Is it any marvel that it is not only the world and the fallen churches of Babylon, but, distressingly, our own precious church, which is now fulfilling yet another of Paul's last prophecies as he awaited the executioner's axe.

¹This know also, that in the last days perilous times shall come. ²For men shall be lovers of their own selves, covetous, boasters, proud, blasphemers, disobedient to parents, unthankful, unholy, ³Without natural affection, trucebreakers, false accusers, incontinent, fierce, despisers of those that are good, ⁴Traitors, heady, highminded, lovers of pleasures more than lovers of God; ⁵Having a form of godliness, but denying the power thereof: from such turn away. (2 Timothy 3:1-5).

Perhaps the most illuminating aspect of this entire Summit were the quoted words of one overseas invitee, Dr. Jon Paulien, who holds the crucial post of head of the New Testament Faculty at Andrews University. He commented positively on the

standard of scholarship demonstrated by members of Avondale College faculty, who presented at the summit. "The Avondale guys have been particularly helpful providing a good summary of the biblical material.... They've done an outstanding job and the church should be proud about the standard of work going on here. The people they pulled together and the quality of the presentations has been enlightening." (South Pacific *Record*, February 21, 2004).

It would have been far better if those flattering words had not been spoken, or if they had, the editors of the *Record* had declined to report them. These laudatory remarks do not sit well with those who sincerely value the perfect Seventh-day Adventist faith.

6 Stratagem II – Prophets Are Human

Dr. Graeme Bradford's book, launched at the Ellen G. White Summit by the South Pacific Division President on February 3, 2004, was not written in a rush of blood, or surge of adrenalin. Dr. Bradford, writing in the introduction to *Prophets Are Human*, Signs Publishing Company, Warburton, Australia, 2004, stated:

> This book has been 20 years in preparation. This is the length of time I have been wrestling with what appeared to be problems. (Dr. Bradford, *Ibid*, p. 10).

Nor was Dr. Bradford's book written without the benefit of wide consultation. In his introduction Dr. Bradford singled out Drs. Robert Olsen, Ron Graybill and Arthur Patrick for gratitude for,

> while attached to the White Estate in the 1980's, [they] first opened my eyes to some of the material I will share. (*Ibid*).

Dr. Ray Roennfeldt – whose grandfather in 1915 was in the first group of German Lutherans to accept the Seventh-day Adventist faith among the settlers in the Barossa Valley, South Australia – was thanked

> for reading the manuscript and his helpful advice. (*Ibid*).

Coincidentally, our Lutheran great-grandfather, Samuel David Standish, whose mother was German, was also baptized with Dr. Roennfeldt's grandfather in that 1915 baptism. We wonder how each would have viewed the vast doctrinal schism in our church today. We met them both when we were little lads.

About a year prior to the launching of *Prophets Are Human*, Dr. Patrick foreshadowed its publication in a paper entitled, *Learning from Ellen White's Perception and use of Scripture: Toward an Adventist Hermeneutic for the Twentieth Century*. In that paper Dr. Patrick requested the reader to

> observe the way this concept [see below for an elucidation of the concept here mentioned] is placed within a helpful context in Graeme Bradford's forthcoming volume on White's writings. Bradford's content, honed with the help of some twenty others, has been intimated in his preaching, teaching and writing of the past decade. (See *Ministry*, August 1999, 25-27).
>
> (*Ibid*, endnote 29, page 16, parenthesis in the original).

It is incredible that a book such as *Prophets Are Human* passed the scrutiny of twenty individuals. It would have been helpful if Dr. Patrick had named these individuals. It seems likely that Dr. Bradford confined his advisors to those who possessed similar views to his own on the subject of inspiration as related to Sister White and Scripture.

Nevertheless, Dr. Bradford's book merits serious examination, having taken twenty years to prepare and been honed by twenty advisors, especially as it received the following recommendations:

> *Prophets Are Human* is one of those books that is born out of adversity and controversy. The catalyst for it centres around the increasing criticism and accusations that have been leveled at Ellen G. White and her writings by those intent on destroying her credibility as an inspired writer and one through whom the gift of prophecy was manifest. Much has been published, circulated via videos and promulgated on the Internet with this objective in mind.
>
> This book has been written to show the arguments brought against Ellen White are, in the main, based on an incorrect understanding of inspiration and how this gift is manifest through the biblical prophets. The author, by analysing the human side of Bible writers as revealed in Scripture, shows clearly that the problems encountered, which have caused many to lose their faith, are not so much with her writings as they are with unbiblical expectations of them. In short, the book makes the very important point that the same criticisms brought against Ellen White can to a large degree be brought against many of the authors of Scripture.
>
> The book has been written in a captivating and engaging story form that makes it easy to read and difficult to put down. The main characters ask questions that thoughtful people have pondered and stumbled over for decades. The answers given by "the pastor" are both biblical and faith affirming.
>
> Graeme Bradford has done an excellent job in dealing with issues in connection with Ellen White and inspiration that for far too long have gone unaddressed. This book is long overdue, and will do much to restore confidence in the authority and validity of the gift of prophecy as evident in the writings of this woman who has left such a rich legacy not only for the Seventh-day Adventist Church, but for the world at large.
>
> I commend the author for recognising the need to provide answers to difficult questions, and strongly recommend the reading of this book, which I believe will be rewarding to the honest seeker of truth.
>
> (Pastor Laurie Evans, President, South Pacific Division, *Ibid*, Foreward, pp. 7, 8).

Graeme Bradford is an honest seeker who writes honest answers to questions about Ellen White. *Prophets Are Human* should give help to many other seekers. I commend this book.

> (Dr. William Johnsson, Editor, *Adventist Review*, *Ibid*, back cover of book).

It is vital that every Seventh-day Adventist have a clear understanding of the issues discussed in this book. For too long too many, both friend and foe, have been drawing conclusions on this topic on the basis of little information, misinformation or suppositions that do not stand up under scrutiny. Graeme Bradford has my highest admiration, not only for the very readable manner in which he has addressed some significant issues surrounding the life and writings of Ellen White, but also for his personal integrity and commitment to the truth. I strongly commend this book to the reader and thank Graeme for his work.

(Dr. Barry Oliver, General Secretary, Seventh-day Adventist Church in the South Pacific, [Secretary, South Pacific Division] *Ibid*).

Neither the critics nor the defenders of Ellen White have given adequate attention to the full range of biblical and historical evidence. That makes this book much more important than the easy-to-read style might suggest. Bradford's book is must reading for anyone interested in Ellen White's inspiration.

(Dr. Jon Paulien, Chair, New Testament Department, Andrews University, *Ibid*).

Dr. Bradford has provided the church with a much-needed resource. While the reader will find the book confronting at times and very likely will not agree with everything it contains, the author is to be commended for bringing long-standing and difficult issues out into the open and addressing them in a manner that is not only credible but congruent with Scripture. In short, it is a stimulating and provocative read for the intelligent Christian.

(Dr. Lester Devine, Director, Ellen G White SDA Research Centre, Avondale College, *Ibid*).

That the *Ministry* monthly magazine – produced by the General Conference Ministerial Association – would provide a platform for the concepts of Dr. Bradford in respect of this identifying feature of the remnant church, (see Dr. Patrick's end note, p.16 quoted above), will raise some eyebrows, but not ours.

In 1998, the year prior to Dr. Patrick's reference to Dr. Bradford's article in the *Ministry* magazine, the Ministerial Association published a book, written by a Southern Baptist pastor and his wife, upholding Sunday sacredness. This book, *The Confessions of a Nomad*, Pacific Press, was authored by Carolyn and William Self. The book remained on sale at the Potomac Conference Adventist Book Center – located about one mile from the General Conference – at least until October 17, 2000, when Sister Betty Larson, wife of Dr. Ralph Larson, purchased a copy. This book was copyrighted by the Ministerial Association of the General Conference.

We cite four excerpts from the book to illustrate that which the General Conference Ministerial Association published and freely distributed.

> All busy people yearn for a day of rest. God Himself gave His permission, a command even, for a day to allow the soul and spirit to be refreshed. This is God's gift to us. He will take care of us physically and spiritually if we follow His plan. Our systems need the replenishment. Sunday is a special day for this worship and refreshment. (*Confessions of a Nomad*, p. 86).

Stratagem II – Prophets Are Human

The early Christians were obsessed with the fact that they came out of a Jewish background. Yet God did something new and real for them in the Easter experience, so they would have the Sabbath, and so they would gather together as the Christian sect on Sunday morning and celebrate the resurrection.

But there is a difference between the Sabbath and Sunday. You work until the Sabbath, and then you rest. Sunday is the day that gives you strength to work the six days in front of you. The Sabbath is the end of the week. Sunday is the beginning. The Sabbath is from sundown to sundown, but Sunday is from midnight to midnight. The Sabbath is a day of rest, but Sunday is a day of worship. The Sabbath has a penalty to it, if you break it. Sunday has no penalty, except that you shortchange yourself.

The Christian draws his strength from Sunday. It's a time to let God talk to the inner man. It's a time when we make real that practice which says, in effect, "Be still and know that I am God." The Christians took the value of the Hebrew Sabbath and added to it the great joy of the Christian resurrection. We have a marriage of the two in the Christian community.

The commandment said, "Remember the Sabbath Day." So we come together as a body of Christ and remember what God has done. It's a sacrament. Worship and Bible study make Sunday a day when the soul is rekindled, as well as a day when the body is rested. (*ibid*, p. 118).

Thoreau [an American poet and writer] said if you want to destroy the Christian faith, first take away Sunday. He was right; it's a holy day. For those who know Jesus Christ as Savior it cannot be a holiday. For those of you who have gathered around the cross and have been saved and washed clean by His blood, it's a sacrilege to do anything else on that day except to celebrate what God has done.

If we abuse Sunday, we're going to destroy something beautiful that God has given. No Sunday means no church; no church means no worship; no worship means no religion; no religion means no morality; no morality means no society; no society means no government; no government means anarchy. That's the choice before us. (*Ibid*, p. 120).

Worship: Real worship is not optional. You do not have to decide each Sunday morning whether or not you'll worship each Sunday morning; it should be programmed into your life.

Good conduct: It's a time when you should do things that are holy. If you do a little planning, you don't have to do your shopping on Sunday. There can be time to do things like that on other days. Remember that every day is His. We are not to give Him one day and do as we please the other six.

Be aware of your witness. What about your neighbor? Can he set his clock by the fact that your car pulls out of the driveway at a certain time on Sunday morning, and you're on your way to the worship of God? Don't forget the power of your witness: no man lives to himself, or dies to himself. (*Ibid*, p. 121).

We include this material to demonstrate the fact that the publication of Dr. Bradford's views in the *Ministry* magazine provided no grounds to conclude that his article possessed the imprint of truth. It also illustrated that within the General Conference are men who have embraced such a degree of ecumenism that they not only published a book promoting Sunday observance, but defended their action when some challenged it. Elder James Cress, the Ministerial Association Secretary, was re-elected to his post at the General Conference Session at Toronto, 2000, two years after he published the book. That the Pacific Press agreed to publish this publication, full of error, also demonstrated that this press, too, was culpable.

In our chapter entitled *February 2004*, we have identified several serious weaknesses in *Prophets Are Human*.

1. Unfounded doubts were generally left unrefuted in the book. These stated doubts were:

    > But now there are doubts. There are so many unanswered questions. The Internet site has listed them:
    >
    > Mrs. White taught the door of salvation was shut after 1844.
    >
    > Mrs White wrote that some races are a mixture of man and beast.
    >
    > Mrs White said wearing wigs causes insanity.
    >
    > Mrs White plagiarized materials from other writers and then denied she had done so. There is proof that Ellen White's "I was shown" visions were even copied.
    >
    > Mrs White did not always practice what she preached regarding unclean foods.
    >
    > Mrs White contradicts herself. She wrote, "Pork is a nourishing food." Later she wrote, "Pork should not be eaten under any circumstances."
    >
    > Mrs White said, in the 1850's, that Jesus was to return in a few months. She said she would be alive when Jesus returns.(*Prophets Are Human*, pp. 13, 14).

    (See chapter entitled, "Dispelling False Accusations" for answers to these claimed errors).

2. The insinuation that there had been a conspiracy of silence within the denomination concerning the doubts expressed in the 1919 General Conference Bible Conference, chaired by the President, Elder Arthur Grosvenor Daniells. This repeated claim was not addressed in the book.

    > What could be in those [1919 Bible Conference] minutes that are so important for us to read? (*Ibid*, p. 89).

> I'm beginning to wonder whether I was deceived when I joined the church. (*Ibid*, p. 18).
>
> Why haven't we been told some of these things before? (*Ibid*, p. 38).

3. The claim that Sister White's writings are riddled with error was sustained by the author, for he did not dispel that claim.
4. The Bible was said to contain "a mixture of the Human and the Divine." (*Ibid*, p. 29).
5. The seriously faulted New International Version of Scripture was consistently used. (*Ibid*).

Of course, we have never supported the indefensible concept that the Bible was verbally inspired. Sister White properly presented the truth.

> The Bible points to God as its author; yet it was written by human hands; and in the varied style of its different books it presents the characteristics of the several writers. The truths revealed are all "given by inspiration of God" (2 Timothy 3:16); yet they are expressed in the words of men. The Infinite One by His Holy Spirit has shed light into the minds and hearts of His servants. He has given dreams and visions, symbols and figures; and those to whom the truth was thus revealed have themselves embodied the thought in human language. (*Great Controversy*, p. v).

The living Word and the written Word, alike were perfect, yet both united the divine with the human.

> The Ten Commandments were spoken by God Himself, and were written by His own hand. They are of divine, and not of human composition. But the Bible, with its God-given truths expressed in the language of men, presents a union of the divine and the human. Such a union existed in the nature of Christ, who was the Son of God and the Son of man. Thus it is true of the Bible, as it was of Christ, that "the Word was made flesh, and dwelt among us." John 1:14. (*Ibid*, pp. v, vi).

While at times there appear to be contradictions in the writings of different Scriptural authors, Sister White upheld the perfect harmony of Scripture. This could only be sustained if inspiration directed the minds of every writer, despite their use of different languages, differing styles of expression and their disparate cultural backgrounds.

> Written in different ages, by men who differed widely in rank and occupation, and in mental and spiritual endowments, the books of the Bible present a wide contrast in style, as well as a diversity in the nature of the subjects unfolded. Different forms of expression are employed by different writers; often the same truth is more strikingly presented by one than by another. And as several writers present a subject under varied aspects and relations, there may appear, to the superficial, careless, or prejudiced reader, to be discrepancy or contradiction, where the thoughtful, reverent student, with clearer insight, discerns the underlying harmony. (*Ibid*, p. vi).

May each of us be "thoughtful, reverent [students] with clear insight" discerning "the underlying harmony" of Scripture and the Spirit of Prophecy.

God carefully selected writers of different talents, background and literary skills, knowing that such would employ expressions of the truth which would strike the hearts of us humans whose life experiences are as varied as those of the messengers selected by God. In this way, all mankind is equally able to taste the good things of the Lord.

> As presented through different individuals, the truth is brought out in its varied aspects. One writer is more strongly impressed with one phase of the subject; he grasps those points that harmonize with his experience or with his power of perception and appreciation; another seizes upon a different phase; and each, under the guidance of the Holy Spirit, presents what is most forcibly impressed upon his own mind—a different aspect of the truth in each, but a perfect harmony through all. And the truths thus revealed unite to form a perfect whole, adapted to meet the wants of men in all the circumstances and experiences of life.
>
> (*Ibid*, p. vi).

Note the words above, "the truths thus revealed unite to form a perfect whole." Sister White strongly upheld the fact that Scripture presents Heaven's message and that it is the truthful testimony of God – not the faulted testimony of man.

> God has been pleased to communicate His truth to the world by human agencies, and He Himself, by His Holy Spirit, qualified men and enabled them to do this work. He guided the mind in the selection of what to speak and what to write. The treasure was entrusted to earthen vessels, yet it is, nonetheless, from Heaven. The testimony is conveyed through the imperfect expression of human language, yet it is the testimony of God; and the obedient, believing child of God beholds in it the glory of a divine power, full of grace and truth. (*Ibid*, pp. vi, vii).

Finally, the servant of the Lord left no doubt that the Holy Scriptures are the infallible revelation of God's will for man.

> In His word, God has committed to men the knowledge necessary for salvation. The Holy Scriptures are to be accepted as an authoritative, infallible revelation of His will. They are the standard of character, the revealer of doctrines, and the test of experience. (*Ibid*, p. vii).

We can rest securely in God's assurance that

> [16]All scripture is given by inspiration of God, and is profitable for doctrine, for reproof, for correction, for instruction in righteousness: [17]That the man of God may be perfect, thoroughly furnished unto all good works. (2 Timothy 3:16, 17).

Despite this evident confirmation of the infallibility of Scripture, *Prophets Are Human*, in claiming to support Sister White's prophetic role, has presented a faulted Scripture, tainted by the social milieu. This faulted view was sustained by the South Pacific Division President in his foreword, paragraph two, to Dr. Bradford's book quoted earlier in this chapter. This matter has been documented in our chapter entitled, *Drifting Away From Bible Truth*.

The doubts cast upon the Holy Bible should suffice to disqualify *Prophets Are Human* as an appropriate book in the defense of the Spirit of Prophecy. Sister White ever uplifted the full trustworthiness of the Sacred Scriptures.

Dr. Bradford's suggestion that

> I personally think God was working with people who were living in a culture that was less than ideal, and was trying to lift them to a higher plane.
>
> (*Prophets Are Human*, p. 26),

is offered as an explanation for his conjecture that the Israelites used "brutality" against the Canaanites at the behest of God. (See *Ibid*). This is no minor charge. If sustained, it would seriously undermine the value of God's Word and make our God altogether as vengeful as evil mankind. It is small marvel that within our church, Scripture is in retreat. Instead of fearing God, we fear church leadership. Instead of seeking God's wisdom to guide us, we seek the guidance of human "experts." Forsaking our liberty in Christ, we barter it for the "security" of leadership approval.

In his book, Dr. Bradford stated that the prophet of the First Advent, John the Baptist, taught error. We cite Dr. Bradford's words:

> John the Baptist had some things to learn and some to unlearn. Remember when he was asked what was required for eternal life, he didn't outline salvation by grace, but rather told his enquirers to reform their lives. [Luke 3:11-14]. Later his converts had to be rebaptized when they grew in their understanding beyond what he imparted. [Acts 19:1-5]. (*Ibid*, p. 67, square brackets in the original).

Plainly, the New Theology's diminution of the place of divinely-empowered works in the lives of the redeemed – works which are a total impossibility to perform without the enabling grace of Christ – has clouded Dr. Bradford's thinking in charging John the Baptist with error. By extrapolation, the charge of error is extended to the prophet of the Second Advent. If in his prophetic office John the Baptist could err then Sister White's "errors" must, too, be overlooked and excused. This is Dr. Bradford's reasoning:

Christ, Himself, could be accused of the same "error" if we are to follow Dr. Bradford's reasoning. Notice Christ's counsel:

> [25] And, behold, a certain lawyer stood up, and tempted him, saying, Master, what shall I do to inherit eternal life? [26] He said unto him, What is written in the law? how readest thou? [27] And he answering said, Thou shalt love the Lord thy God with all thy heart, and with all thy soul, and with all thy strength, and with all thy mind; and thy neighbour as thyself. [28] And he said unto him, Thou hast answered right: this do, and thou shalt live. (Luke 10:25-28).

Christ today would likewise be accused of legalism by some – were they unaware of whom He was – when He answered the rich young ruler's quest for eternal life.

> ¹⁶And, behold, one came and said unto him, Good Master, what good thing shall I do, that I may have eternal life? ¹⁷And he said unto him, Why callest thou me good? there is none good but one, that is, God: but if thou wilt enter into life, keep the commandments. (Matthew 19:16, 17).

But Christ fully taught that enabling grace was crucial for the successful fulfilment of His inspired advice. He expressed to Paul,

> ...My grace is sufficient for thee: for my strength is made perfect in weakness. (2 Corinthians 12:9).

Proponents of the New Theology appear to fail to discern the power of the miracle of grace. To neglect the transformation of character wrought by Christ's grace in the heart is to emasculate this wonderful gift and to accept Satan's counterfeit of grace, which is an insipid, powerless entity.

Dr. Bradford also proffered the view that Sister White's ministry contributed no element of doctrinal authority. We would have thought that as an experienced pastor, evangelist, ministerial secretary and teacher of ministerial trainees, Dr. Bradford would have studied the many passages where Sister White did claim such inspired authority. Apparently he has not, for the only alternative would be that he is aware of her claims in this matter and he has judged these claims to be invalid and thus deceitful.

To diminish Sister White's value in the arena of doctrine, Dr. Bradford presented a truth.

> The prime purpose of the gift of prophecy is a spiritual one.
> (*Prophets Are Human*, p. 61).

Of course this is the role of every prophet including the prophet Paul who included in that role the greatest body of Christian doctrine found in the epistles of the New Testament. He extolled sound doctrine:

> ⁶If thou put the brethren in remembrance of these things, thou shalt be a good minister of Jesus Christ, nourished up in the words of faith and of good doctrine, whereunto thou hast attained.... ¹⁶Take heed unto thyself, and unto the doctrine; continue in them: for in doing this thou shalt both save thyself, and them that hear thee. (1 Timothy 4:6, 16).

> ¹Let as many servants as are under the yoke count their own masters worthy of all honour, that the name of God and his doctrine be not blasphemed.... ³If any man teach otherwise, and consent not to wholesome words, even the words of our Lord Jesus Christ, and to the doctrine which is according to godliness; ⁴He is proud, knowing nothing, but doting about questions and strifes of words, whereof

> cometh envy, strife, railings, evil surmisings, ⁵Perverse disputings of men of corrupt minds, and destitute of the truth, supposing that gain is godliness: from such withdraw thyself. (1 Timothy 6:1, 3-5).
>
> All scripture is given by inspiration of God, and is profitable for doctrine, for reproof, for correction, for instruction in righteousness: (2 Timothy 3:16).
>
> ⁹Holding fast the faithful word as he hath been taught, that he may be able by sound doctrine both to exhort and to convince the gainsayers.... ¹But speak thou the things which become sound doctrine:... ⁷In all things showing thyself a pattern of good works: in doctrine showing uncorruptness, gravity, sincerity.... ¹⁰Not purloining, but showing all good fidelity; that they may adorn the doctrine of God our Saviour in all things. (Titus 1:9; 2:1, 7, 10).

Where do we discover these enlightening doctrines? We discover them, of course, in the writings and recorded words of the prophets. Dr. Bradford, however, sought to distance Sister White's mission from doctrine, perhaps deeming that theologians like himself are more qualified to arbitrate on such matters.

In this he seriously erred if this was his conclusion. By referring to the doubts of Elder H. C. Lacey – with which Elder A. G. Daniells agreed – expressed at the 1919 Bible Conference – Dr. Bradford implied that the prime spiritual role of our end-time prophet does not embrace doctrinal authority. But Sister White frequently claimed such authority. We cite two instances.

> At this time there was fanaticism among some of those who had been believers in the first message. Serious errors in doctrine and practice were cherished, and some were ready to condemn all who would not accept their views. God revealed these errors to me in vision and sent me to His erring children to declare them; but in performing this duty I met with bitter opposition and reproach.
> (*Testimonies for the Church*, Vol. 5, pp. 655, 656).

It would appear that this reproach directed against Sister White's settlement of doctrinal issues remains to this day. That Sister White's work encompassed elucidation of Bible doctrine, cannot and must not be doubted.

> We are to be established in the faith, in the light of the truth given us in our early experience. At that time one error after another pressed in upon us; ministers and doctors brought in new doctrines. We would search the Scriptures with much prayer, and the Holy Spirit would bring the truth to our minds. Sometimes whole nights would be devoted to searching the Scriptures, and earnestly asking God for guidance. Companies of devoted men and women assembled for this purpose. The power of God would come upon me, and I was enabled clearly to define what is truth and what is error.
>
> As the points of our faith were thus established, our feet were placed upon a solid foundation. We accepted the truth point by point, under the demonstration of the

Holy Spirit. I would be taken off in vision, and explanations would be given me. I was given illustrations of heavenly things, and of the sanctuary, so that we were placed where light was shining on us in clear, distinct rays.

(*Gospel Workers*, p. 302).

Dr. Bradford's book is a low point in the publishing work in Australia. It is yet another evidence that the Signs Publishing Company has departed from its established purpose, a purpose which it followed in its earlier history, to publish the pure truth of God. It's bold acknowledgment that,

> This book [is] proudly printed and published in Australia by Signs Publishing Company, Victoria   (South Pacific *Record*, February 14, 2004)

contains a hint of frenzy from publishers who have already blighted their reputation by the inclusion of many faulted articles in their publications, the *Record*, the *Signs*, and the *Edge* magazines.

Dr. Bradford used the Letters column of the South Pacific *Record* in an attempt to dispel the evident impact of Sister White's warning which he quoted. Below we quote his entire letter as published.

> I want to thank "Name supplied" (April 17) for their kind words about my book *Prophets Are Human* as well as share a little of my "homework."
>
> The statement, "The very last deception of Satan will be to make of none effect the testimony of the Spirit of God" (*Selected Messages*, Book 1, page 48) has been quoted a number of times in recent Letters. It comes from *Letter 12*, 1890. Unfortunately the compilers of *Selected Messages* left out the words that identify what that deception is to be, for Ellen White goes on to state that "He will bring in spurious visions."
>
> I'm not aware of anyone involved in the recent discussions being involved this way. We must not be afraid to meet Ellen White's critics openly and honestly. We can do so with a right understanding from Scripture of the gift of prophecy.
>
> Ellen White can pass every biblical expectation of a true prophet. The problem is that after her death the church began to use her in ways that she would never have approved.   (South Pacific *Record*, May 22, 2004, p. 13).

Praise God that Dr. James Nix, Director of the General Conference Ellen G. White Estate, took issue with Dr. Bradford's wrongful interpretation. Dr. Nix's letter to the same periodical plainly documented the intent of Sister White. His letter, too, is quoted in full:

> In Letters (May 22) reference was made to Ellen White's statement, "The very last deception of Satan will be to make of none effect the testimony of the Spirit of God" (*Selected Messages*, Book 1, page 48). The letter stated that the compilers of *Selected Messages* left out words – "spurious visions" – identifying what that deception will be.

The quotation comes from a long letter written on August 12, 1890, to a Brother and Sister Garmire. Ellen White expressed several areas of concerns to Brother Garmire, including his support of his daughter's claim to be receiving visions.

The quotation in *Selected Messages* is found in the part of the letter that deals with the daughter's spurious visions. The next paragraph expands upon Mrs. White's understanding of the means Satan will use to destroy confidence in the testimonies.

"The very last deception of Satan will be to make of none effect the testimony of the Spirit of God. 'Where there is no vision, the people perish.' Satan will work ingeniously, in *different* ways and *through different agencies*, to unsettle the confidence of God's remnant people in the true testimony. He will bring in spurious visions to mislead and mingle the false with the true, and so disgust people that they will regard everything that bears the name of visions, as a species of fanaticism....

"Likewise, he works through persons who have been reproved for some inconsistency in their religious life, for some course of action which was dangerous to themselves and others; and instead of receiving the testimony as a blessing from God, they refuse the means God uses to set them right. Such may be apparently very zealous for God, but they put their own interpretation upon the Word, and make it contradict what the Lord has revealed in the testimonies. They think they are doing God's service, but such work God has not given them to do." (Letter 12, 1890, emphasis supplied).

Clearly, Mrs. White was describing more than just "spurious visions." The quotation as printed does not violate its context. Rather, it reflects fairly her view of Satan's last deception. (South Pacific *Record*, July 10, 2004, p.29).

One wonders why Dr. Bradford took issue with Sister White's statement and failed to present the full intent of it when he had, as he testified, done his "homework." Dr. Bradford claims in his book, *Prophets Are Human*, that he is defending the Spirit of Prophecy against the internet attacks on Sister White's reliability. If he sincerely believes this, then Sister White's statement applied to the internet critics and not to him. Some will wonder whether Dr. Bradford harbors at least a sneaking suspicion that he, too, is making of none effect the testimony of the Spirit of God, and may fall under the condemnation of Sister White's letter. Such a fear would provide a logical reason for him to desire to neutralize the impact and implications of this statement, upon which he did his "homework."

The General Conference White Estate followed up Elder Nix's letter to the *Record* with a none-too-positive evaluation of Dr. Bradford's book, *Prophets Are Human* which it sent to the South Pacific Division. Praise God for this righteous action. God still has his Nicodemus and Joseph of Arimathaea at the World Headquarters of our Church. In the claimed spirit of openness the

Executive Editor of the South Pacific *Record* should direct the Editor of the *Record* to publish salient extracts of the report so that those who have been deceived by *Prophets Are Human* may be warned of its upholding of soul-destroying error.

The report correctly stated that Dr. Bradford's book contained "gross inconsistencies and factual errors." The White Estate strongly regretted that the book was given approval for printing before the world church had been afforded the opportunity to evaluate this new approach to the Spirit of Prophecy. The report also stated that the material in the book did not line up with historical facts, and quotations were used out of their proper context. The General Conference White Estate recommended that the book be withdrawn from sale and be re-issued free of these major defects. The White Estate is also aware that, tragically, the Pacific Press in the United States has ordered one thousand copies of the book for sale.

Today in the South Pacific Division, through the artifices of the Avondale College Theology Department, supported by the South Pacific Division leadership, is constantly altering the fundamental truths of our faith, without any reference to the General Conference in full quinquennial session. It is time to call "Halt!"

It must not be overlooked that Dr. Bradford has long promoted error in our midst. A long video-tape which he prepared in the 1980's is still extant. Not content to challenge doctrines such as the fallen human nature of Christ and the sanctuary message, Dr. Bradford felt it proper to malign one minister who *did* stand solidly behind these truths, New Zealand evangelist, Pr. Austin Cooke, one of the South Pacific Division's most-successful public evangelists.

Dr. Bradford concluded his presentation with a series of interviews concerning Pastor Cooke and the supposed value of the training of Avondale College. In Dr. Bradford's interview with Avondale College retired professor, Dr. Noel Clapham, the latter libeled Pastor Cooke, a warrior for truth. At a presentation at Avondale College, Pr. Cooke had inadvertently placed the date of the marriage of Martin Luther a little earlier in time on the basis of one authority, a most insignificant matter, in respect to his presentation. Seizing upon the triviality, Dr. Noel Clapham, a stout supporter of the New Theology, exploded, referring to Pr. Cooke's response to Dr. Clapham's later correction,

> I can hardly believe it. He [Pr. Cooke] said, "What does it matter, Noel? What does it matter?" He feels free to make defamatory statements which outside this denomination would cost him money, defamatory statements about people and institutions and does it with an inane, neurotic laugh you'd expect from a firebug or a saboteur.   (Transcript from Dr. Bradford's videotape).

Dr. Bradford possessed ample opportunity to remove these insulting words against a preacher of righteousness, prior to distributing the videotape. He chose not to do so. In the intervening years he has not apologized to Pr. Cooke for his neglect of this responsibility. Pastor Cooke, still actively preaching the truth in Australia, New Zealand and England, celebrated his eighty-seventh birthday in July, 2004. So zealous is he for the defense of the faith that when, in 2002, he fell from a ladder while lopping branches off a tree and sustained serious fractures of his pelvis in three places, Pastor Cooke travelled a thousand miles from Brisbane to Melbourne in order to preach the word to God's flock only two months later.

It is worthy of report that the South Pacific *Record* of February 14, 2004 emblazoned in color on its cover the words,

> United in the Warmth of Fellowship.

With such a faulted basis for unity it is no source for astonishment that our church has never previously been so disunited in the South Pacific. We can attend football clubs, ex-servicemen's clubs, the Roman Catholic Church or a thousand other organizations and find fellowship, but only in Seventh-day Adventist faithful churches may be found truth. It is the common possession of this body of faith which alone unites us and which results in genuine warm fellowship. Genuine fellowship is a result of unity, not its cause.

The word *phantasmagoria* was coined in the early nineteenth century, having been derived from a magic-lantern show which produced optical illusions. As we review the events of February 2004 in the South Pacific Division, how we cry out, "If only this alien doctrine could pass away like the phantasmagoria of a fevered dream!" But alas, the omega of apostasy, as prophesied by our prophet for these days, is a reality; it is here to remain until the sealing work is completed and, indeed, a thousand years longer until

> ... the day cometh, that shall burn as an oven; and all the proud, yea, and all that do wickedly, shall be stubble: and the day that cometh shall burn them up, saith the LORD of hosts, that it shall leave them neither root nor branch.
>
> (Malachi 4:1).

7
Stratagem III – An Ellen White Reality Check

The article occupied less than a page in the February 7, 2004 edition of the South Pacific *Record*, yet in the annuls of denominational publishing, the editorial, *An Ellen White Reality Check*, must rank along side the most blatant, overt attempts to dismantle truth.

It commenced as a summary of the activities of the South Pacific Division during the first week of February, 2004. This was a week of unparalleled shame in our home Division.

> This week's *Record* begins a series of four articles entitled "Ellen White for today." These articles coincide with a summit at Avondale College, which ran this past week, about the church's understanding and application of Ellen White's writings.
>
> This is a series of interviews or, more correctly, conversations with Dr Arthur Patrick. A respected church historian within and outside the Seventh-day Adventist Church, Dr. Patrick has served in a variety of capacities within the church, including: pastor-evangelist; chaplain; theology lecturer and, importantly, the director of the Ellen G White/Seventh-day Adventist Research Centre.

The editor claimed that

> As you will discover, he [Dr. Patrick] has confidence in the God-given inspiration and leading in the ministry of Ellen White

It would seem today that the "God-given inspiration" in which some claim to have confidence, is a most faulty one, for later in the month of February Pastor Bruce Manners, the editor of the *Record* posed the following question to Dr. Arthur Patrick:

> So even an inspired person can be partly right and partly wrong?
> (*Record*, February 28, 2004).

Dr. Patrick's response was:

> You've got it! My cancer specialist doesn't fix my lawnmower. My wife is excellent at teaching children, but hopeless at dealing with email viruses. Because Ellen White was shown in a two-hour panorama the age-long struggle between righteousness and sin does not mean that she was an expert on the life and times of John Huss. (*Ibid*).

Since the accuracy of Sister White's account of John Huss in the chapter "Huss and Jerome" in *The Great Controversy*, pp. 97-119, is under stern attack, this response is tantamount to having "confidence" in an inspiration which is "partly right and partly wrong." May God preserve us from such a counterfeit inspiration. Such would merit absolutely no confidence whatsoever.

Pastor Manners presented his editorial as a defense of the internet attack upon the Spirit of Prophecy.

> We asked him [Dr. Patrick] to speak with *Record* because Ellen White's ministry is coming under sustained attack, particularly on the Internet. Yet many of these attacks are based on information that has been researched and known within the Adventist Church for some time. Unfortunately, the more recent research into the life and writings of Ellen White and the discussion surrounding her ministry has tended to be available only in a limited way. That has made it difficult for church members to respond to the sometimes malicious attacks being made.
> (*Ibid*).

However, the editor moved on to confirm the correctness of the information, while denying the conclusions drawn.

> Often these attacks are based on correct information, but draw conclusions that give little consideration for both the historical content and a mature understanding of prophetic ministry. (*Ibid*).

What Pastor Manners here referred to as "a mature understanding of prophetic ministry" is one, as we have seen above, which is "partly right and partly wrong." Is this the best defense we can mount against the internet attacks of former Seventh-day Adventist ordained pastors who are now Sunday-keepers and have, in some cases, been guilty of adultery? It must not escape notice that some of these ex-pastors were leaders in the Celebration worship when Seventh-day Adventist pastors. One, at least, had even received praise in the *Adventist Review* for raising up a "successful" Celebration Church, which is now defunct. Under the headline "Adventist Worship – Celebration Style" and the sub-heading, "Pastors With a Vision for Change," it was declared:

> Dave Snyder of Milwaukee [Oregon] dreamed of a different experience for [his] congregation – of a spiritually healing community, where warm Christian fellowship would permeate every aspect of church life, where members would become excited about worshipping and following God, and where former members could return and feel safe and comfortable.
> (*Adventist Review*, October 1, 1990).

The *Ministry* monthly magazine, the organ of the General Conference Ministerial Association, also weighed in on the side of celebration worship in its issue of October, 1991 entitled "WORSHIP: Coming together in God's presence." Among other articles one, written by Darryl Comstock, Principal at Central Valley Junior Academy, Tangent, Oregon, was entitled "Selling Change – How to bring about change without losing your members." The President of the Oregon Conference who encouraged the introduction of these celebration services, South African Pastor Alf Birch, was nominated President of the South Pacific Division at the 1990 General Conference Session and voted into that position. He accepted it, but two days later he resigned the post and Pastor Bryan Ball was elected in his place. This nomination pointed to the direction the South Pacific Division had set fourteen years ago.

Pastor Manners promoted a new and different understanding of Sister White's ministry based upon new evidence.

> The conversations with Dr Patrick are an attempt to look at the findings that have come to light in the past 30 years, and the challenges they raise for what could be called the traditional understanding of Ellen White's special role within the Adventist Church. The evidence is clear: we have to understand Ellen White differently from the way we have in the past. (*Ibid*).

Let it be remembered that the past thirty years have encompassed the decades of the rapid growth of the assault upon our faith by the ministry. The parallel between open distrust of the *Testimonies* and the efforts to alter almost every essential-established article of our faith is no coincidence. The *Testimonies*, if believed, establish our Bible-based doctrines and plants them in the reinforced foundations of truth.

The *Record* editor openly attacked the accuracy of Sister White's inspired writings. The evidence is plain for all to read.

> For instance, it is now well documented that she, at times, used historical sources that included factual errors in *The Great Controversy*. She was not guided to correct those facts. But that admission must be followed by asking about her purpose. She did not intend to write history, but to "unfold the scenes of the great controversy between truth and error" (*The Great Controversy*, page xii). Having in mind the overall picture she had of this controversy, she then used the best Protestant sources available to her, including their now known factual errors. (*Ibid*, parenthesis in original).

When this editorial was penned, Pastor Manners was under appointment as Senior Pastor of the Avondale College Church. He has now taken up this post. Will the students training for service in God's work be strengthened in the faith by this appointment? Will Pastor Manners, himself, be turned to truth by his inevitable association with the Avondale College theologians? These are questions born out of concern for the salvation and ministry of those mentioned.

Pastor Manners further emphasized the thesis that inspiration is "partly right and partly wrong."

> For those who have not kept abreast of research into the writings of Ellen White, that last paragraph may prove difficult. Errors of fact in inspired writings? Can that be? While we, as a church, take the position that inspired writings are not inerrant (that is, without error), there has always been the suspicion that God would somehow protect His writers from even the simplest mistakes.

This has tended, perhaps, to be the unspoken understanding of Ellen White's writings. We now need to face the reality that this is not so.
(Ibid. Words in parenthesis are in the original).

The editorial then moved into territory of extreme authorship.

> With Ellen White two extremes are to be avoided. The first takes such a high view of her inspiration that it is unrealistic, unworkable and unbiblical. The temptation here is to view her like a pope or to proclaim her Saint Ellen. The second takes a low view of her ministry and suggests she was unethical, underhanded and unworthy of consideration. The temptation is to say her writings have no more value than a thousand others. *(Ibid)*.

Sister White like a pope? Saint Ellen? Surely these misguided comparisons cannot be accorded serious status. The pope claims the power to overrule Scriptural imperatives such as the Law of God. Sister White never arrogated such authority to herself nor has any Seventh-day Adventist we have met ever accorded her such blasphemous authority. The name Saint Ellen possesses overtones of Saint Mary who was accorded freedom from sin throughout her entire life by the Papal Dogma of the Immaculate Conception proclaimed by Pope Pius IX, December 8, 1854. All agree that Sister White, like all past prophets, was a sinner in need of the grace of her Savior.

It is most disturbing that:

> Before publishing these conversations, they were submitted to a broad range of people at various levels within the church. The counsel we received has proved very helpful, as was the desire that this information should be published. However, we understand that this topic will prove difficult for some time, and a few may even see it as another attack on Ellen White's ministry. *(Ibid)*.

We can only ask the question, "Are there none in leadership posts in the South Pacific to counsel in the most effective manner that such a debasing of faith has no place in any Seventh-day Adventist publication?" Even if some leaders have provided such wise advice, which has been rejected, is there not one prepared to raise his voice publicly to warn God's people that they are being led astray by men in positions of high influence in our midst?

At the conclusion of the editorial is a footnote written in italics. It states:

> In Fundamental Belief 1, a phrase borrowed probably from Ellen White's introduction to *The Great Controversy* is used to state that the Bible is the "infallible revelation of His will." This claim is quite different from saying the Bible is infallible or inerrant. *(Ibid)*.

Really? Has the English language become a meaningless series of incomprehensible vocal noises? Not surprisingly our *Oxford English Reference Dictionary*, Oxford University Press, Oxford, 1996, defines *infallible* as "incapable of error" and *inerrant* as "not liable to err." For American readers, *The*

International Edition of the Heritage Illustrated Dictionary of the English Language, American Heritage Publishing Co. Inc., Boston, 1973, defines *infallible* similarly – "incapable of error" and *inerrant* as "making no errors."

Sister White explicitly declared that

> God's Word is infallible. (*Selected Messages*, Vol. 1, p. 416).

She also recorded the fact, with evident approval, that the sixteenth century reformer, Ulrich Zwingli (1484-1531),

> presented the word of God as the only infallible authority.
> (*Great Controversy*, p. 177).

Clearly Sister White's statement confirming the Bible as the infallible revelation of God's will is in no wise different in its intent. Her use of the term the "infallible revelation of His will" applied to Scripture, does mean it is infallible, inerrant. "Ellen White reality check" may best be evaluated as a flight into fantasy.

8 Stratagem IV – Ellen White for Today

The four "conversations" between Pastor Bruce Manners, editor of the South Pacific *Record*, and Dr. Arthur Patrick, (*Record*, February 7, 14, 21 and 28, 2004), must rank among the most disingenuous material ever to blight a Seventh-day Adventist denominational publication.

The conversations presented a remarkable tangle of faint praise for the Spirit of Prophecy, unwarranted laudatory remarks for some who have sought to destroy the credibility of Sister White's writings, illogical conclusions, a naïve acceptance of the many claims leveled against Sister White in the form of her supposed literary "errors", a failure to research the powerful evidence now available which answers these claims, claims that Sister White presented some materials which were erroneous, and misdirected and implausible assertions to have strengthened faith in her prophetic mission.

As a "conversation" piece, these articles suffered from stilted questions more akin in style to those of popular newspaper column writers answering questions they have never been asked. The questions posed, too often, were largely expressions of the questioner's opinion rather than a search for the interviewee's considered conclusions. The responses, on the other hand, lacked spontaneity. They evidenced the structure of the well-rehearsed and carefully-polished answers of a written response, rather than those one would expect from the transcript of a tape-recording of a genuine, spontaneous "conversation."

Despite this manifestly negative review of the material in these four "conversations", this assessment, although our genuine appraisal, is not presented with the least animus in respect to Dr. Patrick or Pastor Manners. Rather do we write in sincere concern for our two brothers and the influence of their work upon the cause God in these final days of earth's history.

It would not serve God's people well if we did not document the elements of this assessment. Before we proceed to this duty, we would record the stated purpose of these conversations, a purpose which they fell short of achieving.

> The conversations beginning in today's *Record* are an attempt to look at some of these issues in a way that remains true to Ellen White's own intention for her writings. (*Ibid*, February 7, 2004, p. 2).

Pastor Manners' aim, as we shall see, was not achieved in this published series of conversations. The issues to which he referred, the numerous internet attacks on Sister White's prophetic calling, rather than being met in a manner "that remains true to Ellen White's own intention for her writings," the conversations sustained. Rather than presenting the numerous defects in the false internet assertions, the conversations promoted their validity. Instead of offering material true to Sister White's intentions for her writings, Pastor Manners and Dr. Patrick chose to destroy their influence in a manner Sister White most certainly did not intend. Sister White was not the author of twenty-five-million words in order to confuse God's saints with a subtle mixture of materials which are partly correct and partly erroneous, leaving us to rely upon theologians to arbitrate by deciphering which portions are correct and which are in error. Only Satan "inspires" a mishmash of truth and error. God never does.

We searched in vain in the four conversations to discover anything which would assist God's people by removing the veil of falsehood which served the purposes of the internet assailants upon the Spirit of Prophecy. The conversations meekly followed the lines of attacks taken by these assailants, placing an implausible explanation upon Sister White's asserted "errors" which are set forth in the first conversation.

> Ellen White is currently under vigorous attack. A wide variety of web sites and some video productions claim such things as: Ellen White was a plagiarist and a liar who knowingly misled people; she did not follow her own counsel; and she changed her position on vital teachings or contradicted herself.
>
> Some of these charges go back to the 19th century, but other attacks are based on information that has come to light in the past 30 years. In this series of conversations Dr Arthur Patrick talks about recent findings and how they relate to Ellen White's ministry and her role in the church today. (*Ibid*, p. 9).

See where Dr. Patrick's defense leads us. (In these conversations Pastor Manners' questions are printed in bold type and Dr. Patrick's replies in normal type):

> **What is the greatest need for the church today in relating to Ellen White?** The current concern is not so much to *defend* her as to *understand* her in view of all the known evidence. Obviously we're not able to present all that material in this discussion, but hopefully we can encourage a better understanding….
>
> **It seems that until about the 1970s, most research within the church on Ellen White was what could be called triumphalistic, apologetic or defensive. Can you give an overview of what happened then?** The Western world was changing rapidly, and those changes impacted Adventists and their mission. At last we had people who could "hear" prophets. Jesus and the apostles speaking in their own languages. That is, they knew Hebrew, Aramaic and Greek.
>
> Teachers at all levels were asked questions quite different from those that had been standard for a century. Fresh issues were brought to pastors by members. Members brought fresh issues to their pastors. So questions that had not been asked before stimulated the spirit of enquiry. (*Ibid*, italics in the original).

Here we clearly see that early in the conversations the "defense" of Sister White's writings is discarded. In place of such defense is substituted stout defenses of these false charges accompanied by pleas of "understanding" of the claimed manifold "mistakes."

As seen above, the 1970's are identified, correctly, as the period in which denominational workers actively commenced their diligent efforts to remove Sister White's writings as influential in confirming the faith and establishing Bible truth.

> **How's that?** As noted last week, 1970 marked a watershed in the study of Ellen White and her writings. New questions started to be asked in college lecture rooms and Sabbath school classes. New resources were becoming available to help provide the answers. (*Ibid*, February 14, 2004, p. 3).

> **As you have researched and listened to the findings of other researchers, how has your appreciation of Ellen White changed?** I've become more aware of the big picture. One illustration may help to explain that a bit. I used to read Ellen White's classic volume *The Desire of Ages* to answer a host of questions like: Which Mary is the one in this story? At what point in the ministry of Jesus did this event occur? Now I read *The Desire of Ages* much more for its spiritual significance. Ellen White expressed its theme on page 22: "To know God is to love Him." The book is 835 pages about falling in love with God as He is revealed in the ministry of Jesus. (*Ibid*, February 7, 2004, p.9).

The perceptive reader will recognize that it was in the era of the 1970's that the New Theology adherents at all levels of our church launched their successful effort to control the organization worldwide. At first this task was met with stern resistance by some leaders within the church organization, especially Elder Robert Pierson, President of the General Conference, (1966-1979).

In the early 1970's the leadership of God's Church began a call for reformation and revival. Pastor Robert Pierson, then General Conference president, initiated the call. This challenge to our church membership was taken up in the editorials and articles in the *Adventist Review*. At the Annual Council of the General Conference held in 1973 a most earnest plea to God's people was adopted by the delegates in session. In our lifetime a more stirring appeal has never been made to God's people. The tone of this appeal was set in the first paragraph:

> We believe that the return of Jesus has been long delayed, that the reasons for the delay are not wrapped in mysteries, and that the primary consideration before the Seventh-day Adventist Church is to re-order its priorities individually and corporately so that our Lord's return may be hastened.
> (General Conference *Annual Council Appeal*, October, 1973).

The Annual Council then turned its attention to the great message of 1888 and questioned,

> What has happened to the message and experience that by 1892 had brought the beginning of the earth's final message of warning and appeal? (*Ibid*).

The leaders of God's Church answered their own question very frankly. There was no arrogant effort to put all the blame on the laity. The Church leadership fully and humbly acknowledged its own deficiencies; nevertheless the failures so evident in God's people were not overlooked. The statement from the Annual Council made the following points:

> As a body the Church still is in the Laodicean condition as set forth by the True Witness in Rev. 3:14-19. Therefore in attempting to find the specific present causes for failure and delay, the Council has noted three main factors:
>
> 1. Leaders and people have not fully accepted as a personal message Christ's analysis and appeal to the Laodiceans. (Rev. 3:14-22);
>
> 2. Leaders and people are in some ways disobedient to divine directives, both in personal experience and in the conduct of the Church's commission;
>
> 3. Leaders and people have not yet finished the Church's task. (*Ibid*).

In order to place the finger on the source of the problem, the gathered church leaders quoted from other writings of God's servant:

> Those who come up to every point, and stand every test, and overcome, be the price what it may, have heeded the counsel of the True Witness, and they will receive the latter rain, and thus be fitted for translation.
>
> (*Testimonies for the Church*, Vol. 1, p. 187).

So important was this appeal from the 1973 General Conference that we are constrained to present selections from the appeal, for it has stood as an awesome challenge to the Church of God to this day.

> The message to Laodicea involved a personal relationship to Jesus Christ that will produce a quality people, a conquering people, a people who, in Christ's own words, will conquer "as I myself conquered." (Rev. 3:21 RSV). This message will produce a people whom God can set forth without embarrassment as exhibits of those who "keep the commandments of God and the faith of Jesus. "(Rev. 14:12 RSV); a people who have learned through experience that all godliness is a result of being sustained by divine power. Such people can be entrusted with special power because they will use it the way Jesus used power; indeed, in all aspects of life they will reflect the character of Jesus.
>
> Becoming like Jesus in word and deed is the goal of the process called righteousness by faith. (*General Conference 1973 Appeal*, op. cit.).

The document then set forth another passage from the Spirit of Prophecy, which was anathema to those who had accepted the New Theology. This passage stated:

> The righteousness of Christ is not a cloak to cover unconfessed and unforsaken sin; it is a principle of life that transforms the character and controls the conduct. Holiness is wholeness for God; it is the entire surrender of heart and life to the indwelling of the principles of heaven. (*Desire of Ages*, pp. 555, 556).

Elder Kenneth Wood, Editor of the *Review and Herald* (1966-1982) also stood out as a vocal protestor of the era, as did others.

Elder Wood openly appealed for godly changes in our Colleges almost a quarter of a century ago. In an editorial entitled, "Colleges in Trouble," he wrote:

> We confess that we are alarmed by the fact that some of our colleges seem to be drifting away from the standards and objectives established for them by their founders. We are alarmed by the secular climate that prevails on some campuses. We are alarmed by the strange winds of doctrine that blow on some campuses. (*Review and Herald*, February 21, 1980).

In the past twenty-five years, that which aroused earnest church leaders in 1980, has greatly escalated. Yet we seldom any longer read or hear any cries of concern from leaders today. When we lose standards, when we substitute secularism for spirituality, when we espouse doctrinal error and present it as truth and when we condone or tolerate immorality, then are we spiritually bankrupt.

The retirement of these two men commenced the tragic era which led rapidly to unbridled apostasy which now pervades throughout the church organization worldwide.

Well do we remember Elder Wood speaking to us at the General Conference Session in Dallas, in 1980, at which Russell was a delegate. Elder Wood spoke of the shock he experienced when he received a letter from Dr. Richard Hammill, at the time Vice President of the General Conference, who retired at the 1980 Session in Dallas, Texas, describing Elder Wood as the Seventh-day Adventist Ayatolah Khoumeni, the fanatical Islamic President of Iran of that era. Dr. Hammill was commenting upon Elder Wood's editorial cited above. Dr. Hammill, who died in the very late 1990's later stated,

> Animals [were] living in the earth ... millions of years ago before these [continental] plates separated. And, moreover, as I got to looking into the geologic column, I had to recognize ... that the geologic column is valid, that some forms of life were extinct before other forms of life came into existence. I had to recognize that the forms of life that we are acquainted with mostly, like the ungulate hoof animals, the primates, man himself, exist only in the very top little thin layer of the Holocene, and that many forms of life were extinct before these ever came in, which, of course, is a big step for a Seventh-day Adventist when you are taught that every form of life came into existence in six days.... I had felt it for many, many years, but finally there in about 1983 I had to say to myself, That's right. The steadily accumulating evidence in the natural world has forced a reevaluation in the way that I look and understand and interpret parts of the Bible. (*Spectrum*, March 1996, pp. 27, 28).

Yet, not only had Dr. Hammil risen to the rank of General Conference Vice President, he had previously held the influential post of President of Andrews University (1963-1976), for thirteen years. Sadly, increasingly men who know not this precious truth of the Seventh-day Adventist faith occupy high ecclesiastical office.

In 1985, on our way through North Carolina, to the General Conference Session in New Orleans, we were invited to lunch by Elder Robert Pierson. He was then in retirement. New Zealand evangelist, Pastor George Burnside accompanied us. We had presented meetings in the Henderson Church, North Carolina, in the town where Elder Pierson had retired. Elder Pierson attended all but one of our meetings. At the conclusion he publicly stated to the congregation that those present had heard the truth of God. There Elder Pierson expressed to us the pain in his heart over a recent issue of the *Adventist Review* in which virtually abortion on demand was sanctioned. He also expressed deep concern that Pastor Geoffrey Garne, the South African who was then editor of the South Pacific *Record* had been "muzzled" by the South Pacific Division leadership, after writing an excellent series of truth-filled editorials. Neither church paper has recovered from those assaults upon it.

Colin also reminded Elder Pierson that he had been a delegate to the General Conference Session in Vienna, Austria, in 1975. Colin had anticipated the Session with great hopes that plans to implement the reforms mooted at the 1973 and 1974 General Conference Annual Councils would be implemented. To Colin's dismay no such initiatives were discussed. It was one of the most disheartening experiences in Colin's life. He enquired of Elder Pierson the reason for this failure to move forward. Sorrowfully, Elder Pierson replied, "I could not move foreward because neither ministry nor laity were ready, on the whole, to implement them." A crucial point in our denominational history passed as we rejected God-ordained reform and rushed headlong into the implementation of the New Theology which has all but destroyed the faith and mission of our beloved Seventh-day Adventist Church. We say "all but," for the very small remnant of the Seventh-day Adventist Church will ever block the success of the New Theology and will ultimately and gloriously finish God's allotted work for His church on earth.

> Except the LORD of hosts had left unto us a very small remnant, we should have been as Sodom, and we should have been like unto Gomorrah.   (Isaiah 1:9).

> [27]Esaias also crieth concerning Israel, Though the number of the children of Israel be as the sand of the sea, a remnant shall be saved: [28]For he will finish the work, and cut it short in righteousness: because a short work will the Lord make upon the earth. [29]And as Esaias said before, Except the Lord of Sabaoth had left us a seed, we had been as Sodoma, and been made like unto Gomorrha.
>
> (Romans 9:27-29).

Thus the "new questions" arising in the 1970's were simply a reflection of the rapid inroads of the New Theology during the same period. They did not arise out of an atmosphere of revival and heightened faith, but in an era when belief was fading.

The conversations between Pastor Manners and Dr. Patrick upheld the unwarranted doubts of church leaders expressed at the 1919 Bible Conference. As we document in this book, those doubts were quite unjustified. (See Part IV of this book). Yet now those tragic doubts of many decades ago are being used by contemporary doubters to depart far beyond where those 1919 doubters would have been willing to travel. Little did those doubters count the cost of their faithless statements. (See Part IV – Divine History).

The discovery of the transcripts of the 1919 Bible Conference startled many Adventists in the late 1970s. What insights did we gain from them?
We learned the questions that seemed so new and threatening in the 1970s and beyond were quite well known and were illumined by the experience and understanding of Ellen White's contemporaries. But the church had largely forgotten both the questions and the answers during the long years we sheltered in the fundamentalist camp where inerrancy [without any error even in incidental details] was expected of inspired writings.

Can you briefly explain some of the issues raised at the 1919 conference?
The verbatim reports are available and repay careful reading. They help us to see Ellen White's life and writings through the eyes of people who worked closely with her. One important issue is how we should understand her writings in relation to mundane detail – like chronology and history. Another is the way in which her writings speak to the heart more than the head.

The transcripts from the 1919 conference show the fear that anything less than an inerrant view of Ellen White's writings would bring protests, so concepts of her inspiration as understood by those who spoke at the conference were withheld from church members. Is this a warning?
Definitely. The 1919 records were packaged and stored for more than 50 years. Their existence and content was [sic] forgotten. One by one those who had close association with Ellen White died. Key people, like Pastor Arthur White, who became secretary of the White Estate in 1937, didn't even know the conference had convened. (South Pacific *Record*, February 7, 2004, p. 10. Square brackets in the first answer were in the original).

No effort was directed by Dr. Patrick to demonstrate that those 1919 church leaders were in grave error in their conclusions. We replaced the authority of the inspired writings of Scripture and the Spirit of Prophecy with those of church leaders and scholars.

But as director of the Ellen G. White/Seventh-day Adventist Research Centre for the Australasian Division (as it was then called) in the late 1970s, you had a front-row seat. How did the drama unfold?
Within a year it was clear that not only did Ellen White prize well over a thousand books in her library, she used many of them copiously in her various types of writing.

The church appointed me to attend the first-ever International Prophetic Guidance Workshop that convened during 1982 in Washington, DC, near the church's world headquarters. That was the most stimulating event of its type I've ever attended. At last we had scores of the most devoted and best informed leaders and scholars together from all over the Adventist world, actually face-to-face, looking at the relevant documents and engaging in vibrant discussions.

(*Ibid*, February 14, 2004, p. 4. Parenthesis in the original).

The cover-up conspiracy suggested in Dr. Bradford's book, *Prophets Are Human* was also supported in these conversations.

Why do you believe there was a reticence to share about these issues?
Almost no-one wants to hear bad news, let alone bear it. This new understanding seemed a threat to long-cherished beliefs. Probably, since church leaders hadn't been able to research the matter themselves, they hoped further study might reveal all the new evidence was wrong or unimportant. Some thought the devil was attacking the church with false information.

What about *Record*? Did it play a role at the time?
Indeed it did. In good faith. I believe, to steady the Adventist ship at the height of the storm over literary relationship, *Record* published an article suggesting that Ellen White probably borrowed from the writings of others about 0.002 per cent of what she wrote. [Robert J. Wieland, Ellen White's inspiration; authentic and profound." *Record*, May 31, 1982, page 9.]

But *Record* later reported information very different from that.
It took seven years for the situation to be clarified. You might like to check the *Record* of 1989 where it is clearly stated that the 1982 figure needs to be multiplied about 15,000 times, insofar as *The Desire of Ages* is concerned.

Note this quote from that article: "Dr Veltman believes about 31.4 per cent of *The Desire of Ages* is verbally parallel or similar to the sources she used. Beyond this literary relationship, a given chapter may reveal a broader 'similarity of ideas' or 'reflect the same thematic development as found in the sources'" [Arthur Patrick, "*The Desire of Ages*; Under the microscope," *Record*, April 15, 1989, pages 6, 7].

(*Ibid*, p. 4. Reference of Dr. Patrick in the original).

In these conversations God's people were left to believe that Sister White's writings contained a body of material which, though faulted, was the use of "the best resources she could lay her hands on."

> **So, from the vantage point of 2004, how can you summarise the literary issue?**
> Ellen White was a diligent, intelligent woman who used the best resources she could lay her hands on. That included writings of the finest minds within the church and even beyond it. God gave what she and her son described as "views", "scenes," "representations" or "flashlight pictures." Themes were revealed to her as well as, on occasion, details.
>
> God expected her to convey these ideas to His church and she struggled to do that in the best possible way during her ministry of 70 years. We need to understand both the "perspiration" and the "inspiration" of the writings we so much treasure.
> (*Ibid*).

Even in his defense of the plagiarism charge Dr. Patrick left room for doubt, choosing to quote an unnamed "competent Adventist historian" who charged Sister White with plagiarism.

> **So is Ellen White a plagiarist?**
> A careful study two decades ago by a non-Adventist lawyer, [Attorney Vincent L. Ramik] raised as a Catholic, experienced in North American copyright law says no. A competent Adventist historian who has just written 60 pages on the issue says yes. I have never applied the term "plagiarist" to Ellen White, because in my opinion to do so would cloud the importance of looking, first of all, at the there and then (her context) and, second, at the here and now (our context).
> (*Ibid*, February 21, 2004, p. 9. Material in round brackets in original).

Another area of concern was Dr. Patrick's "Sister White versus the Holy Spirit" claim. This issue is surely not whether we replace the guidance of the Holy Spirit with the counsel of the Spirit of Prophecy. In truth this is an outrageous proposition. Like inspired Scriptural writings, Sister White's writings can only be truly understood by minds guided by the Holy Spirit. No genuine researcher for truth believes that he must choose between inspired writings and the Holy Spirit. Both are equally necessary to lead us to truth.

> **Are you implying we may not have been doing that effectively, and this could be an important reason why the conflict occurred?**
> Yes. For many Adventists, by the middle of the last century Ellen White's writings had become an authoritative, all-inclusive encyclopaedia of Adventist faith and practice. They were using her spiritual gift to deny the role of the Holy Spirit in relation to the Bible and the spiritual gifts of the company of believers. The furore over sources helped us – perhaps we should say, forced us – to consider anew Ellen White's role in the church.

Can you be specific and give an example?
Take that wonderful book, *The Great Controversy*, for instance. Most Adventists took it as authoritative on such matters as history and chronology. From the detailed study of part of the handwritten draft, Don McAdams identified clearly a main source Ellen White used (for instance, the book she consulted as she wrote about John Huss) and the way she followed that source page after page, using its framework and language, even incorporating some of its historical errors and moral exhortations.

Of similar importance was Ron Graybill's study of the way Ellen White used the writings of a well-recognised Adventist author, Uriah Smith. Looking at the abundant evidence it is now clear that Ellen White was not writing history; she was interpreting it. That was a far more important task with a much greater significance. (*Ibid*, p. 10. Parenthesis in the original).

But didn't she claim she was dependent on the Holy Spirit as she wrote out what she had seen?
Right again! Like the prophets of the Bible. Ellen White received the gift of revelation (divine disclosure) and inspiration (divine assistance in communicating the message received). Remember how Paul puts responsibility on the community of believers when he says, "Do not treat prophecies with contempt. Test everything" (1 Thessalonians 5:20, 21, NIV). In other words, to read the Bible is also to learn our duty as a faith community.

Another example: Because Ellen White was shown 10 important things in her great health reform vision of 1863 doesn't mean she knew the 990 other things we might find useful with reference to healthful living.
(*Ibid*, February 28, 2004, p. 10. Words in parenthesis are in the original).

These statements do not sit well in the minds of God's remnant flock. As the conversations progressed, the charges of error grew:

Has careful study identified actual mistakes in material that Ellen White has borrowed?
Many. But they are in the details, and do not destroy the big picture, the all-important interpretation. Let me again reflect the essence of what a careful researcher wrote in his doctoral study early in the 1970s: Ellen White learned history by ordinary means; the activity of God in history was disclosed to her. The church can, now it has far better access to primary resources and many well-trained historians, correct the detail – even while we learn to better appreciate the God-given pattern.

So Ellen White's authority is now understood as being more specific than as the all-knowing authority given her writings a few decades ago?
Yes. This circumstance has made us more aware of the essence of her writings.

Does this kind of understanding have an application for Ellen White's writings on health?
Indeed! Our need was to recognise the importance of human wellbeing in God's plan for us and the world. It is our spiritual duty to foster good health. That core understanding helped the Adventist health emphasis survive the decline of the American health reform movement. It now challenges us to keep abreast of scientific perceptions of the lifestyle that best implements the biblical pattern.

So you're suggesting that Ellen White's writings have a higher purpose, a more demanding role, than being an encyclopaedia on diet, disease and details of healthful living.
Far more demanding, far more significant. Ellen White offers meaning – the reason why God would have us live healthfully. Once we establish the guiding principles, science can help us with the details of how to be balanced vegetarians, the amount of sleep we need under precise circumstances in view of our age and related factors, or to figure out the answers to a host of other issues.

It seems that sort of observation echoes a theme in your book on a century of health care at Sydney Adventist Hospital.
True. The hospital would close within a month if it took a literal approach to diagnosing diseases on the basis of Ellen White's writings. It survives (and mostly thrives) after a century because it took principles that Ellen White expresses and implemented them in a fast-changing culture, progressively informed by scientific research. (*Ibid.* Parenthesis in original).

These statements require no comment from us. Their intent will be discerned by all readers.

Dr. Patrick's fourth conversation, (*Ibid*, February 28, 2004) came forth authoritatively declaring Sister White to be a purveyor of inaccurate materials. We cannot remain in silence when such remarks are stated:

But you seem to put limits on that guidance?
Definitely. Limitation is an important part of what it means to be a human being. Even the apostle Paul says bluntly, "Now I know in part; then shall I know fully" (Corinthians 13:12, NIV). (*Ibid*, p. 10).

So even an inspired person can be partly right and partly wrong?
You've got it! My cancer specialist doesn't fix my lawnmower. My wife is excellent at teaching children, but hopeless at dealing with email viruses. Because Ellen White was shown in a two-hour panorama the age-long struggle between righteousness and sin does not mean she was an expert on the life and times of John Huss. (*Ibid*).

The following question posed and the response cited, refer to the shut door theory.

So you rate this as a significant theological error?
I do. But I prize and often speak affirmatively of Ellen White's account of her first vision where the incorrect expression first occurs. This flaw is akin to that of William Miller in setting a date for the Second Advent. God used Miller's emphasis on the return of Christ to awaken the world, despite the specific error.
(Ibid).

The issue of the shut door is addressed in this book. (See chapter entitled "Dispelling False Accusations.")

The implication that Sister White misinterpreted Scripture is a most serious charge.

What other points require modification?
They could be stated this way, "She made effective use of the Bible in her writings even though she employed Scripture in a variety of ways, not all of which express the meaning and intent of the Bible. While she often helped the church develop and express its theology, her doctrinal understanding underwent both growth and change during her lifetime of ministry. She retained a position of control over her literary output, but her literary assistants and advisers had more than a minor mechanical role in the preparation of her writings for publication. Her writings reveal a remarkable literary beauty, but her use of sources and the role she assigned her assistants or advisers indicates that this literary excellence should not be used as a proof of her divine inspiration."

Do others agree with this position?
Only people who have ignored the evidence or chosen not to keep abreast of the successive waves of information seem to question the basic stances indicated. Of course, there is plenty of room for both refinements and extensions.

Seventh-day Adventism is a quest for truth. We're determined to seek the truth of Scripture and follow it no matter what it costs, for truth is dearer and more precious than life itself. Bible truth makes us free in Jesus Christ; it centres in a knowledge of God and is focused on His purpose for each of us and for the planet. We not only want the truth of the Bible; we want the truth about the way the Lord has led and taught us as His last-day people. That includes historical accuracy, gained from faithful research in the primary sources that are now so abundant. *(Ibid, p. 11).*

Dr. Patrick surely is aware that not a few of the New Testament writers, in quoting Old Testament Scriptural passages were guided by the Holy Spirit to expand their meaning beyond that implied by the Old Testament prophet. Note, for example, how Paul applied the prophecy of Israel concerning the return of the remnant of Jews from Babylon to Jerusalem to the Second Coming of the Lord:

> For though thy people Israel be as the sand of the sea, yet a remnant of them shall return: the consumption decreed shall overflow with righteousness.
>
> (Isaiah 10:22).

> Esaias also crieth concerning Israel, Though the number of the children of Israel be as the sand of the sea, a remnant shall be saved: (Romans 9:27).

The translators of the King James Version of Scripture were quite correct when they stated of the first eight verses of the twenty-second Psalm,

> David complaineth in great discouragement.

Now read those verses:

> 1 My God, my God, why hast thou forsaken me? *why art thou so* far from helping me, *and from* the words of my roaring?
>
> 2 O my God, I cry in the daytime, but thou hearest not; and in the night season, and am not silent.
>
> 3 But thou *art* holy, O *thou* that inhabitest the praises of Israel.
>
> 4 Our fathers trusted in thee: they trusted, and thou didst deliver them.
>
> 5 They cried unto thee, and were delivered: they trusted in thee, and were not confounded.
>
> 6 But I *am* a worm, and no man; a reproach of men, and despised of the people.
>
> 7 All they that see me laugh me to scorn: they shoot out the lip, they shake the head, *saying,*
>
> 8 He trusted on the LORD *that* he would deliver him: let him deliver him, seeing he delighted in him. (Psalm 22:1-8).

But the gospel writers clearly apply this passage, a great Messianic prophecy, to our Savior. Both interpretations are valid, for they are both inspired by God. (Mark 15:34).

The February 2004 issues of the *Record* will ever stand as a bold announcement, condoned by some in church leadership, that we no longer regard the writings of the servant of the Lord as worthy of our trust. The Senior Consultant Editor of the *Record* is the South Pacific Division Secretary, Dr. Barry Oliver. We weep. However, Colin in dialogue with an Administrator of the General Conference was left in no doubt that he was alarmed with the stand taken in Australia in respect of the Spirit of Prophecy. Colin urged direct action be taken to redress the issue.

9 Stratagem V – ClearView

The fifth stratagem also commenced on February 7, 2004. The South Pacific *Record* was again used as a vehicle to introduce the fearful errors of Evangelical Protestantism into our faith. A new series of inserts of four pages – each together with a second four-page insert – first appeared in the *Record* in the February 7 issue. These inserts appeared monthly for seven months, appearing in the first *Record* of each month, February-August, 2004. This series was subtitled, *a way of seeing prophecy*.

The editor was Pastor Paul Petersen, the Danish-born Field Secretary of the South Pacific Division. The editorial committee was:

> Dr. Stenio Gungadoo, Cross-Cultural Ministries Director, Victorian Conference;
>
> Pr. Erika Puni, Director Sabbath School, Personal Ministries and Stewardship, South Pacific Division;
>
> Brother Brenton Stacey, South Pacific Division news correspondent;
>
> Pr. Ken Vogel, Secretary of the Australian Union Conference, previously President of the Western Australian Conference, and later, the South Queensland Conference.

Materials expanding these articles were placed on the South Pacific Division website.

This was the fifth prong in the assiduous efforts to diminish the doctrinal and prophetic authority of Sister White's writings.

On the third page of *ClearView* No. 4, May 1, 2004 *Record*, the subject "Christ – and antichrist" is addressed. Read thoughtfully, this is an abject destruction of prophetic truth:

> The beast in Revelation parodies the sacrifice of Jesus. Just like Jesus, it preaches and exercises its authority for 3.5 years, and is killed (*slaughtered*, the word in Revelation 13:3 is identical to the one used about the Lamb in [Revelation] 5:6) and comes back to life. This power is a counterfeit while presenting itself as Christian.
>
> (*ClearView*, No. 4, page 3, inserted in South Pacific *Record*, May 1, 2004 – material in round brackets is in the original).

Let us notice the following points:
1. "The beast in Revelation [chapter 13] parodies the sacrifice of Jesus."

> Is the deadly wound inflicted upon the Papacy in 1798 a parody of the death of Christ on Calvary? Of course not! Here we see the first evidence

that Pastor Petersen appears not to believe that the Papacy is the antichrist of Bible prophecy. Indeed, although *ClearView* No. 4 claimed to be "a way of seeing prophecy," in this article on the antichrist, not once is the Papacy mentioned nor even alluded to. Sister White correctly and plainly stated:

> The infliction of the deadly wound points to the downfall of the papacy in 1798. (*The Great Controversy*, p. 579).

By ignoring this fact, both Scripture and the Spirit of Prophecy are seriously diminished.

2. "Just like Jesus, it [the beast, antichrist] preaches and exercised authority for 3.5 years."

> This interpretation really is astounding! Yes, Jesus preached for 3.5 years, but not the antichrist. The antichrist exerted fearful authority for 3.5 prophetic years – 1260 literal years.

> > And now began the 1260 years of papal oppression foretold in the prophecies of Daniel and the Revelation. Daniel 7:25, Revelation 13:5-7. (*The Great Controversy*, p. 54).

> In reducing the period of the Papal oppression, Pr. Petersen has revealed that he either does not believe or is unfamiliar with the Spirit of Prophecy in this matter. In ignoring the papacy in his "way of seeing prophecy," it is evident that he does not believe that the Papacy is the antichrist. Further, by limiting the 1260 day prophecy to 3.5 literal years, the author has conceded to the blatant Jesuit-designed (Francisco Ribera) error of Evangelical Protestantism and the faulted futuristic interpretation of prophecy which centers upon the secret rapture, the rebuilding of the Temple in Jerusalem and an earthly millennium. (See our book, *The Rapture, the End Time and the Millennium*).

> > The 1260 years of papal supremacy began in AD 538, and would, therefore, terminate in 1798. (*The Great Controversy*, p. 266).

> Further, Christ most certainly did not, as did the Papacy, "exercise authority on earth" during His earthly sojourn.

> > Even as the Son of man came not to be ministered unto, but to minister, and to give his life a ransom for many. (Matthew 20:28).

3. "The beast... is killed (*slaughtered* the word in Revelation 13:3 is identical to the one used about the Lamb in 5:6) and comes back to life."

> It is true that the word *slain* in Revelation 5:6 which refers to Christ's incomparable sacrifice for our salvation is the same Greek word from which the words *deadly wound* are translated in Revelation 13:3. (See the

> margin in the King James Version Bible for this text). But to compare the papal deadly wound as a counterfeit of Christ's death on Calvary doesn't bear analysis. The Papacy does possess a counterfeit of Christ's death – the blasphemous mass. The deadly wound is not that counterfeit. Rather it is an historical fact which provides one of the identifying features of the Papacy.

4. "This power is a counterfeit, while presenting itself as Christian."

> In isolation, this statement fits the Papacy correctly. But when in context of an antichrist exerting authority for only 3.5 years, we see it to be a false antichrist aligned with that of the futurist doctrine of the fallen churches of Babylon.

We mentioned that *ClearView*, the four-page insert in the *Record*, itself included a four-page insert of pages of smaller size to the *Record* pages. This set forth two Bible Studies, each of two pages. Numbers Seven and Eight: "Universal Judgment" and "Christ and His Enemies" respectively, appeared in the *Record* of May 1, 2004. Bible Study No. 8 was a parallel to the "Christ – and antichrist" feature referred to above. Once again, despite this Bible Study referring to the little horn, not a single mention was made of the Papacy. The introduction of this Bible Study No. 8 stated:

> Yet, the historical enemy of Christ and His saints is described as "a little horn...." Knowing who and how He [Christ] is, will help to recognize the characteristics of the little horn, too.

One can study the details provided in the Bible Study No. 8 without discovering any materials which would identify the Papacy as the little horn of Daniel 7.

In this same *ClearView* issue was presented another article alluding to the Investigative Judgment, entitled "Universal judgment – when God received back His power." It appeared on page 2 of this issue No. 4. Significantly, although the article referred to the judgment scenes in Daniel 7:9-14, not a single reference was made to Daniel 8:14 which pinpoints to the very day that Judgment commenced, October 22, 1844. (See our book *The Rapture, the End Time and the Millennium* and also Dr. William H. Shea, *Selected Studies on Prophetic* Interpretation, General Conference of Seventh-day Adventists, 1982, pp. 132-137, for the evidence of the certainty of this date).

This May 1, 2004, *ClearView* article concluded with the following words:

> After the legal verdict in heaven, the result of the deliberations are realized on earth (Daniel 7:14, 18, 27), when the visible Kingdom of God is established.

Here we see expressed that the visible kingdom of God, the Kingdom of Glory, is realized on earth when the investigative judgment, a term Pr. Petersen ignored, is completed. These statements even in their lack of precision leave the reader with the concept of the fallen churches of Babylon, that the one thousand years following the judgment are spent on earth.

In the inserted Bible Study No. 7 entitled "Universal Judgment," once again no mention was made of the 2300-days prophecy of Daniel 8:14 and the very same conclusion is drawn. We quote the final summary provided. The first four conclusions are correct, but the fifth sustains the error of apostate Protestantism.

> The judgment in Daniel 7 contains five central elements. (1) God "comes" to His throne to judge, (2) Dominions and Kingdoms of history are evaluated and rejected, (3) The "Son of man" is given authority to reign forever, (4) Judgment is passed in favour of the saints, (5) following the legal verdict in heaven, the kingdom is realised on earth.

As one senior evangelist stated after reading this article, "It appears to be intentionally vague." Pastor Petersen's statement above could be shared with evangelical Protestants in the spirit of ecumenism and they would see it as supporting their erroneous concept of the earthly millennium. On the other hand, when challenged by a truth-believing Seventh-day Adventist, it could be said, "Well, I didn't write specifically that there was an immediate setting-up of the Kingdom of Glory on earth; there is a lapse of 1000 years before this transpires." Our presentations must be as clear as the sun on a cloudless day.

We notice that both Bible Studies stated:

> Produced by the Field Secretary, South Pacific Division.

While Pr. Petersen's imprecision of expression may be seen to provide him some latitude to speak in two directions,

1. That God's kingdom is established on earth at the conclusion of the "universal judgment," OR
2. That there is a "gap" of 1000 years between the conclusion of the judgment and the establishment of His kingdom on earth in the New Jerusalem,

this latter interpretation is not sustainable in his *ClearView* presentations, in view of three incontrovertible facts:

1. No mention was made of a time lapse of any duration between the conclusion of the "universal judgment" and the establishment of Christ's kingdom upon earth.
2. Pr. Petersen's preference for the futuristic view of a 3.5-year reign of the antichrist, certifies his support of the end-time scenario of the Evangelical Protestant position.
3. He ignored the significance of the 2300-years prophecy of Daniel 8:14, so central to the investigative judgment and the Seventh-day Adventist end-time scenario.

In *ClearView*,, No. 3, April 2004, p. 2, yet another error was presented. We quote it:

> Adventists have used another idiomatic expression, "Jesus went into the Most Holy." It originates with the service of the Day of Atonement and designates the beginning of the judgment. It indicates a new phase of His heavenly ministry, but it is not meant to be understood that He had no contact with His Father until then. It is not about geography, but about function.

Christ's entry into the Most Holy Place is not idiomatic. Sister White clearly stated it to be a literal event. Her words are not entwined in symbolism. They are literal:

> I was shown what did take place in heaven at the close of the prophetic periods in 1844. As Jesus ended His ministration in the holy place and closed the door of that apartment, a great darkness settled upon those who had heard and rejected the message of His coming, and they lost sight of Him. Jesus then clothed Himself with precious garments. Around the bottom of His robe was a bell and a pomegranate. A breastplate of curious work was suspended from His shoulders. As He moved, this glittered like diamonds, magnifying letters which looked like names written or engraved upon the breastplate. Upon His head was something which had the appearance of a crown. When fully attired, He was surrounded by angels, and in a flaming chariot He passed within the second veil.
> (*Early Writings*, p. 251).

Sister White further described this event in different words, earlier in the book:

> I saw the Father rise from the throne, and in a flaming chariot go into the holy of holies within the veil, and sit down. Then Jesus rose up from the throne, and the most of those who were bowed down arose with Him. (*Ibid*, p. 55).

The words "It is not about geography, but about function," stated by Pastor Petersen, echo Dr. Ford's insistence that the geography or architecture of the heavenly sanctuary were unimportant. This concept was first heard by Colin from Dr. Ford at the first National Convention of Seventh-day Adventist University Students at Crosslands camp site in Sydney in 1962. From these statements Dr. Ford usually deduced two false principles:

1. The sanctuary in heaven did not possess two apartments or that the distinction was dissolved when the earthly second veil was rent in twain at the moment of Christ's death and/or

2. The whole of heaven is the sanctuary.

Neither of these positions can be sustained from the Bible or Spirit of Prophecy.

At first reading, yet another plain error is sustained in *ClearView*, No. 1, February 7, 2004, p. 3.

> Apocalyptic [Prophetic revelations especially of the end time] literature flourished from 200 BC to 100 AD and permeated the New Testament. The book of Daniel was the first fully-developed example and became the inspiration and source for later apocalyptic thinking in Judaism and Christianity.

This statement, when first read, provides the impression of supporting the higher critics' view that the prophecies were written, not by Daniel, but by someone after 200 BC following Rome's defeat of the Greek Empire and thus were an historical record, not a prophetic utterance. Yet Christ plainly stated that Daniel wrote that prophetic book.

> When ye therefore shall see the abomination of desolation, spoken of by Daniel the prophet, stand in the holy place, (whoso readeth, let him understand:) (Matthew 24:15. Parenthesis in the original text).

However, as we read on to a third paragraph after this statement, we find:

> The catalyst for the creation for apocalyptic literature were three national disasters. The first was the exile in Babylon. During this period, Ezekiel, Daniel and Zechariah produced books dominated by apocalyptic ideas.

Thus this paragraph places Daniel's book in the correct era. Care should have been taken to make this clear in the first paragraph quoted lest some read it and form an erroneous conclusion, and fail to read to the later explanation of the article. Of course this is a small point, one merely of style.

Systematically, the faith of God's people in Scripture and the Spirit of Prophecy – as the certainty of our irrefutable faith – has been undermined by the leadership of the South Pacific Division. Like Sister White, Daniel and John possessed the divine gift of the Spirit of Prophecy. In these efforts to destroy the faith of Seventh-day Adventists there has been – and continues to be – a concerted effort to destroy the Remnant church and merge us with the ecumenical movement. God alone, will preserve His true people. It is our solemn responsibility as ministers of the gospel to warn God's people of the dangers of such presentations.

In the foundations of the Seventh-day Adventist Church, the book of Daniel, of all the sixty-six books of the Bible, is the most significant. Of its twelve chapters, chapter 8 is of greatest importance. Of the twenty-seven verses in this chapter, verse 14 stands out as the dynamic, the inspiration, the great hope of Seventh-day Adventism. One book in sixty-six; one chapter in 1,189 and one verse in the 31,102 verses which comprise the written word of God, holds the key to the greatest body of truth ever bestowed upon humans.

In the cleansing of the sanctuary, is found the climax to Christ's unmatched work of redemption – the key to the only infallible judgments in eternity and the ultimate triumph of God's infinite plan of salvation. No single verse of

Scripture encapsulates such an expanse of salvational elements as does Daniel 8:14. Yet in Scripture, this marvel of salvation is condensed into a mere eighteen English words:

> And he said unto me, Unto two thousand and three hundred days; then shall the sanctuary be cleansed.

However, in the fifth *ClearView* edition, published in the South Pacific *Record*, June 5, 2004, the article, authored by the editor, Pr. Paul Petersen, "history, judgment and sanctuary – Daniel 8:14 in context," was bereft of any mention of the crucial relevance of this verse to Seventh-day Adventist understanding of the investigative judgment. No calls for God's people to afflict their souls were issued. Yet, Scripture mandates such affliction in no less than five passages (Leviticus 16:29, 31; 23:27, 32; Numbers 29:7) in relation to the typical Day of Atonement. Sister White applied these passages to our day – the antitypical Day of Atonement.

> We are now living in the great day of atonement. In the typical service, while the high priest was making the atonement for Israel, all were required to afflict their souls by repentance of sin and humiliation before the Lord, lest they be cut off from among the people. In like manner, all who would have their names retained in the book of life should now, in the few remaining days of their probation, afflict their souls before God by sorrow for sin and true repentance. There must be deep, faithful searching of heart. (*Great Controversy*, pp. 489, 490).

Further, in this article, the year – much less the day, 22 October – received no mention, although Clifford Goldstein, Senior *Sabbath School Quarterly* editor, in an article on the first page, does twice mention 1844. Yet even in Brother Goldstein's article is no mention of the urgent need for God's people to seek character perfection in God's strength, so that we may have Christ as our advocate. Rather, Clifford Goldstein used the faulted abbreviated translation of Romans 8:1 found in the New International Version, which omits the condition upon which Christ's atoning grace is provided. Compare the two versions of this text:

> Therefore, there is now no condemnation for those who are in Christ Jesus.
> (*New International Version*).

> There is therefore now no condemnation to them which are in Christ Jesus, who walk not after the flesh, but after the Spirit. (*King James Version*).

Only those who are afflicting their souls will walk not after the flesh, but after the Spirit.

The precise date, October 22, 1844, is important. Sister White specifically confirmed this date.

> The tenth day of the seventh month, the great Day of Atonement, the time of the cleansing of the sanctuary, which in the year 1844 fell upon the twenty-second of October, was regarded as the time of the Lord's coming. This was in harmony with the proofs already presented that the 2300 days would terminate in the autumn, and the conclusion seemed irresistible. (*Great Controversy*, p. 400).

In an outstanding piece of research, Dr. William H. Shea, Professor of Theology at Andrews University at the time of his research, discovered that on the date of the commencement of the 2300-year prophecy, 457 B.C., this Day of Atonement was scheduled for October 22. This is marked confirmatory evidence of the accuracy of Sister White's inspired statement above, which conflicts with the opinions of most scholars. The 2300-day prophecy was fulfilled with exactitude, on the very day. (For a more comprehensive account of this matter, see our book *The Rapture, The End Time and the Millennium*, Hartland Publications; or Dr. Shea's report, *Selected Studies on Prophetic Interpretation*, General Conference of Seventh-day Adventists, College View Printers, Lincoln Nebraska, 1982, pages 132-137).

The date 457 B.C., and its relation to Daniel 9:25, received no mention in edition 5 of *ClearView*, although it was mentioned in *ClearView*, edition 6 (published in the South Pacific *Record*, July 3, 2004). Once more, the articles contained no enlightenment from the Spirit of Prophecy.

However, Dr. Paul Petersen's article did include one useful statement from a non-Seventh-day Adventist author, useful in that for one who is unacquainted with the full understanding of Daniel 8:14, he does demonstrate a remarkable level of insight into this passage of Scripture, Daniel 8:13, 14.

> Finally there is an agonized question in chapter 8: "How long?" The second major theme of this chapter is that the time of wrath is limited and thus the people's suffering is limited as well. This is surely one of the most powerful appeals of apocalyptic literature and apocalyptic movements. Theologically it is one of the most important messages of the book of Daniel for a modern world. It is the promise of the gospel that darkness will not last forever, that innocence will not be crushed forever, that justice will be done. Surely this is the most important function of the "last judgment" scenes, such as the division of the sheep and goats in Matthew 25.
> (Daniel L. Smith-Christopher, *The New Interpreter's Bible*, Abingdon Press, 1996, Vol. 7, p. 118).

We must say that it is refreshing to discover a non-Seventh-day Adventist scholar who perceived that this passage of Daniel "is one of the most powerful appeals of apocalyptic literature," that it is "one of the most important messages of the book of Daniel for the modern world," and who recognized the theme of the "last judgment" in Daniel 8.

Even in Bible Study No. 10, Pr. Petersen studiously refrained from any mention of the date 22 October, 1844 – despite the fact that the topic of the

Bible Study is "For How Long?" He left the "How Long?" question dangling with no specific answer. The closest this Bible Study came to answering the "How Long" question, was contained in two separated sentences:

> The cry for God's intervention is the typical "how long?" (literally "until when?") of the psalms of lament.
>
> (Bible Study No. 10, p.1 – parenthesis is in the original).

> The heavenly counterpart of that festival (the day of atonement) began at the end of the time period in Daniel 8:14. (*Ibid*, p. 2).

An earlier generation of Seventh-day Adventists longed and thirsted for prophetic exposition. They avidly read every such presentation in our denominational periodicals. Even as lads, we eagerly read them. We, as a people, were proud of our prophetic roots and our advanced knowledge of prophetic interpretation. We possessed the "more sure word of prophecy." (2 Peter 1:19). But today, such is not the case. Russell has undertaken a number of surveys of groups of denominational church attendees who receive the South Pacific *Record*, and discovered that of approximately two hundred polled, only two had taken the time to review the *ClearView* articles. If Russell were to include himself, that number would be increased fifty percent, to three!

We may well ask "Why?", for many of these people are serious students of prophecy. However, they desire competent, inspiration-based enlightenment, not sterile presentations which skirt around Seventh-day Adventist prophetic distinctives and eschew the inspired insights of the Spirit of Prophecy.

We are in the last days. If ever there were a prophetic imperative to prepare our hearts and characters through Christ's power and His grace, Daniel 8:14 presents it. That text – while representing only 0.003 percent of the total verses of the Bible – permeates every passage of Scripture dealing with salvation issues. It is too important to be addressed with vague comments which serve only to conceal vibrant, salvational truths; comments which do not strike the soul with the urgent need of preparation for the Judgment, nor warn of the awesome Day of the Lord.

In *ClearView*, edition 6, published in the South Pacific *Record*, July 3, 2004, it was refreshing to see the dates 457BC, 27AD, 31AD and 34AD surface, and be accorded their correct significance. The year-day principle was supported, even though Dr. Petersen did not invoke it for the 1260-day prophecy, according the antichrist power for a literal 3.5 years. (See *ClearView*, edition 4, South Pacific *Record*, May 1, 2004).

The *ClearView*, edition 6, also stated (p.2):

> Gabriel begins his prophetic oracle by speaking about the time period that has been determined – or "cut off" – for Daniel's people and Daniel's holy city, Jerusalem.

In the fourth page of the enclosed Bible Study of the July, 2004 *ClearView* it was well stated that:

> Of the long period of the 2300 years a period of 490 years were cut off for Daniel's people and holy city. In the last of the 70 weeks, Jesus would be the perfect sacrifice and the heavenly sanctuary would be anointed. It was in this sanctuary the cleansing and judgment will take place after the period of 2300 years.

This is an accurate statement. We still await, however, a clear statement that Christ entered the Most Holy Place in 1844, not 31AD as promoted by the New Theology.

Dr. Petersen also appeared to be disinclined, not only to designate the Papacy as the antichrist, but also to designate the little horn of Daniel 8 as more than the Roman Empire. (See *ClearView*, July 2004, p.2). It, of course, designated Rome in both its imperial and papal form.

The final ClearView article, included in the South Pacific *Record*, August 7, 2004, spoke in warm terms of the New Jerusalem.

The most disturbing feature of this seven-part series on end-time prophecy is the signal failure in seven articles and fourteen Bible studies to identify the Papacy as the antichrist, the little horn of Daniel 7, the man of sin, the first beast of Revelation 13, the beast of Revelation 17, the scarlet woman of Revelation 17, the Mother of Harlots or the leader of the fallen churches of Babylon.

This glaring omission defines, in a most public manner, a new era in our understanding of Bible prophecy, a turning of our backs upon inspired revelation, and an acceptance of the blindness of current Apostate Protestantism on Roman Catholic aims and prophesied prominence and persecution in these last days. Such an implied denial of these matters is an issue of enormous magnitude. The little horn of Daniel 8 will alarm every converted Seventh-day Adventist and draw him or her in this day of the Omega of Apostasy closer to our Lord, seeking His righteousness, fidelity and courage, as never before.

10 Stratagem VI – Understanding the Gift

In the South Pacific *Record*, 22 May, 2004, Pastor Laurie Evans, the President of the South Pacific Division, authored an editorial entitled, "Understanding the Gift." He commenced and concluded the editorial with praise for Sister White's ministry. In his concluding paragraph, Pastor Evans stated:

> There is no question we have been greatly blessed and enriched by this gift [of the Spirit of Prophecy], and continue to be.

Yet, as we read the middle paragraphs of the editorial, it appeared that Pastor Evans' logic is riding insouciantly on two horses of apparent contradiction. Speaking of the "matchless charms of Jesus" as presented in Sister White's writings, Pr. Evans proceeded to use words now all-too-often spoken by those who are destroying Sister White's writings, damning them with faint praise. He stated that:

> Nearly fifty years on [since his acceptance of the Seventh-day Adventist faith], nothing has changed, except I have a clearer understanding how inspiration operates through the prophetic gift.

Pastor Evans also grieved over the fact that,

> Sadly I have noticed that, over time, there has been a loss of interest in her writings by many of our members. People have 'switched off' on Ellen White and have come to believe her writings are largely irrelevant or lacking credibility.

Here, Pastor Evans correctly acknowledged the pitiful general situation in our church in the South Pacific, in respect of the gift of prophecy in our midst. This is true also in many other parts of the world field.

What Pastor Evans failed to acknowledge was the fact that it is the theology professors at Avondale College who are the source of this state of affairs and that, for years now, the leadership of the South Pacific Division has supported the re-interpretation of the Spirit of Prophecy; the failure of our preachers to use the inspired writings of Sister White in their sermons; and the promotion of the fantasy that Sister White's writings contain many serious errors. What is taught in our Colleges, is preached a little later in our churches, and believed shortly thereafter by our Church membership. It must never be overlooked that each Division President is the ex-officio Chairman of the Avondale College Board.

In speaking of the internet attacks upon the Spirit of Prophecy, Pastor Evans cited three of the "errors," appearing on the Internet:

Stratagem VI – Understanding the Gift

- In writing The Great Controversy, she [Sister White] copied both words and pictures;

- When she wrote, "I was shown", what followed was at times copied from other sources;

- She taught that the Tower of Babel was built before the Flood.

Following what is now a well-honed strategy, Pastor Evans provided no documentation for these charges, in order that the readers may examine them. Nor did he in any way attempt to explain the valid responses to these allegations. Is it then, any wonder that our people today are seeing Sister White's writings as "lacking credibility?" Pastor Evans, himself, had, in this editorial, fuelled such a conclusion, instead of upholding the prophetic gift, his editorial offered us only moth-eaten phylacteries!

If Sister White is represented – as Pastor Evans has done – as having copied materials from other writers while claiming to have been shown them in vision, then Sister White is set forth as a bare-faced liar. Of course this term is unlikely to be used, rather is her implied falsehood likely to be spoken of in words which may be described as terminological inexactitude. It is as simple as that. Now, we notice that Pastor Evans did not state that he believed this, but because he neither set forth the credible explanations which refute these claims, nor even stated that such valid answers exist, he left the readers to draw their own, unenlightened, conclusions. No doubt only a few bothered to search for the truth. This search was made all the more difficult because Pastor Evans did not think it necessary to quote even one of the passages to which he referred, or even provide the reference.

Yet, if the statement that Pastor Evans cited,

> When she wrote, "I was shown", what followed was at times copied from other sources,

is correct, we need not search through her works in order to verify Pastor Evans' undocumented assertion and then read reams of historical works in order to ascertain for ourselves if her "I was shown" statements included, in some cases, the words of secular writers, for Sister White, herself, openly stated that this had transpired. Let us refresh the readers' minds on this matter.

> Through the illumination of the Holy Spirit, the scenes of the long-continued conflict between good and evil have been opened to the writer of these pages.... As the Spirit of God has opened to my mind the great truths of His word, and the scenes of the past and the future, I have been bidden to make known to others that which has thus been revealed.... In some cases where a historian has so grouped together events as to afford, in brief, a comprehensive view of the subject, or has summarized details in a convenient manner, his words have been quoted; but in some instances no specific credit has been given, since the quotations are not given for the purpose of citing that writer as authority, but because his

statement affords a ready and forcible presentation of the subject. In narrating the experience and views of those carrying forward the work of reform in our own time, similar use has been made of their published works.

(Great Controversy, pp. x-xii).

We summarize Sister White's words above:
1. She was illuminated by the Holy Spirit in writing *The Great Controversy*;
2. The Spirit of God opened the scenes of the past to Sister White's mind – no doubt in vision – "I was shown";
3. Sometimes she quoted secular historians when their words were true to the visions she had received;
4. Sometimes she chose not to reference these quotations for she did not desire to credit these men with matters the Holy Spirit had provided her.

Was Sister White truthful when she stated in these passages "I was shown?" Most assuredly she was! Did she express what she had been shown, sometimes through the words of secular history when they accurately reported such history? Yes she did! Was this deceptive? Absolutely not! Was this appropriate? Most certainly it was! Was Sister White a liar? Emphatically no!

As her son, Elder William White, stated at the General Conference Council on October 30, 1911, at the time of the launch of the 1911 edition of *The Great Controversy*:

> Mother has never claimed to be authority on history. The things which she has written out, are descriptions of flashlight pictures and other representations given her.... In connection with the writing out of these views, she has made use of good and clear historical statements to help make plain to the reader the things which she is endeavoring to present. (*Selected Messages*, Vol. 3, p. 436).

The reader is encouraged to read this documentation from *The Great Controversy* and *Selected Messages*, Vol. 3, in full, to ensure the material omitted above (see ellipsis), in nowise alters the sense of that which has been quoted above. Rather, such a reading will establish faith in the Spirit of Prophecy.

In answering the second problem cited by Pastor Evans, we have also effectively answered the first.

Did Sister White teach that the Tower of Babel was built before the flood? Let us briefly examine her writings upon this matter. For brevity we quote the very first words of the chapters devoted to the Tower of Babel. All these chapters (addressing the Tower of Babel) follow the chapters concerning the Noachian Flood in various books:

> *Spiritual Gifts*, Vol. 3, p. 96:
> Some of the descendants of Noah soon began to apostatize.

> *Spirit of Prophecy*, Vol. 1, p. 91:
> Some of the descendants of Noah soon began to apostatize.

Stratagem VI – Understanding the Gift

> *Patriarchs and Prophets*, p. 117:
> To re-populate the desolate earth, which the Flood has so lately swept from its moral corruption....
>
> *Story of Redemption*, p. 72:
> Some of the descendants of Noah soon began to apostatize.

Plainly, Sister White well knew that which every young child raised in a Christian home knows – the Tower of Babel post-dated the Flood. In *Spiritual Gifts*, Vol. 3, which was published in 1864, Chapters VII and VIII, "The Flood" and "After the Flood," respectively, both appear before Chapter X, "The Tower of Babel."

What, then, is the source of this accusation? We quote the passage to which, we believe, Pastor Evans referred.

> The Lord first established the system of sacrificial offerings with Adam after his fall, which he taught to his descendants. This system was corrupted before the flood by those who separated themselves from the faithful followers of God, and engaged in the building of the tower of Babel.   (*Spiritual Gifts*, Vol. 3, p. 301).

That critics would quote this statement as evidence of the errancy of Sister White's inspired writings is quite reprehensible. Even an uninspired writer with but a scant knowledge of Scripture would not make such an elementary error.

Uriah Smith soon provided the solution to this problem – a comma together with the word "and" had been inadvertently omitted by the type-setter. Elder Smith's words were,

> An unfortunate typographical error which has crept in here, makes the language place the building of the Tower of Babel, before the flood. After the word 'flood', a comma and the word 'and' have been left out.
> (*Review and Herald*, July 31, 1866, p. 66).

It is of interest that in the Facsimile Edition produced by the Trustees of the Ellen G. White Publications in 1945, no correction was made. However, in the "Preface to Facsimile Edition", the typographical error was pointed out. Perhaps Pastor Evans read only the original edition, or if he researched the 1945 facsimile edition, he may not have read the preface. It stated:

> Being here reproduced photographically, the papers carry with them, of course, such typographical errors as occurred in the first printing. One outstanding case of this kind will be noted in Volume III, page 301, in line 4 of the last paragraph, where through a printers error, a comma and the word "and" were inadvertently omitted, creating a seeming historical discrepancy in an incidental reference, which has given some careless readers, who wholly ignored the plain teaching of the earlier chapters, an opportunity to declare that the book teaches that the tower of Babel antedated the flood. This typographical error was soon discovered and was corrected in the next printing of the matter in 1870 in *Spirit of Prophecy*,

Volume I. As corrected in the second printing, the sentence in question, referring to the sacrificial system established at the gate of Eden reads: (see quotation *Spirit of Prophecy*, Volume I, page 266, below).

It would have been far better if this statement had been placed in the body of the Facsimile as a footnote on the page where the mistake occurred, even though we concede this may have been difficult to do in a Facsimile edition. At least a cross-reference to the Preface could have been placed as a footnote.

Six years later, when *Spirit of Prophecy*, volume I was published (1870), no such typographical error remained. It clearly stated:

> This system was corrupted before the flood, and by those who separated themselves from the faithful of God and engaged in the building of the tower of Babel. (*Spirit of Prophecy*, Vol. 1, p. 266).

That Pastor Evans added the comment,

> There are hundreds of pages on different [web] sites with these kinds of statements." (*South Pacific Record*, op. cit.),

was not designed to encourage confidence in the Spirit of Prophecy, nor did his words

> ...there are other more serious allegations that are unsettling for some of our members.

Pastor Evans then proceeded to cite men "of the caliber of A. G. Daniells" and Elders F. W. Wilcox, W. W. Prescott and H. M. S. Richards [Snr] who professed less than full confidence in the Spirit of Prophecy. He did not distance himself from the doubts of these four well-known Seventh-day Adventists, nor did Pastor Evans rebuke their alleged faithlessness. If Pastor Evans' claims concerning these men are correct, we plainly conclude that they were in serious error.

11 Stratagem VII – Ministers' and Elders' Summits – Revelation, Inspiration and Ellen White

In various areas of Australia and New Zealand, Elders' Summits were conducted, entitled "Revelation, Inspiration and Ellen White." On Sabbath, June 19, 2004, an Elders' Summit was conducted by the Victorian Conference from 2pm to 7pm. The guest speakers were Dr. Ray Roennfeldt, Chairman of the Theology Department, Avondale College, and Dr. Graeme Bradford, Theology Department, Avondale College.

Some time prior to the Elders' Summit the Victorian Conference Pastoral Staff were reported to have been

> Blessed by the teaching of Drs. Ray Roennfeldt & Graeme Bradford.
> (*Intravic* – Victorian Adventist Church News, May, 2004, page 2).

The article recounted the nature of the meeting of the theologians with the Conference pastors:

> They shared valuable insights on inspiration and the prophetic ministry of Ellen White, a ministry they both treasure.
>
> This was a foretaste of what Elders will share at the Elders' Summit, on June 19, from 2pm to 7pm (*Ibid*).

The aim of these Summits was enunciated:

> With a large volume of negative material available on the internet, Pastors and Elders are in need of having credible answers to be able to give to members. The Summit will provide many of those answers. Also, if you are familiar with the video, "The Spirit Behind the Church," you will find the Summit very helpful. (*Ibid*).

The video, "The Spirit Behind the Church," which Russell viewed in 2000, was produced by a Protestant organization. It featured a number of former Seventh-day Adventist ordained ministers, who used the time provided them in reviling our beloved church, its precious truths and the inestimable gift of the Spirit of Prophecy. Their fidelity to Scripture and God's law may be gauged by the knowledge that some of these men were pastoring Sunday-keeping churches. Their accusations against the Spirit of Prophecy were shallow, and in a large part they were simply ineptly re-echoing nineteenth-century charges which have long since been answered.

One charge laid was that Sister White had falsely prophesied that England would enter the American Civil War. Superficially read, Sister White's words can be misconstrued to mean that which is alleged. Writing in 1862, during the Civil War (1861-1865), Sister White declared that:

> When England does declare war, all nations will have an interest of their own to serve, and there will be general war, general confusion.
> (*Testimonies for the Church*, Vol. 1, p. 259).

That there was an expectation that Britain may enter the Civil War on the side of the South, is an indisputable historical fact.

> He [Jefferson Davis – 1808-1889, President of the Confederate States of America] hoped that within twelve months at most Britain and France would come to his aid. (*Encyclopaedia Britannica*, 1963 edition, Vol. 1, p. 732).

Once more, the question arises, Was Sister White simply echoing this expectation which was never fulfilled? The answer again is – Absolutely no! When the entire paragraph in which she made the statement concerning England is read in detail, it is evident that Sister White was speaking conditionally, not prophetically. Notice the conditional words of Sister White.

> England is studying whether it is best to take advantage of the present weak condition of our nation, and venture to make war upon her. She is weighing the matter, and trying to sound other nations. She fears, if she should commence war abroad, that she would be weak at home, and that other nations would take advantage of her weakness. (*Testimonies for the Church*, Vol. 1, p. 259).

Here we notice the adverbial clause of condition in this passage – "*if* she should commence war abroad." (*Ibid*, emphasis added). We continue this paragraph up to the sentence which detractors of Sister White cite as error.

> Other nations are making quiet yet active preparations for war, and are hoping that England will make war with our nation, for then they would improve the opportunity to be revenged on her for the advantage she has taken of them in the past and the injustice done them. A portion of the queen's subjects are waiting a favorable opportunity to break their yoke; but if England thinks it will pay, she will not hesitate a moment to improve her opportunities to exercise her power and humble our nation. (*Ibid*).

Once more we see the use of a conditional clause – "but *if* England thinks it will pay. (*Ibid*, emphasis added). The British Prime Minister in 1862 was the Third Viscount Henry John Temple Palmerston (1784-1865), seventy-eight years of age. There is no doubt that he was pleased with events which led to the Civil War, for

> his own opinion led him rather to desire than to avert the rupture of the union [of the American nation]. (*Encyclopaedia Britannica*, 1963 edition, Vol. 17, p. 159).

It is plain that Sister White was correct in her record of the contemporary history of which she then wrote. We have, also, documented the conditional frame-work in which she penned her words, "When England does declare war...." Then how may we reconcile her words within a single paragraph – "If"..., "If"..., and "When...." The resolution is quite simple. We must understand the full meaning of the English word, "when." *The Heritage Illustrated Dictionary*, American Heritage Publishing Co. Inc., New York, 1973, provides one definition of *when* to be *if*.

Sometimes we use the word *when* to mean *whenever*, or *if*. It is clearly this use of the word *when* that Sister White intended, as confirmed by the conditional nature of the previous sentences. *The Oxford Reference Dictionary* defines whenever as:

> at whatever time.
>
> (*The Oxford Reference Dictionary*, Oxford University Press, Oxford, England, 1996).

We commonly use *when* in the sense of *if*. We, ourselves, have no plans to visit the Antarctic Continent. However we would state that "When we do go to Antarctica, we would like to observe the wildlife there." And we would. But it is almost certain that we will never visit that continent. Commonly people use words such as "When I can find time, I'd like to write my memoirs." This is not said in an assurance that they will accomplish this desire, rather it is conditional upon finding the free time to do so.

Even Scripture uses the word *when* to mean *if*. Jeremiah is translated to have said:

> ... when ye shall enter into Egypt: and ye shall be an execration, and an astonishment, and a curse, and a reproach; and ye shall see this place no more.
>
> (Jeremiah 42:18).

Of course Judah did not go into Egypt during Jeremiah's lifetime, nor at any subsequent time. Even when taken captivity by Babylon, they did see Judah again after the restoration. If the previous verses are read we see that the preposition *if* is used, certifying the conditional nature of this prophecy. (See Jeremiah 42:10, 13, 15).

It is a pity that when the first fifteen minutes of the video, "The Spirit Behind the Church," was shown at the Victorian Conference Summit, it was stopped at the point where the accusation was made that Sister White erred in stating that Britain would enter the American Civil War. No explanation of this false allegation was offered during the Elders' Summit. At best this negligence was designed to leave doubts in the minds of attendees concerning the veracity of the Servant of the Lord's writings.

Dr. Ray Roennfeldt spoke first at the Elders' Summit. His presentation could best be characterized by the words, "What Scripture is Like." We quote from a transcript of an audiotape of the presentation which was presented to us. During his discourse, which was largely confined to Biblical "errors," Dr. Roennfeldt took issue with Paul's statements concerning women – that they should remain silent in the church (1 Corinthians 14:34), that man was made in God's image and that woman was made in man's image (1 Corinthians 11:7, 8) and Paul's statement that man was created first (1 Corinthians 11:8, 9). Dr. Roennfeldt cited no Biblical references for his complaints, so we have suggested the passages to which we believe he referred. Dr. Roennfeldt then posed a question which he followed with a "defense" of Paul's words, clearly indicating his belief that they were contrary to other parts of the Bible. We quote verbatim from his presentation.

> Is Paul contradicting Scripture? No, I don't think he is. He's arguing like a rabbi would argue. He's arguing just like a Jewish rabbi would argue. And a Jewish rabbi would argue, "Now this argument is not really up to scratch, but it's a good argument. That's how rabbis actually argued....[1] I'm just saying what Scripture is like. (Transcript of audiotape, Elders' Summit, Melbourne, June 19, 2004).

To assert that Paul's inspired writings consisted of some statements which did not "really come up to scratch," but he used them anyway because they were good arguments; to say that he was only writing like a Jewish rabbi; surely is thoroughly offensive to any man or woman who treasures the Holy Word of God. Rather than correctly representing Scripture, Dr. Roennfeldt's statement may reflect the thinking and strategy of some theologians (rabbis) of the era of the Second Coming.

We emphatically declare that Scripture is NOT like that! It does not use passages which do not bear divine veracity (that don't "really come up to scratch"): it ever possesses the hallmark of divine truth. That a peal of laughter burst forth from not a few of the attendees when those words were spoken, suggests that the general tenor of the lecture was that in which the sacredness of Scripture was not considered. Paul was privileged to author fourteen of the twenty-seven books of the New Testament. God's principles of faith, written under inspiration by him, do not contain slick phrases meant to cover up weak arguments and make invalid points.

Writing in Australia on March 28, 1893, Sister White aptly described that which our theologians are setting themselves to achieve.

> Those who trust in their intelligence he [Satan] will make believe that they can correct the Scriptures. You are going to meet this infidelity in high places.
>
> (*Upward Look*, p. 101).

Dr. Roennfeldt also brought out the age-old "incompatibilities" in the four gospel accounts. Rather than explaining them, he simply said,

> "I'm saying to myself, Who cares?" (*Ibid*).

Well, *we* do! To cast doubt upon Scripture is no minor issue. Dr. Roennfeldt had spoken of a number of apparent disparities between the numbers one and

---

1 The ellipsis was inserted because Dr. Roennfeldt broke off his train of thought and did not complete a sentence he had commenced. We all, occasionally do this in spoken presentations. For the record, the entire words omitted were, "Now a few years ago the Scripture started saying."

two – the number of times the cock crowed after Peter's denial of Christ, the number of angels at Christ's tomb, the number of demoniacs Christ healed at Gergesa, and the number of blind men healed in Jericho.

Let us review the accounts of the number of times the cock crowed after Peter's denials, both in Christ's prophecy and in its fulfillment. First we look at the accounts of Christ's prophecy:

> Jesus said unto him, Verily I say unto thee, That this night, before the cock crow, thou shalt deny me thrice. (Matthew 26:34).

> And Jesus saith unto him, Verily I say unto thee, That this day, even in this night, before the cock crow twice, thou shalt deny me thrice. (Mark 14:30).

> And he said, I tell thee, Peter, the cock shall not crow this day, before that thou shalt thrice deny that thou knowest me. (Luke 22:34).

> Jesus answered him, Wilt thou lay down thy life for my sake? Verily, verily, I say unto thee, The cock shall not crow, till thou hast denied me thrice.
> (John 13:38).

Here we notice two matters. Only Mark mentioned the fact that the cock would crow twice and the other three gospel writers did not record the number of times the cock was to crow.

We now record the four accounts of the fulfillment of Christ's prophecy.

> And Peter remembered the word of Jesus, which said unto him, Before the cock crow, thou shalt deny me thrice. And he went out, and wept bitterly.
> (Matthew 26:75).

> But he denied, saying, I know not, neither understand I what thou sayest. And he went out into the porch; and the cock crew. (Mark 14:68).

> And Peter said, Man, I know not what thou sayest. And immediately, while he yet spake, the cock crew. (Luke 22:60).

> Peter then denied again: and immediately the cock crew. (John 18:27).

In these four accounts of the fulfilled prophecy, none mention any number of times the cock crowed (or "crew" as Scripture states). But with significance we record that while Mark recorded the number, twice, in the prophecy, he did not in the fulfillment. Clearly, the significant fact was that the cock crowed. That it crowed twice is beyond all dispute. The consequence of Peter's first denial is recorded in inspired writings.

> Peter felt compelled to answer, and said angrily, "Woman, I know Him not." This was the first denial, and immediately the cock crew.... Peter now denied his

> Master with cursing and swearing. Again the cock crew. Peter heard it then, and he remembered the words of Jesus [Mark 14:30 quoted].
>
> (*Desire of Ages*, pp. 711, 712).

Thus the two crowings of the cock are confirmed in inspiration, once after Peter's first denial and once after his third. That no mention was made of the number of times the cock would crow cannot be misconstrued to state that it would only crow once. In these accounts there is no contradiction.

The same may be stated concerning the presence of two angels at Christ's tomb on the resurrection day. Matthew and Mark refer to but one angel while Luke and John mention two. We quote the four gospels' records.

> And, behold, there was a great earthquake: for the angel of the Lord descended from heaven, and came and rolled back the stone from the door, and sat upon it.
>
> (Matthew 28:2).

> And entering into the sepulchre, they saw a young man sitting on the right side, clothed in a long white garment; and they were affrighted. (Mark 16:5).

> And it came to pass, as they were much perplexed thereabout, behold, two men stood by them in shining garments: (Luke 24:4).

> ¹¹But Mary stood without at the sepulchre weeping: and as she wept, she stooped down, and looked into the sepulchre, ¹²And seeth two angels in white sitting, the one at the head, and the other at the feet, where the body of Jesus had lain.
>
> (John 20:11, 12).

Once again, Sister White confirmed the presence of the larger number – two angels.

> A young man clothed in shining garments was sitting by the tomb. It was the angel who had rolled away the stone. He had taken the guise of humanity that he might not alarm these friends of Jesus.... Again they look into the tomb, and again they hear the wonderful news. Another angel in human form is there, and he says, "Why seek ye the living among the dead? (*Desire of Ages*, pp. 788, 789).

Clearly, at first one angel only was visible in the tomb, but later the second angel appeared. Thus there is no conflict between the four accounts. Two gospel writers reported the first impression of the women, two reported the later appearance of a second angel. Thus Scripture cannot be credibly declared to be in error in these accounts. Both are correct.

Sister White also cleared up any question of how many demoniacs Christ healed at Gergesa. Christ healed two. Yet of the three gospel writers who recorded this miracle, only Matthew certified that two were healed.

> And when he was come to the other side into the country of the Gergesenes, there met him two possessed with devils, coming out of the tombs, exceeding fierce, so that no man might pass by that way. (Matthew 8:28).

> And when he was come out of the ship, immediately there met him out of the tombs a man with an unclean spirit (Mark 5:2).

> And when he went forth to land, there met him out of the city a certain man, which had devils long time, and ware no clothes, neither abode in any house, but in the tombs. (Luke 8:27).

When the full account is read we discover that Mark and Luke provided an added piece of information not found in Matthew's account. Mark (5:9) and Luke (8:30) both recorded that in Christ's dialogue that the spirit named himself as Legion. Clearly these two writers focused their account upon the most prominent of the two demoniacs, while Matthew, who alone of these three writers was present when the miracle transpired, included in his account, the presence of the second demoniac.

Sister White's record of the event confirmed the presence of two demoniacs.

> From some hiding place among the tombs, two madmen rushed upon them as if to tear them in pieces. (*Desire of Ages*, p. 337).

The value of the Spirit of Prophecy is illustrated in each of these three supposed "errors." Scripture is not in error. The gospels are a written mosaic, designed of God, to present a wider picture of events, panoramas, which when united, challenge our thinking and greatly expand our vistas of truths and events.

The fourth of Dr. Roennfeldt's singularity versus duality "errors", that of the healing of the two blind men of Jericho, is a most interesting one for it is dual dimensional. Not only is there a question of the number of blind men healed but also one of whether he/they were healed as Christ traveled to Jericho or from Jericho. We set forth the passages from the synoptic gospels. John made no reference to this episode in Christ's earthly ministry.

> [29]And as they departed from Jericho, a great multitude followed him. [30]And, behold, two blind men sitting by the way side, when they heard that Jesus passed by, cried out, saying, Have mercy on us, O Lord, thou Son of David.
> (Matthew 20:29, 30).

> [46]And they came to Jericho: and as he went out of Jericho with his disciples and a great number of people, blind Bartimaeus, the son of Timaeus, sat by the highway side begging. [47]And when he heard that it was Jesus of Nazareth, he began to cry out, and say, Jesus, thou Son of David, have mercy on me. (Mark 10:46, 47).

> [35]And it came to pass, that as he was come nigh unto Jericho, a certain blind man sat by the way side begging: [36]And hearing the multitude pass by, he asked what it meant. [37]And they told him, that Jesus of Nazareth passeth by. [38]And he cried, saying, Jesus, thou Son of David, have mercy on me.... [1]And Jesus entered and passed through Jericho. (Luke 18:35-38; 19:1).

Unlike the claimed "discrepancies" discussed above, the Spirit of Prophecy provides no assistance in this matter. In the book *Desire of Ages*, Sister White made no mention of the healing of the blind men. While Sister White referred a number of times to this healing in other books, she did so in order to use the passages to illustrate spiritual blindness or to use the words "Jesus of Nazareth passeth by" (Luke 18:37) in another context. Luke 18:41 is also used this way. (*Seventh-day Adventist Bible Commentary*, Vol. 5, p. 1111; *Evangelism*, pp. 444, 553; *Ministry of Healing*, p. 107; *Sons and Daughters of God*, p. 126; *Spiritual Gifts*, Vol. 2, p. 202; *Testimonies for the Church*, Vol. 3, p. 32; Vol. 4, pp. 178, 355; Vol. 6, p. 226).

In order to provide a proper evaluation of the accuracy of the records of each of the three gospel authors concerned – the account of this miraculous healing of one/two blind men and the claimed "discrepancy" concerning the site of the healing – upon entering or upon exiting Jericho – we turn to an non-inspired author. We have chosen to do so for three reasons:

1. Sister White has not written in respect of the details of this miracle;
2. Dr. Roennfeldt spoke quite dismissively of the book from which we will quote, despite the many excellent and highly credible defenses the author has marshaled against more than two hundred assaults on Scripture, including those which Dr. Roennfeldt has chosen to resurrect;
3. Dr. Archer's calm, valid account of the reconciliation of the three gospel records bears the hallmark of veracity.

> It is only after we compare the testimony of all three witnesses that we obtain a fuller understanding of the whole episode. From Luke 18:35 we learn that Bartimaeus first learned of Jesus' visit to Jericho as He and His followers were entering the town. Then, as the crowd was passing by, he tried to gain Christ's attention by calling out directly to Him from where he was sitting. Yet it would seem that he was not at first successful; for it was not until Jesus had entered the town, had His contact with Zacchaeus, taught the people the parable of the pounds (or, minas), and was on the point of leaving the city that Bartimaeus finally managed to engage Christ's attention. Possibly this was because the crowd was quieter on Jesus' departure than it had been at His arrival. At any rate, it was not until that point that Jesus stopped walking and gave orders to Bartimaeus to be brought to Him.
>
> Mark 10:46, 47 makes this clear: "And they come to Jericho. And as he was going out from Jericho ... Bartimaeus ... was sitting by the road. And hearing that it was Jesus the Nazarene, he began to cry out and say, 'Jesus, Son of David, have mercy on me!'" We cannot be certain whether vv. 47-48 refer to his first (and unsuccessful) appeal, or whether it was his subsequent outcry on Jesus' departure. From Matthew 20:30 we get the clear information that it was the latter. For Matthew 20:29 states quite explicitly that this dialogue with Jesus took place as the Lord was emerging from the city. Matthew also informs us that Bartimaeus had picked up a blind colleague in the meantime. It seems that Bartimaeus

spoke to him of his high hopes of getting through to Jesus when he would depart from the city, by the same gate He had entered. It may not have been a close friend of his, since Bartimaeus seems to have called out on his own behalf, in the first instance at least (Mark 10:18; Luke 18:39).

Bartimaeus and his unnamed companion moved forward at more or less the same time to where Jesus was standing. As they made their way to the Savior, they jointly petitioned Him (Matt. 20:33). Yet for some reason it was Bartimaeus who showed the greater energy in his importunity to Christ, and it was therefore to him that Jesus addressed His remarks and questions. He next healed the other man as well, and apparently touched their sightless eyes with His hand, thus restoring their sight to them (Matt. 20:34). The result was that both men joined Jesus' following and rejoiced as they witnessed to everyone they saw concerning what the Lord had done for them.

The three accounts supplement one another very helpfully in such a way as to bring out the facts that (1) Bartimaeus was the prime mover and the undiscourageable man of faith in this approach to Jesus for healing, while his companion was a less aggressive personality who was content to chime in with whatever Bartimaeus said: (2) Bartimaues' persistence was such that he would not take no for an answer, no matter how sternly the public ordered him to be silent. He even kept waiting for a second opportunity to contact Jesus, no matter how long it took for our Lord to accomplish His purposes in Jericho. Therefore he was most intently waiting for Jesus as He finally emerged once more through that same city gate.

(Dr. Gleason Leonard Archer – born 1916 –
Encyclopedia of Bible Difficulties, Zondervan Publishing House,
Grand Rapids, Michigan, 1982, pp. 332, 333).

During the discourse at the Elders' Summit it seemed that no effort was spared in order to assert that Scripture is riddled with deficiencies. The truth that Jude 1:14, 15 quotes from the book of First Enoch, one of the group of non-inspired writings which are known as the pseudepigrapha, written in the first and second centuries BC, was used to support the claim that some passages of Scripture are derived from copying the writings of those who were not inspired. While this is correct, no attempt was made to assure the Elders' Summit attendees that God led Jude to include this accurate material in Scripture, thus placing the stamp of divine inspiration upon it.

While claiming Scripture is accurate in guiding us to salvation, Dr. Roennfeldt's remarks were peppered with doubts that the Bible was free of error, as originally written. Veiled questions were repeatedly raised. We notice but four of these which came forth in rapid succession.

The Bible is reliable, but here and there in the Bible there are some incidental details which do not affect the essential meaning of the Scripture.
(Dr. Ray Roennfeldt, "Elders Summit," June 19, 2004).

> We have evidence that the Bible is the Word of God but here and there there are things that puzzle us in Scripture. (Ibid).

> There can be some differences of details but it does not affect the essential meaning of Scripture. (Ibid).

> We do not believe the Bible is inerrant, but [it] is an infallible revelation of God's will. (Ibid).

Our question is, If the Bible is not inerrant in its original autographs, as written by the God-chosen authors, then how can anyone possibly assert it is "infallible in its revelation of God's will?" At the best this could only be guesswork if it is conceded the Bible is not inerrant, for we would possess absolutely no guarantee that it was not mistaken in its claims concerning the way of salvation. Manifestly, the sources of error in the so-called "incidental," "minor" errors, would also operate on the minds of the prophets as they wrote the details of the plan of salvation.

But we have absolute certainty that the Bible is infallible, inerrant, in all that the writers wrote. To this the Spirit of Prophecy emphatically attests, as documented in the chapter entitled, "Are God-Inspired Writings Sometimes Correct and Sometimes Incorrect?"

Dr. Roennfeldt did not resist the temptation to distort denominational history in order to pursue his theory that the Spirit of Prophecy, like Scripture, is errant in "incidentals" and "minor" matters. This view has led many to find fault with very major aspects of Sister White's inspired messages, including the sanctuary message, the human nature of Christ, and Christian character perfection. This fact must not be lost upon each reader.

We record one statement which Dr. Roennfeldt made at the Elders' Summit which played fast and loose with denominational history.

> At the turn of the century, the nineteenth to the twentieth century, there were men like [A.T.] Jones, and there were men like [John Harvey] Kellogg – "whatever the prophet has written, I blot out my mind. It has to be truth, [the] Word of God." That's how Kellogg was, how Jones was.
>
> There were others like Willie, the son [Elder William White], who worked with her, and also [Elder A. G.] Daniells and [Elder W. W.] Prescott, who worked with her, and they had a more flexible view of what to expect from her, from first-hand experience working with the prophet.
>
> When the crunch came, who left the church? No other [one word here indecipherable on tape]. "Whatever the prophet said, it always has to be right." They were forced to face information that their little narrow world could not contain and they went out and opposed us, and I would say, too, that we are going to lose many people who are very, very rigid." (Ibid).

Denominational History clearly attests that Dr. John Harvey Kellogg did not leave the Seventh-day Adventist Church because he had held Sister White's writings to be inerrant and then discovered her writings to be fallible. He left for two major reasons – his desire for kingly power over the church's medical work, which at the time employed more workers than the rest of the denomination, and because he espoused pantheism and the General Conference, quite rightly, refused to permit the Review and Herald Publishing House to print his pantheistic book, *The Living Temple*, as an official denominationally-approved volume.

That Dr. Kellogg did not rigidly believe the instruction of the Lord is documented in denominational history for all to see. When Sister White counseled him to raise up many small sanitariums, he rejected this divine advice and chose to build a massive institution at Battle Creek. When Sister White rightly evaluated Dr. Kellogg's book, *The Living Temple*, to be promoting serious doctrinal error, he again defied Sister White's counsel.

Elder A. T. Jones too, evidenced a disinclination to accept Sister White's strong recommendations that he not join with Dr. Kellogg in his work. Instead Elder Jones chose to follow his own faulted reasoning. He did not "blot out his mind" as Dr. Roennfeldt asserted. Both Elder Jones and Dr. Kellogg placed their fallible minds against the counsel of the Lord. In choosing this course both men set themselves upon a path which jeopardized their eternal salvation.

A number of reliable Seventh-day Adventist Histories have traced the events leading up to the departures from the church of Dr. Kellogg and Elder Jones. We know of none which have confirmed Dr. Roennfeldt's account of these events, although some recent, revisionist histories may have. We present two such historical accounts in brief.

> Shortly after the turn of the century Dr. Kellogg came into conflict with the leaders of the General Conference over his attempts to get control of all SDA medical institutions with which he had been associated. He finally did succeed in getting control of the Battle Creek Sanitarium, the Battle Creek Food Company and the health institution in Mexico. His book, *The Living Temple*, was permeated with the principles of pantheism.
>
> Everything was done to help him see his error. Ellen White worked with him personally and sent him many messages, but in vain. In 1907 he lost his membership in the church.
>
> (*Seventh-day Adventist Encyclopedia*, Review and Herald Publishing Assocation, 1996, Vol. 1, p. 852).

> While president of the California Conference (1901-1903) he [Elder A. T. Jones] accepted an invitation from Dr. J. H. Kellogg, who was then actively seeking to separate the Battle Creek Sanitarium from denominational control, to join his staff. Against the counsel of Sister White he accepted the invitation.
>
> (*Ibid*, p. 833).

Elder Jones very briefly rejoined the General Conference in the Religious Liberty Department – but within months

> He became sympathetic with the doctor [J. H. Kellogg] in his warfare against the General Conference. This resulted in separation from denominational employment, and finally, in loss of church membership. (*Ibid*).

Clearly, both Dr. Kellogg and A. T. Jones left the church, not because they believed Sister White's counsel "very, very rigidly," but for the diametrically opposite reason, that they spurned such counsel when it opposed their own desires.

> The work of undercutting the testimonies began with meetings held by Dr. Kellogg and A. T. Jones [in 1905] with the [Battle Creek] Sanitarium workers and was advanced by correspondence with Seventh-day Adventist youth throughout the field.
> (Elder Arthur L. White, *Ellen G. White*, Review and Herald Publishing Association, Washington D.C., 1982, Vol. 6, p. 61).

Contrary to Dr. Reonnfeldt's claim that Dr. Kellogg was "rigid" in his faith in the Spirit of Prophecy counsels, there is strong evidence that he made a practice of accepting only those which met his desires and rejected Sister White's counsels when they crossed his desires. This was the ultimate cause of his departure from the faith. We cite one testimony to this fact. At the 1919 Bible Conference, M. E. Kern recalled:

> Many years ago I was in a meeting where Dr. Kellogg and others were considering a business matter. Dr. Kellogg there took a position exactly contrary to something Sister White had said. When asked how he explained what she had said, he replied that she had been influenced to say it. He was running down the Testimonies there. A short time after that I read one of his articles in the paper, in which he was laying down the law on the basis of the Testimonies. That made me lose my confidence in Dr. Kellogg. On one point that he did not agree with, he said she had been influenced. Then he took this other thing that pleased him and he said it was from the Lord. Perhaps he thought one was from the Lord and the other was not.
> (Transcript of 1919 Bible Conference, *Spectrum*, Vol. 10, No. 1, p.46).

Could it be that the theologians (rabbis) of the era of Christ's First Advent were not alone in using arguments which they well knew "were not really up to scratch, but [were] good arguments" for their own purposes? Has the same tactic re-surfaced among the theologians of the era of the Second Advent?

This breach of historical accuracy was not the only occasion during the Elders' Summit on which a false interpretation was placed upon denominational history. During the question and answer period it was stated, speaking of the twentieth century, that in the twenties, thirties and forties we went into a fundamentalist mode placing Ellen White where she never intended to be. In the nineteen-fifties we started to recover from this.

A study of those four decades, three of which form the early years of our lifetime, present a very different picture. As our forthcoming book, Volume two in our Seventh-day Adventist History Septenate – *Preparing for the Barnhouse-Martin Crisis* – which traces the history of our church in the decades of the thirties, forties and first half of the fifties, demonstrates many moves were made at high levels of our church which prepared the way for the shameful Barnhouse-Martin dialogue – a dialogue between Presbyterian clergyman Dr. Donald Barnhouse and Baptist theologian, Dr. Walter Martin and members appointed by the General Conference including, Dr. Leroy Froom, Dr. Roy Allen Anderson, Elder W. E. Read and Elder T. E. Unruh – from which emerged the book, above all denomination publications, which signaled a change of faith by attempting to weaken the sanctuary message and attempting to alter the Biblical truth of Christ's human nature and lowering the value of Sister White's ministry, *Seventh-day Adventists Answer Questions on Doctrine*, usually known by the last three words of the title.

The claim that we began to recover from our "fundamentalist" mode of the previous decades in the 1950's, was tantamount to the claim that the apostasy promoted in *Questions on Doctrines*, published in 1957, was a return to true faith. This is deception of a most marked nature. The state of our all-but-destroyed church today is clear evidence of this fact.

A number of breaches of standards were suggested by attendees during the question time and through interjections. The speakers provided no godly counsel to help these individuals to reach the highest level of fidelity. Sabbath observance was one target of these questions, raised by the audience. Two examples suffice. One attendee suggested that Sister White's counsel concerning cleaning shoes prior to Sabbath (*Child Guidance*, p.528; *Testimonies for the Church*, Vol. 6, p.355) did not apply today because in those days they wore boots which were often very muddy and took a considerable time to clean. This person was not cautioned by the theologians that the principle of true Sabbath keeping is to complete all possible preparations for the Sabbath during secular hours.

Similarly the principle of taking baths prior to Sabbath (see *Child Guidance*, p. 528; *Testimonies for the Church*, Vol. 6, p. 355) was suggested to be unnecessary today because it takes far less time with modern conveniences. Dr. Roennfeldt appeared to support this view by telling of his experience as a child where the water was boiled in the copper and transported by buckets to the bath. We, too, experienced this as children, but it has not led us to excuse ourselves from following divine counsel under less arduous circumstances.

One elder set forth a specious view that theater-going (see *Testimonies for the Church*, Vol. 6, pp. 406, 407) was banned in Sister White's counsels because the theater-houses were associated with brothels. No documentation of this association on a large scale was understandably cited. Nor did the theologians counter this misguided suggestion by pointing out that fiction, either written or viewed, was condemned by God through his servant. Even more importantly, they did not warn the elder that theater-goers will be destroyed with Satan. (*Testimonies for the Church*, Vol. 6, p. 407).

One man present enthusiastically sought to have the Spirit of Prophecy deleted from our statement of faith. He, too, received no godly counsel. It was in this atmosphere that the Elders' Summit progressed. There was scarcely a hint that any believers in the gift of prophecy in our midst were present.

Despite these obvious major shortcomings in the presentations at the Elders' Summit, there were those who, while strong proponents of truth, were beguiled by the presentations. This is a phenomenon all too often seen at such meetings. Why does such a phenomenon prevail? We illustrate with a personal family experiences.

In January, 1974, our Mother, Hilda Standish, along with our Father, Darcy Standish, attended the Victorian Conference Camp Meeting. It was to be our dear Mother's last Camp Meeting, for she died suddenly four months later, on May 5 of that year, at only sixty-one years of age.

Our parents, being devout Seventh-day Adventists, had commenced to notice gradual alterations in our faith and, having previously greatly appreciated Dr. Desmond Ford's presentations, were now somewhat apprehensive when they found he was listed to speak at the divine service on one of the two Sabbaths of the Camp.

However, although their "antennas were up," they discerned no deviation from Seventh-day Adventist Bible-based doctrine in Dr. Ford's message. This our Mother reported in her usual weekly letter, in a long series of letters, which were unfailingly of interest to us, then forty years of age. Nevertheless, she did remark that three brethren in the congregation did express concerns with the material presented. "But Dad and I believe that these men were simply nit-picking," she wrote in her beautiful handwriting.

Since Colin was then at Columbia Union College in Greater Washington D.C. and Russell was in Sydney serving at Sydney Adventist Hospital, we accepted our Mother's and Father's evaluation.

In 1976, unrequested, Russell was sent an audio tape and a transcript of Dr. Ford's divine service presented two years earlier at that Camp. Russell was amazed that our parents had not evaluated it as did the three complainants. Without stating the time and location of this sermon transcript, Russell passed it to our Father and requested his evaluation. His laconic response was, "Russ, that's a fearful destruction of truth."

When Russell acquainted him with the venue and date, our Father replied, "Russ, how could Mum and I have missed these words at the time?" The answer is that we all are distracted in our thoughts at times when listening to orations. To maintain full concentration throughout a presentation of forty-five to sixty minutes is a feat seldom achieved. Further, some speakers possess a talent for carrying their audiences with them in such a manner that the listeners are almost mesmerized by the roseate phrases employed, and do not ponder to estimate their accuracy, for the speaker moves on, providing scarcely a moment for reflection upon the subject matter.

Stratagem VII – Ministers' and Elders' Summits – Revelation, Inspiration and Ellen White

One clear Biblical error in Dr. Ford's message three decades past, was the concept that we are simultaneously servants of God and servants of Satan, as he emphasized the carnality of our natures. Contradicting such a concept, Christ stated:

> No servant can serve two masters: for either he will hate the one, and love the other; or else he will hold to the one, and despise the other. Ye cannot serve God and mammon. (Luke 16:13).

During a visit to Weimar College in California when Colin was College Dean there, 1979, Russell met a godly, truth-believing couple. They were highly educated, the husband holding a Ph.D. degree in biochemistry. They staunchly opposed Dr. Ford's theology. He was then a theology professor at Pacific Union College. They had the opportunity to hear Dr. Ford in person during a visit to Pacific Union College. The couple reported to us that Dr. Ford was on his "best behavior," since that which he preached accorded with truth.

Colin, rather rashly, Russell thought, said, "I'll guarantee he promoted ten errors in the first ten minutes." Colin did not know that the couple had brought back an audiotape of the presentation. We were invited to listen. Colin, fairly stated, "I'll only count as an error anything which both of you agree is error."

The first sentence was error. It included the words, "I can't keep the commandments for a fraction of a second." Colin stopped the tape. "Do you agree with that?" he asked. In asserting that they certainly did disagree, they added, "How did that get past us?" Before the tape had run five minutes, the couple had agreed to ten errors, despite the fact that we put not the least pressure on them to so judge the material. They were aghast at their former evaluation of Dr. Ford's service.

How careful we need to be if we choose to listen to those whom we know to present error.

At the Elders' Summit in Melbourne, June 19, 2004, some in attendance possessed no recollection of some of the most serious breaches of truth spoken.

In 1904, when the error of pantheism was being promoted by Dr. Kellogg and Dr. Waggoner, Sister White issued an urgent warning. This pantheistic error Sister White designated as the Alpha of Apostasy. She warned that the Omega of Apostasy was to follow:

> Be not deceived; many will depart from the faith, giving heed to seducing spirits and doctrines of devils. We have now before us the alpha of this danger. The omega will be of a most startling nature.
>
> (*Selected Messages*, Vol. 1, p. 197. Also *Special Testimonies*, Series B, No. 2).

We are now deep into the Omega of Apostasy. Read Sister White's dire warnings concerning the present situation, since her message is even more applicable today in the midst of the Omega than it was during the ascendancy of the Alpha. The Alpha was far less damaging than the Omega is, for church leadership did not espouse or support it. Volume 8 of *The Testimonies for the Church* was published in March, 1904, specifically to meet the crisis of the Alpha. (See

Testimonies for the Church, Vol. 8, p. 5). The warnings are more urgent and even more pointed today as some of the "very elect" are being deceived.

> The experience of the past will be repeated. In the future, Satan's superstitions will assume new forms. Errors will be presented in a pleasing and flattering manner. False theories, clothed with garments of light, will be presented to God's people. Thus Satan will try to deceive, if possible, the very elect. Most seducing influences will be exerted; minds will be hypnotized.
> (*Testimonies for the Church*, Vol. 8, p. 293). ....
>
> Satanic agencies are clothing false theories in an attractive garb, even as Satan in the Garden of Eden concealed his identity from our first parents by speaking through the serpent. These agencies are instilling into human minds that which in reality is deadly error. The hypnotic influence of Satan will rest upon those who turn from the plain word of God to pleasing fables.
>
> It is those who have had the most light that Satan most assiduously seeks to ensnare. He knows that if he can deceive them, they will, under his control, clothe sin with garments of righteousness, and lead many astray.
>
> I say to all: Be on your guard; for as an angel of light Satan is walking in every assembly of Christian workers, and in every church, trying to win the members to his side. I am bidden to give to the people of God the warning: "Be not deceived; God is not mocked." Galatians 6:7. (*Ibid*, pp. 293, 294).

This is the very reason why the Servant of the Lord has warned us:

> I was shown the necessity of those who believe that we are having the last message of mercy, being separate from those who are daily imbibing new errors. I saw that neither young nor old should attend their meetings; for it is wrong to thus encourage them while they teach error that is a deadly poison to the soul and teach for doctrines the commandments of men. The influence of such gatherings is not good. If God has delivered us from such darkness and error, we should stand fast in the liberty wherewith He has set us free and rejoice in the truth. God is displeased with us when we go to listen to error, without being obliged to go; for unless He sends us to those meetings where error is forced home to the people by the power of the will, He will not keep us. The angels cease their watchful care over us, and we are left to the buffetings of the enemy, to be darkened and weakened by him and the power of his evil angels; and the light around us becomes contaminated with the darkness. (*Early Writings*, p. 124, 125).

When this dire warning goes unheeded, it is little wonder that the minds of very elect are opened to deception.

Since we have fully commented upon Dr. Bradford's views in his book *Prophets Are Human* (see chapter entitled, "Stratagem II – Prophets Are Human"), we do not wish to extend this book by commenting upon the views he presented at the Elders' Summit.

After the conclusion of the Elders' Summit one brother asked a very important question of Dr. Bradford. This brother read from a question he had prepared in writing.

> In your book, you state that in their inspired writings Bible prophets sometimes made mistakes. My question is: How can I tell the difference between Satan's inspired writings which mix truth with error and God's inspired writings which also mix truth with error? And how can I sort out the error in Satan's inspired writings and the truth in God's inspired writings?

Dr. Bradford's reply was:

> The true prophet always leads people to Christ and to obedience to God; the false prophet never does this. Matthew chapter 7 is the answer to your question. By their fruit you can recognize them.

This was a patently unsatisfactory answer for it suffered from two defects; one logical, the other factual.

1. If the Bible contains error, then it is futile quoting from the Scripture in order to discover which words are true and which are false, for the passage referred to in Matthew 7:16 could itself be one of the errors of Scripture.
2. We notice that Dr. Bradford implicitly agreed that he had stated in his book that Bible prophets included some mistakes in Scripture.

Sadly, throughout there was no evident sense that the subjects of the presentations, the holy Word of God and the Spirit of Prophecy, were addressed in the true sacredness of this body of God-inspired truth. When we read from and speak of these revelations of the Mighty God, the Everlasting Father, we hold in our hands sacred tomes, and speak of holy words. Too often the words of the Spirit of Prophecy were spoken from faulted recollections rather than read from the inspired writings themselves. This, too, was a feature of the discussion of Scripture. Too frequently the off-handed, pithy, faulted comments of the speakers were met with waves of laughter. The atmosphere of levity followed by a number of rounds of applause in the question session, left us with a sense of sorrow, for men, rather than God, were thus honored.

God's inspired word has a telling impact upon us today.

> That we henceforth be no more children, tossed to and fro, and carried about with every wind of doctrine, by the sleight of men, and cunning craftiness, whereby they lie in wait to deceive; (Ephesians 4:14).

Christ's agonized question,

> when the Son of man cometh, shall he find faith on the earth? (Luke 18:8),

rings down through almost twenty centuries to our day. He continues to weep for His professed people.

12 Stratagem VIII – Editorial Comments on Letters

Not infrequently magazine editors courteously invite article contributors to make a brief response in their letters to the editor column when a correspondent proposes a contrary view to that of the article author.

However, it is most unusual for the editor to invite someone to comment upon a letter which is not addressing an issue which the invited commentator has raised. Yet this unusual course was taken in the South Pacific *Record*, July 31, 2004. The letter which engendered this unusual response, was written by Pr. Jan Knopper, retired South Pacific Division Publishing Director.

Pr. Knopper was responding to an editorial written in the *Record* of February 7, 2004 by Pr. Bruce Manners. (See chapter entitled, "Stratagem III – An Ellen White Reality Check"). We quote Pr. Knopper's letter.

> After the editorial of February 7, 2004 ("An Ellen White reality check"), and following the directions given to go to the Ellen G. White Research Centre at Avondale College to find the facts regarding "errors" in *The Great Controversy*, we can now let the readers of Record know that there are no errors in *The Great Controversy* and neither were Ellen White's historical sources in error.
>
> We found only two alleged errors: the first regarding the Waldenses and Sabbath-keeping; and the second regarding the John Huss story.
>
> For everybody to read, we now have two documents. One deals with the Waldenses and gives evidence without a shadow of doubt that there were Sabbath-keepers among the Waldenses. The second document provides evidence that the story of John Huss as stated in *The Great Controversy* is 100 per cent correct.
>
> If there is a reader who maintains that there are other historical errors, of which we have not been informed, please tell us.

If a response to this letter was deemed desirable, surely it was Pr. Manner's prerogative to make that response. Between February 7, 2004 and July 31, 2004, the editorship of the *Record* had transferred from Pr. Bruce Manners to Bro. Nathan Brown.

Russell had received the same documents as Pr. Knopper from the Avondale College Ellen G. White Research Centre. He had studied them and drawn precisely the same conclusions as Pr. Knopper. (See chapter entitled "Historical Accuracy"). The response was made by Dr. Lester Devine, Director of the Avondale College Ellen G. White Research Centre. We record Dr. Devine's words in full.

Jan Knopper wants a list of the "historical errors" in *The Great Controversy*. The practical issue for me is does he want "errors" when she wrote in 1911 or "2004 errors?" Ellen White went to enormous effort to ensure her 1911 revision of *The Great Controversy* was as perfect as she could make it (see *Selected Messages*, Book 3, appendices a, b and c) and congruent with the best historians of her day. If she wrote in 1911 what we know today, her first readers would have considered some aspects of her historical commentary inaccurate. The bottom line is that Ellen White cannot win in either time frame if people insist on a verbal inspiration, inerrant view of her ministry. For this type of "inerrancy" to continue to work over 100 years there must be no increase in knowledge during that time – a concept in conflict with Adventist belief that knowledge will increase to the end of time. Ellen White makes no claim to being authoritative as a historian – rather she is using historical events descriptively to illustrate the great principles of the great controversy. She points this out in the introduction to her book and which we all need to read carefully in order to understand the claims she made for her ministry on these issues – claims more limited than some sincere church members today make on her behalf.

Dr. Devine proposed six propositions, each of which merit consideration, in his response to Dr. Knopper's letter. These were:

1. Dr. Devine pitted historical knowledge of 1911 against such knowledge in 2004;
2. The readers of *The Great Controversy* in 1911 would have judged her history inaccurate if Sister White had used the knowledge we have in 2004 of those historical events;
3. Sister White "cannot win in either time frame if people insist on a verbal inspiration, inerrant view of her ministry";
4. For inerrancy to work there must be zero increase in knowledge over a period of a century;
5. Seventh-day Adventists believe that knowledge will increase to the end of time;
6. Sister White did not claim to be an authoritative historian.

We examine the first of these propositions.

The concept that historical records of past eras written in 2004 are more accurate than those authored ninety-three years earlier is, at best, an *ad hoc* assumption. In the chapter entitled "Disparities Between the 1888 and 1911 *Great Controversy* Editions," we document the fact that numbers of older historical volumes which were quoted in the 1888 edition of *The Great Controversy*, could not be located twenty-three years later when the 1911 edition was compiled. It must be remembered that it is not only flora and fauna of this world which are becoming extinct at an alarming rate, but this is true also of historical works. While occasionally a long-lost record of an historical event surfaces, the overwhelming trend is the loss of ancient or older records. Thus older historical records, records in closer temporal proximity to the events which are described, and which on balance, are more likely to be accurate, are rapidly disappearing from library shelves.

Of far greater concern is Dr. Devine's apparent disregard of the inspired nature of Sister White's writings. God's knowledge of every detail of historical events of the past has neither grown nor diminished in the past ninety-three years.

The second proposition also suffers from a lack of credibility. Sister White did not write with regard to the current knowledge of her readers or the academic community at large of her day. Had she pursued such a policy she would never have declared that germs could initiate cancer and that smoking led to malignancy, for neither of these, now verified, facts, were known in her lifetime.

Some have claimed that in one vision of Sister White, God did provide her with inaccurate information in order to accord with the knowledge of her day. On August 30, 1846 Sister White received a vision in which she saw three planets and a number of moons circling these planets. Sister White's record of this event follows:

> August 30th, 1846 I was married to Elder James White. In a few months we attended a conference in Topsham, Me. Bro. J. Bates was present. He did not then fully believe that my visions were of God. It was a meeting of much interest. But I was suddenly taken ill and fainted. The brethren prayed for me, and I was restored to consciousness. The Spirit of God rested upon us in Bro. C.'s humble dwelling, and I was wrapt in a vision of God's glory, and for the first time had a view of other planets. After I came out of vision I related what I had seen. Bro. Bates asked if I had studied astronomy. I told him I had no recollection of ever looking into an astronomy. Said he, "This is of the Lord." I never saw Bro. Bates so free and happy before. His countenance shone with the light of Heaven, and he exhorted the church with power. (*Spiritual Gifts*, Vol. 2, p. 83).

From various reports we glean that Captain Joseph Bates, who was present, took it upon himself to identify the planets based upon the moons then thought to circle those planets. Sister White did not identify the planets. We now know that these planets identified by Captain Bates have many more moons than were known in 1846.

Even in the past forty years there has been a vast increase in the knowledge of the number of moons circling these planets. In 1963 only twelve moons were known to circle Jupiter (*Encyclopaedia Britannica*, 1963 edition, Vol. 13, p. 191), nine Saturn (*Ibid*, Vol. 20, p. 10) and five Uranus (*Ibid*, Vol. 22, p. 891). In 2004 the number of moons now known, respectively, for these planets are fifty-six (information received from the Astronomical Society of Melbourne, August 3, 2004), thirty-three (*Scientific American*, June, 2004 and SBS News Service, 17th August, 2004) and twenty-two (Astronomical Society of Melbourne, *op. cit.*). There is a general expectation that further moons will be discovered in the future.

Nowhere did Sister White identify the planets which she was shown. Thus the charge that Sister White was provided information in her astronomical vision of 1846, which merely reflected current knowledge stands refuted. Captain Bates' identification must not be attributed to Sister White or to God's inspiration. Let it not be overlooked that Sister White saw a planet with seven moons outside our solar system in an 1846 vision where she was shown a planet to which Enoch was visiting. Some have designated this as the same vision (see *Early Writings*, pp. 39, 40). This may be so, but proof is wanting. Clearly the planet described here is not one in our solar system, all of which are uninhabited, except for our earth.

Elder J. N. Loughborough's account of the August 30, 1846 vision gave credence to the idea that Sister White had viewed Jupiter and Saturn, but he was not a first-hand witness and undoubtedly was dependent upon Captain Bates' identifications. Captain Bates, being a sea captain, was, of necessity, an amateur astronomer. (See J. N. Loughborough, *The Great Second Advent Movement*, pp. 260, 261).

There is no evidence which has been cited to confirm the theory that God provided Sister White with false information on this matter. Indeed the evidence is all to the contrary, for although Elder Loughborough mentioned Jupiter and Saturn by name, on the basis of the Captain's theory, he described Sister White as viewing people on those planets. In this case he quoted Sister White's words, placing them in quotation marks, "The inhabitants are tall, majestic people." (*Ibid*). Here is sound evidence that Sister White saw planets outside our solar system.

Dr. Devine's third proposition that Sister White "cannot win in either time frame" is incredible. We are not dealing with Sister White's historical knowledge, we are dealing with God's. While we most certainly believe that God-inspired writings are inerrant, we do not believe in verbal inspiration. Further, Pr. Knopper made no such statement or inference in his letter and thus this comment was quite irrelevant to the discussion.

Proposition four, in which Dr. Devine asserted that inerrancy can only operate over a period of a century if knowledge does not increase in that period is quite startling. What are the implications of this proposition for Scripture which, in its earliest writings, has existed, not for a single century, but for thirty-five centuries? We must ask ourselves whether we serve a finite god or a God whose knowledge of the past, present and future is infinite. Such statements as this proposition surely must not be uttered much less placed in print, prior to them being thoroughly examined and thought through after prayerful and diligent study of inspiration, and their implications for God's people and His truth evaluated.

Proposition five – that Seventh-day Adventists believe that knowledge will increase to the end of time – is, of course, correct. But such knowledge will expand truth, not contradict it.

Proposition six is also correct. Sister White never claimed to be an expert on history. This fact is impressive, for God inspired her to write history of unquestionable accuracy. We read nowhere where Moses claimed to be a historian, yet, despite the destruction of all the records of the antediluvian world, he wrote the only account of that period which exists today. He even traced the genealogies of the patriarchs during that period, as well as the history of the world beyond the Flood, for a total era of approximately two thousand five hundred years. His was the most remarkable feat of history ever undertaken. Why? Simply because God revealed that history to him.

Dr. Devine's response to Pr. Knopper's letter was not the first instance in which the *Record* published a response to a letter related to the revisionist view of the Spirit of Prophecy. (See *Records* March 13 and March 20, 2004). We note with deep concern that no such editorial comment has been felt expedient to correct the misinformation in a number of letters upholding the new South Pacific Division stance on Scripture and the Spirit of Prophecy. It appears that only letters upholding the accuracy of the Bible and the Spirit of Prophecy are subject to editorial contradiction. Such a stratagem serves the aims of the enemy of truth.

13 Are Inspired Writings Sometimes Correct and Sometimes Incorrect?

The answer to this question posed by this chapter heading is an emphatic "Yes!" – if they are writings inspired by Satan. Eve first discovered in her first contact with him, the fact that Satan, often cleverly, united truth and error.

> [1]Now the serpent was more subtle than any beast of the field which the LORD God had made. And he said unto the woman, Yea, hath God said, Ye shall not eat of every tree of the garden? [2]And the woman said unto the serpent, We may eat of the fruit of the trees of the garden: [3]But of the fruit of the tree which *is* in the midst of the garden, God hath said, Ye shall not eat of it, neither shall ye touch it, lest ye die. [4]And the serpent said unto the woman, Ye shall not surely die: [5]For God doth know that in the day ye eat thereof, then your eyes shall be opened, and ye shall be as gods, knowing good and evil. (Genesis 3:1-5).

We notice that this statement by Satan contained more truth than error. We list these truths:

1. God had stated that Adam and Eve may not eat of EVERY tree in the Garden of Eden;
2. Eve did not drop dead when she ate the fruit;
3. She did receive the knowledge of the difference between good and evil. Thus her eyes were opened to this difference as Satan promised.

In fact, what error did Satan assert? He used two techniques. Firstly, he asked an "innocent" question, "hath God said?" Here was error, not in the precise words spoken but in the inferred doubt. Secondly, in expressing the truth that, because of God's love and His tender grace, He did not immediately blot Eve out of existence, Satan did not tell the full truth – the final annihilation of the unrepentant wicked and the prior death of Eve on this old earth. In these subtle subterfuges is seen the error which Satan united with truth.

Eve aided and abetted Satan by adding to God's Word the words "...neither shall ye touch it" (see verse 3 above). What God had actually said was:

> [16]And the LORD God commanded the man, saying, Of every tree of the garden thou mayest freely eat: [17]But of the tree of the knowledge of good and evil, thou shalt not eat of it: for in the day that thou eatest thereof thou shalt surely die. (Genesis 2:16, 17).

Sister White commented in a number of places in her writings concerning Eve's addition to God's Word:

> Eve had overstated the words of God's command. He had said to Adam and Eve, "But of the tree of the knowledge of good and evil, thou shalt not eat of it: for in the day that thou eatest thereof thou shalt surely die." In Eve's controversy with the serpent, she added "Neither shall ye touch it." Here the subtlety of the serpent appeared. This statement of Eve gave him advantage; he plucked the fruit and placed it in her hand, using her own words, "He hath said, If ye touch it, ye shall die. You see no harm comes to you from touching the fruit, neither will you receive any harm by eating it." (*Confrontation*, p. 14).

How careful we must be never to proceed beyond Scripture!

Today, there are those in our midst who wholeheartedly concur that Satan subtly unites truth and error but they proceed one infinite step further and state, concerning the inspired writings of Scripture and the Spirit of Prophecy that they, too, possess an admixture of truth and error. We cite documentation.

> Having in mind the overall picture, she [Sister White] had of this [great] controversy, she then used the best Protestant sources available to her, including their now-known factual errors.
>
> (Pastor Bruce Manners, South Pacific *Record*, 7 February, 2004, p. 2).

> While we as a church, take the position that inspired writings are not inerrant (that is, without error), there has always been the suspicion that God would somehow protect His writers from even the simplest mistakes.
>
> This has tended, perhaps, to be the unspoken understanding of Ellen White's writings. We now need to face the reality that this is not so.
>
> (*Ibid* – parenthesis in the original).

At which General Conference Session did the delegates vote that inspired writings are not inerrant? We can discover no such voted decision.

In an interview conducted by Pastor Bruce Manners, then editor of the South Pacific *Record*, and now Senior Pastor of the Avondale College Seventh-day Adventist Church, this alleged mixture of truth with error in Scripture and the Spirit of Prophecy was stated by Dr. Arthur Patrick, former director of the Avondale College Ellen G. White Research Centre. After stating that in his mind Sister White had supernatural guidance "beyond reasonable doubt," Dr. Patrick asserted that he "put limits on that guidance." Pastor Manners then posed the question cited below, Dr. Patrick's answer follows:

> **So even an inspired person can be partly right and partly wrong?**
> You've got it!... Because Ellen White was shown in a two-hour panorama the age-long struggle between righteousness and sin does not mean she was an expert on the life and times of John Huss [Dr. Patrick alluded here to the claim of others, for example, Dr. Ron Graybill, that in the book, *The Great Controversy*, pp. 100, 101, Sister White included four historical errors].   (*Ibid*, February 28, 2004, p. 10).

Here we see documented evidence of the view that inspired writings, both those in Scripture and those in the Spirit of Prophecy, contain truth contaminated by error.

Dr. Bradford, through the words of his fictional theologian, Dr. Harold Smithurst, referred to Paul's words in 1 Corinthians 1:14, 15:

> [14]I thank God that I baptized none of you, but Crispus and Gaius; [15]Lest any should say that I had baptized in mine own name.   (1 Corinthians 1:14, 15).

Pastor Bradford judged this passage of Scripture to be false.

> Now that isn't true.   (*Prophets Are Human*, op. cit., p. 32).

That is a very serious charge against Scripture. Further, it is a false charge. This accusation is dealt with in the chapter entitled "Drifting Away From Bible Truth," in this book. Dr. Bradford presented this comment under a sub-heading, "The Bible is a Mixture of the Human and the Divine." This, of course, is true, but in a very limited sense. It is only true in the sense that inspired thoughts were written in the language and words of the canonical writer. It is untrue when such a statement is associated with the imputation that any passage of Scripture "isn't true."

Let us examine the serious dilemma in which we are placed if both of the following claims are factual:

1. Satan inspires men and women to proclaim by voice and pen that which is truth mixed with that which is erroneous;
2. The Holy Spirit inspires men and women to proclaim by voice and pen that which is truth mixed with that which is erroneous.

The searching believer – if both of these propositions are accepted – is left with no basis upon which to discern between that which is inspired by the devil and that which Christ inspires through the Holy Spirit. This is a quandary of insuperable proportions. Within this view is the implied charge that God's Word is no more accurate than Satan's.

One particle of error destroys truth irrespective of the quantity of truth remaining. No doubt we are all aware of the illustration which we cite below. We present it not because of its originality but for its age-old aptness. A glass of pure distilled water becomes toxic when contaminated by a single drop of poison. Truth is only truth when it is uncontaminated by error. This matter highlights the folly of those who excuse error in a presentation on the grounds that "there was, however, a lot of truth in the presentation." There was not! That sermon was error through and through, as the glass of water containing just one drop of poison is toxic throughout the liquid content of the glass.

Some counter that we can discern the difference on the basis of the Scriptural assurance that,

> Wherefore by their fruits ye shall know them.   (Matthew 7:20).

But this text solves absolutely nothing, for if the Scripture is a mixture of truth and error, how do we know that this advice is not polluted by error?

God has plainly stated the one criterion upon which truth is based!

> To the law and to the testimony: if they speak not according to this word, it is because there is no light in them. (Isaiah 8:20).

It is no mere happenstance that this verse is preceded by the words of verse 19:

> And when they shall say unto you, Seek unto them that have familiar spirits, and unto wizards that peep, and that mutter: should not a people seek unto their God? for the living to the dead? (Isaiah 8:19).

Here is presented in these successive verses, the stark contrast between Satan's inspired words and God's. God's people are guided by the law and the testimony. If the words of Scripture and the prophetic testimony of the Spirit of Prophecy were partly right and partly wrong, then we would be bereft of the least distinction between the words of Christ's servants and the servants of Satan's. We would never discover the pathway to heaven.

Consider Sister White's inspired words:

> Error is never harmless. It never sanctifies, but always brings confusion and dissension. It is always dangerous. The enemy has great power over minds that are not thoroughly fortified by prayer and established in Bible truth.
> (*Testimonies for the Church*, Vol. 5, p. 292).

Let us not pass by these words, paying scant attention and according them none of their force, in our search for the narrow road which leads to life eternal. Several positions which are paramount in the firm establishment of God's plan for salvation in our lives, are set forth, in this short passage:

1. Error is NEVER harmless;
2. Error NEVER sanctifies;
3. Error is ALWAYS dangerous;
4. Error is dispelled by prayer and truth is established by the Bible.

So we must address a number of resultant questions:

1. Would God inspire his "penmen" to include error which is always harmful?
2. Would He inspire His prophets to present error so that we remain unsanctified?
3. Is it God's plan to leave us in the certain danger of our loss of eternal life?
4. If the Bible is errant, could it dispel that which it, itself, inculcates – error?

To answer any one of these questions in the affirmative is to lay the charge against God of leading us away from our salvation. God does not inspire His prophets and then permit them to record His words erroneously. Such a view charges God with permitting His sacred word to be defiled.

But, in contradistinction to this state of plangent melancholy and hopelessness, our God – who is love – has offered us the certainty of His inspired Word and the joy of His salvation. He has assured us that:

> [16]ALL scripture is given by inspiration of God, and is PROFITABLE for doctrine, for reproof, for correction, for instruction in righteousness: [17]That the man of God may be perfect, thoroughly furnished unto all good works.
>
> (2 Timothy 3:16, 17 – emphasis added).

Now, if some Scripture contained uninspired material which contains human error, this statement would be yet another example of error.

Would ALL Scripture then be profitable for doctrine?

Would ALL Scripture then be profitable for reproof and for correction?

Would ALL Scripture then be profitable for instruction in righteousness?

Would ALL Scripture then be profitable to make godly men perfect?

Would ALL Scripture then thoroughly furnish mankind to perform all good works?

Each question is rhetorical. This passage of Scripture means what it plainly states. It would make nonsense of God's Word if Scripture did not contain truth alone.

It is time to reject this fallacious error, that we may walk in the light of all God-inspired writings, illuminated by the Holy Spirit and empowered by Christ's grace. It is too late in earth's history to follow folly. Satan's inspired words are an admixture of truth and error; Christ's words, by contrast, present perfect truth. They fully illuminate the path to heaven.

Our theologians who teach the fallibility of God's Word have departed from Protestantism. Unrepented, they will never be among those whom God has called to complete the Reformation.

> Wycliffe now taught THE DISTINCTIVE DOCTRINES OF PROTESTANTISM – salvation through faith in Christ, and the sole infallibility of the Scriptures.
>
> (*The Story of Redemption*, p. 337, emphasis added).

> The grand principle maintained by these Reformers—the same that had been held by the Waldenses, by Wycliffe, by John Huss, by Luther, Zwingli, and those who united with them—was the infallible authority of the Holy Scriptures as a rule of faith and practice. (*Great Controversy*, p. 249).

Over the past three decades the proponents of the New Theology have loudly proclaimed their aim to take our church back to the theology of the Reformation. Here we see that this claim has been a subterfuge to take us away from those Reformation principles which were correct.

We praise God for the Spirit of Prophecy for it uses plain words to dispel the sophistries of those who would remove trust from inspired writings.

Notwithstanding the claims of these theologians to support the Bible and the Spirit of Prophecy writings as safe guides to salvation, their very words, claiming the errancy of these inspired works, loudly deny their claim.

> In His word, God has committed to men the knowledge necessary for salvation. The Holy Scriptures are to be accepted as an authoritative, infallible revelation of His will. (*Great Controversy*, p. vii).

> The Bible presents a perfect standard of character; it is an infallible guide under all circumstances, even to the end of the journey of life.
> (*Testimonies for the Church*, Vol. 5, p. 264).

Twenty-one years later Sister White repeated the very words of the last quotation in *Signs of the Times*, March 21, 1906. they were later incorporated into the compilation, *My Life Today*, p. 25.

We repeat Sister White's affirmation:

> God's Word is infallible. (*Selected Messages*, Vol. 1, p. 416).

God's inspired writings compel us to utterly reject the faith-destroying words of those who would degrade the integrity of Scripture.

Part III
Conferences to Alter Faith

14 Conferences

Increasingly conferences are being called, sometimes under conditions of secrecy, in order to re-examine previously-settled matters of faith. In his paper, presented before the February 2-5, 2004 Summit held at Avondale College, (*op. cit.*, p. 1), Dr. Patrick set forth a series of preceding conferences called in 1978, 1982 and 2002, re-evaluating Sister White.

The calling of other conferences re-examining various subjects of faith which we had believed to be well established, such as the matter of women's ordination and the literal accuracy of the first eleven chapters of Genesis, appear to be escalating. These conferences are costly. But are they valuable?

We have concluded that these summits, conferences, workshops, seminars reality checks and other such gatherings, whatever their designations, called to re-examine established truth, inevitably lead to the denigration of truth; indeed to open denial of our precious faith. They are artful efforts of Satan to abolish the one body of truth which, possessed by sanctified Seventh-day Adventists, will lead to the climax of the great controversy between Christ and Satan. Never have we seen one of these Conferences, from the 1919 General Conference Bible Conference to the 2004 Summit at Avondale College where,

> More than 100 ministers, church educators and administrators met at Avondale College, NSW [New South Wales] from February 2 to 5 to gain a better understanding of the role and ministry of Ellen White.
> (South Pacific *Record*, February 21, 2004),

lead to an advancement in truth.

Notice the word *better* in the *Record* article. The use of this adjective is – to place it in its best light – totally misleading. The headline of the *Record* article quoted above explained the real purpose much more accurately – "Church leaders reassess Ellen White." So, too, did Pr. Bruce Manners' editorial headline in the same periodical of February 7, 2004, "An Ellen White Reality Check."

Ever since the introduction of the New Theology through the book *Questions on Doctrine* in the late 1950's, there has been a growing trend to call *ad hoc* committees together in order to re-examine the principles of our faith. Back in 1979 when Colin was Dean of Weimar College, he was appointed a member of an *ad hoc* committee called in order to examine the principles of Righteousness by Faith. Dr Desmond Ford was also a member of that *ad hoc* committee. At the time this seemed like a wonderful opportunity to uplift the principles of Bible truth in an important committee called by the General Conference.

Amazingly all six sub-committees, no doubt guided by the Holy Spirit, brought back strong affirmations of the fundamental, inspired principles of the doctrine of righteousness by faith. Tragically Dr. Ford and a number of like-minded thinkers were appointed by the chairman to "refine the findings." Eventually that "refinement" of the findings appeared in the *Adventist Review*. Along with many other members of those sub-committee Colin could not recognize the "refinement" as representing that which was agreed by the committees. By appointing the minority of New Theology proponents in the original committees, to the refinement committee, the Chairman had ensured that the six truth-sustaining reports would be suppressed and the New Theology position would be advanced in the minds of the *Adventist Review* readers. With such tactics were the aims of those promoting the New Theology forwarded.

Colin was also appointed to another *ad hoc* committee looking into four separate issues prior to the 1975 General Conference Session held in Vienna, Austria. He was President of Columbia Union College at the time. This General Conference *ad hoc* committee chairman, Elder Willis Hackett, a Vice President of the General Conference, appointed Colin as the chairman of one of the subcommittees.

The sub-committee Colin chaired, diligently studied Scripture and the Spirit of Prophecy on the issue of the ordination of women elders and pastors. The group of twelve individuals were unanimous that there was no inspired warrant for ordination of either women elders or pastors. Yet when the chairman of the Committee spoke strongly against their finding and recommendation, only two of the sub-committee members, of which Colin was one, in the final vote, voted in accordance with the committee's findings despite the fact that they were firmly based upon inspiration.

The two General Conference leaders had offered not one passage of Scripture or the Spirit of Prophecy in support of their objections to the findings of the sub-committee. But it seemed that the almost fifty members of the four sub-committees, including the ten from the sub-committee Colin had chaired, were far more influenced by the voices of human leaders than the voice of God.

Glacier View in 1980 was the venue for an examination by over one hundred and twenty theologians and church administrators, of Dr Ford's doctrinal position, which he had expressed in a nine-hundred-page document. Presently, *ad hoc* committees are examining Sister White's health message and others are investigating the principles of creation as found in the Bible. What has been the result of these investigations? In the case of Dr Ford's doctrines, the result has been widespread acceptance of his false theological views, not only among laity, but also among the ministry and many administrators in high office within our church. Women's ordination is now not uncommon in churches – the Southeastern California Conference recently approved a common credential for women in the ministry on an equal basis with men: many of our theologians and scientists now teach the unscriptural view that the earth is millions of years old and deny the six-day creation week; numerous pastors and lay-people spurn Sister White's writings today. Even in Botswana, women ministers are now appointed.

We are now, in hindsight, clearly able to see the results of these committees which have been set up with the avowed purpose of re-examining established truths – truths established firmly upon the Bible and the Spirit of Prophecy. Is it not time for us to see a pattern which is occurring at all levels of our Church? Is it not time for us to ask the question, 'Are these *ad hoc* committees and conventions leading to the confirmation of truth, or are they simply ruses whereby the faithless elements in our church find a thin edge of the wedge through which they can establish a platform from which they may insinuate their God-disdaining beliefs into our midst?' The current evidence would answer this question by affirming the second of the two propositions stated above.

Is it not time for us to ask ourselves the question, 'Is it proper to examine the validity of truths which have been accepted on the plainest words of Scripture and the Spirit of Prophecy?' Are we doubting that God has led us and – even more importantly – that His Word means precisely what it says? How can humans believe that they can take votes upon the unchanging truths of inspiration? We should have learnt from history. Every Church Council called from the fourth century ended with a further departure from settled Biblical truth.

Is it not time for us to see the mendacious claims of these conferences to be upholding truth, to be unfounded? This is not the time to re-examine truth. It is time to *teach* all members, young and old, new or longstanding, ministry or laity, the infallible truth entrusted to the Seventh-day Adventist Church to know, believe, live in the power of Christ and to share with the whole world.

In the July/August 1998 edition of the American magazine *Touchstone*, Alan P. Medinger, a perceptive author of the Episcopalian Church in the United States, described a most interesting dialogue which was introduced into his own church. Several ministers and lay members approached a bishop of the Episcopalian Church with a proposal. They said that they believed the Episcopalian Church should re-study the subject of whether it was appropriate for their denomination to cut off all assistance to the poor and needy. They cited in defence of their view that we are now living in a modern economy where jobs are available for all and that the Scripture plainly states,

> If any would not work, neither should he eat. (2 Thessalonians 3:10).

They very conveniently forgot that Christ Himself, after placing upon Christians the requirement to assist the poor and needy, had stated of those who declined the obligation,

> [41]Then shall he say also unto them on the left hand, Depart from me, ye cursed, into everlasting fire, prepared for the devil and his angels: [42]For I was an hungered, and ye gave me no meat: I was thirsty, and ye gave me no drink: [43]I was a stranger, and ye took me not in: naked, and ye clothed me not: sick, and in prison, and ye visited me not. [44]Then shall they also answer him, saying, Lord, when saw we thee

> an hungered, or athirst, or a stranger, or naked, or sick, or in prison, and did not minister unto thee? ⁴⁵Then shall he answer them, saying, Verily I say unto you, Inasmuch as ye did it not to one of the least of these, ye did it not to me. ⁴⁶And these shall go away into everlasting punishment: but the righteous into life eternal. (Matthew 25:41-46).

Manifestly, this is a plain command of God. There was no need for *ad hoc* committees to discuss the issue. The plainest Word of God has settled it. Paul – in 2 Thessalonians 3:10 – was clearly referring to lazy people who could well work in order to obtain the necessities of life, not to those who were in dire straits through no fault of their own – the sick, those seriously deformed, the mentally incompetent and the aged. Even if such needy souls were not to be found in affluent countries, which of course they are, surely the untold numbers of needy in less affluent nations should attract our compassionate benevolence.

The head of the Episcopalian Church was shocked by this suggestion from the delegation, and even declared it to be ridiculous. He was quoted as saying,

> We are not going to cut off all our programs for the poor and needy.
> (*Touchstone*, op. cit).

But the head of the delegation responded,

> No, no, I am not saying that we should cut them off, just that we should study the subject. After all, how can we know whether or not we should do this if we do not discuss it? We have new economic and psychological understandings now – knowledge that was not available two thousand years ago. We really don't know what God is saying about charity. Let's just keep an open mind and enter into dialogue about it. Appoint a commission of experts in the field and let's see what they come up with. What harm can it do?' (*Touchstone*, op. cit.).

While the leader of the church was quite opposed to the idea, he nevertheless did not want to be regarded as narrow-minded. He gathered together the requested committee which predictably could come to no firm decision on the matter. That committee met in the 1970's.

When no conclusion was arrived at by the first committee, regional groups were appointed to study the subject. Eventually the local churches were asked to enter into dialogue upon the topic. What were the consequences of this procedure?

Many of the members, weak in the faith, now felt that the wisdom of doing charity work was a matter of opinion. Many who had strong convictions on the matter became so involved in these many discussions that their time and energy were taken away from the provision of God-ordained charity. What were the results of these prolonged dialogues?

> During this process, starting slowly, but with increasing frequency the church's soup kitchens and homeless shelters started closing down. Programs for the physically handicapped and for the addicted, ceased operations. While one

faction in the church was fighting for their closure, another fought as strenuously to keep them open, but the great mass of people in the denomination – those in the middle – were just confused by it all and gradually lost any enthusiasm for keeping the programs open. Making matters worse for the advocates of Christian charity, the people who ran soup kitchens, the shelters, and the support groups found all of their time being taken fighting out the battles on the commissions, and their ministries floundered. (*Touchstone*, July/Aug, 1998).

While the Seventh-day Adventist Church is not dealing with charity as a prime issue, we have fallen into the same trap. Committees have been formed to dialogue the matter of whether Dr. Ford should be used in our pulpits. At church levels, music committees have been formed in order to determine what sort of music is acceptable and even preferable in our churches. Every time the liberal element of the church is determined to introduce its agenda, committees are formed and the result is that little by little, they succeed in eroding the foundational truths and/or practices and standards of God's chosen church. Our desire is to speak to pastors and administrators in our church together with church elders and other officers of local churches. Is it not time to put an end to that which has all but destroyed the mission and purity of the Seventh-day Adventist Church? Is it not time to state that matters which have been clearly mandated by Divine unction are not open to negotiation? Dare we open to the thoughts of our believers, issues which are manifestly in grave opposition to Divine mandate, fearing that we would be regarded as bigots if we did not?

One of the great issues facing Seventh-day Adventists today is, DARE WE RE-EXAMINE ISSUES FOR WHICH INSPIRATION HAS PROVIDED A PLAIN "THUS SAITH THE LORD"? Is God's guidance negotiable? Are we a church which does not know our faith and the Bible principles of our truths?

Let us illustrate. When a decision was made to form an *ad hoc* review committee to examine Dr Ford's ideas in 1980, the General Conference issued a request that the matter of Righteousness by Faith be removed from discussions and our publications until the Glacier View Committee had reached a consensus on the matter. Can you imagine the damage that such a request did to our church? Now believers were left to assume that church leaders did not even know after one hundred and thirty-six years what we believed on the subject of Righteousness by Faith.

We were completing our first co-authored book, *Adventism Vindicated*, when this request was published in major denominational papers. Russell was very open about what he was writing in defence of the doctrine of righteousness by faith and had told the President of the Southeast Asia Union what he was authoring. Russell was, at that time, President of Bangkok Adventist Hospital (Thailand).

Russell was quite surprised to receive a letter from the Union President stating that, in view of that which the General Conference President, Elder Neal Wilson, had requested, he should not proceed with the book until after a decision on the matter of Righteousness by Faith was made at Glacier View. Russell replied courteously, but firmly, that he had no intention of desisting in his aim to complete and publish the book. He pointed out that we knew perfectly well what the Bible and the Spirit of Prophecy taught on the subject of Righteousness by Faith. There is no doubt in the Bible. There is no equivocation in the Spirit of Prophecy. It is a settled matter of inspiration. He also explained that he had no doubt that if people like himself and Colin ceased to uplift the truth of the doctrine, that the devil would not call a truce in his efforts to introduce the New Theology into our church.

Russell fully expected to be dismissed for his failure to acquiesce to the Union President's request. He did offer that, if his stand were an embarrassment, he would quietly return to Australia where he knew he could obtain a position in a University of Melbourne hospital where his work had been appreciated earlier.

Twenty-five years have passed since Russell wrote that letter. He received no reply and the Union President and Russell became close friends; the Union President, Elder Robert Heisler, supported Russell's work with great enthusiasm. Incredibly, the following year it was this Union President who chaired the Union Committee which recommended Russell's ordination to the ministry and who strongly supported him in that ministry. Russell has often wondered if God was testing his fidelity to truth before calling him to this sacred office.

Surely, it is time for church leaders and members to cease acting as if we, as a people, do not know what we believe on issues which have been settled – and settled firmly – on the basis of inspiration. We need administrators who will refuse to call together *ad hoc* committees which are "balanced" between those who believe the truth and those who do not, for all we are accomplishing – as the current state of our church amply demonstrates – is the introduction of that which defames Scripture and denies God's precious truth.

15 General Conference International Conferences

The tragedy of Conferences called to re-evaluate truth lies in the fact that our church leaders do not trust the laity. They largely call church workers to these conferences. It is not in Australia alone that these conferences are called. The General Conference is now making a habit of calling such meetings in order to reinvent the Seventh-day Adventist faith.

In 2002 two Conferences were called. In August of 2002, The International Faith and Science Conference was convened. The General Conference President, Pr. Jan Paulsen, attended and spoke. Reporting upon this conference, Richard J. Bottomley M.B.A., Ph.D. (University of Toronto), Professor of physics and business at Canadian University College, a Seventh-day Adventist tertiary institution, reported:

> Most Seventh-day Adventists are aware of the apparent conflict between the findings of science and our traditional view of origins. To many Adventists, it is a simple case of scientists, who, under Satan's influence, deny the plain facts of the flood and the young earth all around us.... But to those who have looked at this issue more deeply it is apparent that there is a much greater problem that defies such a simple-minded characterization.
> (*Spectrum*, Vol. 30, Issue No. 4, Autumn 2002, p. 52).

Are we, who in full trust in God's Word and the Spirit of Prophecy, "simple-minded"? There is nothing savoring of simplicity in God's mind and He is the author of these books. There is a growing arrogance in the hearts of many educated, professing Seventh-day Adventists today. While those upholding the Biblical and Spirit of Prophecy accounts of science and the origin of this earth are far from simple-minded, we do, however, possess a simple and unshakeable faith in God's inspired writings.

Let us notice the aura of secrecy in which this conference was conducted:

> To address this problem in a responsible way, the church convened The International Faith and Science Conference in Ogden, Utah, late in August [23-29 August, 2002]. Since this is a sensitive issue and the Church didn't want to signal any movement on the issue, the conference was limited to a small group, mostly church employees, and closed to most outside observers. Participants were counseled to be careful in discussing the content of the conference after the conclusion. (*Ibid*).

Here we see the strategy of some leaders in the General Conference in its bid to destroy the six-day creation record of Genesis chapter one and the words of the Spirit of Prophecy – repeated at least eighty-three times – that the creation of this world occurred approximately six thousand years ago. While there are faithful scientists who staunchly support the inspired record, probably a majority of our College and University professors in the western world do not.

Russell's son, Dr. Timothy Standish (born 1963), a geneticist and a research scientist at the General Conference Geoscience Research Institute, is one who supports the inspired record. He was one of the contributors to the book, *In Six Days*, edited by Dr. John F. Ashton, New Holland Publishers, Sydney, 1999. He also presented a paper in support of the "simple-minded" view at the 2002 International Science and Faith Conference. He was not alone in this.

A year later, from August 13-20, 2003 a North American Division Faith and Science Conference was convened at Glacier View, Colorado. Similar conferences were, alas, also conducted in other Divisions around the world. On this occasion North American administrators, scientists and theologians were invited. Larry Evans, a staff member of *Adventist News Network* (ANN) of the General Conference reported that,

> This was the second in a series of three meetings that will culminate in a 2004 international conference. (South Pacific *Record*, September 13, 2003).

We notice the theme of the 2003 conference.

> The conference allowed some of the church's best scientists and theologians to talk about contradictory evidence regarding the many facets surrounding Creation. (*Ibid*).

While proclaiming that according to church leaders,

> its goals were not to change the church's beliefs or draw up criteria to define orthodoxy, (*Ibid*),

Larry Evans went on to say,

> It did, however, attempt to outline a process where serious and caring dialogue could take place so scholars could explore conflicting views of difficult issues raised by scientific data that suggest that there could be more than one interpretation. Among these are questions such as the age of the earth and whether the Noachian flood was truly "universal." (*Ibid*).

Do we truly doubt the plainest words of inspiration that our earth is approximately six thousand years old? Do we genuinely doubt that Noah's flood was not worldwide? Tragically, an increasing number of Seventh-day Adventist leaders, theologians, scientists, ministers and laypeople do.

Only the credulous reader would fail to discern the use of these conferences to subvert the faith. Even though words are carefully selected in preparing these reports for the laity, the trend cannot be mistaken. Large numbers of our scientists and theologians no longer believe Scripture or the Spirit of Prophecy. Their views are now prevailing at the highest levels of our church; "Caring dialogue" indeed!

Professor Bottomley was correct when he chose the ominous words for the title of his report on the 2002 International Faith and Science Conference – "A Work in Progress." There is a determination to destroy the faith of God's people. This work most certainly is in progress and it must be met head-on by all God's faithful people who will not be intimidated by what Sister White defined as

> science, falsely so called [which] is wearing away the foundation of Christian principle, and those who once were in the faith drift away from the Bible landmarks, and divorce themselves from God, while still claiming to be His children. (*Evangelism*, p. 362).

Dr. Edwin A. Karlow, professor of physics at La Sierra University, who served at Columbia Union College in the 1970's when Colin was President, and has been a member of the Geoscience Research Institute board since 1991, presented brief insights into that presented at the International Conference in 2002. When Colin knew Dr. Karlow on the staff of Columbia Union College as Chairman of the Mathematics and Physics Departments, Colin recalls him then as a highly-regarded staff member who believed the words of inspiration that our earth is about six thousand years old. These snippets from papers delivered are found in his article entitled "A Family Affair," *Spectrum*, Vol. 30, No. 4, Autumn 2002, pp. 47-51. His brief summaries of this Conference, which cost $55,000 to hold, and included eighty-four participants from every Division of our church, including

> Twenty church administrators, four pastors, eighteen theologians, thirty-five scientists, and seven invitees from the General Conference including the editors of *Ministry*, *Adult Bible Study Guides*, *Adventist Review* and *Signs of the Times*. In addition six lay members attended, (*Ibid*, p. 47),

will alarm faithful servants of God.

Even Pr. Paulsen dared not to declare that the earth was created about six-thousand years ago, stating that its age was

> a young one. (*Ibid*, p. 48).

In Seventh-day Adventist circles today, this claim is usually employed as short-hand for saying that "while I do not believe the earth is millions of years old, nevertheless, I doubt Sister White's six thousand years statements." We cannot know if this was Pastor Paulsen's intent. But why is it so seldom that we now dare to use the number 6000 in relation to the age of the earth? Even the avowed "Conservative" Adventist Theological Society moved in 2003 to remove from its constitution the words 'Six-thousand years' in relation to the age of the earth and substitute the words 'a short chronology' in its place. This notice was sent to all members along with the Spring, 2003, edition of *The Journal of the Adventist Theological Society*.

Why are even "conservative" scientists and theologians afraid to support Scripture and the Spirit of Prophecy? They must not concede the first step towards doubt in divine revelations. Let them boldly and confidently state that the earth is about six thousand years old.

We were shocked to learn that Dr. Richard M. Davidson, Chairman of the Old Testament Department at the Adventist Theological Seminary, a man with whom we have spent days in dialogue, and found faithful, proposed:

> the 'passive gap' interpretation of texts from Genesis 1:1, 2 to Genesis 1:3, which allows for the possibility of much older ('millions of years') prefossil rocks.
> (*Ibid*, p. 48 – words in parenthesis were in the original).

Surely God's own handwriting contradicts such a suggestion.

> For in six days the LORD made heaven and earth, the sea, and all that in them is, and rested the seventh day: wherefore the LORD blessed the sabbath day, and hallowed it. (Exodus 20:11).

Moses was inspired to confirm God's words:

> [16]Wherefore the children of Israel shall keep the sabbath, to observe the sabbath throughout their generations, for a perpetual covenant. [17]It is a sign between me and the children of Israel for ever: for in six days the LORD made heaven and earth, and on the seventh day he rested, and was refreshed. (Exodus 31:16, 17).

Here we see the intimate relationship between the creation of the earth and all that is in it in six days, and the Sabbath. To even consider the "passive gap" theory is to not only doubt God's Word and that of the Spirit of Prophecy but to open the way to desecration of the Sabbath. It is significant that in Exodus 31:17 the heaven and earth alone are designated as having been created in the six days.

In Exodus 20:11 God plainly states He made heaven and earth AND "all that in them is", in six days not just the "all that in them is." This is incontrovertible evidence of Dr. Davidson's error. Sister White is also very clear on this issue. She specifically declared that the world itself along with the Sabbath day were created in the self-same seven-day week. Read Sister White's words with care.

> They make void the law of God by their traditions. The sophistry in regard to the world's being created in an indefinite period of time is one of Satan's falsehoods. God speaks to the human family in language they can comprehend. He does not leave the matter so indefinite that human beings can handle it according to their theories. When the Lord declares that He made the world in six days and rested on the seventh day, He means the day of twenty-four hours, which He has marked off by the rising and setting of the sun.
>
> God would not present the death sentence for a disregard of the Sabbath unless He had presented before men a clear understanding of the Sabbath. After He had created our world and man, He looked upon the work that He had done, and

pronounced it very good. And when the foundation of the earth was laid, the foundation of the Sabbath was laid also. (*Testimonies to Ministers*, pp. 135, 136).

Notice with care the last sentence in this passage. The foundation of the earth was laid at the same time as the foundation of the Sabbath. This statement is explicit. It provides no room for doubt.

Further, Sister White specifically stated:

> The work of creation can never be explained by science. What science can explain the mystery of life?
>
> The theory that God did not create matter when He brought the world into existence is without foundation. In the formation of our world, God was not indebted to pre-existing matter. On the contrary, all things, material or spiritual, stood up before the Lord Jehovah at His voice and were created for His own purpose. The heavens and all the host of them, the earth and all things therein, are not only the work of His hand; they came into existence by the breath of His mouth. (*Testimonies for the Church*, Vol. 8, pp. 258, 259).

Notice the words "all things material." Too often theologians stand in awe of scientists. Rather let all stand in awe of God. Dr. Davidson, on the contrary, stated in the paper he presented:

> First, as John Hartley points out, in his NIB Commentary, 'The consistent pattern used for each day of creation tells us that verses 1-2 [of Genesis chapter 1] are not an integral part of the first day of creation. That is, these first two verses stand apart from the report of what God did on the first day of creation....' Fifthly, already in the creation account of Genesis 1:3 [and following verses] there is an emphasis upon God's creating by differentiation or separation involving previously-created materials.
>
> (*Journal of the Adventist Theological Society*, Vol. 4, No. 1, Spring 2003, pp. 21-23).

Sister White's statement quoted above from *Testimonies for the Church*, Vol. 8, pp. 258, 259 clearly refutes this supposition. It is alarming that *The Journal of the Adventist Theological Society* would choose to publish such clear error.

We do not, of course, propose the faulty view that the universe was created during the six days of the creation of this earth. But we do propose that the solar system was. Certainly the sun and moon were created during this six-day period.

> [14] And God said, Let there be lights in the firmament of the heaven to divide the day from the night; and let them be for signs, and for seasons, and for days, and years: [15] And let them be for lights in the firmament of the heaven to give light upon the earth: and it was so. [16] And God made two great lights; the greater light to rule the day, and the lesser light to rule the night: he made the stars also. [17] And God set them in the firmament of the heaven to give light upon the earth, [18] And to rule over the day and over the night, and to divide the light from the darkness:

and God saw that it was good. ¹⁹And the evening and the morning were the fourth day. (Genesis 1:14-19).

We believe that the most acceptable explanation of the stars mentioned in the parenthetical statement of Genesis 1:16 is that they refer to the planets of our solar system, since it is manifestly the bodies of the solar system which are the subject of Creation in Genesis chapter one. Some have suggested that the word "stars" in Genesis 1:16 must refer to the countless billions of stars in the sky for the Hebrew word *Kowkab* is used. Strong defines this word as *star* (on page 72 of his Concordance's Hebrew dictionary cited below). It is true that most times in Scripture this word is used either to refer to suns or meteorites. But it is plainly used to refer to planets also as we see in the following words.

> When the morning stars sang together, and all the sons of God shouted for joy? Job 38:7.

The word *stars* here is translated also from *kowkab*. Surely the sons of God were singing their anthems of joyous praise on planets, not on suns.

We do not believe that the heaven mentioned in Genesis 1:1 is the starry heaven or the totality of the universe, for good reason. The Hebrew word from which *heaven* in this verse is translated is *shamayim* which has been defined as follows:

> The sky...alluding to the visible arch in which the clouds move.
> (*Abingdon's Strong's Exhaustive Concordance of the Bible*, Abingdon Press, Nashville, Tennessee, 1986, p. 156 in the Hebrew and Chaldee Dictionary).

The passive gap theory may be faulted on several grounds:
1. The sun and the moon were created on the fourth day of Creation Week. Genesis 1:16 plainly states "And God MADE two great lights" (emphasis added). We do not believe the record of these creative acts in Genesis 1:14-19 provides evidence for the conjecture that these bodies were present prior to Creation Week and that on the fourth day the nuclear fusion which provides the light (energy) of the sun was activated on that day. The Bible plainly declares:

> And God set them [the sun and the moon] in the firmament of the heaven to give light upon the earth. (Genesis 1:17).

The firmament was not in existence until the second day of Creation Week.

> ⁶And God said, Let there be a firmament in the midst of the waters, and let it divide the waters from the waters. ⁷And God made the firmament, and divided the waters which were under the firmament from the waters which were above the firmament: and it was so. ⁸And God called the firmament Heaven. And the evening and the morning were the second day. (Genesis 1:6-8).

If the sun and moon were created within Creation Week, there can be no possible reason to support the theory that the earth was not.
2. The Spirit of Prophecy certifies that the earth and every living thing were to be created together for neither existed prior to the war in heaven. Read the following words with care. Before the entire heavenly host, as Lucifer's rebellion in heaven itself reached its crescendo, the angels were informed that the creation of the earth was yet future.

> The Father then made known [to Lucifer and his angelic supporters] that it was ordained by Himself that Christ, His Son, should be equal with Himself; so that wherever was the presence of His Son, it was as His own presence. The word of the Son was to be obeyed as readily as the word of the Father. His Son He had invested with authority to command the heavenly host. Especially was His Son to work in union with Himself in the anticipated creation of the earth and every living thing that should exist upon the earth. His Son would carry out His will and His purposes but would do nothing of Himself alone. The Father's will would be fulfilled in Him. (*The Story of Redemption*, pp. 13, 14).

3. It was only after the angelic rebels were exiled from heaven that the world was created.

> Not a taint of rebellion was left in heaven. All was again peaceful and harmonious as before. Angels in heaven mourned the fate of those who had been their companions in happiness and bliss. Their loss was felt in heaven.
>
> The Father consulted His Son in regard to at once carrying out their purpose to make man to inhabit the earth. He would place man upon probation to test his loyalty before he could be rendered eternally secure. If he endured the test wherewith God saw fit to prove him, he should eventually be equal with the angels. He was to have the favor of God, and he was to converse with angels, and they with him. He did not see fit to place them beyond the power of disobedience.
>
> The Father and the Son engaged in the mighty, wondrous work they had contemplated – of creating the world. The earth came forth from the hand of the Creator exceedingly beautiful. There were mountains and hills and plains; and interspersed among them were rivers and bodies of water. The earth was not one extensive plain, but the monotony of the scenery was broken by hills and mountains, not high and ragged as they now are, but regular and beautiful in shape. (*Ibid*, pp. 19, 20).

Here we see that the Earth and all its contours were created shortly after Satan's expulsion from heaven. Thus the Earth could not have been created in the ages past.

4. Exodus 31:17 clearly proclaims, as we have seen above, that the "heaven [atmospheric] and earth," were themselves created in the six days prior to the first Sabbath on the seventh day.
5. Exodus 20:11 (see above) separates the earth and heavens from all that in them is, thus including both the non-biological and the biological creation within the same period of six days. Dr. Davidson created a distinction between what he terms the dyad of "heavens and earth" in Genesis 1:1, which he applied to the universe and the triad of heaven, earth and sea of Exodus 20:11. We believe this is an artificial distinction for which there is no inspired verification. On the other hand, Scripture applies both the dyad "heaven and earth" (See Exodus 31:17 above) and the triad (See Exodus 20:11) to the same time period and both are encompassed in precisely the same six days of creation. We can never err if we accept a plain "thus saith the Lord."
6. The above quoted passage from *Testimonies for the Church*, Vol. 8, pp. 258, 259 merits further scrutiny in the light of that gleaned from Scripture above in point 5. Significant are the all-inclusive words "the heavens and all the host of them, the earth and all things therein." Here are included the sky, the bodies of the solar system apart from our earth ("the host of them – sun, moon and planetary system, our earth and the biological creation). Some may argue that human creation does not fit the pattern of coming "into existence by the breath of His mouth." Did not God rely upon pre-existing dust from the earth for the creation of Adam?

> And the LORD God formed man of the dust of the ground, and breathed into his nostrils the breath of life; and man became a living soul.
> (Genesis 2:7).

Did not God depend upon Adam's pre-existing rib for the creation of Eve?

> [21] And the LORD God caused a deep sleep to fall upon Adam, and he slept: and he took one of his ribs, and closed up the flesh instead thereof; [22] And the rib, which the LORD God had taken from man, made he a woman, and brought her unto the man. (Genesis 2:21, 22).

Further, did not God create animals and birds from the pre-existing soil of the earth?

> And out of the ground the LORD God formed every beast of the field, and every fowl of the air; and brought them unto Adam to see what he would call them: and whatsoever Adam called every living creature, that was the name thereof. (Genesis 2:19).

Let it not be ignored that Sister White wrote with Biblical authority when she stated that "they came into existence by the breath of His mouth." (Patriarchs and Prophets, p. 44).

> 6 By the word of the LORD were the heavens made; and all the host of them by the breath of his mouth.
>
> 7 He gathereth the waters of the sea together as an heap: he layeth up the depth in storehouses.
>
> 8 Let all the earth fear the LORD: let all the inhabitants of the world stand in awe of him.
>
> 9 For he spake, and it was done; he commanded, and it stood fast.
> (Psalm 33:6-9).

> Let them praise the name of the LORD: for he commanded, and they were created. (Psalm 148:5).

> And God said, Let there be light: and there was light. (Gensis 1:3).

We do not dare to go beyond inspiration for we well know that God has spoken:

> For my thoughts are not your thoughts, neither are your ways my ways, saith the LORD. (Isaiah 55:8).

Undoubtedly we will not fully understand the reconciliation of Genesis 2:7, 19, 21, 22 with Genesis 1:3, Psalms 33:6-9 and 148:5 until we sit at Jesus feet. There we will most certainly truly understand. Suffice for our mortal minds to believe God's inspired words and accept Sister White's clear revelation which combines "the heavens and all the host of them, the earth and all things therein" in the one creative act. We would do well to humbly contemplate God's reminder:

> 5 Who is like unto the LORD our God, who dwelleth on high,
>
> 6 Who humbleth himself to behold the things that are in heaven, and in the earth! (Psalm 113:5, 6).

7. Sister White dispelled the interpretation of the words "without form and void" of Genesis 1:2 as referring to a long age of the earth.

> The Bible recognizes no long ages in which the earth was slowly evolved from chaos. (*Patriarchs and Prophets*, p. 112).

8. The Spirit of Prophecy plainly declares that the foundations of both the Sabbath and the earth were laid at the same time. We repeat this statement:

> And when the foundation of the earth was laid, the foundation of the Sabbath was laid also. "When the morning stars sang together, and all the sons of God shouted for joy," God saw that a Sabbath was essential for man, even in Paradise. (*Testimonies to Ministers*, p. 136).

9. Hebrew scholars believe that Genesis 1:1, 2 permits no gap within these verses.

> In an article written by Raymond F. Surburg, Th.D., Ph.D., Associate Professor of Theology, Concordia Teachers' College, Seward, Nebraska, the following report was included:
>
>> In 1948 at the Winona Lake School of Theology M. Henkel polled 20 "Is there any exegetical evidence for the view that there was a gap between vv.1 and 2 [of Genesis Chapter 1]? Their reply was an emphatic "no."
>>
>> (Quoted from "Fundamental Christianity and Evolution," *Modern Science and the Christian Faith*, Wheaton, Van Kampen Press, 1950, p. 49, Note 30 in Paul A. Zimmerman B.D., Ph.D., President Concordia Teachers College, editor, *Darwin, Evolution and Creation*, Concordia Publishing House, St. Louis, Michigan, 1959, pp. 53, 54).
>
> Dr. Surburg pointed out that:
>
>> Today this theory is very popular among many Fundamentalists and evangelical Christians because it has been sponsored by the Scofield Reference Bible.... Although held by many Christians today, this theory can not be substantiated from the Bible. It attempts to give some explanation for the different strata which, geologists say make up the surface of the earth. But the gap gives no explanation for the fossils in the rocks unless, as Berkhof says, "it is assumed that there were also successive creations of animals, followed by mass destruction." (*Ibid*, pp. 52, 53).

It must not be overlooked that the Scofield Reference Bible supported the Secret Rapture theory, dispensationalism (the view that salvation was based upon law in the Old Testament and grace in the New Testament), the earthly millennium and the end-time antichrist who will exert power for three and a half years, together with many other errors. Its added notes possess a very poor record of Biblical accuracy.

Again we would emphasize that on the principles of the faith we have found Dr. Davidson to be faithful. Few have written more convincingly in defense of the sanctuary message. We feel sure he will re-evaluate this aberration. Russell recalls traveling with him by air from Chicago to South Bend, Indiana. They were seated across the aisle of the plane. Dr. Davidson expressed his joy that Russell's son, Timothy, had then been appointed an Associate Professor of Biology at Andrews University for he knew Timothy to be faithful to the Biblical account of creation.

A second time we would emphasize our admiration of Dr. Davidson's stand for the salient truths of the Seventh-day Adventist faith. But on the matter of the gap theory we believe he does not have the support of inspired writings.

16 The International Conference on Faith and Science, 2002

Below we list some of the comments made in the 2002 International Conference on Faith and Science as recorded in Professor Karlow's report. We recognize that *Spectrum* places the strongest liberal slant upon such Conferences, minimizing the contributions of faithful scientists and theologians; however, while conceding this fact, it is nevertheless disgraceful that such concepts as those selected by Professor Karlow were voiced by presenters of scientific or theological papers, many of whom are teachers in our Colleges. We again point out that not only is Dr. Karlow a professor at La Sierra [Adventist] University, he is a member of the Board of the General Conference Geoscience Research Institute.

Randall Younker:

> the texts [of Genesis chapters 1 and 2] are historical and accurate though not to be taken as "science" in today's terms. (Dr. Karlow, op. cit.,p. 48).

Fritz Guy:

> Argued for reading the Genesis accounts as primarily theological in nature. He reminded the attendees that reading the text "literalistically" is itself an interpretation and that "no interpretation has a preferred status." (Ibid, p. 48). [We, Russell and Colin Standish, would point out that such a view would totally destroy every literal interpretation of any passage of Scripture].

Gerhard Pfandl:

> Almost every instance Ellen White wrote about the age of the earth she did so without intending to measure time since creation. [Dr. Karlow went on to comment – "surprisingly no one contested Pfandl's conclusion"]. (Ibid, p. 48).

In fact Dr. Pfandl chose to make a number of totally unsubstantiated assertions in the actual paper he presented to the International Conference. *Spectrum* uncharacteristically understated his plain error. Dr. Pfandl stated that:

> According to E. G. White laser-disc concordance, there are forty-two 6000-year and forty-one 4000-year statements in her writings. The former refer to the time since creation, the latter to the time from creation to the birth of Christ.... However, most of her references to these time periods are not for the sake of establishing the age of the earth, but incidental to some other thought she wanted to present. (*Journal of the Adventist Theological Society*, op. cit., p. 187).

Dr. Pfandl, who is in the General Conference Biblical Research Institute, is plainly wrong as one quotation from Sister White which mentions neither the numbers 6000 nor 4000, but rather 2500 and 1600, demonstrates conclusively.

> During the first twenty-five hundred years of human history, there was no written revelation. Those who had been taught of God, communicated their knowledge to others, and it was handed down from father to son, through successive generations. The preparation of the written word began in the time of Moses. Inspired revelations were then embodied in an inspired book. This work continued during the long period of sixteen hundred years—from Moses, the historian of creation and the law, to John, the recorder of the most sublime truths of the gospel. (*The Great Controversy*, p. v).

Here Sister White specifically set out the period from creation to the end of the writing of Scripture to be 2500 plus 1600 years – a total of 4100 years. Since John ceased his writings around 100 AD, this passage plainly and incontrovertibly declares our earth today to be about 6000 years old. (Jamieson, Fausset and Brown, *Commentary, Critical, Experimental and Practical*, William Collins and Sons, Glasgow, 1868, Vol. 7, pp. lvii, lxvi, lxi, place the writing of 2 John, 3 John and Revelation after AD.95). Once again we express our surprise that the Adventist Theological Society would publish such error.

H. Thomas Goodwin and Kevin E. Nick:

> Their presentation included an overview of the geologic column and an analysis of how the paradigm of long ages (millions of years) successfully unifies many disciplines dependent upon data from the columns, whereas a shorter chronology does not. (Dr. Karlow, *op. cit.*, p. 48 – parenthesis in original).

Lee Spencer:

> Made a case for taxonomic [arrangement of order] similarity of fossil hominids [human-like creatures] which carries a strong suggestion of evolutionary development. (*Ibid*, p. 48).

Ron Carter:

> Evolutionary hypothesizing can be placed squarely in the camp of legitimate science. (*Ibid*, p. 48).

Marco Terreros:

> Tackled the topic of death before sin. In his view, thinking about the possibility of death before the fall could offer an attractive way out of the problems of ancient fossils in the geological column and evidence of ancient humans. Terreros suggested that death of bacteria and vegetable composts should not be included in the curse of death which resulted from the fall. (*Ibid*, p. 50).

If Dr. Terreros made a claim for death before sin this would defy the plainest statement of Scripture.

> Wherefore, as by one man sin entered into the world, and death by sin; and so death passed upon all men, for that all have sinned: (Romans 5:12).

Death came because of sin. The Spirit of Prophecy plainly counters the false claim that the death of vegetation occurred prior to the entry of sin into the earth.

> As they witnessed in drooping flower and falling leaf the first signs of decay, Adam and his companion mourned more deeply than men now mourn over their dead. The death of the frail, delicate flowers was indeed a cause of sorrow; but when the goodly trees cast off their leaves, the scene brought vividly to mind the stern fact that death is the portion of every living thing. (*Patriarchs & Prophets*, p. 62).

If vegetable composts were present upon the earth before sin entered, Adam and Eve could hardly have been so distressed by the falling of leaves after their expulsion from the Garden of Eden.

The report of Dr. Terreros' paper demonstrated where, in the minds of some, our church is now heading.

We have reported this account of Dr. Terreros' presentation at the International Faith and Science Conference with caution and no little hesitancy. We have read Dr. Terreros' paper "Is All Death a Consequence of Sin?: Theological Implications of Alternative Models," (*Journal of the Adventist Theological Society, op. cit.*, pp. 150-175), and nowhere in it do we find the words which Professor Karlow has attributed to him. Five possibilities exist:

1. Professor Karlow deliberately misrepresented Dr. Terreros' words. This seems most unlikely.
2. Dr. Terreros stated these words during the discussion which ensued at the conclusion of his presentation.
3. Dr. Terreros omitted these words from his paper in order to provide a more "conservative" view akin to that he deemed to be more acceptable to the editorial staff of the Journal.
4. The editorial staff modified Dr. Terreros' paper to accord with its stated aims.
5. Dr. Karlow quoted from another paper written by Dr. Terreros.

One matter stands out. Not a few contributors to *Spectrum* who uplift plain error are welcome attendees and contributors to these General Conference Conferences. Further, it is clear that *Spectrum* reports lack balance. They focus upon that which suits their liberal agenda and emphasize presentations which destroy faith and even when faithful presentations are reported they demean them with negative comments.

In his article in the *Journal of the Adventist Theological Society* Dr. Terreros stated,

> The disjunction of death and sin undermines the biblical teaching on death as a penalty for sin. (p. 171).

This is quite contrary to the quotations cited by Dr. Karlow from Dr. Terreros' Conference presentation.

In a personal telephone conversation on May 11, 2004, which Russell had with Dr. Edwin Karlow, Professor of Physics at La Sierra University, the author of the *Spectrum* article on the 2002 Faith and Science Conference, Dr. Karlow kindly referred to the copious notes he had taken during the Conference. He emphasized that he had not quoted Dr. Terreros' words verbatim and that these were his impressions of the tenor of Dr. Terreros' words at the time.

Dr. Karlow noted that some of the speakers, at times, departed from their prepared papers to provide additional views. He also, in response to Russell's question, stated that no one, including the attendees at the Conference, had questioned the accuracy of his report in the eighteen months since it had been published. Dr. Karlow received an invitation to attend the August, 2004 International Conference on Science and Faith.

In view of the results of our investigation of this report we cannot arbitrate upon its accuracy.

However, Russell contracted Dr. Terreros by telephone on May 19, 2004. Dr. Terreros confirmed that he had not stated the words attributed to him in Spectrum. He confirmed that the words printed in the *Journal of the Adventist Theological Society* correctly presented his presentation.

Dr. Terreros did state, however, that he had sold some copies of his Andrews University Ph.D. thesis entitled, *Theistic Evolution – It's Theological Implications*, at the Conference. In the early stages of that thesis Dr. Terreros defined that which he meant, for the purpose of his thesis, as the death which resulted from the entry of sin into the world.

To do justice to Dr. Terreros, we quote from his thesis:

> Death: First, this term is used here in reference to its biological or physical aspect. Physical death refers in this dissertation to a loss of life, or a separation from the body of the life principle, and the onset of decay or corruption, in reference to the individual organism. In this sense I apply the concept "death" to human individuals and the animal kingdom (higher animals, in particular, and at least birds).
>
> Some scholars consider humanity's original eating of seeds and fruit in the Garden of Eden and even the digestion of the cells in a blade of grass as "death" or as conducive to it. However, according to the creation account (of Gen. 1:29, 30), plants were intended to provide nourishment for humans and animals including birds, which required that a part of a plant be removed and digested and, consequently, that in the process some cells ceased to exist. Such cellular "death" as applied to plants, which were provided by God as food for humans and animals and having, therefore, no effect on atonement theology, is not considered in this dissertation as relevant to the theological question of death before sin. (pp. 11, 12. Parenthesis is in the original).

In footnotes on page 11 Dr. Terreros referred to C. S. Lewis and John Wesley as the grounds for not including vegetation and lower forms of life such as microbes in his definition of the death which resulted from the curse of sin. However, he did not make a dogmatic statement excluding these from death referred to in the Bible, as a result of sin.

> As C. S. Lewis notes, "Biologists in distinguishing animal from vegetable do not make use of sentience or locomotion or other such characteristics as a layman would naturally fix upon. At some point, however (though where, we cannot say), sentience almost certainly comes in for the higher animals have nervous systems very like our own." C. S. Lews, *The Problem of Pain*, (New York: Macmillan Company, 1944), p. 119.

> Birds are the lowest form of animal life whose death was used in the Old Testament as a symbol of the atonement (Lev 7:26 cf. 17:11; 14:6) by the sacrificial death of Christ. And, though the whole of creation is the recipient of God's care, Jesus in the New Testament specifically mentioned birds as the lowest form of animal life object of God's particular concern (Matt 6:26; Luke 12:24; cf. Deut 22:6, 7; Job 38:41; Pss 50:11; 147:9). John Wesley considered – as had Lactantius in the fourth century – that birds are beings "far superior to either insects or reptiles." John Wesley, *Sermon LXI*.13 (*Wesleys Works*, 14 vols. [London: Wesleyan Methodist Book Room, 1831], 6:212-213). (Dr. Marco Terreros' thesis footnotes 3 and 4).

We believe that Sister White's statement from *Patriarchs and Prophets*, p. 62, quoted earlier in the previous chapter of our book, would have served a far better purpose than the writings of C. S. Lewis and John Wesley. We would hope that the Seventh-day Adventist Theological Seminary would promote, where appropriate, the inspired words of the Spirit of Prophecy which we can fully trust, rather than those of other men who, although highly respected, were apt to error in their writings.

We have reported this matter in full for it does illustrate many aspects of this discussion. We refer to reports of two other presentations at the 2002 International Faith and Science Conference.

Brian Bull:

> Offered a tentative "long ages" synthesis of his "two incommensurate worlds" – the world of science encountered during the work week, and "by faith," the world of Genesis he encountered on Sabbath.... However, he admitted that if the long chronology is really true, then "the world that lies at the center of my spiritual understanding drifts away from my outstretched fingers and I am left with a dark and featureless void." (p. 50).

How tragic it is that Dr. Bull had correctly pointed his listeners to where these views will lead, not only himself, but all Seventh-day Adventists who share them.

Perhaps one spirit evident in this convention is best understood by Professor Karlow's negative comments upon one speaker, Dr. Frank Hasel, Professor of Theology at Bogenhofen College, Austria, who did uphold Bible truth. We quote these comments:

> Hasel's respondents found his position problematic, however. They claimed that it derives its motivations from the legitimately tentative and incomplete nature of science, but it also assumes that faith and doctrine derived from Scripture, have an absolute, unchanging nature. Furthermore, they faulted Hasel's line of reasoning for failing to acknowledge that science and theology are both human activities. (p. 50).

Professor Karlow pointedly did not record the negative responses to the presentations of those who espoused and promoted error, not because none were made, but because he chose not to do so.

These conferences certainly further Satan's aims. The Biblical Research Institute of the General Conference has no business organizing them. They are, in general, an arena in which the Bible and the Spirit of Prophecy are discarded, replaced by the folly of men. Those upholding truth will soon discover that their righteous stands are gradually eliminated from such Conferences. That another such Conference for North America was held in 2003 and another International Conference is planned for August, 2004, as we write, demonstrated a persistent determination to allow the spread of error within our midst and to supply a platform for those who desire to promote evolutionary concepts, views which they are no doubt sharing with students in Seventh-day Adventist Colleges.

Any denigration of the seven-day creation week is a fatal diminishing of our faith, including a destruction of the Sabbath. Even the so-called passive-gap theory is an affront to the holy Sabbath day. To place the creation of the earth separate from the creation of the biological entities on the earth is not sustained by inspiration, no matter how diligently efforts are made to support this clear error. The words of Sister White brook no controversy in this matter. We repeat them:

> And when the foundation of the earth was laid, the foundation of the Sabbath was laid also. "When the morning stars sang together, and all the sons of God shouted for joy," God saw that a Sabbath was essential for man, even in Paradise.
> (*Testimonies to Ministers*, p. 136).

Clearly there would be no purpose for a Sabbath prior to the creation of man. Thus the foundations of the earth were laid in the first week of earth's existence. And let it be ever remembered that,

> When the Lord declares that He made the world in six days and rested on the seventh day, He means the day of twenty-four hours, which He has marked off by the rising and setting of the sun. (*Ibid*).

When God, speaking through His servant is so clear, it is little wonder that faithless Seventh-day Adventist theologians and scientists seek to destroy Sister White's witness. They are thus exposed as impostors.

Just prior to his 1979 retirement as General Conference President, Elder Robert Pierson, had detected the inroads of evolution into our midst. We re-echo his plaintive plea:

> Already, brethren and sisters, there are subtle forces that are beginning to stir. Regrettably there are those in the Church who belittle the inspiration of the total Bible, who scorn the first eleven chapters of Genesis, who question the Spirit of Prophecy's short chronology of the earth, and who subtly and not so subtly attack the Spirit of Prophecy. There are some who point to the Reformers and contemporary theologians as a source and the norm for Seventh-day Adventist doctrine. There are those who allegedly are tired of the hackneyed phrases of Adventism. There are those who wish to forget the standards of the Church we love. There are those who covet and would court the favor of the Evangelicals; who would throw off the mantle of a peculiar people; and those who would go the way of the secular materialistic world.
>
> Fellow leaders, beloved brethren and sisters – don't let it happen! I appeal to you as earnestly as I know how this morning – don't let it happen! I appeal to Andrews University, to the Seminary, to Loma Linda University – don't let it happen! We are not Seventh-day Anglicans, not Seventh-day Lutherans – we are Seventh-day Adventists! This is God's last Church with God's last message!
>
> *(Adventist Review*, Oct. 26, 1978).

The second 2002 conference was the First International Conference on Ellen G. White and Seventh-day Adventist History. It was hosted at the Historic Adventist Village in Battle Creek, Michigan, May 15-19, 2002. This Conference also cast serious doubts upon the inspiration of the Spirit of Prophecy. It will be examined later in this book.

17 Did We Not Know?

Throughout Dr. Graeme Bradford's book, *Prophets Are Human*, his fictional characters, Doug and Jean, repeatedly questioned why the denomination had not earlier disclosed the alleged many "mistakes" in Sister White's writings. Thus Doug questioned:

> Why haven't we been told some of these things before?
> (Graeme Bradford, *op. cit.* p.34).

That question continued throughout the book and was never resolved.

Again we return to personal experience in order to examine this matter. Our father, Darcy Rowland Standish (1912-1997), while still in his thirties, returned home from work one evening in the late 1940's, full of exciting news.

Dad had been relieving his fellow Hamilton Church elder, Brother Dugald Dunlop, a relative of the famous Australia war hero who – as an army doctor in the Second World War – had been captured by Japanese forces in Singapore. "Weary" Dunlop, as he was nicknamed, saved many of his fellow captured Australian servicemen from death in the infamous Changi Prisoner of War Camp sited close to Singapore's now-famous Changi Airport. "Weary" Dunlop received many awards after his return to Australia.

Brother Dugald Dunlop was the manager and, except around the Christmas period, the lone worker in the small Sanitarium Health Food Store in the old Arcade in Newcastle, Australia's sixth largest city and its largest industrial urban region. Hamilton is a suburb of Newcastle.

The cause of our father's excitement was soon revealed. In his hand was a large volume. It was J. H. Merle D'Aubigné's *History of the Sixteenth Century Reformation*. Dad shared his experience of that day with our mother, Hilda Marie Joyce Standish (nee Bailey; 1912-1974), and with us.

A man had entered the shop offering this volume to our father for purchase. He explained that the book held no interest for him; although he had descended from a family of Seventh-day Adventists, he had never embraced the faith. He was asking ten shillings (now one dollar) for the second-hand book which had come into his possession upon the death of his parents.

It is unlikely that Dad would have expended ten shillings to purchase the book had the man not opened it up, exposing the inside front cover. There was a card adhering to the cover. It stated: "From the private library of Ellen G. White." Sister White, prior to her departure from Australia in August, 1900, had sold the book to a member of this man's family who lived in Maitland, a town twenty miles north of Newcastle and thus not far from Avondale where Sister White resided. In pencil is written, "Purchased by me on the departure of

Sister White from Australia, August, 1900, J.N." The brother had later written his name in the book – "James Nancarrow."

We will never forget our father's enthusiastic words, "You know this book could well be the very book Sister White used to help her write the history of the Reformation in *The Great Controversy*". Whether she had referred to that specific tome when she wrote the 1888 edition of *The Great Controversy* we do not know. Many years before his death our father gave this valued book in his library, which he considered to be a family heirloom, to Colin.

There is every possibility that Dad's supposition was correct, for Sister White had arrived in Australia in 1891, only three years after the 1888 *Great Controversy* was published and she manifestly did not purchase D'Aubigné's book at an Adventist Book Centre in Australia. While we cannot rule out the possibility that she had purchased it at a religious book store in Australia, we believe that to be unlikely. In the 1970's Colin showed the book to Sister White's grandson, Elder Arthur White (1907-1991), then Director of the White Estate at the General Conference. After perusing it Elder White concluded that it was quite likely the very volume from which his grandmother had generously quoted in writing the 1888 edition of *The Great Controversy*. This volume of D'Aubigné's book was published in 1883.

When our father spoke of Sister White as using the writings of a non-inspired author in her inspired book, we expressed no surprise. Although we were only mid-teenagers at the time, we were acquainted with the fact that God guided Sister White to use such sources, where they accurately portrayed history or other matters important to God's church. In the 1940's we were perfectly aware of this fact.

Our God is a wise God. He does not use inspiration to "reinvent the wheel." Secular men have correctly discerned the truth that one plus one equals two and that one multiplied by one equals one. No divine revelation was expended in confirming these facts of truth.

Similarly, while the writings of historians, scientists and health professionals are typically fraught with error, nevertheless, such academics have also written many accurate matters, as we shall set forth in our discussions in these areas later in this volume.

In 1951 Pastor Francis David Nichol (1897-1966), Editor of *The Review and Herald*, 1945-1966, raised in Australia in the town of Thirlmere just a short distance southwest of Sydney, published his well-researched book, *Ellen White and Her Critics*. As young men we heard Elder Nichol preach in our church in Hamilton, a suburb of Newcastle. We were intrigued to learn that he was born only about two hundred yards (approximately 200 metres) from where we were born thirty-six years later. Our father purchased a copy of the book soon after and we had access to it as we returned to the family home, for as eighteen-year olds we graduated from the two-year Theological Normal Course, as the Primary Teaching Course was then termed, in 1951. Pastor Nichol's book was published in the same year.

Make no mistake, we read much of it with no little interest. Here was no cover-up of the alleged "mistakes" of Sister White including those of plagiarism and the great majority of those claimed "errors" now being "revealed" by academics who would destroy her inspired works. While many scientific and health matters known today were not available or understood more than half-a-century ago, Pastor Nichol did a masterly work in defense of the attacks upon the Spirit of Prophecy. He would have done even better had he lived and written in the twenty-first century.

Claims that Sister White's errors were covered up are incorrect. What has transpired in the last half century, especially following the 1957 publishing of *Seventh-day Adventists Answer Questions on Doctrine*, has been a period where the Spirit of Prophecy has been de-emphasized in our pulpits and in our publications. Where once our *Sabbath School Lesson Quarterlies* consisted of questions with answering Bible texts and Spirit of Prophecy insights, the Spirit of Prophecy is now far less quoted and the Sabbath School students are subject to comments by uninspired authors which they have to evaluate for truth or error. Not a little error has been insinuated. (See the subject of 666 in the Lesson Quarterly of the second quarter, 2002, p. 85).

The reason why the accusations of a cover-up by unnamed leaders concerning the "errors" in Sister White's writings now possess currency, is that for years few members have bothered to interest themselves in a body of material which they have been told possesses manifold "mistakes." The gross disinterest in personal study of the *Testimonies* has been paralleled by a loss of knowledge concerning the various specific attacks upon the veracity of Sister White's writings. The alleged "cover-up" is, in fact, a result of a general disinterest in the Spirit of Prophecy in our midst. Those who are earnest students of the Spirit of Prophecy have investigated and dismissed the alleged errors in the Spirit of Prophecy. With the unfolding of new scientific discoveries which support Sister White's advanced declarations, our faith has been augmented.

While one of the papers presented at the February 2-5 Summit on Sister White's Role in the Church held at Avondale College provided the impression that there has been much more adverse matters uncovered concerning Sister White's writings in the past half-century (See Dr. Arthur Patrick, "Ellen White and the South Pacific Adventism: Retrospect and Prospect"), in reality only two major matters have been brought forth in this period. One was the discovery of the minutes of the 1919 General Conference Bible Conference, which we will address later in this book, and the other was the accumulated works of a number of authors including Walter Rea and Ronald Numbers who have asserted the discovery of more evidence of Sister White's reliance upon non-inspired sources. Even if this latter claim were correct, this would in no wise diminish Sister White's inspired writings. Indeed, they add confidence in the fact that she was inspired as she chose valid material and ignored spurious claims. Sister White's use of valid materials from other authors is repeatedly acknowledged in her counsels on health issues and her historical writing.

As we stated above, God has frequently guided prophets to secular sources which possessed absolute accuracy. In Sister White's case, as no doubt in the case of other prophets, God has provided visions which set forth unerring facts and then guided the prophets to the accurate account in secular sources already available.

In this way Ezra was able to select from the secular Chronicles of the monarchs of Judah and Israel and prepare them for inspired writings. A Jehovah's Witness book rightly records that:

> The Bible books of Chronicles as well as the book bearing Ezra's name give evidence that Ezra was an indefatigable researcher, with discernment in dividing between various readings of the copies of the Law existing then. He exhibited unusual zeal in searching the official documents of his nation, and it is evidently due to his efforts that we have the accurate record Chronicles gives us. We must remember, however, that he had God's spirit of inspiration and that God guided him with a view to preserving a great portion of Israel's history for our benefit.
> (*Insight on the Scriptures*, International Bible Students Association, New York, 1988, Vol. 1, p.798).

Sister White confirmed that Ezra diligently studied the historical and poetical books of the Bible (*Seventh-day Adventist Bible Commentary*, Vol. 3, p. 1134). In the same passage Sister White described him as a man of learning. He also:

> ...gathered all the copies of the law that he could find. He published copies of these among God's people, and became a teacher of the law and the prophecies in the schools of the prophets. The pure Word, thus diligently taught by Ezra, gave knowledge that was invaluable at that time. (*Ibid*).

There is excellent circumstantial evidence that Ezra gathered the accurate accounts found in the Chronicles of the Kings of Judah and Israel for,

> Originally Chronicles and Ezra formed a single book.
> (*Encyclopaedia Britannica*, 1963 edition, Vol. 5, p. 715).

Just as Ezra was inspired by God to select records of the kings which bore the imprint of accuracy, so too, was Sister White. In the chapter entitled, "Sister White's Historical Selections", we have examined these matters more fully.

We must ever be careful not to set ourselves up as arbiters of that which is accurate and that which is inaccurate in accounts of history presented years after the historical events transpired. Wisdom surely reminds us that while God's inspired history is faultless, man's rarely is. When we find discrepancies between the two accounts, it would be folly to accept the secular account as accurate.

PART IV
Divine History

18 Sister White's Historical Selections

We studied History for three years at the University of Sydney completing a major in the discipline. We well remember our first term paper early in 1955. Following the British system of "survival of the fittest" we knew that the majority of the class of about six hundred students would fail the course. The scale of marking will seem strange to many non-Australian readers. There were just three grades – Fail 0-3 out of ten; Pass 4 or 5; Credit 6-10. We never heard of anyone receiving a grade above 8, which was regarded, in the minds of the students, as the pinnacle of brilliance.

Now four marks out of ten, on the surface, may appear to be a simple attainment. That was not the view of the large number of students who were assessed at three or less on their term paper. In that term paper we each received four marks – a bare pass. Written on the paper as part of the professor's assessment was "You failed to use primary documents." That was a mistake we never repeated and our results for the rest of the year and the subsequent years reflected our learning of this requirement.

By primary documents were meant first-hand records of contemporary events of the past and reports of participants in those events. In addition, where applicable, documents such as parliamentary and congressional proceedings are regarded as primary sources of history. While it was permissible to use the historical works of historians living centuries after the event, these had to be balanced and evaluated in the light of extant primary documents. The obvious wisdom of this is clear.

Yet, are primary documents of necessity reliable accounts of history? Sometimes they are most unreliable. Let us imagine that contemporary histories of the 2003 War on Iraq were to be written, one by President George Bush and the other by President Sadam Hussein. Unquestionably these hypothetical historical works would qualify as primary documents and would be eagerly read by their contemporaries, but would either history fully and accurately reflect the genuine historical data of the war? Certainly we would encounter a marked difference in these two works of history. It is likely that, except for the date and the location of the war, the readers of these two hypothetical histories could be forgiven if they concluded that the two Presidents were writing about different events.

Even if eminent, qualified historians chose to write a history of the 2003 Iraqi War, these could contain false conclusions drawn from biased accounts tainted by selectively reporting the documentary evidence available, if each approached his task from a different perspective of the conflict.

Of course, historians, writing centuries after events, either from a bias or inadvertently, do not pass the test of accuracy in all which they write. Yet there are many accurate facts presented in virtually every history. The hypothetical histories of the two Presidents in the Iraqi War would be bound to contain many facts which were undeniable.

However, there is one type of historical account which is unfailingly reliable.

> The Bible is the most instructive and comprehensive history that has ever been given to the world. Its sacred pages contain the only authentic account of the creation. Here we behold the power that "stretched forth the heavens, and laid the foundations of the earth." Here we have a truthful history of the human race, one that is unmarred by human prejudice or human pride.
> (*Fundamentals of Christian Education*, pp. 84, 85).

Yet how often is the infallible history provided by inspiration judged by the writings of faulted secular historians. To measure inspired history in this manner surely reaches a level of human folly which must amaze and distress angels.

Dr. Arthur Patrick (born 1934) in the third of his conversations with Pr. Bruce Manners, Editor of the South Pacific *Record* and also the *Signs*, charged that Dr. Donald R. McAdams, a former President of Southwestern Adventist College (1975-1984) had

> identified clearly a main source Ellen White used (for instance, the book she consulted as she wrote about John Huss) and the way that she followed that source page after page, using its framework and language, even incorporating some of its historical errors and moral exhortations.
> (South Pacific *Record*, 21 February, 2004, p.10 – parenthesis in original).

Dr. McAdams made a serious charge against Sister White and this charge has been echoed by Dr. Patrick. Well might we ask both of these scholars, "Upon what basis was this charge laid?" How did they evaluate the historian referred to by Dr. McAdams, whom Dr. Patrick failed to identify, as being in error in the presentation of the historical data from which Sister White quoted? We can only assume that Dr. McAdams, with whom Colin became acquainted when they were both contemporary Presidents of denominational Colleges in the 1970's (in Colin's case Columbia Union College. Dr. McAdams was then President of Southwestern Adventist College, Texas), found other historical accounts of Huss' life which disagreed with the source Sister White was led by God to employ.

Sister White used highly credible Reformation historians in writing Chapter 6 of *The Great Controversy* entitled "Huss and Jerome." These included Presbyterian cleric Dr. James Aitken Wylie, *The History of Protestantism*; Bonnechose, *The Reformers Before the Reformation*; Jacques Lenfant, *History of the Council of Constance*; J. H. Merle D'Aubingé, *History of the Reformation of the Sixteenth Century*; Ezra Hall Gillett, *Life and Times of John Hus*. While none of these men were infallible in their historical writings, undoubtedly, under inspiration, Sister White selected accurate material, verified by the only One who knows all.

In view of what we have written earlier in this chapter concerning historical accuracy and the place played by the perspective and bias of the historian in his writing, is any one of us in a position to arbitrate upon events which transpired in Bohemia six centuries past? Would we not do well, privileged as we are, to possess a divinely inspired account of the events of the era, to thank God that we do not have to arbitrate, for He has spoken through His servant?

We recall Pastor George Burnside (1908-1994), the renowned New Zealand evangelist, who told us of the experience of an atheist brother of an Australian pastor. This pastor had prayed for his infidel brother for many years. When the brother heard the Seventh-day Adventist truth through evangelistic presentations, he embraced it with great joy. He determined to emulate his brother and train for the ministry.

During his training at Avondale College this ministerial trainee was taught that,

> the Bible is perfect for the purpose God had in mind when He gave it to us.
>
> (Graeme Bradford, *op. cit.*, p. 33).

Dr. Bradford was not his teacher.

We first heard the gist of this quotation three decades ago from the lips of Dr. Ford. "The Bible is perfect for its purpose." Of course it is. This assertion bears the hallmark of a truism. But underneath this correct statement is a liberal interpretation. When this statement is repeated it may be interpreted to mean, "The Bible is perfect for its purpose – to provide us a guide to our heavenly home, but in matters peripheral to that aim, such as science, chronology and history, it contains mistakes."

This would-be pastor heard during his lectures that the Bible contained errors of History and Science, yet provided a perfect guide to salvation. A logical man, he reasoned that up to a point he could validate history and he could confirm Biblical statements concerning science. If the Bible contains serious deviations from accuracy in these matters which he could check, how could he accept the Biblical statements concerning salvation, statements which, outside an inerrant Word of God, he could not verify. He terminated his studies and once more walked the road of atheism.

We should not be surprised that the same charges have been leveled against God's second body of counsels for when sixteen men, eleven pastors and five laymen, of which Russell was one, took Dr. Desmond Ford before the Biblical Research Institute of the Australasian Division on February 3 & 4, 1976, Pastor Frank Breaden (died 1999) was compelled to deliver a paper which effectively destroyed Dr. Ford's claim that there were millions of mistakes in the Bible.

In his reply Dr. Ford defended his assertion by claiming that he was not referring to the original writings of Scripture, but rather to the copyist errors which now appear in the Greek and Hebrew manuscripts.

Even if we accept Dr. Ford's explanation, which would only be proper, the destruction of any value of Scripture would be complete. There are less than three-quarters of a million words in the Bible. If, even by "millions of mistakes" Dr. Ford meant the lowest possible number, two million, then there would be approximately three mistakes for every word in Scripture. The Holy Word of God contaminated by such mass pollution would be fit for the garbage bin and nothing else.

Would any reader visit a health professional for health advice if the textbooks he had studied were equally crammed with mistakes? It would be rank foolishness to entrust one's health to such a practitioner. The consequences for our souls of such a massive vitiation of Scripture would be vastly more disastrous.

Once charges are laid that inspired writings are errant they lose their authority, for who is to arbitrate which portions are inaccurate and which statements possess veracity? Do some theologians dare to set themselves up as such arbiters? Do some scientists? Do some health professionals? Do certain historians? In fact some do. Such deserve the Victoria Cross (in the United States, the Congressional Medal of Honor) for demonstrating such an extreme level of "valor."

When Sister White turned to the greatest, truest, and most accurate of Protestant Historians, Jean Henri Merle D'Aubingé (1794-1872), and James Aitken Wylie (born 1808), undoubtedly God inspired her selection, as He did with other authors. Dr. Patrick cast doubt upon Sister White's statement that the commencement of the Massacre of St. Bartholomew's Day in France was signaled by the tolling of the palace bell. (See *The Great Controversy*, 1888 Edition, p. 272; *Spirit of Prophecy*, Vol. 4, p. 191), by asking was it the palace bell or the castle bell or the church bell, as some historians have asserted? (See South Pacific *Record*, February 21, 2004). Surely it is time for divine history to be accounted its place above all relevant secular, faulted history. God has spoken through His servant. Surely this settles the issue. Let fallible historians argue over this detail, but not Seventh-day Adventists.

Accusations of plagiarism have been leveled against Christ. It is said that He borrowed the golden rule from an ancient rabbi. But who gave that rule to the rabbi in the first place? Please notice Sister White's words once more:

> Christ did not disdain the repetition of old and familiar truths in prophecies if they would serve His purpose to inculcate ideas. He was the originator of all the ancient gems of truth. Through the work of the enemy these truths had been displaced. They had been disconnected from their true position and placed in the framework of error. Christ's work was to readjust and establish the precious gems in the framework of truth.... Christ rescued them from the rubbish of error, gave them a new, vital force, and commanded them to shine as precious jewels, and stand fast forever. (Manuscript 25, 1890).

Sister White went on to write:

> Christ Himself could use any of these old truths without borrowing in the smallest particle, for He had originated them all. He had cast them into the minds and

thoughts of each generation, and when He came to our world, He rearranged and vitalized the truths which had become dead, making them more forcible for the benefit of future generations. It was Jesus Christ who had the power of rescuing the truths from rubbish, and again giving them to the world with more than their original freshness and power.

As Christ presented these truths to minds, He broke up their accustomed train of thought as little as possible. Nevertheless a new and transforming economy of truth must be woven into their experience. He, therefore, aroused their minds by presenting truth through the agency of their familiar associations. (*Ibid*).

Elder William White set forth the clear manner in which his mother was guided by inspiration to extract truth from error:

In her early experience when she was sorely distressed over the difficulty of putting into human language the revelations of truths that had been imparted to her, she was reminded of the fact that all wisdom and knowledge comes from God and she was assured that God would bestow grace and guidance. She was told that in the reading of religious books and journals, she would find precious gems of truth expressed in acceptable language, and that she would be given help from heaven to recognize these and to separate them from the rubbish of error with which she would sometimes find them associated.

(W. C. White and Dores Robinson, *Brief Statements*, St. Helena, California, Elmshave Office, August, 1933, p.5 – Reprinted in *Adventist Review*, June 4, 1981).

Again we exhort, "Let us believe God's inspired words."

Dr. Samuele Bacchiocchi of late has specialized in casting doubt upon the accuracy of the historical accounts of *The Great Controversy*. He has stated that,

The sample of [historical] statements we have just examined, suffice to show us that there are still inaccuracies in The Great Controversy that ought to be corrected. (Samuele Bacchiocchi's E-mail Newsletter, August 1, 2002).

Sister White plainly stated:

Through ages of darkness and apostasy there were Waldenses who denied the supremacy of Rome, who rejected image worship as idolatry, and who kept the true Sabbath. Under the fiercest tempests of opposition they maintained their faith. (*Great Controversy*, p. 65).

...some of whom [Waldenses] were observers of the Sabbath. (*ibid*, p. 577).

Dr. Bacchiocchi contended:

I spent several hours searching for an answer in the scholarly volumes Storia dei Valdesi – (History of the Waldenses), authored by Almedeo Molnar and Augusto Hugon. These two books were published in 1974 by the Claudiana, which is the official Waldensian publishing house. They are regarded as the most comprehensive history of the Waldenses. To my regret I found no allusion to Sabbathkeeping among the Waldenses.

(Bacchiocchi, *op. cit.* parenthesis in the original).

Dr. Bacchiocchi's failure notwithstanding, history attests to the accuracy of Sister White's statement. Dr. Johann Joseph Ignaz von Döllinger, Th.D. (1799-1890), German Roman Catholic Professor of Church History and Ecclesiastical Law at the University of Munich, who was excommunicated in 1871 when he rejected the Dogma of Papal Infallibility, wrote:

> ...not a few [Waldenses of the fifteenth century] celebrated the Sabbath with the Jews.
> (*Beitrage zur Sektengeschichte des Mittelalters* [Reports on the History of the Sects in the Middle Ages], Munich, 1890, second part, p. 661).

Other historians support the fact that many Waldenses kept the Sabbath.

> One of their [the Waldenses'] opinions, that the Law of Moses is to be kept according to the letter, and that the keeping of the Sabbath ... ought to take take place.
> (Peter Allix, *The Ancient Churches of Piedmont*, Richard Chiswell, London, 1690, p. 154).

> Observance of the Sabbath ... is enjoined [by the Waldenses].
> (Adam Blair, *History of the Waldenses*, Adam and Charles Black, Edinburgh, 1833, Vol. 1, p. 220).

Dr. Bacchiocchi also challenged the accuracy of Sister White's statement that:

> Behind the lofty bulwarks of the mountains...the Waldenses found a hiding place. Here the light of truth was kept burning amid the darkness of the Middle Ages. Here for a thousand years, witnesses for the truth maintained the ancient faith.
> (*The Great Controversy*, pp. 65, 66).

Here Dr. Bacchiocchi fell into the common trap of dating the Waldenses from the era of the man whose name was eventually attached to them in the twelfth century, Peter Waldo, a rich merchant of the city of Lyons in France who sold his goods and gave the means to the poor, following a life of poverty.

Speaking of the last statement cited above, Dr. Bacchiocchi asserted that,

> the Waldenses did not exist for "a thousand years." (Bacchiocchi, op. cit).

He based his false claim upon one source, a "Dictionary of Church History."

Yet had Dr. Bacchiocchi searched History more diligently he would not have made his false accusation. It is he and not Sister White who is inaccurate. We cite one authority:

> He [Peter Waldo] and his followers formed a centre around which gathered the Arnoldisti and the Humiliati of Italy, the Petrobrusions and Albigensians of France, and perhaps the Apostolics of the Rhine Valley.... Some claimed Claude, Bishop of Turin (822-839) as their founder; others held that they were the successors of a small group of good men who had protested against the degradation of the Church in the days of Sylvester I [Pope, 314-335] and [Emperor] Constantine [280-337].... It is certain, at all events, that the Waldensians of Piedmont were a fusion of various sects.
>
> (Ellen Scott Davison (died 1921), *Forerunners of St. Francis and Other Studies*, Edited by Gertrude R. B. Richards, Houghton Miffen Company, Boston, 1927, pp. 237, 252, 253).

Ellen Davison was a specialist in historical research on the life of common people in the Middle Ages.

Another writer stated:

> Their [The Waldenses] beginning we have fixed according to the common reckoning of ancient writers, A.D. 1170; but it appears that they existed long before. (Thieleman J. van Braght, *Martyrs Mirror*, p. 290).

Dr. Bacchiocchi has challenged us to search books in Church History – one such book written by Albert Henry Newman, D.D., LL.D. (1852-1933), stated concerning the early Waldenses that the followers of Jovinianus

> took refuge in the Alpine valleys and there kept alive the evangelical teaching that was to reappear with vigor in the twelfth century.
>
> (*A Manual of Church History*, The American Baptist Publication Society, Philadelphia, 1933, Vol. 1, p. 376).

Dr. Benjamin George Wilkinson (1892-1968) discussed this matter fully in his book, *Truth Triumphant*, Pacific Press Publishing Association, Oakland, California, 1944, pp. 214-267.

Dr. Bacchiocchi's newsletters are scattered worldwide and are influential. Unfortunately he has set himself up as an expert critic of the accuracy of Sister White's inspired historical references in *The Great Controversy* including the significance of the dates 538 and 1798 bounding the period of the 1260 years of papal supremacy. Sister White stated:

> The 1260 years of papal supremacy began in AD 538, and would therefore terminate in 1798. (*Great Controversy*, p. 266).

> The period [of 1260 years] ... began with the supremacy of the papacy, AD 538, and terminated in 1798. (*Ibid*, p. 439).

The arguments of Dr. Bacchiocchi on these matters have been thoroughly dispelled in *The Remnant Herald*, No. 75, September, 2002, pp. 1194-1196, which Russell edits.

It is a matter of no little moment that Seventh-day Adventists now feel themselves competent to arbitrate between divinely inspired history and fallible, secular historical works. Is this not a level of academic pride which does not befit servants of God?

19 Historical Accuracy

On January 30, 1978, the White Estate in the General Conference published an article written by Ron Graybill entitled, *Historical Difficulties in the Great Controversy*. We quote from a June, 1982 revision. The author took issue with the following account concerning a period in the life of John Huss.

> Tidings of the work at Prague were carried to Rome, and Huss was soon summoned to appear before the pope. To obey would be to expose himself to certain death. The king and queen of Bohemia, the university, members of the nobility, and officers of the government united in an appeal to the pontiff that Huss be permitted to remain at Prague and to answer at Rome by deputy. Instead of granting this request, the pope proceeded to the trial and condemnation of Huss, and then declared the city of Prague to be under interdict.
>
> In that age this sentence, whenever pronounced, created widespread alarm. The ceremonies by which it was accompanied were well adapted to strike terror to a people who looked upon the pope as the representative of God Himself, holding the keys of heaven and hell, and possessing power to invoke temporal as well as spiritual judgments. It was believed that the gates of heaven were closed against the region smitten with interdict; that until it should please the pope to remove the ban, the dead were shut out from the abodes of bliss. In token of this terrible calamity, all the services of religion were suspended. The churches were closed. Marriages were solemnized in the churchyard. The dead, denied burial in consecrated ground, were interred, without the rites of sepulture, in the ditches or the fields. Thus by measures which appealed to the imagination, Rome essayed to control the consciences of men.
>
> The city of Prague was filled with tumult. A large class denounced Huss as the cause of all their calamities and demanded that he be given up to the vengeance of Rome. To quiet the storm, the Reformer withdrew for a time to his native village. Writing to the friends whom he had left at Prague, he said: "If I have withdrawn from the midst of you, it is to follow the precept and example of Jesus Christ, in order not to give room to the ill-minded to draw on themselves eternal condemnation, and in order not to be to the pious a cause of affliction and persecution. I have retired also through an apprehension that impious priests might continue for a longer time to prohibit the preaching of the word of God amongst you; but I have not quitted you to deny the divine truth, for which, with God's assistance, I am willing to die."—Bonnechose, The Reformers Before the Reformation, Vol. 1, p. 87. Huss did not cease his labors, but traveled through the

surrounding country, preaching to eager crowds. Thus the measures to which the pope resorted to suppress the gospel were causing it to be the more widely extended. (*The Great Controversy*, pp. 100, 101).

Dr. Graybill, who worked for a number of years in the General Conference White Estate, identified four statements in the above passage which he concluded were historical errors. He wrote,

> I am fairly certain that items one and three are not correct, and I am fully certain that items two and four are not correct. (Ron Graybill, op. cit., p. 2).

He came to these conclusions upon

> the basis of primary and secondary sources. (*Ibid*).

The four points to which Dr. Graybill referred were:
1. That the Pope was the one who issued the order placing Prague under interdict;
2. That during this interdict, all the churches in Prague were closed, and all religious services were suspended;
3. That as a result of the tumult, Huss left Prague for a time;
4. That Huss wrote the letter quoted on page 101, paragraph 2, at this time to explain why he left Prague. (*Ibid*).

Dr. Graybill went to strenuous lengths in order to place the date 1411 on the quotation he cited from *Great Controversy*, pages 100, 101 above. But one reads in vain to discover the date 1411 in Sister White's account. Further, in the entire twenty-three pages of Chapter 6, entitled "Huss and Jerome," we could not discover a single date mentioned in Sister White's comments or in any words of the historians she cited. Yet Ronald Graybill confidently stated that Sister White was referring to the specific year 1411. He also wrote that she was following Wylie's *History of Protestantism* at this point, and Wylie's narrative and Mrs. White's account of the 1411 interdict have all of the same factual difficulties. (*Ibid*, pp. 2, 3).

Ron Graybill also further asserted that,

> Mrs. White is really describing the 1412 interdict. (*Ibid*, p. 2).

We have reviewed James Wylie's account of Huss' life seeking this date of 1411 demanded by Dr. Graybill. In Dr. Wylie's account we have discovered the following dates:

863	Letter written by the King of Moravia to the Greek Emperor. (p. 131).
1079	Date of Pope Gregory VII's bull. (p. 131).
1347	University of Prague founded. (p. 134).
1373	John Huss born. (p. 134).
1374	Death of Milicius. (p. 133).
1376	The stake decreed against all dissenters. (p. 133).

1392	Bethlehem Chapel founded. (p. 134).	
1393	Huss obtains Bachelor's degree. (p. 134).	
1393	Prague Jubilee (p.134)	
1394	Death of Janovius. (p. 133).	
1394	Huss obtained Bachelor of Theology degree (p. 134).	
1396	Huss obtains Master's degree. (p. 134).	
1402	Huss appointed preacher at Bethlehem Chapel. (p. 134).	
1404	Visit of two English theologians to Prague. (p. 135).	
1405	Publication of Episcopal prohibition. (p. 136).	
1409	Huss' protest. (p. 136).	
1413	Sigismund becomes Emperor of Holy Roman Empire. (p. 144).	
1414	Pope John XXIII convenes the General Council. (p. 146).	
1415	Eighth Session of the Council held. (p. 149).	
1415	Pope John XXIII deposed. (p. 153).	
1415	Last Council. (p. 156).	
1415	Huss' martyrdom. (p. 161).	
1419	Bridget canonized by Pope Martin V (p. 149)	

>(J. A. Wylie, *The History of Protestantism*, Mourne Missionary Trust, Kilkeel, Northern Ireland, 1985, Vol. 1).

We have cited these dates in order to demonstrate that Dr. Wylie was not averse to recording dates. Yet his account of John Huss' life from the latter's birth to his martyrdom contains not a single mention of the year 1411, nor did he mention the year 1412.

When this fact, associated with Sister White's failure to mention the date 1411, are placed side by side, Dr. Graybill's pamphlet loses much of its force.

Further, Dr. Graybill failed to mention that during John Huss' period three popes "reigned" simultaneously, Balthazar (**or** Baldassarre) Cossa (John XXIII), Angelo Corrario (Gregory XII) and Pedro de Luna (Benedict XIII). In one respect all possessed great wisdom.

> If they asked John XXIII, he told them that Gregory XII was "a heretic, a demon, the Antichrist," Gregory XII obligingly bore the same testimony respecting John XXIII, and both John and Gregory united in sounding in similar fashion the praises of Benedict XIII, whom they stigmatised as "an imposter and schismatic," while Benedict paid back with prodigal interest the compliments of his two opponents. (Dr. Wylie, *op. cit.*, p. 141).

It came to this, that if these men were to be believed, instead of three popes there were three antichrists in Christendom. It was amazing just how accurately each pope judged the characters of the other two. All three were perfectly correct in their estimate of the other two.

But of more significance is the fact that in order to bolster their own ambitious claims to be the only legitimate pope, there is no doubt that many original documents were filled with bias and others were tampered. Dr. Graybill made no reference to the chaotic condition of the papacy during the last years of John Huss' life and the distortion of original documents in consequence. Further, the fact that Jesuit scholars have honed their skills in slanting "credible" history in ways favorable to the Roman Catholic Church, seems to have escaped his attention.

Roman Catholic author Dr. Peter De Rosa gained his education at the Gregorian University in Rome. A former Professor of Metaphysics and Ethics at the English Roman Catholic Westminster Seminary and Dean of Theology of Corpus Christi College, London, he left the priesthood – but not the Roman Catholic Church – in 1970 in order to marry. He aptly spoke of the papal scandal in the era of Huss' trial. Speaking of Pope John XXIII who ruled over the beginning of Huss' trial and was later arbitrarily declared an antipope, Dr. De Rosa recorded that some cathedrals were required to remove his name from their engraved list of popes. This pope was indicted by the Council of Constance over which he had presided.

> Cossa [John XXIII] saw the indictment, a huge catalogue of his misdemeanors drawn up with wicked accuracy. The madams in charge of every whorehouse in Christendom must have testified against him. When he heard the growing demands, especially from the English, that they should burn him and be done with it, he agreed to resign, provided the other two popes followed suit.
> (Peter de Rosa, *Vicars of Christ*, Corgi Books, London, 1989, p. 131).

De Rosa recorded that the Council of

> Constance ... proceeded to use its authority, first to depose Benedict [XIII].
> (*Ibid*, p. 132).

The expulsion from the Papal seat of John XXIII soon followed:

> John XXIII was next.... The fathers of the Council agreed he was the legitimate pope.... The charges against him were reduced from fifty-four to five. As Gibbons characteristically remarked in *The Decline and Fall*, 'the most scandalous charges were suppressed; the Vicar of Christ was only accused of piracy, murder, rape, sodomy and incest.' It was well known that since becoming the Vicar of Christ, the only exercise he took was in bed. It was significant that John XXIII was absolved from heresy, probably because he had never evinced sufficient interest in religion to be classed as heterodox ... he was given only a three-year prison term.
> (*Ibid*).

De Rosa compared the Pope to Huss who was incarcerated with John XXIII in the same prison:

> Huss, brave, chaste, incorruptible, stern opponent of simony and clerical concubinage, met a harsher fate. Forbidden counsel, tried on a trumped-up charge, interrogated by Dominicans who had not read his book, even in translation, he was sentenced to death.
> (*Ibid*).

It was not surprising that John XXIII was convicted of such crimes as De Rosa recorded:

> He was rumoured never to have confessed his sins or taken the sacrament. Nor did he believe in the soul's immortality [we guess he had to be right about something] or the resurrection of the dead. It was doubted by some that he believed in God.
> (De Rosa, *op. cit.*, p. 629).

The third papal claimant, Gregory XII, the only one of the three now regarded as a legitimate pope

> solemnly convoked the Council which had been in session for months, and then resigned. With these formalities complete, all three popes were taken care of.
> (*Ibid*, p. 133).

We quote this material in order to enlighten the reader that it was in this era of three competing popes – each with his supporters placing their biased accounts of the period – that the contemporary history of events in Prague during 1411 and 1412 were written. It is little wonder that some find it difficult to decipher any lucid, accurate history of the era. On the other hand, divinely selected history suffers none of these defects.

Even in modern times a Jesuit priest was appointed Chief Librarian of the New York City Library. In the United States, only the Library of Congress is larger than this library. He held his post throughout the decade of the 1990's before retiring. It is possible he had achieved all he wished to achieve during those ten years in office.

A study of Sister White's books and those of Dr. James Wylie demonstrated that neither Sister White nor Dr. James Wylie mentioned the dates 1411 or 1412 in their accounts of the history of John Huss' reformatory ministry. However, we would agree that on the balance of evidence, Sister White in *Great Controversy* pages 100, 101, may have, in part, referred to events in 1411 and not 1412 as Dr. Ron Graybill asserted. However we do not concede that Sister White was referring always to the year 1411; nor do we grant that the evidence supplied by Dr. Graybill confirmed that Sister White's account merited his judgment that items one and three were "fairly certain" to be incorrect; nor do we agree that Dr. Graybill was justified in declaring that he was "fully certain" that items two and four were "not correct."

To refresh the memory of the reader we here again include Dr. Graybill's four listed claims against Sister White's words:
1. That the Pope was the one who issued the order placing Prague under interdict;
2. That during this interdict, all the churches in Prague were closed, and all religious services were suspended;
3. That as a result of the tumult, Huss left Prague for a time;
4. That Huss wrote the letter quoted on page 101, paragraph 2, of *The Great Controversy* at this time to explain why he left Prague. (*Ibid*).

Pastor Jan Voerman of the Netherlands, in a carefully researched monograph entitled, *Historical Difficulties in the Great Controversy*, has amply supported the accuracy of Sister White's recorded history concerning the events in Prague in 1411. This should not cause surprise, for the Holy Spirit inspired her work. For much of that which follows we are indebted to Pastor Voerman.

Quoting from the credible information provided in the German Theological and Protestant Church encyclopedia, *Real-Encyklopädie für prttestantische Theologie und Kirche*, In Verbindung mit vielen protestantischen Theologen und Gelehrten, Stuttgart und Hamburg, Band 6, S.330, it seems almost certain that, as Dr. Graybill claimed, Sister White was largely referring to events in Prague during the year 1411.

> In February 1411 [Cardinal Otto] Colonna pronounced over Huss the Excommunications in absence, and threatened the place, where he would reside, with the Interdict. *(Ibid)*.

King Wenceslas (1361-1419), King of Bohemia, supported Huss (see *Encyclopaedia Britannica*, 1963 Edition, Vol. 23, p. 512). Pope John XXIII, in response to the king's pleas on behalf of Huss, appointed Cardinal Brancas to manage events in Prague. But the ban on Huss was not removed and on June 18, 1411 Archbishop Zbynek of Prague placed an interdict on Prague.

Here we address Dr. Graybill's claim that he is "fairly certain" that it was not the Pope who issued the interdict in 1411. Dr. Graybill's claim was that it was issued on the initiative of the Archbishop. But an authoritative work provides firm support for Sister White's statement that it was the pope who initiated the interdict.

> Popular riots followed in the city [Prague], and Huss, backed by the people, still maintained, nor did he yield one jot even after the entire city was laid under a papal interdict in 1411.
>
> (*Chamber's Encyclopaedia, A Dictionary of Universal Knowledge*, Vol. VI, p. 16).

Notice – "the entire city [of Prague] was laid under a papal interdict in 1411." This confirms Sister White's words:

> The pope ... declared the city of Prague to be under interdict.
>
> (*Great Controversy*, p. 100).

This statement is further confirmed as accurate, this time by a Roman Catholic source:

> Since he [Huss] neglected the summons of the papal judicial investigator, Cardinal Otto Colonna, followed in February the excommunication by the Pope, that on March 15 was read in nearly all churches in Prague.
>
> (*Lexicon für Theologie und Kirche*, Herder and Co., Freiburg im Breisgau, Band 5, S.206).

Here once more, the 1411 excommunication was declared to have been issued by the Pope. Clearly, the interdict which followed in June, while announced by the Archbishop of Prague, had been initiated by Pope Alexander V, who was later designated as an antipope. (There is strong evidence that this pope was poisoned at the instigation of his successor John XXIII). That the pope initiated the interdict is clear from the words of another credible source:

> The consequence was that Hus was excommunicated, and Prague laid under a Papal interdict – measures which failed, however, to achieve their object.
> (James Hastings, editor, *Encyclopaedia of Religion and Ethics*, Vol. VI, p. 887).

Clearly this was the 1411 interdict, for it failed to achieve its object. The 1412 interdict proved more successful.

It causes no little surprise that a trained and experienced scholar would jump to his unwarranted conclusions, especially when working in the General Conference White Estate and handling divinely inspired writings.

Since the interdict of 1411 did not achieve its object, a fact which the weight of historical evidence plainly supports, is then Dr. Graybill's claim that Sister White stated, "that during this interdict, all churches in Prague were closed and all religious services were suspended," incorrect?

Of course it is incorrect. It is true that the interdict was ineffective because of the support, not only of royalty, but of the populace. But did Sister White make a statement concerning the 1411 interdict, claiming all the churches of Prague were closed? Of course not!

One only has to read the second paragraph quoted above, found in the first paragraph of the *Great Controversy*, p. 101 to recognize that Sister White was here speaking in general terms concerning interdicts when they were enforced. The term "In that age", speaks not to a single year but to a period of time, an era.

Those who recall thirteenth century English history will remember that Pope Innocent III (1160-1216, Pope 1198-1216) in his dispute with King John (1167-1216, King 1199-1216) over the choice of the Achbishop of Canterbury, placed an interdict upon England which involved that which Sister White correctly wrote as occurring "in that age."

There is nothing in the paragraph which Dr. Graybill cites to "confirm" an error in Sister White's historical writings which would lead us to conclude that she was applying this to the ineffective interdict of 1411. Sister White was simply pointing out the intended severity of such a papal declaration. In the case of King John of England he was forced to capitulate after six years and offer the English kingdom as a fiefdom to the Pope. A large annual tribute was paid to Rome for over one hundred and fifty years as a consequence, until John Wycliffe wisely advised Parliament to default.

The third questioned matter of whether Huss left Prague in 1411 as the result of the tumult is now examined. Let us again quote credible history.

> The breach became wider and wider and led to popular riots in Prague, so that at length the king, who was still on Huss' side found it necessary to induce him, for the sake of peace to leave Prague (1411). Huss did so.
> (*Encyclopaedia of Religion and Ethics*, op. cit., Vol VI, p. 887).

Dr. Graybill's claim that John Huss wrote this letter, to which Sister White refers in the third paragraph we have quoted at the commencement of this chapter, in December, 1412, is pure supposition. As Pastor Jan Voerman pointed out, Dr. Graybill's reasoning is inadequate to prove his point. Dr. Graybill asserted that:

> The letter could not have been written in December of 1411 because even if we grant, for the sake of argument, that Huss left Prague in 1411, the interdict was a thing of the past and Huss was certainly back in the city by December. We have him writing the Pope from Prague on the "Day of St. Giles" (1 September, 1411) (Spinka, *The letters of John Huss*, pp. 54-56). Thus we know that Mrs. White's citation of this letter in this context is a historical error.
> (Ron Graybill, *op. cit.*, p. 6, parenthesis in original).

We concur with Pastor Voerman's assessment:

> This assertion does not seem to make sense. Hus [The Bohemian spelling of Huss' surname was Hus] could have written the pope from Prague on 1 September, 1411 without any problem and left Prague near the end of the year.
> (Pastor Voerman, *op. cit.*).

We would suggest that on the balance of probabilities, Dr. Graybill was straining every piece of evidence in order to uphold his thesis that Sister White did not select her historical statements under the guidance of inspiration. We would ask, Why is it so difficult to accord inspired history the status of accuracy it deserves, while according faulted secular history a higher status? We assume that Dr. Graybill presented the most cogent arguments he could muster in order to demonstrate Sister White's record of Huss' life, to be errant. If we are correct in this assumption, we must conclude that he has failed in his purpose.

20 Disparity Between the 1888 and 1911 Great Controversy Editions

The book, The Great Controversy, has received much negative comment in respect of its historical accuracy, of which the history of Huss, discussed in chapter entitled "Historical Accuracy," was just one instance.

It is clear that many ordained ministers, theologians and church administrators cast serious doubt upon Sister White's word. In the Introduction to the 1911 *Great Controversy*, she wrote:

> As the Spirit of God has opened to my mind the great truths of His word, and the scenes of the past and the future, I have been bidden to make known to others that which has thus been revealed—to trace the history of the controversy in past ages, and especially so to present it as to shed a light on the fast-approaching struggle of the future. In pursuance of this purpose, I have endeavored to select and group together events in the history of the church in such a manner as to trace the unfolding of the great testing truths that at different periods have been given to the world, that have excited the wrath of Satan, and the enmity of a world-loving church, and that have been maintained by the witness of those who "loved not their lives unto the death." (*Great Controversy*, p. xi).

Significantly, Sister White also revealed the reason why she did not always provide specific references for ideas she used from other authors. She did not cover up such matters as many would have us believe. Remember it was "the Spirit of God [who] opened the great truths of [God's] word, and the scenes of the past and the future." (See quotation above).

> The great events which have marked the progress of reform in past ages are matters of history, well known and universally acknowledged by the Protestant world; they are facts which none can gainsay. This history I have presented briefly, in accordance with the scope of the book, and the brevity which must necessarily be observed, the facts having been condensed into as little space as seemed consistent with a proper understanding of their application. In some cases where a historian has so grouped together events as to afford, in brief, a comprehensive view of the subject, or has summarized details in a convenient manner, his words have been quoted; but in some instances no specific credit has been given, since the quotations are not given for the purpose of citing that writer as authority, but because his statement affords a ready and forcible presentation of the subject. In narrating the experience and views of those carrying forward the work of reform in our own time, similar use has been made of their published works.
> (*Ibid*, pp. xi, xii),

Sister White's reason for omitting some references appeals to the mind of reason as valid. As a prophet, unlike ourselves, she required no need to bolster her material on the basis of human credibility. Sister White's credibility lay with her inspired knowledge of truth.

On January 9, 1979, Elder Robert Olson, later Director of the Ellen G. White Estate at the General Conference, published a manuscript entitled *Ellen G. White's Use of History*. In this twelve page paper seven differences between the 1888 and the 1911 editions of *The Great Controversy* were cited. The inference was left that the reason Sister White altered these references was because she discovered that some of her 1888 historical statements were in error and she wished to correct these in 1911.

In selecting the seven examples of alterations between the 1888 and 1911 editions, Dr. Olson declared these to be:

> some of the more important changes approved by Ellen White as incorporated in the 1911 edition of *The Great Controversy*. (*op. cit.*, p. 8).

A few months later Elder Olson issued a second, nine-page manuscript entitled *Historical Discrepancies in the Spirit of Prophecy*. These two manuscripts are still relevant today for when Pastor Jan Knopper, retired South Pacific Division Publishing Department Director, wrote in a letter to the editor of the South Pacific *Record*, published in the February 28, 2004 edition, requesting the *Record* to

> supply documented facts regarding those sources and alleged errors (p. 13),

as asserted in the editorial of the February 7, 2004 edition of the paper, the *Record* editor stated that such information was freely available from the Ellen G. White Research Centre located on the campus of Avondale College. Dr. Olson's two manuscripts together with Dr. Ron Graybill's cited earlier in this book were among the four documents provided.

Dr. Olson did not choose to quote from Elder William White's statement upon these alterations. Sister White's son commented upon these items during her lifetime in a statement made before the General Conference Council held October 30, 1911, in the very year the last edition of *The Great Controversy* was issued.

> In a few instances, new quotations from historians, preachers, and present-day writers have been used in the place of the old, because they are more forceful or because we have been unable to find the old ones. In each case where there has been such a change, mother has given faithful attention to the proposed substitution, and has approved of the change. You will find that changes of this character have been made on pages 273, 277, 306-308, 334, 335, 387, 547, 580, and 581. (*Selected Messages*, Vol. 3, p. 435).

There were other reasons for alterations between the 1888 and 1911 editions, which were published twenty-three years apart. One obvious need for alteration was cited by Elder W. C. White in the same presentation.

> In eight or ten places, time references have been changed because of the lapse of time since the book was first published. (*Ibid*).

A third problem which confronted Sister White in the production of the 1911 edition was:

> There are still some score or more quotations in the book whose authority we have so far been unable to trace. Fortunately, these relate to matters regarding which there is not a probability of there being any serious contention. (*Ibid*).

Yet a fourth cause for alteration concerned editorial consistency, because the 1911 edition became the fifth volume in the Conflict of the Ages series.

> In spelling, punctuation, and capitalization, changes have been made to bring this book into uniformity of style with the other volumes of this series. (*Ibid*).

Another concern of Sister White led to further alterations. No doubt the remarkable change in Protestant attitudes to Roman Catholicism between 1888 and 1911 engendered these alterations. In 1888 the Protestant generation then living possessed a fresh memory of Pope Pius IX's outrageous Syllabus of Errors reviling religious liberty, issued December 8, 1864 and his declaration of Papal Infallibility issued on the same month and day, 1870. By 1911 a new generation of Protestants had arisen who, although not in the comfort zone with Roman Catholics of today's ecumenical spirit, were, nevertheless, rapidly casting off the conviction that the Papacy was the antichrist of Bible prophecy, as the secret rapture error and its end-time antichrist gathered doctrinal momentum among evangelical Protestants.

> In several places, forms of expression have been changed to avoid giving unnecessary offense. An example of this will be found in the change of the word "Romish" to "Roman" or "Roman Catholic." in two places the phrase "divinity of Christ" is changed to "deity of Christ." and the words "religious toleration" have been changed to "religious liberty." (*Ibid*, pp. 435, 436).

There were occasions where inspired words from 1888 were slightly altered because it was deemed necessary to convince non-Seventh-day Adventists of the inspired fact presented by providing actual documentation from historical sources.

> On pages 50, 563, 564, 580, 581, and in a few other places where there were statements regarding the papacy which are strongly disputed by Roman Catholics, and which are difficult to prove from accessible histories, the wording in the new edition has been so changed that the statement falls easily within the range of evidence that is readily obtainable.

> Regarding these and similar passages, which might stir up bitter and unprofitable controversies, mother has often said: "what I have written regarding the arrogance and the assumptions of the papacy is true. Much historical evidence

regarding these matters has been designedly destroyed; nevertheless, that the book may be of the greatest benefit to Catholics and others, and that needless controversies may be avoided, it is better to have all statements regarding the assumptions of the pope and the claims of the papacy stated so moderately as to be easily and clearly proved from accepted histories that are within the reach of our ministers and students.

If you hear reports that some of the work done on this latest edition was done contrary to mother's wish or without her knowledge, you can be sure that such reports are false, and unworthy of consideration. (Ibid, p. 436).

We invite the reader to review the above quotation noting that:
1. Sister White's statements in 1888 and assumptions were true;
2. Historical evidences had been DESIGNEDLY destroyed;
3. She permitted some modifications so that the book would be more helpful to the minds of Roman Catholics in the new era of the twentieth century. This demonstrated that as a prophet, God not only inspired Sister White with knowledge but also with wisdom from on high.

Sister White had a distinct advantage over authors such as ourselves when we seek the best historical material in order to bring important matters before our people. Notice:

Mother has never claimed to be an authority on history. The things which she has written out, are descriptions of flashlight pictures and other representations given her regarding the actions of men, and the influence of these actions upon the work of God for the salvation of men, with views of past, present, and future history in its relation to this work. In connection with the writing out of these views, she has made use of good and clear historical statements to help make plain to the reader the things which she is endeavoring to present. (Ibid).

With this background understanding of the alterations made between the 1888 and 1911 editions of *The Great Controversy*, we summarize these reasons:
1. To increase the forcefulness of the presentation even further;
2. Because twenty-three years had lapsed between editions, time references were altered appropriately;
3. Inability to trace earlier references because the histories had been removed from libraries and other depositories of these books;
4. Need to alter spelling, punctuation and capitalization to agree with other books in the Conflict of the Ages series;
5. To remove terms concerning Roman Catholicism which had become more offensive during the twenty-three-year period of dramatic change in the views of Protestants;
6. Introduction of new documentation.

Now it is proper to reveal the seven comparisons between the two editions which Dr. Olson listed. Bear in mind the six matters above; and all these differences will be resolved.

Disparity Between the 1888 and 1911 Great Controversy Editions

1888 Edition	1911 Edition

Page 50

It is one of the leading doctrines of Romanism that the pope is the visible head of the universal church of Christ, invested with supreme authority over bishops and pastors in all parts of the world. More than this, the pope has arrogated the very titles of Deity. <u>He styles himself</u> "Lord God the Pope," assumes infallibility, and demands that all men pay him homage. Thus the same claim urged by Satan in the wilderness of temptation is still urged by him through the Church of Rome, and vast numbers are ready to yield him homage.	It is one of the leading doctrines of Romanism that the pope is the visible head of the universal church of Christ, invested with supreme authority over bishops and pastors in all parts of the world. More than this, the pope has been given the very titles of Deity. <u>He has been styled</u> "Lord God the Pope," and has been declared infallible. He demands the homage of all men. The same claim urged by Satan in the wilderness of temptation is still urged by him through the Church of Rome, and vast numbers are ready to yield him homage.

1

Page 65

The Waldenses were <u>the first</u> of all the peoples of Europe to obtain a translation of the Holy Scriptures.	The Waldenses were <u>among the first</u> of the peoples of Europe to obtain a translation of the Holy Scriptures.

2

---

[1] Sister White's 1888 claim may be amply documented. Both Popes Innocent III (ruled 1198–1216) and Leo X (ruled 1513–1521) used the title of the Roman Caesars – *Dominus et Deus imprimateur*, (Our Lord and God). (Baron Alfred Procelli, *The Antichrist*, Eric C. Peters, Blackwood, New Jersey, p. 28).

Further, "It is quite certain that the Popes have never reproved or rejected this title [Our Lord God the Pope], for the passage in the Gloss [explanatory note] referred to appears in the edition of the Canon Law published at Rome in 1580 by [Pope] Gregory XIII [Pope 1572–1587] and the *Index Expurgatorius* of [Pope] Pius V [Pope 1566–1572] – who was canonized (Pereira, *Tentativa Theologica*, English translation, 1847, p. 180 quoted in Porcelli, *op.cit.*, p. 28).

Clearly the words of the 1888 Edition stating that the Popes, themselves, claimed the title of Lord God the Pope were not altered in the 1911 edition because of inaccuracy, as Sister White's detractors suggest, but for the reasons cited above by Elder William White.

[2] There is no reason to doubt this divinely-inspired statement of 1888. Secular history does not record the date of the first Bible translation prepared by the Waldenses. No doubt the alteration was made in 1911, not because the 1888 edition was in error, but because proof from secular sources does not exist. This in no way invalidates the fact that God revealed to Sister White that the Waldenses were the first to provide a translation of Scripture into their native tongue. In 1911, Sister White probably altered the wording to meet the minds of non-Seventh-day Adventists, skeptical of God's inspired word revealed to her.

The Greatest of All the Prophets

1888 Edition	1911 Edition

Page 272

But blackest in the black catalogue of crime, most horrible among the fiendish deeds of all the dreadful centuries, was the St. Bartholomew Massacre. The world still recalls with shuddering horror the scenes of that most cowardly and cruel onslaught. The king of France, urged on by Romish priests and prelates, lent his sanction to the dreadful work. <u>The great bell of the palace</u> tolling at dead of night, was a signal for the slaughter. Protestants by thousands, sleeping quietly in their homes, trusting to the plighted honor of their king, were dragged forth without a warning and murdered in cold blood.	But blackest in the black catalogue of crime, most horrible among the fiendish deeds of all the dreadful centuries, was the St. Bartholomew Massacre. The world still recalls with shuddering horror the scenes of that most cowardly and cruel onslaught. The king of France, urged on by Romish priests and prelates, lent his sanction to the dreadful work. <u>A bell</u> tolling at dead of night, was a signal for the slaughter. Protestants by thousands, sleeping quietly in their homes, trusting to the plighted honor of their king, were dragged forth without a warning and murdered in cold blood.

3

Page 273

"The beast that ascendeth out of the bottomless pit shall make war against them, and shall overcome them, and kill them." The atheistical power that ruled in France during the Revolution and the reign of terror, did wage such a war on the Bible as the world had never witnessed. <u>The Word of God was prohibited</u> by the national assembly. Bibles were collected and publicly burned with every possible manifestation of scorn.	"The beast that ascendeth out of the bottomless pit shall make war against them, and shall overcome them, and kill them." The atheistical power that ruled in France during the Revolution and the Reign of Terror, did wage such a war against God and His holy word as the world had never witnessed. <u>The worship of the Deity was abolished</u> by the National Assembly. Bibles were collected and publicy burned with every possible manifestation of scorn.

4

---

[3] Dr. Arthur Patrick rightly stated, referring to the tolling of the bell, "Was it the palace bell? The castle bell? The church bell? Let the historians continue to argue over that sort of thing." (*South Pacific Record*, February 21, 2004). We need not doubt that God arbitrated on this dispute. Yes, let the historians argue. Let us believe God, who inspired Sister White's writings. No doubt Sister White altered the 1911 words on this matter, omitting to designate the specific bell which tolled, because of the dispute among historians, which could have been a distraction to readers.

[4] Since the French National Assembly in 1793 passed a decree "which abolished the Christian religion and set aside the Bible" (*Great Controversy*, 1911 edition, p. 287), both the 1888 and the 1911 statements are correct as Sister White testified on p. 287 below.

1888 Edition   1911 Edition

Page 286-7

1888 Edition	1911 Edition
God's faithful witnesses, slain by the blasphemous power that "ascendeth out of the bottomless pit," were not long to remain silent. "After three days and a half, the Spirit of life from God entered into them, and they stood upon their feet; and great fear fell upon them which saw them." It was in 1793 that <u>the decree which prohibited the Bible</u> passed the French Assembly. Three years and a half later a resolution rescinding the decree, and granting toleration to the Scriptures, was adopted by the same body.	God's faithful witnesses, slain by the blasphemous power that "ascendeth out of the bottomless pit," were not long to remain silent. "After three days and a half, the Spirit of life from God entered into them, and they stood upon their feet; and great fear fell upon them which saw them." Revelation 11:11. It was in 1793 that <u>the decrees which abolished the Christian religion and set aside the Bible</u> passed the French Assembly. Three years and a half later a resolution rescinding the decree, and granting toleration to the Scriptures, was adopted by the same body.

5

Page 287-288

1888 Edition	1911 Edition
For the fifty years preceding 1792, little attention was given to the work of foreign missions. No new societies were formed, and there were but few churches that made any effort for the spread of Christianity in heathen lands. But toward the close of the eighteenth century a great change took place. Men became dissatisfied with the results of rationalism, and realized the necessity of divine revelation and experimental religion. The devoted Carey, who in 1793 became the first English missionary to India, kindled anew the flame of missionary effort in England. In America, twenty years later, the zeal of a society of students, among whom was Adoniram Judson, resulted in the formation of <u>the American Board of Foreign Missions under whose auspices Judson went as a missionary from the United States to Burma</u>. From this time the work of foreign missions attained an unprecedented growth.	For the fifty years preceding 1792, little attention was given to the work of foreign missions. No new societies were formed, and there were but few churches that made any effort for the spread of Christianity in heathen lands. But toward the close of the eighteenth century a great change took place. Men became dissatisfied with the results of rationalism, and realized the necessity of divine revelation and experimental religion. From this time the work of foreign missions attained an unprecedented growth. (<u>See Appendix</u>). Appendix Note: In the United States <u>the American Board of Commissioners for Foreign Missions</u> was formed in 1812, and <u>Adoniram Judson was sent out that year to Calcutta. He established himself in Burma the next year.</u>

5

---

[5] The readings of pages 286, 287 and 287, 288, while the words are slightly altered are stating essentially the same matters.

1888 Edition	1911 Edition
"Almost if not altogether alone as the most mysterious and as yet unexplained phenomenon of its kind,... stands the dark day of May 19, 1780, – a most unaccountable darkening of the whole visible heavens and atmosphere in New England." That the darkness was not due to an eclipse is evident from the fact that the moon was then nearly full. It was not caused by clouds, or the thickness of the atmosphere, for in some localities where the darkness extended, the sky was so clear that the stars could be seen. Concerning the inability of science to assign a satisfactory cause for this manifestation, <u>Herschel the astronomer declares</u>: "The dark day in North America was one of those wonderful phenomena of nature which philosophy is at a loss to explain."	"Almost, if not altogether alone, as the most mysterious and as yet unexplained phenomenon of its kind,... stands the dark day of May 19, 1780, – a most unaccountable darkening of the whole visible heavens and atmosphere in New England." – R. M. Devens, *Our First Century*, page 89. An eyewitness living in Massachusetts describes the events as follows: "In the morning the sun rose clear, but was soon overcast. The clouds became lowery, and from them, black and ominous, as they soon appeared, lightning flashed, thunder rolled, and a little rain fell. Toward nine o'clock, the clouds became thinner, and assumed a brassy or coppery appearance, and earth, rocks, trees, buildings, water, and persons were changed by this strange, unearthly light.

Page 306

[6]

No fair-minded reader would judge the passage disparities above to provide the least evidence that Sister White was here altering "mistakes" she had included in her 1888 edition. It is a matter of alarm that men such as Elder Arthur Grosvenor Daniells (1858-1935) and Elder William Warren Prescott (1855-1944) – who were well aware of these explanations and reasons and who both attended the 1911 General Conference Council where Elder Willie White commented on these explanations – spoke as they did at the 1919 Bible Conference.

Those who declare that the Church has covered up these alterations and the reasons for them, thus entertaining a conspiracy theory, possess no grounds to make such claims. Pr. William White addressed them at the 1911 General Conference Council and, as we have seen, for almost a quarter of a century, since the third volume of *Selected Messages* was published in 1980, the words he spoke in 1911 have had widespread exposure.

---

[6] Notice that in 1888 Sister White referred to "some localities," not all, where "the sky was so clear that the stars could be seen." She did not state "everywhere." It is important to notice this fact. In 1911 Sister White revealed that this situation did not prevail in *all* locations for she referred to an area where black and ominous clouds also accompanied the darkness. There is no room to doubt the inspired words of the 1888 edition nor those of the 1911 edition. Let us not permit doubters in our midst to destroy our faith. (See R. M. Devens, *Our First Century*, C. A. Nichols & Co., Springfield, Massachusetts, 1876, pp. 88–96, for descriptions (in a number of locations) of various conditions during the dark day.)

We will not spend time on the so-called "disparities" between the 1884 and 1888 editions of *The Great Controversy*. Suffice to remind the reader that the 1884 edition was prepared for the Seventh-day Adventist readership while the 1888 and 1911 editions were prepared for the world. We quote one such example. The 1885 edition to which Pr. White referred was the 1884 edition.

> In *Great Controversy*, Volume IV, published in 1885, in the chapter "Snares of Satan," there are three pages or more of matter that was not used in the later editions, which were prepared to be sold to the multitudes by our canvassers. It is most excellent and interesting reading for Sabbathkeepers, as it points out the work that Satan will do in persuading popular ministers and church members to elevate the Sunday sabbath, and to persecute Sabbathkeepers.
>
> It was not left out because it was less true in 1888 than in 1885, but because mother thought it was not wisdom to say these things to the multitudes to whom the book would be sold in future years…. (*Selected Messages*, Vol. 3, p. 443).

That deleted material may be read in the book, *Testimonies to Ministers*, pages 472-475, which was published over eighty years ago, in 1923.

We have written many books specifically for Seventh-day Adventists. We have later altered some for new editions prepared for non-Seventh-day Adventists. One such book is *Adventism Imperiled* which was altered to *Education for Excellence – the Christian Advantage*. Both books are still in circulation. The alterations were not made in order to correct "mistakes." It was prudent to make these alterations in order to address the readership not of our faith.

21 Administrators, Editors and Academics Evaluate the Spirit of Prophecy – The 1919 Bible Conference

Since Dr. Smithurst, the fictional theologian in Dr. Bradford's book, *Prophets are Human*, raised the issue of the General Conference Bible Conference in 1919 but chose not to evaluate it, except to accept the doubts of these leaders, we here examine this Bible Conference. In his book Dr. Bradford's character, Dr. Smithurst, stated:

> In a meeting back in 1919, where some of our leaders were discussing some of these issues, H. C. Lacey {Herbert Camden][1871-1950][Bible lecturer, Washington Missionary College, now Columbia Union College] made this comment: 'In our estimate of the Spirit of Prophecy, isn't its value to us more in the spiritual light it throws into our own hearts and lives than in the intellectual accuracy in historical and theological matters? Ought we not to take these writings as the voice of the spirit of our hearts, instead of the voice of the teacher to our heads? And isn't the final proof of the Spirit of Prophecy its spiritual value rather than its doctrinal accuracy?'
>
> A. G. Daniells, the General Conference president, agreed with this statement by Lacey when he replied, 'Yes, I think so.'
>
> Remember, Daniells had done a lot of work in assisting her with her writings. That makes his comment here very significant. Ellen White is so frequently the pastor or evangelist who wants to help us in our relationship with Jesus Christ. In doing this she will take some ideas from her culture. Some of these ideas were readily accepted in her time, but we would question them today.
>
> (Dr. Bradford, *op. cit.*, p. 61).

Here we see that Elders Herbert Lacey and Arthur Daniells both considered Sister White's "historical and theological matters" were not to be trusted for their "intellectual accuracy in historical and theological matters." It was not historical accuracy alone, but theological reliability that was questioned in 1919. Such charges utterly destroy the value of the Spirit of Prophecy if substantiated. The 1919 Bible Conference was a disgrace to our church. Yet Dr. Bradford supported the idea that Sister White was inaccurate not only in history but also in her theology. Dr. Smithurst then proceeded to challenge Sister White's health and scientific statements. There was no attempt to show the error of Elders Lacey and Daniells, for in serious error they most certainly were. The following three chapters and this one, take up this challenge.

In December 1975, F. Donald Yost, Archivist of the General Conference, discovered a stenographic record of the Bible Conference held in Washington, D.C., July 1-21, 1919. This record had long been lost. Its discovery was regarded as a triumph for the proponents of the New Theology as some attendees at the 1919 Conference expressed less than full faith in the inspiration of Sister White's writings.

The expressed objective of the 1919 Conference was:

> To unite in definite, practical, spiritual study of the Word of God in order to gain more light and greater unity. (*Review and Herald*, August 21, 1919, pp. 3, 4).

The result announced after the conclusion of the Conference was reported to be:

> The Bible and history teachers, the editors, and the members of the General Conference Committee, who came together from all parts of North America, rejoiced to find themselves in agreement on all the great fundamental truths of the Bible. (*Ibid*, p. 4).

The subjects addressed were:
1. The Person and Mediatorial Work of Christ
2. The Nature and Work of the Holy Spirit
3. The Two Covenants
4. The Principles of Prophetic Interpretation
5. The Eastern Question (Turkey and Armageddon in Bible Prophecy)
6. The Beast Power in Revelation
7. The 1260 Days
8. The United States in Prophecy
9. The Seven Trumpets
10. Matthew Twenty-four
11. The Identification of the Ten Kingdoms

The list of attendees included the following men. (We include the later service of some of these men to illustrate the scope of their influence after the 1919 Bible Conference):
1. E. F. Abbotsworth
2. Jacob Nelson Anderson (1867-1958), Teacher, Washington Missionary Seminary (1910-1928) and Biblical Languages at Union College, Nebraska (1934-1943).
3. C. L. Benson
4. Calvin P. Bollman (1853-1943), Associate Editor, Liberty Magazine; Associate Editor, *Review and Herald*, (1920-1938).
5. Leon Leslie Caviness (1884-1955), Associate Editor, *Review and Herald*; Departmental Secretary, Latin Union (Algeria, Belgium, France, Italy, Morocco, Portugal, Spain Switzerland [1920-1924]); Director Seminaire

Adventiste du Saléve (1921-1922); Sabbath School and Educational Secretary, European Division (1924-1928); and Southern European Division (1928-1932); Professor of Biblical Languages, Pacific Union College (1932-1952).
6. Arthur Grosvener Daniells (1858-1935), General Conference President; (1901-1922); Secretary (1922-1926)
7. Thomas Marion French (1883-1949), Head, School of Theology, Emmanuel Missionary College; Sabbath School Secretary, African Division (1922-1925); Editor, African *Signs of the Times* (1925-1927); President Natal-Transvaal Conference (1927-1929); Head of Theology, Atlantic Union College (1929-1934); Associate Editor, *Review and Herald*, (1934-1938); Chairman of Bible Department, Walla Walla College (1938, 1939); President West Virginia Conference (1939-1942); President East Pennsylvania Conference (1942, 1943).
8. B. L. House
9. Warren Eugene Howell (1869-1943), Editor, *Christian Education*; Director of the General Conference Department of Education (1918-1930).
10. Milton Earle Kern (1875-1961), Former President, Washington Foreign Missionary Seminary; Chairman of the Home Commission of the General Conference (1922-1930); General Conference Associate Secretary (1930-1933); General Conference Secretary (1933); Dean of the Advanced Bible School (1933-1936); Dean of the Seventh-day Adventist Theological Seminary (1936-1943), Field Secretary of the General Conference and President of the Board of Trustees of the Ellen White Publications (1943-1950).
11. Herbert Camden Lacey (1871-1950), Bible and Biblical Language teacher at Washington Foreign Missionary Seminary; for a time Professor of Biblical Exegesis, Loma Linda University.
12. Charles Smull Longacre (1871-1958), Secretary of the General Conference Home Missionary Department; he later became a high profile proponent of religious liberty.
13. D. A. Parsons
14. William Warren Prescott (1855-1944), General Conference Field Secretary; Principlal, Australasian Missionary College (1922); President and head of the Bible Department, Union College, Nebraska (1924-1928); Head of Bible Department, Emmanuel Missionary College (1930-1934).
15. C. A. Shull
16. Christian Martin Sorenson (1874-1965), History Teacher, Emmanuel Missionary College (1920-1932); History Teacher, La Sierra College (1932); Principal, Fireside Correspondence School
17. Asa Oscar Tait (1858-1941), Editor, *Signs of the Times*
18. Clifton Linley Taylor (1882-1963), Head, Bible Department, Canadian Junior College; Principal, Fireside Correspondence School (1922-

1924); Head of Bible Department, Atlantic Union College (1924-1929).
19. George B. Thompson (1862-1930), General Conference Field Secretary
20. W. H. Wakenham, Bible Teacher, Emmanuel Missionary College
21. Bro. Waldoff
22. Francis McLellan Wilcox (1865-1951), Editor, *Review and Herald*, (1911-1944).
23. Milton Charles Wilcox (1853-1935), Book Editor, Pacific Press
24. Flora Harriet Williams (1865-1944), Education Supervisor of the East Michigan Conference; Editor of *Home and School*, (1930-1938).
25. W. G. Wirth, Religion Teacher, Pacific Union College.

In total there were fifty in attendance, but we have been unable to discover documentation listing all the attendees' names. Of those attendees whose life details we have discovered, the last to die was Dr. Christian Sorenson in 1965, forty-six years after the 1919 Bible Conference, a decade after the Barnhouse-Martin Dialogue and eight years after the publication of the book which opened the way for the introduction of the New Theology worldwide, *Questions on Doctrine*.

In this book we confine ourselves to the matters discussed in relation to the writings of Sister White. These discussions centered on three issues:
1. Word-inspiration of Sister White's writings
2. Infallibility of Sister White's writings
3. The Spirit of Prophecy as an interpreter of Scripture.

That time was spent on the first of these propositions surprises us. We have never heard a single individual promote the concept that Sister White's writings were word inspired. Sister White plainly denied that concept. Perhaps a few ill-informed people expressed this view at that time.

> As spoken by the heavenly agencies, the words are severe in their simplicity; and I try to put the thoughts into such simple language that a child can understand every word uttered. (*Selected Messages*, Vol. 3, p. 92).

In an incident to which all over-busy people can relate, Sister White told of the frustration of her son, Elder W. C. White, when Sister Marian Davis brought trivialities concerning Sister White's writings to his attention. At the time, 1889, Elder William White was overworked in his post of acting General Conference President. The first time we read this passage we chuckled at Elder White's means of controlling his frustration. For us it was a moment of *déjà vu*. But the passage does illustrate the fact that Sister Davis sometimes suggested small alterations to the wording used. Of course, all alterations that impinged upon meaning had to receive Sister White's approval.

> Willie [William C. White, son Of Ellen White, at the time serving as Acting President of The General Conference.] is in meeting early and late, devising,

planning for the doing of better and more efficient work in the cause of God. We see him only at the table.

> Marian will go to him for some little matters that it seems she could settle for herself. She is nervous and hurried and he so worn he has to just shut his teeth together and hold his nerves as best he can. I have had a talk with her and told her she must settle many things herself that she has been bringing Willie.
>
> Her mind is on every point and the connections, and his mind has been plowing through a variety of difficult subjects until his brain reels and then his mind is in no way prepared to take up these little minutiae. She must just carry some of these things that belong to her part of the work, and not bring them before him nor worry his mind with them. Sometimes I think she will kill us both, all unnecessarily, with her little things she can just as well settle herself as to bring them before us. Every little change of a word she wants us to see.
>
> (*Selected Messages*, Vol. 3, pp. 92, 93).

Earlier in Sister White's life she accepted the assistance of her husband, Elder James White, in the preparation of her books.

> The instruction I received in vision was faithfully written out by me, as I had time and strength for the work. Afterward we examined the matter together, my husband correcting grammatical errors and eliminating needless repetition.
>
> (*Ibid*, p. 89).

In view of Sister White's plain words, there is absolutely no need to spend time on the issue of whether her writings were word-inspired. They were not. God inspired her thoughts. This was also the case with the Biblical writers. All were thought-inspired, as was Sister White. Each of the Bible writers used their unique expressions in recording divinely-given principles. In using their own expressions, their words were, nevertheless, accurate and thoroughly reliable.

Why then was this issue brought forward? Our experience is that it is not a view advanced by those who trust the inspired writings of the Servant of the Lord. Rather, this issue is inevitably raised by those who place little or no trust in Sister White's writings. This straw man is raised as if it is some issue bedeviling our believers and then it is effectively demolished in an atmosphere of diminishing Sister White's credibility. Such an attitude would destroy not only the writings of God's servant, but of all Bible writers.

Elder C. L. Taylor spoke wisely when he stated,

> With regard to the verbal inspiration of the Testimonies, I would say that I have heard more about it here in one day than ever before in my life. I think we have made a great big mountain of difficulty to go out and fight against. I do not believe that our people generally believe in the verbal inspiration of the Testimonies.
>
> (Transcript of 1919 Bible Conference, *Spectrum*, Vol. 10, No. 1, p. 47).

However we believe Elder Taylor underestimated the laity when he went on to state,

> I think that the general idea of our people is that the Testimonies are the writings of a sister who received light from God. As to verbal inspiration, I think they have a very ill-defined idea. I think they believe that in some way God gave her light, and she wrote it down, and they do not know what verbal inspiration means.
>
> (*Ibid*).

The General Conference President, Elder A. G. Daniells, appeared to share Elder Taylor's low estimate of the laity's understanding of the issue of verbal versus thought inspiration or, as he designated it, "truth inspired."

> Shall we consider some points as settled, and pass on? Take the matter of verbal inspiration. I think it is very much as Brother Taylor says, that among the most of our people there is no question. It is not agitated. They do not understand it, and they do not understand the technical features of the inspiration of the Bible, either. And the power of the Bible and its grip on the human race does not depend on a technical point as to their belief in it, whether it is verbally inspired or truth-inspired. (*Ibid*).

Speaking from personal experience Elder Daniells stated:

> In Australia I saw "The Desire of Ages" being made up, and I saw the rewriting of chapters, some of them written over and over and over again. I saw that, and when I talked with Sister Davis about it, I tell you I had to square up to this thing and begin to settle things about the spirit of prophecy. (*Ibid*).

It is most unfortunate that Elder Daniells expressed his finding in such a manner that his hearers could not but conclude that he was expressing less than full confidence in the divine inspiration of *The Desire of Ages*.

The General Conference President's following words disgraced his high post. His consistent failure to accept personally the health message is seen in his words.

> If we did that [accept Sister White's writings as word inspired], I would just take everything from A to Z, exactly as it is written, without making any explanations to any one, and I would not eat butter or salt or eggs if I believed that the Lord gave the words in those Testimonies to Sister White for the whole body of people in this world. But I do not believe it. (*Ibid*).

Such words of doubt characterized Elder Daniells' comments. Elder Daniells appeared unable to understand that Sister White only accepted the suggested alterations in wording if she approved. She took great care to ensure that the improvements in expression which others suggested did in no wise alter the meaning of the divine revelations she had received.

> I read over all that is copied, to see that everything is as it should be. I read all the book manuscript before it is sent to the printer. So you can see that my time must be fully occupied. (*Selected Messages*, Vol. 3, pp. 90, 91).

> I feel very thankful for the help of Sister Marian Davis [1847-1904] in getting out my books. She gathers materials from my diaries, from my letters, and from the articles published in the papers. I greatly prize her faithful service. She has been with me for twenty-five years, and has constantly been gaining increasing ability for the work of classifying and grouping my writings. (*Ibid*, p. 93).

While Dean of Weimar College, Colin had invited Elder Robert Pierson, retired General Conference President, to conduct a Week of Prayer at the College in 1980, a year following Elder Pierson's retirement.

Elder Pierson was a man who evidenced full faith in the writings of Sister White. He had not seen the 1919 Bible Conference material probably because in the last years of General Conference Presidency following the discovery of the 1919 Bible Conference Minutes, he had been too busy to read them. Colin shared the minutes with him. After carefully reading them, he was shocked. His one comment was "I wish Elder Daniells hadn't said some of the things which he said at the Bible Conference."

Elder Daniells' expressed doubts at this conference seem to contrast with his frequent expressions of faith in the messages of God's servant. These expressions are also at odds with his strong support for Sister White's writings, expressed in his book, *The Abiding Gift of Prophecy*, written in the 1920's. It is possible that Elder Daniells harbored doubts in the period of his middle age which he did not possess when a young man and which he had reconciled in his old age. Perhaps after leaving the office of General Conference President he had time for proper study and reflection on this issue.

Only four years prior to the 1919 Bible Conference, in his oration at Sister White's funeral, conducted July 24, 1915, Elder Daniells had stated:

> Her life of full surrender, obedience, and prayer for divine help was rewarded by the bestowal of the gift of prophecy, one of the choicest of all the gifts of the Spirit.... Those who have been associated with her through all the years that have passed since that time have never had occasion to alter their conviction that the revelations which have come to her through the years have come from God.
> (*Life Sketches*, pp. 468, 469).

We wonder why these sentiments were not reiterated at the 1919 Bible Conference.

There could be reasons for his doubts in 1919. Sister White had opposed his desire for a presidential, authoritative General Conference structure. She gave him a number of dressing-downs over his desire to dictate inappropriate control over self-supporting ministers. Further, Elder Daniells' life-style, especially in the matter of diet, was at odds with the health message which Sister White had expounded.

Elder Lee, pioneer American missionary to Korea, related to Colin the grounds for the replacement of Elder Daniells as General Conference President at the 1922 General Conference Session held in San Francisco. While serving in Korea, Elder Lee and his wife hosted Elder and Sister Daniells, who were itinerating in the Far East.

Shortly after Elder and Sister Daniells' arrival at the Lee home, Sister Daniells spoke to Elder Lee's Korean house-girl asking her to go to the market and purchase a chicken for Elder Daniells who, Sister Daniells explained, needed such food to maintain his strength. Elder Lee had promoted the health message to the Korean converts. Naturally, the cook disclosed the request she had received to other church members. The poor example of the General Conference President all but destroyed Elder Lee's influence in spreading the health reform message.

Elder Lee was on furlough at the time of the 1922 General Conference Session and attended the meetings. There was a stalemate on the Nominating Committee. Some believed it was wise to extend Elder Daniells' tenure in the office of President. An equal number of members of the Nominating Committee desired a change. Wisely, the Nominating Committee decided to seek the counsel of the few overseas missionaries who were attending the Session. Elder Lee was not the only missionary who had been embarrassed by Elder Daniell's insistence in following a flesh diet. The counsel of these missionaries tipped the balance and Elder W. A. Spicer was appointed to the Presidency.

It is also reported that when Elder Daniells lay dying of cancer, he refused an anointing service. He stated that his illness had been caused, he believed, by his indulgence in a flesh diet, and that it would be inappropriate for him to be anointed. He is reported to have said to a young man who stated that he was praying for Elder Daniells' recovery, "Don't pray for my recovery. I brought this condition on myself. Please pray for my salvation."

We pray that in the latter years of his life Elder Daniells repented of the errors in his life and that our loving God will provide for him a place in His kingdom.

The other two issues listed above were proper matters for examination. These discussions were held separately from the general Bible Conference discussions, on July 30 and August 1, 1919. On the first of these two days the subject investigated was "The Use of the Spirit of Prophecy in Our Teaching of Bible and History." On August 1 the issue addressed was "Inspiration of the Spirit of Prophecy As Related to the Inspiration of the Bible."

Early in the discussion on the matter of the use of the Spirit of Prophecy in interpreting Scripture, some unfortunate remarks were made by Elder Daniells.

> **C. L. Taylor:** I would like to ask you to discuss for us the exegetical value of the Testimonies. Of course I think it is generally understood by us that there are many texts to which she makes no reference. There are many texts that she explains,

and there may be other explanations that are equally true that she does not touch. But my question is really this: May we accept the explanations of scripture that she gives? Are these dependable?

A. G. Daniells: I have always felt that they were. It may be that in some very critical matters there may be some difficulties; but I have used the writings for years in a way to clarify or elucidate the thoughts in the texts of Scripture. Take "Desire of Ages" and "Patriarchs and Prophets." In reading them through I have found many instances of good illumination.

Does that answer your question? Do you mean whether students should resort to the writings for their interpretation of the Bible, or to get additional light? That is to say, is it necessary to have these writings in order to understand the Bible? Must we go to her explanations to get our meaning of the Bible? Is that the question or is that involved in it?

C. L. Taylor: Not directly, but possibly indirectly. But I will give a more concrete example. We will suppose that a student comes for help on a certain scripture, and wants to know what it means. Is it proper for the teacher to explain that scripture, with perhaps other scriptures illuminating the text, and then bring in the spirit of prophecy also as additional light on the text? Or suppose two students differ on the meaning of a text, and they come to the teacher to find out what it means: Should the teacher explain the texts and then use the Testimonies to support the position he takes? Or take still a third case: Suppose that two brethren, both of them believers in the Testimonies, and of course believers in the Bible primarily, have a difference of opinion on a certain text: Is it right for them in their study of that text to bring in the spirit of prophecy to aid in their understanding of it, or should they leave that out of the question entirely?

A. G. Daniells: On that first point, I think this, that we are to get our interpretation from this Book, primarily. I think that the Book explains itself, and I think we can understand the Book, fundamentally, through the Book, without resorting to the Testimonies to prove up on it.

W. E. Howell: The spirit of prophecy says the Bible is its own expositor.

A. G. Daniells: Yes, but I have heard ministers say that the spirit of prophecy is the interpreter of the Bible. I heard it preached at the General Conference some years ago, when it was said that the only way we could understand the Bible was through the writings of the spirit of prophecy.

J. M. Anderson: And he also said "infallible interpreter."

C. M. Sorenson: That expression has been canceled. That is not our position.

A. G. Daniells: It is not our position, and it is not right that the spirit of prophecy is the only safe interpreter of the Bible. That is a false doctrine, a false view. It will not stand. Why, my friends what would all the people have done from John's day down to the present if there were no way to understand the Bible except through the writings of the spirit of prophecy? It is a terrible position to take! That is false, it is error. It is positively dangerous! What do those people do over in Roumania? We have hundreds of Sabbath-keepers there who have not seen a book on the spirit of prophecy. What do these people in China do? Can't they understand this Book only as we get the interpretation through the spirit of prophecy and then take it to them? That is heathenish!

(*Spectrum*, op. cit., p. 30, 31).

The problem with the ebb and flow of this discussion is that much of that which was stated was true, but other words downgraded the Spirit of Prophecy. It is true that the Bible, rightly understood, is its own interpreter. It is equally true, however, that God in His great love and mercy, knowing the degeneracy of the Christian faith, often used Sister White to highlight matters in Scripture which otherwise would have escaped our dull minds. The assistance of the Spirit of Prophecy in this respect cannot be underestimated. Her prophetic insights are even more significant in these days of infidelity and apostasy than were the prophetic utterances of the Old Testament prophets in their era. Without her ministry the Seventh-day Adventist Church would never have developed the cohesive- Biblical platform of truth which is the greatest body of belief ever imparted to sinners.

In the Old Testament era, the Old Testament canon of Scripture, too, was its own interpreter. But God inspired the New Testament writers to elucidate matters which had been hidden under the trash of human traditions by the Jewish Church. Thus the apostles frequently plucked many statements from the Old Testament and revealed their timely relevance as Messianic prophecies. We instance some examples:

> [12]Now when Jesus had heard that John was cast into prison, he departed into Galilee; [13]And leaving Nazareth, he came and dwelt in Capernaum, which is upon the sea coast, in the borders of Zabulon and Nephthalim: [14]That it might be fulfilled which was spoken by Esaias the prophet, saying, [15]The land of Zabulon, and the land of Nephthalim, by the way of the sea, beyond Jordan, Galilee of the Gentiles; [16]The people which sat in darkness saw great light; and to them which sat in the region and shadow of death light is sprung up. (Matthew 4:12-16) – See Isaiah 9:1, 2.

> [16]When the even was come, they brought unto him many that were possessed with devils: and he cast out the spirits with his word, and healed all that were sick: [17]That it might be fulfilled which was spoken by Esaias the prophet, saying, Himself took our infirmities, and bare our sicknesses. (Matthew 8:16, 17) – See Isaiah 53:4.

> [23]He that hateth me hateth my Father also. [24]If I had not done among them the works which none other man did, they had not had sin: but now have they both seen and hated both me and my Father. [25]But this cometh to pass, that the word might be fulfilled that is written in their law, They hated me without a cause. (John 15:23-25) – See Psalm 35:19; 63:4.

This precedent appears to have been lost upon the minds of those gathered at the 1919 Bible Conference. Sister White was called to a similar work at the time of the Second Coming as were the apostles at the First Coming.

Further, there are many pieces of information concerning the Old Testament era, found only in the Old Testament, just as God's last-day prophet has expanded our knowledge of Old and New Testament history. We cite three New Testament contributions to Old Testament history as examples of many.

The New Testament informs us that Moses was forty years old when he killed the Egyptian task-master. (Acts 7:22-24). The New Testament reveals that Enoch prophesied concerning the Second Coming. (Jude 1:14). Finally, Paul revealed that Abraham believed God would have raised Isaac from the dead after he had been sacrificed. (Hebrews 11:19). None of these facts appear in the Old Testament. There are many more additions to Old Testament history found in the New Testament.

22 Doubts and More Doubts

It must not be thought that the doubts expressed by the General Conference President and many others at the 1919 Bible Conference concerning the reliability of the Spirit of Prophecy went by without protest. C. L. Benson stood out as a man who attempted to hold the line. He clearly supported the divine veracity of the Spirit of Prophecy. He demonstrated more courage in expressing disagreement with the position taken by Elder Daniells than many others. C. L. Benson was constrained to remark:

> I have felt very much concerned along the same line; and the question that has raised itself in my own mind goes a little further than has been brought up here; but it seems to me it is almost a logical step. That is this: If there are such uncertainties with reference to our historical position, and if the Testimonies are not to be relied on to throw a great deal of light upon our historical positions, and if the same is true with reference to our theological interpretation of texts, then how can we consistently place implicit confidence in the direction that is given with reference to our educational problems, and our medical school, and even our denominational organization? If there is a definite spiritual leadership in these things, then how can we consistently lay aside the Testimonies or partially lay them aside when it comes to the prophetic and historic side of the message? and place these things on the basis of research work? That question is in my mind, and I am confident that it is in the minds of others.
> (Transcript of 1919 Bible Conference, *Spectrum*, Vol 10, No. 1, p. 46).

Brother Waldorf supported C. L. Benson's position. He had previously cited three rivers which together unite to provide a foundation of truth. Referring to this illustration, Brother Waldorf said in agreement,

> That is in my mind. That is why I brought out that illustration on the blackboard this morning – those three rivers, history, spirit of prophecy, and the Bible. (*Ibid*).

Once more, throwing in the red herring of verbal inspiration, J. N. Anderson demonstrated a less-than-confident view of the accuracy of the writings of Sister White upon historical matters. In his response to Brethren Benson and Waldorf, he spoke with some passion:

> I thought when we dismissed the subject the other day the main question was how we as teachers should deal with this question when we stand before our students. I think we have come to quite a unanimous opinion about this matter among ourselves here, and we stand pretty well together, I should say, as to what position the Testimonies occupy – their authority and their relation to the Bible, and so

on, – but the question in my mind, and in the mind of some others, too, I think, is What shall we as teachers do when we stand before our classes and some historical questions come up, such as we have spoken of here, where we have decided that Sister White's writings are not final? We say there are many historical facts that we believe scholarship must decide, that Sister White never claimed to be final on the historical matters that appear in her writings. Are we safe to tell that to our students? Or shall we hold it in abeyance? And can we hold something in the back of our head that we are absolutely sure about, and that most of the brethren stand with us on? – can we hold those things back and be true to ourselves? And furthermore, are we safe in doing it? Is it well to let our people in general go on holding to the verbal inspiration of the Testimonies? When we do that, aren't we preparing for a crisis that will be very serious someday? It seems to me that the best thing for us to do is to cautiously and very carefully educate our people to see just where we really should stand to be consistent protestants, to be consistent with the Testimonies themselves, and to be consistent with what we know we must do, as intelligent men, as we have decided in these meetings.

Of course these are not such big questions, because I do not teach along this line. Still, they do sometimes arise in my classes. But personally I am not concerned about it. I *am* concerned about the faith of the young men and women that come into our schools. They are to be our leaders, and I think these are the days when they should be given the very best foundation we can give them. We should give them the most sincere and honest beliefs that we have in our own hearts.

I speak with some feeling because it does come close to my convictions that something should be done here in this place, – here is where it can be done – to safeguard our people, to educate them and to bring them back and cause them to stand upon the only foundation that can ever be secure as we advance and progress. (*Ibid*).

Here we see that more than eighty years ago among our College teachers some held less-than-steadfast views on the Spirit of Prophecy. That Elder Daniells fanned this spirit of doubt led to the preparation of a generation of pastors and teachers graduating from our schools in the 1920's and 1930's who provided lip-service to faith in the *Testimonies for the Church*, but who harbored doubts in their hearts. Such a situation was exacerbated when, in the 1930's, the General Conference agreed to accept secular-regional accreditation of our Colleges. The roots of the events which followed the Barnhouse-Martin Dialogue may be traced back at least to the end of the second decade of the twentieth century.

Providentially, in response to J. N. Anderson's ruse of raising the almost irrelevant issue of verbal inspiration, C. L. Taylor brought forth a balance on this issue. We repeat that which we cited in the previous chapter:

With regard to the verbal inspiration of the Testimonies, I would say that I have heard more about it here in one day than ever before in my life. I think we have

> made a great big mountain of difficulty to go out and fight against. I do not believe that our people generally believe in the verbal inspiration of the Testimonies. I think that the general idea of our people is that the Testimonies are the writings of a sister who received light from God. As to verbal inspiration, I think they have a very ill-defined idea. I think they believe that in some way God gave her light, and she wrote it down, and they do not know what verbal inspiration means.
>
> (Ibid).

It is almost certain that C. L. Taylor's words were more in accord with the truth than that of the previous speaker, but he did sound somewhat patronizing to the laity. We believe they were not as ignorant of the subject of verbal inspiration as C. L. Taylor inferred.

Continuing his remarks, C. L. Taylor, too, joined the chorus of those who placed their own judgments above divine revelations:

> But I do see a great deal in the question Professor Benson raised, and that is if we must lay aside what Sister White has said interpreting history, or what we might call the philosophy of history, as unreliable, and also lay aside as unreliable expositions of scripture, the only natural conclusion for me, and probably for a great many others, would be that the same authorship is unreliable regarding organization, regarding pantheism, and every other subject that she ever treated on; – that she *may* have told the truth, but we had better get all the historical data we can to see whether she told the truth or not. That is something I would like to hear discussed. I do not believe we shall get to the foundation of the question unless we answer Professor Benson's question. (Ibid).

M. E. Kern pointed out the double talk of some at the Conference. T h i s strategy was later to be used in a masterly fashion when the New Theology errors made serious inroads into our church. Today many influential thought leaders in our church have raised tergiversation to a well-honed art. We quote the words of M. E. Kern:

> I am not so sure that some of the brethren are right in saying that we are all agreed on this question. I came in here the other day for the first time to attend the Conference, and I would hear the same man in the same talk say that we could not depend on this historical data that was given in the spirit of prophecy, and then assert his absolute confidence in the spirit of prophecy and in the Testimonies. And then a little further along there would be something else that he would not agree with. For instance, the positive testimony against butter was mentioned, and he explained that there are exceptions to that. Later he would again say, "I have absolute confidence in the inspiration of the spirit of prophecy." The question is, What is the nature of inspiration? How can we feel, and believe and *know* that there is an inconsistency there, – something that is not right, – and yet believe that the spirit of prophecy is inspired? Do you get the question? (Ibid).

M. E. Kern continued:

> That is the difficulty we have in explaining this to young people. We may have confidence ourselves, but it is hard to make others believe it if we express this more liberal view. I can see how some might take advantage of this liberal view and go out and eat meat every meal, and say that part of the Testimonies is not reliable. (*Ibid*).

The speaker continued in his positive fashion illustrating his point with a personal experience:

> Brother Benson's question is to the point. We had a council here a few weeks ago, and we laid down pretty straight some principles of education, and also some technicalities of education, and we based our conclusions on the authority of the spirit of prophecy, as it was written. Now we come to those historical questions, and we say, "Well, Sister White was mistaken about that, and that needs to be revised." The individual who did not quite see the points that we made at the educational council may say, "Well, possibly Sister White is wrong about the influence of universities," and it is hard to convince him that she was right, perhaps. I want, somehow, to get on a consistent basis myself.
>
> Many years ago I was in a meeting where Dr. Kellogg and others were considering a business matter. Dr. Kellogg there took a position exactly contrary to something Sister White had said. When asked how he explained what she had said, he replied that she had been influenced to say it. He was running down the Testimonies there. A short time after that I read one of his articles in the paper, in which he was laying down the law on the basis of the Testimonies. That made me lose my confidence in Dr. Kellogg. On one point that he did not agree with, he said she had been influenced. Then he took this other thing that pleased him and he said it was from the Lord. Perhaps he thought one was from the Lord and the other was not. But we certainly do have difficulty in showing the people which is human and which is divinely inspired. (*Ibid*, pp. 48, 49).

Significantly Elder Kern later became a General Conference Secretary (1933) and 1937-1943 was first Dean of the Seventh-day Adventist Theological Seminary.

It was not long before the forces of doubt were reawakened by W. H. Wakeham:

> There is a real difficulty, and we will have it to meet. We may say that the people do not believe in the verbal inspiration of the Testimonies. Perhaps technically they do not know what it means. But that is not the question at all. They have accepted the Testimonies all over the country, and believe that every identical word that Sister White has written was to be received as infallible truth. We have that thing to meet when we get back, and it will be brought up in our classes just as sure as we stand here, because it has come to me over and over again in every class I have taught. It not only comes out in classes, but in the churches. I know we have a very delicate task before us if we meet the situation and do it in the way

the Lord wants it done. I am praying very earnestly for help as I go back to meet some of the things I know I am going to meet. (*Ibid*).

Long before Dr. Samuele Bacchiocchi made his 2002 attack in his e-mail Newsletter, dated July 7, 2002, on the dates 538 and 1798 as the boundaries of the 1260 day prophecy of Daniel 7:25, these dates were being questioned at the 1919 Bible Conference. (See *The Remnant Herald*, No. 75, September 2002, pp. 1194-1996 for evidence of Dr. Bacchiocci's position). Some, such as C. M. Sorenson and W. W. Prescott, were only prepared to accept Sister White's "philosophy of history," not her recorded historical details. This was equivalent to casting Scriptural history aside on the supposed grounds that it includes uninspired scribal errors in the two books of Kings and the two books of Chronicles, while accepting the philosophy of history in the Bible. Surely God can enlighten minds to select accurate secular history for inclusion in His sacred-inspired writings. Even C. L. Benson wavered on this matter. We quote these men's words:

> **C. M. Sorrenson:** Nobody has ever questioned Sister White's philosophy of history, so far as I know, – and I promise I have heard most of the questions raised about it, – along the line of the hand of God in human affairs and the way the hand of God has been manifested. The only question anybody has raised has been about minor details. Take this question as to whether 533 has some significance taken in connection with 538. She never set 533, but if there is a significance attached to it in human affairs, it certainly would not shut us out from using it, and that would not affect the 1260 years. Some people say antichrist is yet to come, and is to last for three and one-half literal years. If you change those positions, you will change the philosophy.
>
> **W. W. Prescott:** Do I understand Brother Benson's view is that such a statement as that in "Great Controversy," that the 1260 years began in 538 and ended in 1798, settles the matter infallibly?
>
> **C. L. Benson:** No, only on the preaching of doctrines in general. If she endorses the prophetic part of our interpretation, irrespective of details, then she endorses it.
>
> **W. W. Prescott:** Then that settles it as being a part of that philosophy.
>
> (*Ibid*, p. 54).

Other dangerous concepts were enunciated. We quote the words of H. C. Lacey by way of example. He reported of Elder Daniells that:

> Those who have not heard you [Elder Daniells], as we have here, and are taking the other side of the question, – some of them are deliberately saying that neither you nor Professor Prescott believe the Testimonies. For instance, I went out to Mt. Vernon [Academy, Ohio] and I met the graduating class there, and when the exercises were over, I had a private talk with three or four of those young people,

and they told me that they certainly understood that our General Conference men down here – they did not mean me or Brother Sorenson – did not believe the Testimonies. (*Ibid*, p. 37).

H. C. Lacey shortly after proposed another dangerous position on the Spirit of Prophecy:

> In our estimate of the spirit of prophecy, isn't its value to us more in the spiritual light it throws into our own hearts and lives than in the intellectual accuracy in historical and theological matters? Ought we not to take those writings as the voice of the Spirit of our hearts, instead of as the voice of the teacher to our heads? And isn't the final proof of the spirit of prophecy its spiritual value rather than its historical accuracy? (*Ibid*, p. 38).

H. C. Lacey here evidenced a weakness shared by not a few attendees at the Bible Conference. He commenced his view with the words, "In our estimate." There was far too much dependence upon men's opinions and too little upon God's. Each delegate appeared to be fueling the doubts of other delegates and in turn reinforcing their own doubts. It seems that the dangerous "group-think" mentality was permitted to take possession of the minds of the attending delegates. Sadly it was the doubters who molded the final consensus.

23 The Doubts Mount

God's attitude to those who spread doubt is seen in the case of Elder Hull. Over half a century prior to the 1919 Bible Conference, Sister White had written plainly to this ordained minister of the Seventh-day Adventist Church. Her letter was dated November 5, 1862. It was a lengthy epistle which may be read in full in *Testimonies for the Church*, Vol. 1, pp. 426-433. We quote a small portion of this letter:

> God is displeased that any of His people who have known the power of His grace should talk their doubts, and by thus doing make themselves a channel for Satan to transmit his suggestions to other minds. A seed of unbelief and evil sown is not readily rooted up. Satan nourishes it every hour, and it flourishes and becomes strong. A good seed sown needs to be nourished, watered, and tenderly cared for; because every poisonous influence is thrown about it to hinder its growth and cause it to die.
>
> Satan's efforts are more powerful now than ever before, for he knows that his time to deceive is short. Brother Hull, I saw that you had injured yourself greatly by exposing your weakness and telling your doubts to those who are Satan's agents. You have been deceived by soft words and fair speeches, and have exposed yourself in a most reckless manner to the attacks of Satan. How could you thus wound yourself and reproach God's word? You have recklessly rushed upon Satan's battleground, and it is no marvel that your mind is so stupid and unfeeling. Already has Satan through his agents poisoned the atmosphere you breathe; already have evil angels telegraphed to his agents upon earth in regard to the course to be pursued toward you. And this is one whom God has called to stand between the living and the dead; this is one of the watchmen stationed upon the walls of Zion to tell the people the time of night. A heavy responsibility rests upon you. If you go down, you will not go alone; for Satan will employ you as his agent to lead souls to death.
>
> I saw that angels of God were looking sorrowfully toward you. They had left your side and were turning mournfully away, while Satan and his angels were grinning in exultation over you. If you had yourself battled with your doubts and not encouraged the devil to tempt you, by talking out your unbelief and loving to dwell upon it, you would not have attracted the fallen angels about you in such numbers. But you chose to talk your darkness; you chose to dwell upon it; and the more you talk and dwell upon it, the darker and darker you grow.
>
> (*Testimonies for the Church*, Vol. 1, pp. 429, 430).

What a warning this is to those who choose to doubt the inspired words of the Spirit of Prophecy! Such play games with their own eternal destiny. They encourage the presence of satanic angels about them and destroy the faith of others.

Even Elder F. M. Wilcox, thinking he was supporting the Spirit of Prophecy, did not express full confidence in Sister White's writings. He said:

> I would like to ask, Brother Daniells, if it could be accepted as a sort of rule that Sister White might be mistaken in details, but in the general policy and instruction she was an authority.
> (Transcript of 1919 Bible Conference, *Spectrum*, Vol. 10, No. 1, p. 53).

Such a view opens the way for Satan to insinuate further and ever more doubts into the hearts of God's people.

C. A. Shull, a College professor, added his doubting concepts to the discussion:

> Just how shall we use the Testimonies in the class room? What shall be our attitude toward them in the line of history, especially? Before I knew that there was any statement in the spirit of prophecy regarding the experience of John, I stated to the class that there was a tradition that John had been thrown into a caldron of boiling oil, and a student immediately produced that statement in the Testimonies that John *was* thrown into the boiling oil. Now, I want to know, was she given a divine revelation that John was thrown into a vat of boiling oil?
>
> Now another question, on the taking of Babylon. Mrs. White in the spirit of prophecy mentions that Babylon was taken according to the historian, by the turning aside of the waters. Modern scholarship says it was not taken that way. What should be our attitude in regard to such things? (*Ibid*, pp 34, 35).

During this entire Conference Elder Daniells was in a prime position to counter the doubts expressed by the college professors and others. He had worked alongside Sister White in Australia and later for fourteen years as General Conference President. These were the last years of her life. He had been very close to her. On numbers of occasions during her lifetime Elder Daniells had publicly expressed faith in her testimonies. But now, four years after her death, he seemed to backtrack on those statements. Instead of strengthening the professors, he fostered their doubts, thus ensuring that our colleges would be less than bastions of support for the wonderful guidance God in His love has given to His Remnant Church. Today, few Seventh-day Adventist college professors establish the writings of Sister White in the hearts of the students. Indeed, rather are they ignored or spurned. The result is a ministry open to the buffetings of Satan. These professors also inevitably treat Scripture lightly.

We quote some of Elder Daniells' comments as recorded in the transcript of the 1919 Bible Conference, repeating one already quoted:

> It is not our position, and it is not our right that the spirit of prophecy is the only safe interpreter of the Bible. That is a false doctrine, a false view. It will not stand.

> Why, my friends what would all the people have done from John's day down to the present if there were no way to understand the Bible except through the writings of the spirit of prophecy! It is a terrible position to take! That is false, it is error. It is positively dangerous. (*Ibid*, p. 30).
>
> I have never gone to her writings, and taken the history that I found in her writings, as the positive statement of history regarding the fulfillment of prophecy. (*Ibid*, p. 34).
>
> I have never understood that Sister White undertook to settle historical questions. (*Ibid*, p. 35).
>
> So when it comes to those historical questions about the taking of Babylon, I think this, brethren, we ought not to let every little statement in history that we find lead us away from the spirit of prophecy. You know historians contradict each other, don't you? (*Ibid*, p. 36).

A number of attendees questioned Sister White's account of the Medo-Persian capture of Babylon. Sister White had written,

> Even while he and his nobles were drinking from the sacred vessels of Jehovah, and praising their gods of silver and of gold, the Medes and the Persians, having turned the Euphrates out of its channel, were marching into the heart of the unguarded city. (*Prophets and Kings*, p. 531).

Some latter-day historians have ignorantly questioned the diversion of the Euphrates River. But Sister White's account was historically correct. The Greek historian of the fifth century B.C., Herodotus, (born about 484 BC) was a credible historian. It has been said of him:

> He was neither naïve nor easily credulous. It is this that makes ... his work ... of such historical importance.
> (*Encyclopaedia Britannica*, 1963 edition, Vol. 11, p. 512B).

Herodotus recorded the capture of Babylon in terms which support Sister White's account:

> Cyrus went 'drawing off the river by a canal into the lake [the artificial lake said to have been made earlier by Queen Nitocris], which was till now a marsh, he made the stream to sink till its former channel could be forded. When this happened, the Persians who were posted with this intent made their way into Babylon by the channel of the Euphrates, which had now sunk about to the height of the middle of a man's thigh. Now if the Babylonians had known beforehand or learnt what Cyrus was planning, they would have suffered the Persians to enter the city and brought them to a miserable end; for then they would have shut all the gates that opened on the river and themselves mounted up on to the walls that ran along the river banks and so caught their enemies as in a trap. But as it was, the Persians

were upon them unawares, and by reason of the great size of the city – so say those who dwell there – those in the outer parts of it were overcome, yet the dwellers in the middle part knew nothing of it; all this time they were dancing and making merry at a festival ... till they learnt the truth but too well. [Compare Da. 5:1-4, 30; Jer. 50:24; 51:31, 32.] Thus was Babylon then for the first time taken.'
>
> (Herodotus Book 1, pp. 191, 192 as quoted *Insight on the Scriptures*, International Bible Students Association, New York, 1988, Vol. 1, p. 567).

Xenophon (430 BC – 355 BC), renowned Greek historian, also confirmed Sister White's account of the fall of Babylon:

> Xenophon's account differs somewhat as to details but contains the same basic elements as that of Herodotus. Xenophon describes Cyrus as deeming it nearly impossible to storm Babylon's mighty walls and then goes on to relate his laying siege to the city, diverting the waters of the Euphrates into trenches and, while the city was in festival celebration, sending his forces up the riverbed past the city walls. The troops under the command of Gobryas and Gadatas caught the guards unawares and gained entrance through the very gates of the palace. In one night 'the city was taken and the king slain,' and the Babylonian soldiers occupying the various citadels surrendered the following morning. – *Cyropaedia*, VII, v. 33; compare Jer. 51:30. (*Ibid*).

There were no grounds for equivocation on this matter. More faith was placed in the views of secular historians living more than two thousand years after the event than in divine inspiration.

At least Elder W. W. Prescott admitted that:

> It is interesting to know that even a higher critic like George Adam Smith agrees with Herodotus on that. (*Spectrum*, op. cit., p. 38).

Who was George Adam Smith? He was Sir George Adam Smith, M.A., D.D., LL.D., Litt.D. (1856-1942). Sir George was a Bible scholar and educator. His possession of a Master of Arts and three doctorates in Divinity, Law and Letters demonstrated that he was no mean scholar. He was Principal and Vice Chancellor of the University of Aberdeen, Scotland and formerly Professor of Old Testament language and literature and theology at the Free Church College, Glasgow, our research discovered. Although a higher critic he certainly was correct in his reliance upon Herodotus' history concerning the method of the fall of Babylon. This he wrote in his book, *The Book of Isaiah*, Vol. 2 in Vol. 11 of *The Expositor's Bible*, A. C. Armstrong and Son, New York, 1908.

It would appear that not one of the attendees at the Conference pointed out that in 1911 Sister White wrote:

> While writing the manuscript of "Great Controversy," I was often conscious of the presence of the angels of God. And many times the scenes about which I was writing were presented to me anew in visions of the night, so that they were fresh and vivid in my mind. (*Selected Messages*, Vol. 3, p. 112).

Again Elder Daniells cast doubt upon Sister White's use of historical data:

> I never understood that she put infallibility into the historical quotations.
> (Transcript of the 1919 Bible Conference, *Spectrum*, op. cit., p. 38).

Answering H. C. Lacey's question:

> And isn't the final proof of the spirit of prophecy its spiritual value rather than its historical accuracy? (*Ibid*)

Elder Daniells replied:

> Yes, I think so. (*Ibid*).

Elder Daniells at times used extreme examples to diminish the health message. Referring to a Brother Olson who was sent to Hammerfest, Norway, north of the Arctic Circle, he recounted how Brother Olson almost starved to death by rigidly pursuing a vegetarian diet consisting largely of potatoes. By use of this illustration, Elder Daniells stated:

> Take this question of health reform. It is well known from the writings themselves and from personal contact with Sister White, and from common sense, that in traveling and in knowledge of different parts of the world, that the instruction set forth in the Testimonies was never intended to be one great wholesale blanket regulation for people's eating and drinking, and it applies to various individuals according to their physical condition and according to the situation in which they find themselves. (*Ibid*, p. 40).

Again Elder Daniells diminished the *Testimonies*:

> That is the way a lot of things got into the Testimonies. They were many of them written for individuals in various states of health, and then they were hurried into the Testimonies without proper modification. That is not to say that they are false things, but it is to say that they do not apply to every individual the world over alike. (*Ibid*, p. 42).

Elder Daniells disparaged Sister White's book, *Sketches from the Life of Paul*, a book from which we have personally received much blessing. He asserted that:

> Just one more thought: Now you know something about that little book, "The Life of Paul." You know the difficulty we got into about that. We could never claim inspiration in the whole thought and makeup of the book, because it has been thrown aside because it was badly put together. (*Ibid*, p. 34).

Those who have read the pages of this book and benefited from it as we have, would dispute Elder Daniell's negative assessment.

Later in the discussions, Elder Daniells threw further doubts on this book. Referring to Sister White's failure to use what is now the accepted means of designated reference for quoted material in writing *Sketches from the Life of Paul*, Elder Daniells asserted:

> She did not claim that that was all revealed to her and written word for word under the inspiration of the Lord. There I saw the manifestation of the human in these writings. Of course I could have said this, and I did say it, that I wished a different course had been taken in the compilation of the books. If proper care had been exercised, it would have saved a lot of people from being thrown off the track. (*Ibid*, p. 52).

Sketches from the Life of Paul was published in 1883. Sister White did quote some passages from William Conybeare's and J. S. Howson's book, *Life and Epistles of St.Paul*. These, of course, accorded with the revelations Sister White had received. During the 1919 discussions, the false rumour that the publishers of Conybeare's and Howson's book, threatened litigation, on the grounds that in her work she plagiarized their book, were given currency. There was absolutely no foundation for this rumor. Conybeare's and Howson's book was first published in England in 1851, 1852. British authors could not receive copyright protection in the United States for their books prior to 1891, eight years **after** Sister White published *Sketches from the Life of Paul*. This 1891 protection was accorded by an Act of March 3, 1891, 26, Stat. 1106 and Presidential proclamation of July 1, 1891, 27 Stat, 981. Elder Francis David Nichol (1897-1966), editor of The Review and Herald, 1945-1966, gathered this information from,

> Louis C. Smith, senior attorney, Copyright Division, Library of Congress, Washington, D.C.
>
> (F. D. Nichol, *Ellen G. White and Her Critics*, Review and Herald Publishing Association, Washington, D.C., 1951, Footnote, p. 455).

Thus, it was no surprise that forty-one years after Sister White published *Sketches from the Life of Paul*, the American publishers of Conybeare's and Howson's book, Thomas Y. Crowell of New York, responding to a letter written by Brother C. E. Holmes, stated:

> Your letter of Jan. 15th received. We publish Conybeare's LIFE AND EPISTLES OF THE APOSTLE PAUL but this is not a copyrighted book and we would have no legal grounds for action against your book and we do not think that we have ever raised any objection or made any claim such as you speak of.
>
> We shall be very glad to see the printed matter to which you refer.
>
> (Letter written to Mr. C. E. Holmes of Oak Park, Illinois, by Thomas Y. Crowell Company, dated January 18, 1924).

Even Elder Daniells conceded that Sister White, when appraised of the formal literary means of identifying quotations, stated:

> Why, I didn't know about quotations and credits. My secretary should have looked after that, and the publishing house should have looked after it.
>
> (Transcript of the 1919 Bible Conference, *Spectrum*, op. cit., p. 52).

The Doubts Mount

With subtle questions Elder Daniells pursued his doubts:

> And should we be surprised when we know that the instrument was fallible, and that the general truths as she says, were revealed, then aren't we prepared to see mistakes? (*Spectrum*, op. cit., p. 51).

Before evaluating Sister White's use of the non-inspired writings of historians and others, let us not forget that Biblical writers also made use of secular material when it accorded with truth:

> For in him we live, and move, and have our being; as certain also of your own poets have said, For we are also his offspring. (Acts 17:28).

Incorporated into Scripture, the words of that uninspired pagan Athenian poet became divine truth. We must never forget that numerous atheists have discovered divine truths. The true fact that $1 + 1 = 2$, as we have previously mentioned, has been discovered by countless millions who know not God.

Many thousands of divine truths concerning God's creative works have been discovered by evolutionary scientists, who spurn the Creator of those laws of physics and biology.

In Sister White's book *Ministry of Healing*, published in 1905, she boldly stated that

> Tobacco is a slow, insidious, but most malignant poison. (p. 327).

We remind the reader that this fact came to her through divine inspiration, though such a statement was considered to be absolute nonsense by medical scientists in her day. Even forty years later one of America's most prestigious medical journals, *The Journal of the American Medical Association*, (JAMA), asserted that there was no scientific evidence that the smoking of tobacco caused lung cancer. Who was correct? Was it eminent medical professors or a third-grade-educated woman, divinely inspired?

Brethren and sisters, it is time to:

> Believe in the LORD your God, so shall ye be established; believe his prophets, so shall ye prosper. (2 Chronicles 20:20).

Even Elder Daniells realized that his words disparaging the work of Sister White, left him open to the charge of insinuating doubts into the minds of the attendees, for twice he sought confirmation from the compliant attendees that he was not doing that which manifestly he was.

> Now, brethren, I want to ask you honestly if there is a man here who has had doubt created in your mind from my attitude and the positions I have taken? [VOICES: No! No!] Or is there one of you that thinks I am shaky on the Testimonies? – I will not say that […] thinks my position is not just right, for you might not agree with me, but from what I have said, is there a tendency to lead

> you to believe that I am shaky, and that some time I will help to get you away from the Testimonies? [Several decided no's were heard.]
>
> (*Spectrum*, op. cit., p. 37. – […] in the quotation indicated that the stenographer could not understand the word).

> What I want to know is this, brethren, Does my position appear to be of such a character that you would be led to think I am shaky? [VOICES: No!] If you think it, just say it right out! I do not want to do that, but I have to be honest, – I can not camouflage in a thing like this. (*Ibid*).

The 1919 Bible Conference stands as a most significant event in the history of the gathering apostasy within our church. While its deliberations were secreted away for fifty-five years, nevertheless the insidious undermining of the inestimably valuable words of the Spirit of Prophecy undoubtedly proceeded unabated in the classrooms of our Colleges, sometimes simply by passively ignoring this source of inspiration, on other occasions by actively denying its value.

Some of the most influential educators in our Colleges attended the 1919 Bible Conference. An agonizing question persists: How did the skepticism pervading that conference impact upon the teaching of the College students? Many of the College students of the post-1919 era rose to positions of influence in later years as they were appointed to high office within the denominational organization. The seeds of today's rejection of the Spirit of Prophecy were sown in 1919.

In view of the covert undermining of the writings of the Spirit of Prophecy in the first half of the twentieth century, it is little wonder that Sister White set forth a contrapuntal statement of major significance.

> We have far more to fear from within than from without. The hindrances to strength and success are far greater from the church itself than from the world.
>
> (*Selected Messages*, Vol. 1, p. 122).

When we studied education at the Australasian Missionary College (now Avondale College) in 1951 and 1952[1] the lone study of the counsels of the Spirit of Prophecy on this crucial subject was advice that we should read through the book *Education* before the conclusion of the academic year. This, to our shame, we did not undertake, on the pathetic grounds that the material in the book was not to be examined. Colin only studied all the counsels of the Spirit of Prophecy on education when he was appointed Chairman of the Education Department at Avondale College in 1965 and found that no one else in the Department desired to teach the subject of Seventh-day Adventist education. It has proven to be a great blessing to him in the subsequent forty

---

[1] In 1951, 1952 the elementary teachers' training course consisted of two years. Academic years commenced in February and concluded in November in Australia.

years of his work in education. We also studied the Pauline Epistles at College without receiving any significant reference to Sister White's inspired insights.

With the reduced emphasis upon the value of the Spirit of Prophecy, despite the work of not a few College lecturers faithful to Sister White's inspired writings, the introduction of the New Theology and the explosion of the Omega of Apostasy into our church was a time-bomb awaiting the inevitable moment to discharge its pernicious energy. Today those devastating explosions have fearfully damaged our church and torn it apart.

Elder Daniells' words may have been phrased in the most noble sentiments, but they resonate doubt down to this present day:

> Now, as I have studied it these years since I was thrown into the controversy at Battle Creek, I have endeavoured to ascertain the truth and then be true to the truth. I do not know how to do it except that way. It will never help me, or help the people, to make a false claim to evade some trouble. I know we have difficulties here, but let us dispose of some of the main things first. Brethren, are we going to evade difficulties or help out the difficulties by taking a false position? [Voices: No!] Well, then let us take an honest, true position, and reach our end somehow, because I never will put up a false claim to evade something that will come up a little later on. That is not honest and it is not Christian, and so I take my stand there. (*Ibid*, pp. 50, 51).

Sister White's counsel regarding doubting inspired writings should have been thoroughly accepted at the 1919 Bible Conference. That it was not, was a portent of the destruction of faith evident in our midst in the almost universal acceptance of the tenets of Evangelical Protestants among us today.

> By faith we may look to the hereafter and grasp the pledge of God for a growth of intellect, the human faculties uniting with the divine, and every power of the soul being brought into direct contact with the Source of light. We may rejoice that all which has perplexed us in the providences of God will then be made plain, things hard to be understood will then find an explanation; and where our finite minds discovered only confusion and broken purposes, we shall see the most perfect and beautiful harmony. "Now we see through a glass, darkly; but then face to face: now I know in part; but then shall I know even as also I am known." 1 Corinthians 13:12. (*Steps to Christ*, p. 112, 113).

24 *The Great Controversy* Attacked

Sister White wrote four editions of *The Great Controversy* in her lifetime. All possessed different titles. These were:

1. 1858 - *The Great Controversy Between Christ and His Angels, and Satan and His Angels*. (This book is generally known as *Spiritual Gifts*, Volume I).
2. 1884 - *The Great Controversy Between Christ and Satan From the Destruction of Jerusalem to the End of the Controversy*. (Generally known as *Spirit of Prophecy*, Volume IV).
3. 1888 - *The Great Controversy between Christ and Satan During the Christian Dispensation*.
4. 1911 - *The Great Controversy Between Christ and Satan, The Conflict of the Ages in the Christian Dispensation*. (Known as The Conflict of the Ages, Volume V).

None of these four editions was identical. Each contained additional material, and, in some cases, portions of the previous editions were deleted.

These facts led to a disparaging of the inspiration of the 1911 edition of *The Great Controversy* at the 1919 Bible Conference. Elder W. W. Prescott was foremost in this matter. He told of his experience in contributing historical material to the 1911 edition of *The Great Controversy*. We quote Elder Prescott's words in full on this matter commencing with a statement by C. L. Benson to which Elder Prescott responded.

> **C.L. Benson:** Yes, in this way: I do not see how we can do anything else but set up our individual judgment if we say we will discount that, because we have something else that we think is better evidence. It is the same with education and the medical science.
>
> **W. W. Prescott:** You are touching exactly the experience through which I went, personally, because you all know that I contributed something toward the revision of "Great Controversy." I furnished considerable material bearing upon that question.
>
> **A. G. Daniells:** By request.
>
> **W. W. Prescott:** Yes, I was asked to do it, and at first I said, "No, I will not do it. I know what it means." But I was urged into it. When I had gone over it with W. C. White, then I said, "Here is my difficulty. I have gone over this and suggested changes that ought to be made in order to correct statements. These changes have been accepted. My personal difficulty will be to retain faith on those things that I

The Great Controversy *Attacked*

can not deal with on that basis." But I did not throw up the spirit of prophecy, and have not yet; but I have had to adjust my view of things. I will say to you, as a matter of fact, that the relation of those writings to this movement and to our work, is clearer and more consistent in my mind than it was then. But still you know what I am charged with. I have gone through the personal experience myself over the very thing that you speak of. If we correct it here and correct it there, how are we going to stand with it in the other places?

F. M. Wilcox: Those things do not involve the general philosophy of the book.

W. W. Prescott: No, but they did involve quite large details. For instance, before "Great Controversy" was revised, I was unorthodox on a certain point, but after it was revised, I was perfectly orthodox.

B. M. Sorenson: On what point?

W. W. Prescott: My interpretation was, (and I taught it for years in *The Protestant Magazine*) that Babylon stood for the great apostasy against God, which headed up in the papacy, but which included all minor forms, and that before we come to the end, they would all come under one. That was not the teaching of "Great Controversy." "Great Controversy" said that Babylon could not mean the Romish church, and I had made it mean that largely and primarily. After the book was revised, although the whole argument remained the same, it said that it could not mean the Roman Church *alone*, just that one word added.

F. M. Wilcox: That helped you out.

W. W. Prescott: Yes, but I told W. C. White I did not think anybody had any right to do that. And I did not believe anybody had any right to use it against me before or afterward. I simply went right on with my teaching.

J. W. Anderson: Would you not claim other portions of the book as on the same basis?

W. W. Prescott: No. I would refuse to do that. I had to deal with A. R. Henry over that question. He was determined to crush those men that took a wrong course concerning him. I spent hours with that man trying to help him. We were intimate in our work, and I used to go to his house and spend hours with him. He brought up this question about the authority of the spirit of prophecy and wanted me to draw the line between what was authoritative and what was not. I said, "Brother Henry, I will not attempt to do it, and I advise you not to do it. There is an authority in that gift here, and we must recognize it."

I have tried to maintain personal confidence in this gift in the church, and I use it and use it. I have gotten great help from those books, but I will tell you frankly that I held to that position on the question of Babylon for years when I knew it was exactly contrary to "Great Controversy," but I went on, and in due time I became orthodox. I did not enjoy that experience at all, and I hope you will not have to go through it. It means something.   (Transcript of 1919 Bible Conference)

Our search of *The Great Controversy* pinpointed the two passages to which Elder Prescott referred in his third last comment above. Notice the two passages side by side.

> The message of Revelation 14, announcing the fall of Babylon must apply to religious bodies that were once pure and have become corrupt. Since this message follows the warning of the judgment, it must be given in the last days; therefore it cannot refer to the Roman Church **alone**, for that church has been in a fallen condition for many centuries.
> (*The Great Controversy*, 1911 edition, page 383, emphasis added).

> The message of Revelation 14, announcing the fall of Babylon, must apply to religious bodies that were once pure and have become corrupt. Since this message follows the warning of the judgment, it must be given in the last days, therefore it cannot refer to the Roman Church, for that church has been in a fallen condition for many centuries.
> (*The Great Controversy*, 1888 edition, page 383, emphasis added).

Now here we notice three distinct alterations in the 1911 edition:
1. The comma after the word "Babylon" has been deleted in the 1911 edition.
2. The comma after "last days" in the 1888 edition is converted to a semicolon in the 1911 edition.
3. To "the Roman Church" in the 1888 edition, the word "alone" has been added in the 1911 edition.

Now we would draw the reader's attention to another passage in both books.

> The term **"Babylon"** is derived from **"Babel,"** and signifies confusion. It is employed in Scripture to designate the various forms of false or apostate religion. In Revelation 17 Babylon is represented as a woman – a figure which is used in the Bible as the symbol of a church, a virtuous woman representing a pure church, a vile woman an apostate church.
> (*The Great Controversy*, 1911 edition, page 381, emphasis added).

> The term **Babylon** is derived from **Babel**, and signifies confusion. It is employed in Scripture to designate the various forms of false or apostate religion. In Revelation 17 Babylon is represented as a woman, a figure which is used in the Bible as the symbol of a church, a virtuous woman representing a pure church, a vile woman an apostate church.
> (*The Great Controversy*, 1888 edition, page 381, emphasis added).

Here again we see three alterations, in this case each is a matter of punctuation. These alterations are:
1. To the first "Babylon" in this passage quotation marks have been added to the word in the 1911 edition. There are no such quotation marks in the 1888 edition.

2. The same difference is found with the word "Babel."
3. The comma after the first use of the word "woman" in the 1888 edition has been altered to a dash in the 1911 edition.

Of course no reasonable individual would see any issue of significance in these minor punctuation alterations. The purpose of punctuation is to assist the reader's understanding of what is written, by making the author's meaning abundantly clear.

But there is another matter in both the 1888 and 1911 editions of the last passage above which demands our attention. Both editions plainly state in exactly identical words that the term "Babylon" is employed in Scripture to designate the various forms of false or apostate religion. Here Sister White, in both passages, indicates that she well understood that the term "Babylon" referred to **the** various forms of false or apostate religions. She was not in the least doubt upon this matter.

On page 382 of both editions, less than one page before the passage on page 383 which caused such doubt and distress to Elder Prescott, Sister White had written:

> The woman **(Babylon)** of Revelation 17 is described as "arrayed in purple and scarlet color, and decked with gold and precious stones and pearls, having a golden cup in her hand full of abominations and filthiness:...and upon her forehead was a name written, **Mystery, Babylon the Great, the mother of harlots.**" Says the prophet: "I saw the woman **drunk** with the blood of the saints, and with the blood of the martyrs of Jesus." Babylon is further declared to be "that great city, which reigneth over the kings of the earth." **Revelation 17:4-6, 18.** The power that for so many centuries maintained despotic sway over the monarchs of Christendom is **Rome**.
>
> (*The Great Controversy*, 1911 edition, page 382, emphasis added, parenthesis in the original).

> The woman, Babylon, of Revelation 17, is described as "arrayed in purple and scarlet color, and decked with gold and precious stones and pearls, having a golden cup in her hand full of abominations and filthiness:...and upon her forehead was a name written, Mystery, Babylon the Great, the mother of harlots." Says the prophet: "I saw the woman drunken with the blood of the saints, and with the blood of the martyrs of Jesus." Babylon is further declared to be "that great city, which reigneth over the kings of the earth." The power that for so many centuries maintained despotic sway over the monarchs of Christendom, is Rome.
>
> (*The Great Controversy*, 1888 edition, page 382 – emphasis added).

Once more we observe alterations which made absolutely no difference to the message of the passage.

1. Commas are either side of the first use of "Babylon" in the passage in 1888, whereas in the 1911 edition "Babylon" has been placed in parenthesis.
2. "Mystery, Babylon the Great, the mother of harlots" is placed in normal type in 1888, but in italics in 1911.

3. The word "drunken" of 1888 was altered to "drunk" in 1911.
4. After "...the kings of the earth" in 1888, no Biblical reference was provided. In the 1911 edition the reference, Revelation 17:4-6, 18 is provided.

The last passage quoted above is most important for it demonstrated beyond all dispute that Sister White held absolutely no doubt that "Babylon [which] is ... the power that for so many centuries maintained despotic sway over the monarchs of Christendom is Rome." This page was the one previous to the page over which Elder Prescott evidenced such doubt.

If Elder Prescott had cared to examine these preceding pages he would have been convinced that Sister White held no doubt whatsoever that the term "Babylon" included the Papacy, the Roman Catholic Church in 1888. Further in the 1884 edition Sister White had written:

> In Revelation 17, Babylon is represented as a woman, a figure which is used in the Scriptures as the symbol of a church. A virtuous woman represents a pure church, a vile woman an apostate church. Babylon is said to be a harlot; and the prophet beheld her drunken with the blood of saints and martyrs. The Babylon thus described represents Rome, that apostate church which has so cruelly persecuted the followers of Christ. (*Spirit of Prophecy*, Vol. 4, p. 233).

Why then did the servant of the Lord omit the word "alone" from the 1888 edition? One conclusion some would draw is that this was either a typographical error or a mistake in typesetting. But this was not a typographical error.

In 1888 Sister White was placing emphasis on the fact that in the rejection of the 1844 message by the formerly noble Protestant churches, they joined Rome in becoming additional constituents of Babylon. The evidence for this fact is strong, for in the 1884 edition Sister White made this matter abundantly plain in the continuation of the paragraph quoted above. We quote the entire paragraph in order that Sister White's reason becomes apparent:

> In Revelation 17, Babylon is represented as a woman, a figure which is used in the Scriptures as the symbol of a church. A virtuous woman represents a pure church, a vile woman an apostate church. Babylon is said to be a harlot; and the prophet beheld her drunken with the blood of saints and martyrs. The Babylon thus described represents Rome, that apostate church which has so cruelly persecuted the followers of Christ. But Babylon the harlot is the mother of daughters who follow her example of corruption. Thus are represented those churches that cling to the doctrines and traditions of Rome and follow her worldly practices, and whose fall is announced in the second angel's message.
> (*Spirit of Prophecy*, Vol. 4, p. 233).

It is likely that Sister White consented to add the word "alone" in 1911 so that readers like Elder Prescott would have no excuse to misconstrue her correct meaning.

In the 1884 edition Sister White had written similarly to 1888 (see *Spirit of Prophecy*, Vol. 4, pp. 232, 233) PRIOR to her explanation that Rome was part of Babylon.

Elder Prescott manifestly possessed no valid grounds for his complaint.

Elder Prescott should have known a whole lot better, but as Brother Hilton Meyers (born 1919) demonstrated in his book, *The Dismantling of Adventism*, (New Millennium Publications, Morisset, New South Wales, Australia, 1996), Elder Prescott was a very faulted influence upon Seventh-day Adventism in a number of ways.

Let us examine the charge that, because of Sister White's use of secular historical material, her omission of certain passages from previous editions and the additions to other editions, these facts provided evidence that *The Great Controversy* was a book which united inspiration with faulty historical data. They most certainly did not! In 1911 Sister White wrote concerning the new edition of *The Great Controversy*:

> The book The Great Controversy, I appreciate above silver or gold, and I greatly desire that it shall come before the people. While writing the manuscript of The Great Controversy, I was often conscious of the presence of the angels of God. And many times the scenes about which I was writing were presented to me anew in visions of the night, so that they were fresh and vivid in my mind.
>
> (*Colporteur Ministry*, p. 128).

> Let there be an interest awakened in the sale of these books [*The Great Controversy* and *Patriarchs and Prophets*]. Their sale is essential; for they contain timely instruction from the Lord. They should be appreciated as books that bring to the people light that is especially needed just now. Therefore these books should be widely distributed. Those who make a careful study of the instruction contained in them, and will receive it as from the Lord, will be kept from receiving many of the errors that are being introduced. Those who accept the truths contained in these books will not be led into false paths. (*Ibid*, p. 130).

Sister White explained the reason why, on some occasions, she provided no references for her source of material.

> The great events which have marked the progress of reform in past ages are matters of history, well known and universally acknowledged by the Protestant world; they are facts which none can gainsay. This history I have presented briefly, in accordance with the scope of the book, and the brevity which must necessarily be observed, the facts having been condensed into as little space as seemed consistent with a proper understanding of their application. In some cases where a historian has so grouped together events as to afford, in brief, a comprehensive view of the subject, or has summarized details in a convenient manner, his words have been quoted; but in some instances no specific credit has been given, since the quotations are not given for the purpose of citing that writer as authority, but

because his statement affords a ready and forcible presentation of the subject. In narrating the experience and views of those carrying forward the work of reform in our own time, similar use has been made of their published works.

(The Great Controversy, pp. xi and xii).

Nevertheless, it must be remembered that in the 1911 edition

> The reader will find more than four hundred references to eighty-eight authors and authorities.
>
> (Statement made by Elder W. C. White before the General Conference Annual Council, October 3, 1911).

Let us once more dispel the claim that there was a sinister motive behind the removal of several pages from the 1884 edition of *The Great Controversy* when the 1888 edition was published. Elder W. C. White provided the rational reason for this omission. From Chapter XXVII, *The Snares of Satan* in the 1884 edition, several pages were deleted when the 1888 edition was prepared. For those studying this matter we suggest they read *Testimonies to Ministers* pages 472-475 where the omitted pages may be found in full. The very fact that these pages, deleted from the 1884 edition, were re-published (*Testimonies to Ministers* was published in 1923, thirty-five years after the publication of the 1888 edition) serves to provide evidence that that material was not discarded because it was deemed to be in error.

We quote Elder W. C. White's explanation for the omission:

> But when it was decided that *Great Controversy*, Volume IV [1884] should be republished in form for general circulation by subscription agents, Ellen G. White suggested that the pages be left out because of the likelihood that ministers of popular churches reading those statements would become angered and would array themselves against the circulation of the book.
>
> (Letter written by Elder W. C. White to Dr. L. E. Froom, dated January 8, 1928).

> In Great Controversy, Volume IV, published in 1885, [we are uncertain of the reason that Elder white consistently referred to the 1884 edition as being published in 1885] in the chapter "Snares of Satan," there are three pages or more of matter that was not used in the later editions, which were prepared to be sold to the multitudes by our canvassers. It is most excellent and interesting reading for sabbathkeepers, as it points out the work that Satan will do in persuading popular ministers and church members to elevate the Sunday Sabbath, and to persecute sabbathkeepers. [Currently found in Testimonies to Ministers, pp. 472-475.] It was not left out because it was less true in 1888 than in 1885, but because mother thought it was not wisdom to say these things to the multitudes to whom the book would be sold in future years....
>
> (Letter written by Elder W. C. White to the Publication Committee, July 25, 1911).

Sister White's assistant, Sister Marian Davis, provided further details of the reason for the omission of this passage from the 1888 edition. We are told that Sister White often explained her reasoning thus:

> These statements are true, and they are useful to our people; but to the general public, for whom this book is now being prepared, they are out of place. Christ said, even to his disciples, 'I have many things to say unto you, but ye cannot bear them now.' and Christ taught his disciples to be 'wise as serpents, and harmless as doves.' Therefore, as it is probable that more souls will be won to Christ by the book without this passage than with it, let it be omitted.
>
> (*Selected Messages*, Vol. 3, pp. 443, 444).

As we have previously noted, God provided Sister White not only with inspired information but with inspired wisdom.

Now let us turn to the accuracy of the history which Sister White chose for the 1911 edition of *The Great Controversy*. Elder White explained this matter cogently.

> Mother has never claimed to be authority on history. The things which she has written out, are descriptions of flashlight pictures and other representations given her regarding the actions of men, and the influence of these actions upon the work of God for the salvation of men, with views of past, present, and future history in its relation to this work. In connection with the writing out of these views, she has made use of good and clear historical statements to help make plain to the reader the things which she is endeavoring to present.   (*Ibid*, p. 437).

Once it is understood that Sister White carefully selected passages from historical authors which accorded with that which God had revealed to her in vision, the use of these secular works of history becomes explicable. Their incorporation in *The Great Controversy* in no wise diminished the inspiration of the book.

In the 1911 edition some of the historical quotations used in 1888 were omitted and replaced by others. Some have wrongly suggested that those alterations were made because the earlier quotations were found to contain items of historical error. The reason for these alterations is easy to understand. Once more, this reason provides a sensible ground for the alterations and provides no warrant to charge Sister White with having used faulted history in her preparation of *The Great Controversy* in 1888.

> When we came to go over this matter for the purpose of giving historical references, there were some quotations which we could not find. In some cases there were found other statements making the same point, from other historians. These were in books accessible in many public libraries. When we brought to mother's attention a quotation that we could not find, and showed her that there was another quotation that we had found, which made the same point, she said, 'use the one you can give reference to, so that the reader of the books, if he wishes

to go to the source and find it, can do so.' In that way some historical data have been substituted. *(Ibid*, p. 439).

Again we would emphasize the fact that Sister White was divinely guided in the writing and compilation of all editions of *The Great Controversy*. Concerning the preparation of the 1884 edition we have the first-hand testimony of her son:

> While mother was writing this book, many of the scenes were presented to her over and over again in visions of the night. The vision of the deliverance of God's people, as given in chapter XL, was repeated three times; and on two occasions, once at her home in Healdsburg and once at the St. Helena sanitarium, members of her family, sleeping in nearby rooms, were awakened from sleep by her clear, musical cry, "They come! They come!"
> (Letter written by Elder W. C. White to members of the Publication Committee, July 25, 1911).

Elder W. C. White's personal testimony of his first-hand knowledge of Sister White's writings is important.

> Regarding mother's writings, I have overwhelming evidence and conviction that they are the description and delineation of what God has revealed to her in vision, and where she has followed the description of historians or the exposition of Adventist writers, I believe that God has given her discernment to use that which is correct and in harmony with truth regarding all matters essential to salvation. If it should be found by faithful study that she has followed some expositions of prophecy which in some detail regarding dates we cannot harmonize with our understanding of secular history, it does not influence my confidence in her writings as a whole any more than my confidence in the Bible is influenced by the fact that I cannot harmonize many of the statements regarding chronology.
> (Statement made by Elder W. C. White to Elder William Walter Eastman (1867-1957), Publishing Department Secretary, Southwestern Union Conference, November 4, 1912).

In the first half of the twentieth century, Sister White's discussion of the amalgamation of man with animals understandably caused much skepticism among those who held doubts concerning Sister White's inspiration. Much has been made of the fact that Sister White presented this fact in the 1858 and 1884 editions of *The Great Controversy*, both of which were written for God's people, but omitted this material from the 1888 and 1911 editions, which were adapted for non-Seventh-day Adventists. The simple answer to this omission is that God in His wisdom guided Sister White to do so. This was once more wisdom, for in the state of human scientific knowledge at the time, this truth no doubt would have led to derision from unbelievers in Sister White's inspiration. In the book *Spiritual Gifts*, Sister White had written:

> But if there was one sin above another which called for the destruction of the race by the flood, it was the base crime of amalgamation of man and beast which defaced the image of God, and caused confusion everywhere. God purposed to destroy by a flood that powerful, long-lived race that had corrupted their ways before him. (*Spiritual Gifts*, Vol. 3, p. 64).

Even after the flood genetic mixing of man and animal occurred, for the descendants of Noah were clearly also acquainted with the techniques of genetic engineering, no doubt revealed to them by Noah's sons.

> Every species of animal which God had created were preserved in the ark. The confused species which God did not create, which were the result of amalgamation, were destroyed by the flood. Since the flood there has been amalgamation of man and beast, as may be seen in the almost endless varieties of species of animals, and in certain races of men. (*Ibid*, p. 75).

It must not be imagined that such men would appear as half-men, half-animal. Perhaps only a single animal gene was placed in the human embryo in order to increase one quality possessed by animals thought to benefit the human race. Such acts doubted God's creative wisdom.

We remind the reader that in the first half of the twentieth century genetic engineering was unknown. Even when American James D. Watson (born 1926) and Englishman Francis H. C. Crick (1918-2004) published their article in *Nature*, April 25, 1953, describing their discovery that the molecules of Deoxyribonucleic acid (DNA), the building blocks of genes, were constructed as a double helix, the potential for inserting foreign genes into the human body was not envisaged.

Even as late as 1962 the eminent Australian immunologist, Sir Macfarlane Burnett (born 1899), who had received the Nobel Prize for Physiology and Medicine in 1960, stated that

> DNA and molecular biology will have no influence on medicine.
> (*Scientific American*, April 2003, p. 50).

However, this opinion dramatically altered when, in 1968, restriction enzymes were discovered which led to the ability to sequence DNA. In the twenty-first century, modern man produced the first complete human genome. All the approximately thirty-thousand human genes are now known. Amalgamation of man and animals is now theoretically possible. Only ethical considerations prevent it. No longer is there reason to doubt Sister White's inspired statement concerning amalgamation.

The statement concerning amalgamation, published in *Spiritual Gifts*, Volume 3, page 64, was republished in *Spirit of Prophecy*, Volume 1, page 69. We cite this example in order to encourage God's people to never concede to the current ignorance of human knowledge and use this ignorance as a grounds to doubt the veracity of Sister White's writings. (See chapter entitled, "The

Amalgamation of Man and Beast" in this book for further discussion of this topic). It is time once more to remember God's counsel.

> Believe in the LORD your God, so shall ye be established; believe his prophets, so shall ye prosper. (2 Chronicles 20:20).

To believe God's prophets will save us embarrassment when time and again Sister White's doubted statements are verified by later increases in human knowledge. We believe that some doubted statements which cause puzzlement today will not be verified by humans until we sit in the Kingdom of Heaven at the feet of the Master Teacher. In the meantime let us possess full faith in Sister White's inspired writings.

We suggest that those interested in the subject of the differences in the four *Great Controversy* editions, read *Selected Messages*, Volume 3, pages 433-465. The reader will observe that not a few of these pages, fifteen in all, are devoted to Elder W. C. White's various letters to Dr. Le Roy Froom, written by Elder White in an effort to clear up Dr. Froom's doubts concerning the accuracy of certain Spirit of Prophecy statements.

We acknowledge that Dr. Froom did God's church a great service in his research presented in the volumes of *The Prophetic Faith of Our Fathers* and *The Conditional Faith of Our Fathers*. Nevertheless, his later work with Australian Pastor Roy Alan Anderson, and Welshman, Pastor W. E. Read in *Seventh-day Adventists Answer Questions on Doctrine* and his discarding of salient doctrines including important aspects of the sanctuary message, the full inspiration of Sister White and the doctrine of the human nature of Christ, was extremely detrimental to our faith. Dr. Froom used his book, *Movement of Destiny*, to further promote views contrary to Scripture and the Spirit of Prophecy. His divergence from truth paved the path to the New Theology. (See our book, *The Gathering Storm and The Storm Bursts*).

The 1919 General Conference Bible Conference was a watershed in Seventh-day Adventism. Behind closed doors church administrators and history professors set the course for both overt and covert attacks on the Spirit of Prophecy and the attempted wholesale destruction of our faith. It was a low point in Seventh-day Adventism.

In revealing these matters related to serious defects in doctrinal fidelity within the church organization, we do not do so in a desire to see self-supporting work walled off from the Seventh-day Adventist Church, like a medieval town. We most certainly are not standing behind the battlements contained within the city's walls, equipped with all the weaponry of war. Our desire is that self-supporting work will play its divinely appointed, elevated, high and holy role in returning the church back to truth and righteousness.

Part V
The Health Message

25 Sister White and Health

In her inspired writings on health Sister White expended a great portion of her time on pointing out the close relationship between health reform and the spiritual life. She described health reform as associated with the Third Angel's Message. Writing in Australia in 1896 in *Special Testimonies to Ministers and Workers*, Series A, No. 7, pp. 36-41, she stated:

> Can He be pleased when half the workers laboring in a place teach that the principles of health reform are as closely allied with the third angel's message as the arm is to the body, while their co-workers, by their practice, teach principles that are entirely opposite? This is regarded as a sin in the sight of God....

Further, the Lord's messenger, writing in St. Helena, California on August 20, 1902, declared:

> True religion and the laws of health go hand in hand. It is impossible to work for the salvation of men and women without presenting to them the need of breaking away from sinful gratifications, which destroy the health, debase the soul, and prevent divine truth from impressing the mind.
>
> (*Testimonies for the Church*, Vol. 7, p. 137).

Writing as early as 1867 God's end-time prophetess referred to those who were

> ... indifferent and have scarcely taken the first step in reform. There seems to be in them a heart of unbelief, and, as this reform restricts the lustful appetite, many shrink back. They have other gods before the Lord.
>
> (*Testimonies for the Church*, Vol. 1, p. 486).

Since the Health Message is such an integral part of our faith, providing us with physical and spiritual benefits, we should express no surprise that piercing attacks have been made upon it and Satan is doing his level best to destroy its impact upon God's people.

Dr. Ronald Numbers, a grandson of 1950-1954 General Conference President, Elder William Henry Branson (1887-1961), published his attacks upon Sister White's health messages. His book, *Prophetess of Health*, Harper and Row Publishers, New York, 1976, was written during his younger days as Assistant Professor of the History of Medicine and the History of Science at the University of Wisconsin.

His attitude to the servant of the Lord may be gauged from his Preface, written in November 1975, which stated in part:

> Ellen G. White, Seventh-day Adventist prophetess, ranks with the Mormon Joseph Smith [1805-1844], the Christian Scientist Mary Baker Eddy [1821-1910] and Charles Taze Russell [1852-1916] of the Jehovah's Witnesses as one of four nineteenth-century founders of a major American religious sect. Yet, outside her own church of two and a half million members, she is probably the least known. Her comparatively unsensational life and her church's reticence to expose her private papers to the scrutiny of critical scholars have contributed to this undeserved obscurity. (p. ix).

There is some evidence that Dr. Numbers' claim that there was a reticence to place her before those not of our faith is true. *The Encyclopaedia Britannica*, 1963 edition, possesses biographies of Joseph Smith, Mary Baker Eddy and Charles Russell but not of Sister White.

Even in the article on Adventism her name does not appear. This is not the fault of the editors for the entire article on Adventism was written by Pastor F. D. Nichol, the then editor of the *Review and Herald*. Only in the references supplied by Pastor Nichol is her name mentioned in the title of his book, *Ellen G. White and Her Critics*. In the 2000 edition of the Encyclopaedia, Sister White's name received a passing mention under *Adventist*.

However, Dr. Numbers must be faulted in placing Seventh-day Adventism under the pejorative category of a *sect*. If our opponents do so, we wear that title with honor, for we know the fierce opposition to truth in the hearts of many who claim to be Bible-believing Christians yet despise certain Bible truths which Seventh-day Adventists happily and correctly espouse.

In writing his book Dr. Numbers acknowledged the assistance he received from two of those called as experts by the South Pacific Division for the February 2-5, 2004 Summit. These were James R. Nix, then at Loma Linda, and Gary Land of Andrews University. Since Dr. Numbers did not reveal the tenor of their contribution to his book we will not speculate. We believe that it is most unlikely that Dr. Nix concurred with Dr. Numbers' conclusions.

Others who received warm words of appreciation for their assistance were two of his cousins, Roy Branson and Bruce Branson, both, of course, also grandsons of Elder W. H. Branson, a former General Conference President. Dr. Roy Branson has long been associated with Adventist Forums in the United States. He was, for a considerable period, an editor of the liberal *Spectrum* magazine. Another former editor of *Spectrum*, dermatologist Dr. Molleurus Couperus, also received Dr. Numbers' words of appreciation as did Dr. Richard W. Schwarz, of Andrews University, who is still seen as an expert by Dr. Arthur Patrick, in his paper presented to the February 2-5, 2004 Summit. (*op. cit.*, pp. xiii, xiv).

Dr. Numbers admitted that he had

> Refrained from using divine inspiration as an historical explanation.
>
> (*op. cit.*, p. xi).

"Why not?" we might question. Do we refrain from using divine explanations for the remarkable health messages conveyed by Moses to the Israelites? Perhaps some professing Seventh-day Adventists today would. Is inspiration of God's chosen prophets not an historical fact?

Quoting from the six volume biography of Sister White, written by her grandson, Elder Arthur Lacey White (1907-1991), *Ellen G. White*, the early manuscripts to which Dr. Numbers had access prior to publication, he admitted quite frankly that he

> had parted company with those Adventist scholars who insist on the following presuppositions: (1) that the Holy Spirit has guided the Advent movement since the early 1840's, (2) "that Ellen Harmon White was chosen by God as his messenger and her work embodied that of a prophet," (3) "that as a sincere dedicated Christian and as a prophet, would not and did not falsify," (4) that the testimony of Mrs. White's fellow-believers "may be accepted as true and correct to the best of the memory of the individuals who reported." (*Ibid*, pp. xi, xii).

Yet many today accept Dr. Numbers' "unbiased" conclusions. While he does not so designate Sister White, nevertheless his conclusions set her forth both as an imposter and a charlatan. Yet some would see him as one who provided the Seventh-day Adventist Church with a coruscation into the writings of Sister White.

Despite the fact that Dr. Numbers seriously denigrated Sister White's prophetic office, Dr. Arthur Patrick assessed that,

> The historical contributions of ... Ron Numbers ... were too often unappreciated or in various ways restricted, laid aside or condemned in the 1970's and 1980's.
> (Dr. Patrick, *Ellen White and South Pacific Adventism: Retrospect and Prospect*. Paper presented at the South Pacific Summit on Sister White's writings, Avondale College, February 2-5, 2004, p. 7).

With Dr. Numbers' failure to understand Sister White's inspired principles it is surprising that a credentialed, ordained minister of the Seventh-day Adventist Church, would choose to speak in complimentary terms of his book.

Another name which has surfaced in the first years of the twenty-first century is that of Australian Ear, Nose and Throat Surgeon, Dr. Don McMahon of Melbourne. His work has been presented to the Ellen G. White Estate of the General Conference, to a conference of world Ellen G. White Research Center directors. Dr. McMahon was also invited to make a seminar presentation in the Victorian Conference Camp Meeting, held in the state of which Melbourne is the capital. He presented a seminar at the South New South Wales Conference Camp, and a paper at the February 2004 Summit at Avondale.

Dr. Patrick reported:

> Dr. Don McMahon has compiled data that facilitates a contemporary analysis, via an undated paper "Adventist health: Inspired or Acquired" and a CD of the same

title, First Edition, 2002, I. It is important to note the comparative fluidity of medical opinion, in other words, medical ideas are subject to change in the way McMahon so convincingly demonstrates.

(Arthur Patrick, *op. cit.*, p. 2 footnote 8).

Another report mentioned that:

> Recently Don McMahon, a surgeon and author who lives in Melbourne, did some research on her [Sister White's] health statements. Being a medical specialist, he wanted to test her statements on health when compared to her contemporaries. He did this by measuring how well her statements and her contemporaries have been verified by modern medicine. He found twice as many of her statements have been verified compared with the next best, and three times more verified than most. For example, 87 per cent of hers were verified, while Dr. Kellogg was only 43 per cent. She was uneducated in medicine, while Dr. Kellogg was considered an outstanding medical man of the times.
>
> (Dr. Bradford, *op.cit.*, p. 62 – Dr. Bradford was referring to "Ahead of Her Time: A Critical Analysis of *Ministry of Healing*, a book by Ellen G. White," Dr. Don McMahon, May 2001, unpublished document).

Note, the figures here presented conflict with those Dr. McMahon presented before the First International Conference on Ellen G. White and History, where Sister White was accorded only a sixty-six percent accuracy. The different figures are easily explained. The eighty-seven percent referred to Sister White's statements where the reasons she provided for her counsel were ignored. The value, according to Dr. McMahon, dropped to sixty-six percent when those reasons were included.

It is time for researchers into the scientific revelations made by Sister White to awaken to the reality that the scientific data – which so many trust in preference to God's inspired words – is dynamic. Dr. McMahon does concede this point. So many of Sister White's medical declarations, which physicians sought to discredit in her day, such as the link between cigarette smoking and germs as causative agents in cancer, the consequences of masturbation and the wearing of wigs, are today known to be correct. In our current academic pride we continue to make the same mistakes of ignorance as did the physicians and medical scientists of the nineteenth century. Will we never learn that the infinite God is trustworthy?

Dr. McMahon's research will be evaluated later.

The inspired writings of the Spirit of Prophecy have been made of none effect in numbers of ways:
1. By denying their usefulness;
2. By ignoring them;
3. By College professors casting aspersions upon them;
4. By forbidding students quoting, in their term papers, from the Spirit of Prophecy, while encouraging them to cite non-Seventh-day Adventist scholars;

5. By disobeying the counsel provided;
6. By claiming that none of her works written after 1884 are valid;
7. By asserting that, while Sister White's writings were true prior to 1898, they applied only to the believers in that time; the only Testimonies relevant to us today are those written after and including 1898 when she first stated that she might not be translated.

We have personally met each one of these efforts to make of none effect the writings of the servant of the Lord.

As a result, flesh eating, including unclean meats, and caffeine and alcohol consumption are no longer rare among professed Seventh-day Adventists. Over ten years ago *Ministry* magazine dealt with alcoholism as a serious problem among church members.

Despite, indeed because of, these facts, the attacks upon Sister White's health messages and her integrity continue to escalate. All scientific studies have demonstrated that those who follow the health message live a healthier and longer life on average.

Instead of criticizing God's wonderful health message, divinely passed to Sister White, we should constantly praise God for His tender love toward us. Our brother-in-law, Dr. David Pennington, Director of Plastic and Reconstructive Surgery at Australia's most respected University Hospital, Sydney's Royal Prince Alfred Hospital, wrote a letter addressed to the editor of the South Pacific *Record*. In this letter he reminded Seventh-day Adventists that,

> Out of the pages of the article "Ellen White for Today," February 28, jumps the phrase "to damn with faint praise." The statement of Arthur Patrick "Because Ellen White was shown 10 important things in her great health reform vision of 1863 doesn't mean she knew the 990 other things we might find useful with reference to healthful living" is to trivialise the most important portfolio of public health advice ever put together by one person, outside of Scripture.

> If all Australians were to faithfully follow from birth all of the eight great principles of health outlined in the spirit of prophecy, consider this:

> Death from coronary disease would be uncommon before advanced age. Death rates from all cancers would at least halve. Death from lung cancer would reduce by 95%. There would be NO AIDS, no sexually-transmitted diseases, virtually no cervical cancer in women, almost no Type 2 diabetes, far less hypertension and stroke, a much higher rate of fertility and successful pregnancies in women, a much lower rate of birth-defects, no risk of diseases transmitted from animal flesh, such as trichinosis, tapeworm, mad cow disease, brucellosis and a host of others. There would be little cirrhosis [of the liver], few ulcers and none of the evil social consequences of alcoholism. There would be no drug overdoses, much less suicide, no hepatitis C, few cases of hepatitis B and few cases of liver cancer. There would be a dramatic reduction in stress-induced mental disease.

And, even more importantly, few of the "990 other things we might find useful" would ever be needed.

I think your readership should ask the question: "What is the agenda behind this series of articles?" I doubt they will find anything positive.

(South Pacific Record, March 20, 2004, p. 13).

Colin, whose doctorate is in Psychology, and Russell, a Consulting Physician, (Internist) fully support our brother-in-law's assessment. Thank God for the Spirit of Prophecy health message.

Our personal testimony is that every day we thank God for another day of life, which He has been pleased to bestow upon us. At seventy years of age, at the time of authoring this book, we recognize that we only reached this milestone because of God's love in providing to our family the health message. Oh that we had ever followed this message as we ought, then, unquestionably our health would have been more robust. But God provides us with remarkable energy and endurance as we follow a very demanding schedule in our administrative duties and written and spoken witness to our Lord's love and His faith.

Unfortunately, the editor of *The Record* sought to partially dispel the impact of the final paragraph in Dr. Pennington's letter, above. The editor commented:

> *Honesty and openness seemed like a good idea at the time.*
>
> (Ibid – italics in the original).

Openness? Honesty? Then let the South Pacific Division be open. Let all the documents presented in the Summit of February 2-5, 2004, be made available for study.

When Russell applied to attend the Victorian Conference Elders' Summit, he received the following e-mail reply:

> Thank you for your request to attend the upcoming Elders Summit.
>
> The Summit is a forum for the Victorian Conference and the Adventist system to communicate researched issues on Ellen G. White. It is to resource our key leadership.
>
> As such you and your wife do not qualify as you do not hold membership in Victoria [Russell's church membership is in the Greater Sydney Conference] and are not current church elders or prospective church elders.
>
> Thank you for the courtesy of requesting permission, but as stated, you and your wife do not qualify for entry, nor is the Victorian Conference willing to make an exception.
>
> (E-mail letter written by Dr. Denis Hankinson, President of the Victorian Conference, to Russell, dated June 2, 2004).

Yet present, without question, were many who had never held any ordained post in God's church and possessed no prospect of ever doing so, and others who held membership outside Australia. Dr. Hankinson supplied the honest reason for his decision to one of the attendees. Dr. Hankinson remarked that Russell Standish applied to attend, but we did not want him here disturbing the meeting. In Russell's more than half-a-century of church membership, he has never disturbed a single meeting. Since Dr. Hankinson and Russell have never met, this implied slur on Russell's character possessed no valid basis. Perhaps the honest reason was that Dr. Hankinson was afraid that Russell would ask a difficult question.

Openness? Honesty? – Hardly!

26 Ticks and Crosses for God

During our years as elementary (primary) school teachers – Russell's three years (1952-1954), and Colin's seven years (1952-1958) – we frequently marked our pupils' work with ticks for correct answers and crosses for answers which were in error. None escaped the misery of receiving crosses for we shortly discovered that, alas, not one of the children we taught was infallible. Nor were we as teachers. Over forty years later, one of his former pupils showed Russell one of the report cards he had written. It contained a spelling mistake. Fortunately the student's parents had not placed a cross upon it.

In this use of these symbols of accuracy and inaccuracy we never progressed in our resort to their use to judge the validity of inspired writings. But something akin to this has been gaining favor in Seventh-day Adventist academic and theological circles in recent years.

In an article entitled "A New Era of Ellen G. White Studies?" (*Spectrum*, Vol. 30, No. 4, Autumn, 2002)., Dr. Douglas Morgan, Chairman of the Department of History and Political Science at Columbia Union College, introduced a summary of a paper presented by Australian Ear, Nose and Throat Surgeon, Dr. Don McMahon, concerning the accuracy of Sister White's health and medical statements in the book *Ministry of Healing*. (*Ibid*, pp. 58, 59). The venue for this presentation was The First International Conference on Ellen G. White and Seventh-day Adventist History, convened at Battle Creek, Michigan, by the General Conference at the suggestion of the General Conference White Estate. The Seventh-day Adventist Theological Faculty at Andrews University assisted in its organization.

Of the sixty-five participants, forty percent, twenty-six attendees, came from outside North America. (*Ibid*, p. 58). Dr. McMahon had undertaken his research in 2001. In a meeting held in 2002 at the Wantirna Church in Melbourne, which Russell had attended upon the invitation of Dr. McMahon, Dr. McMahon spoke of placing ticks and crosses against Sister White's health and medical assertions. In a personal telephone conversation with Dr. McMahon, May 11, 2004, he informed Russell that he no longer speaks of correct and incorrect in reference to Sister White's health messages since he believed such a representation did not correctly reflect his intention.

Dr. McMahon referred to the warm response he had received following his presentation before the International Conference held earlier in the year, May 15-19, 2002. Dr. McMahon's claim was certainly verified by Professor Morgan who reported that,

> No one seemed unduly perturbed by McMahon's conclusion that only sixty-six percent of Ellen G. White's health and medical statements ... would be deemed accurate by modern standards. (*Ibid*, p. 59).

A new measurement standard of prophetic accuracy seems to have been proposed at that Conference – PAQ, prophetic accuracy quotient. Thus Dr. McMahon's results were accorded – by those who used the PAQ scale – a "healthy" score of 66 compared with those of other writers on health reform during the nineteenth century who, although

> more famous health reformers of the era fared far worse – Sylvester Graham (29 percent), William Alcott (27 percent), James C. Jackson (34 percent), and John Harvey Kellogg (37 percent). (*Ibid* – all parentheses are in the original).

Dr. McMahon, himself, made no reference to the PAQ.

One positive result of Dr. McMahon's conclusions was that they laid to rest the impressions left by Ronald Numbers in his book, *Prophetess of Health*, that Sister White copied most of her health principles from the health reformers of her day and deceived God's people into believing that her counsels were inspired.

One important point Dr. McMahon had made, which was not recorded in Dr. Morgan's report, was that a statistical analysis of that which he had presented indicated that there was only one chance in 10^{25} (ten trillion trillion) that Sister White could have obtained her health principles by chance factors. This strongly confirmed that Sister White was inspired by God. Dr. McMahon also believes that his findings as to the accuracy of Sister White's statements in respect to current medical knowledge, is not a final evaluation. Dr. McMahon and we, however, do differ on two issues:

1. That inspiration is inerrant, and
2. That Sister White's physiological statements are inspired. Dr. McMahon believes that Sister White's physiological explanations, as opposed to her health principles, were "a random selection taken from her time, of the physiologists of the day." Thus Dr. McMahon believes many of these statements are in error and these errors do not reflect on her inspiration in the area of health principles.

We believe Dr. McMahon's input is a mixed contribution to our faith. While confirming the inspiration of Sister White's health principles, in his belief that inspiration can be faulted and that the physiological matters she used were simply reflecting the knowledge of her day, Dr. McMahon seriously diminished God's inspired revelations through His servant.

In an earlier private conversation with Dr. McMahon, Russell was told, contrary to Professor Morgan's report, of the response of the sixty-five attendees cited above, that there was some dissent to his report. Dr. McMahon did state that a couple of delegates from South America attending the conference were not happy with the general tone of the Conference. But this dissent was not openly expressed in the Conference Sessions. Possibly among those was Alberto Timm, Director of the Brazilian Ellen G. White Research Center.

> In his plenary address on May 16, Alberto Timm issued a trenchant, programmatic call for defending the authority of Ellen G. White against current threats.
>
> (*Ibid*, p. 58).

Praise God for Pastor Timm! Even if the *Spectrum* report couched his faithfulness in pejorative terms, we thank God for his faithfulness.

We note with increasing concern that these International Conferences, of which more are proposed, increasingly draw delegates from all continents, but usually the delegates from North America outnumber the delegates from each of the other five inhabited continents combined. Yet only about 7.7 percent of Seventh-day Adventist members live in the North American Division which includes only three nations – the United States, Canada and Bermuda. Thus, at this International Conference, a Division representing less than eight percent of Seventh-day Adventists was accorded sixty percent of delegates, while the rest of the world church members comprising over ninety-two percent of members, were represented by only forty percent of the delegates.

In this manner the destabilization of our faith has been transported from the nests of faithlessness in the North American, European and South Pacific Division Colleges and Universities to every other Division of the World Field. Within the last seven years we have preached in every one of the thirteen Divisions – the East Central Africa, Euro-Africa, Euro-Asia, Inter-American, North American, Northern Asia-Pacific, South American, Southern Africa-Indian Ocean, Southern Asia, Southern Asia-Pacific, South Pacific, Trans-European, and Western Africa. In each of these Divisions the destruction of the faith is rampant. Another strategy has been to send promising pastors to Andrews University for post-graduate training. Although the Seminary has some professors true to the faith, they are in the minority and most students leave with their faith destroyed, or greatly compromised.

In 1989 we spent two hours with Pastor Enoch Olivera, then in his ninth year as a Vice President of the General Conference. Prior to his appointment in 1980 to the General Conference post, Pastor Olivera was President of the South American Division for five years. In great distress he recounted the experience of three young Brazilian pastors sent to Andrews University in the early 1980's to undertake doctorate studies. Each returned with a lost faith in the principles of truth and all three were dismissed from the ministry.

In the 1960's, Australian Pr. Lennel (Chubby) Moulds returned home from the Seventh-day Adventist Theological Seminary. He had earned a Master of Divinity degree. Appointed to the Theology Department of Avondale College, Pastor Moulds taught that which he had learned at the Theological Seminary. Dr. Desmond Ford was Chairman of Theology at the time, while Colin was Chairman of the Avondale College Education Department.

Before Pastor Moulds had returned to Australia to take up his appointment, Colin had alerted Pastor Laurence Christopher Naden, (1906-1979), President of the Division (1962-1970) and Chairman of the College Board, that he had heard ominous reports about Pastor Moulds' beliefs and suggested a thorough investigation. In response Colin was informed that the Division had invested considerable funds in Pr. Moulds' post-graduate education and when he returned the Australasian (now South Pacific) Division would explain their expectations to him.

Soon after Pastor Moulds took up his post in the Theology Department, Colin spoke to him about the reports of his heterodoxy, which he had heard. Without making any effort to deny the reports, Pastor Moulds light-heartedly assured Colin that he need not worry for he would not share these with the students. But share them he did!

One student wrote home to his parents to reassure them that they should not fear, despite the fact that he was studying under Pastor Moulds, who was the son of a Union President. The student assured his parents that he intended to keep the faith! Colin enjoyed his social contacts with Pastor Moulds, but was alarmed at the tenor of his theological lectures. Pastor Moulds defended the content of his lectures on the grounds that he was simply sharing what he had learned at Andrews University.

Eventually Pastor Moulds was rightly dismissed from his post, a decision with which Colin concurred. Yet Colin felt a deep sympathy for this promising pastor who had permitted his professors to destroy his faith. Pr. Moulds made a "prophecy" to Colin before his departure. He stated that he would leave denominational employment and would do no damage to the Seventh-day Adventist Church, (a promise he essentially kept), but that Dr. Desmond Ford, whose faith had been subverted by Englishman, Dr. Edward Heppenstall, at the Theological Seminary, would one day seriously damage the church's beliefs.

Colin recalls in 1975 urging an *ad hoc* General Conference Committee to cease the practice of attempting to balance committees by choosing representatives from "both sides of the issue", since this was a formula for compromise. Colin's plea was strongly supported by Elder Reggie Dower, Secretary (1966-1980) of the Ministerial Association of the General Conference. However, no alteration in the policy of "balance" took place. Colin's plea had been that only those loyal to Biblical mandates and the counsels of the Spirit of Prophecy be considered suitable candidates for such important committees. Today those well known to be opponents of truth swamp many of the *ad hoc* committees and deliberative conferences called by our church at all levels. Such a result is the inevitable consequence of the policy of "balancing" candidates who love God's truth with those who oppose it.

In 1989 when Colin spoke in Kenya, the leader of the Central Kenyan Conference shared his deep concern over the presentations of Kenyan ministers who had returned from their studies at the Theological Seminary at Andrews University. We both spoke with this church leader who was a delegate to the

General Conference 1995 Session in Utrecht, the Netherlands. He confirmed his fear that these men were destroying the faith.

Thus by both postgraduate theological training and International Conferences at which delegates are often carefully selected so that a predominance of liberal-minded men and women are invited, the General Conference is using its prestige to spread plain error worldwide. Seventh-day Adventists must recognize this fact, for no less than their eternal destinies are at stake as verily as were those of the members of God's Church at the First Advent who did not discern the agenda of the Sanhedrin.

In this atmosphere it is little surprise that Dr. McMahon's presentations have captured the attention of and received plaudits from men and women bent on "a new era in Ellen G. White studies."

Even the General Conference President made a curious statement, which would not have displeased those who are intent on diminishing Sister White's status as a prophet. Dr. Jan Paulsen (born 1934) was quoted as stating in August, 2002:

> Recognizing that some [of the delegates to the Faith and Science Conference] "come from a perspective which is not where I am," he stated, "you are necessary partners to the conversations we are having." (*Ibid*, p. 48).

We notice that those who faithfully and openly defend truth, especially members who rightly denounce error, are a dwindling number of invitees at these conferences. One welcome exception was Colin's invitation to attend the 2004 International Conference on Science and Faith, as an observer, but not as a participant. Yet these are the very men and women whose voices are most urgently required to be heard at this time. In the days of King Ahab it was not the prophets of Baal whom the people of God most urgently needed to hear but the voice of the most despised prophet in Israel, Elijah. Elijah would receive no greater welcome in the Seventh-day Adventist Church today than he did in God's ancient church. Even the seven thousand who had not bowed the knee to Baal were too timid to stand vocally in defense of the God of Elijah. Elijah was translated – none of the seven thousand were. Those who are awaiting translation, never experiencing death, will not be silent in their defense of precious truth. Their voices may be despised by a majority of church leaders but God will remember these, His faithful servants.

> In the time when His wrath shall go forth in judgments, these humble, devoted followers of Christ will be distinguished from the rest of the world by their soul anguish, which is expressed in lamentation and weeping, reproofs and warnings. While others try to throw a cloak over the existing evil, and excuse the great wickedness everywhere prevalent, those who have a zeal for God's honor and a love for souls will not hold their peace to obtain favor of any. Their righteous souls are vexed day by day with the unholy works and conversation of the unrighteous. They are powerless to stop the rushing torrent of iniquity, and hence they are

filled with grief and alarm. They mourn before God to see religion despised in the very homes of those who have had great light. They lament and afflict their souls because pride, avarice, selfishness, and deception of almost every kind are in the church. The Spirit of God, which prompts to reproof, is trampled underfoot, while the servants of Satan triumph. God is dishonored, the truth made of none effect. (*Testimonies for the Church*, Vol. 5, pp. 210, 211).

Is it proper to evaluate either Scripture or the Spirit of Prophecy, according those statements with which we are in agreement even a symbolic tick and those which disagree with either our preference or the current knowledge of mankind, a symbolic cross? Surely this is not a divine duty. Has all humility left us? Has meekness disappeared from our midst? Do we no longer see the infinite gulf between our knowledge and that of the God of heaven? Yet in the areas of history, science, health and origins of the earth many are now, without the use of these symbols of correctness and error, doing precisely this.

Have these negative evaluations brought strength and purpose to the Seventh-day Adventist Church? When we undertake these rash assessments of the inspired writings of Christ's last day prophet, in what way do we differ from the infidels of the eighteenth and the nineteenth centuries, who brought superficially plausible charges against Scripture? Have we considered that if we were according ticks and crosses to the counsels of Sister White a century ago, the number of crosses would have greatly exceeded those of today? Can we not, in patience, wait for science and history and other disciplines to catch up with God's wisdom, and if not on this earth, await Christ's revelations as we sit at His feet in the courts above?

By any evaluation of our church in the South Pacific and worldwide, we are in sharp decline. In the South Pacific we are effectively losing membership annually, our membership numbers only being maintained by the retention of the names of members long since departed from the faith. In a period of a little over a year, three of our five hospitals in the South Pacific closed their doors: Auckland, North New Zealand; Warburton, Victoria; and Sopas, Western Highlands Province of Papua-New Guinea. In recent years the Sanitarium Health Food Company has closed down all of its more-than-ninety retail shops and also franchised its specialty line division. It also has closed numbers of factories even those in "Jerusalem centers" such as Warburton in Australia and Palmerston North in New Zealand. They have also been closed in other cities.

Our educational program is only limping along on a massive injection of state-aid from the Federal Government, a source of revenue which God forbids. In New Zealand the situation is worse. In order to survive, all our church schools have permitted themselves to be integrated into the state educational system.

Our people have lost interest in evangelistic outreach. When the Victorian Conference appealed for funds for an evangelistic outreach, a single donation was received after several weeks had passed. Not even one of the Conference staff who had initiated the appeal had contributed a single cent themselves.

Tithe and Sabbath School offerings are slipping at an alarming rate when measured in relation to membership numbers and income levels. This is true worldwide where only thirty percent of our members return tithe. In some areas of Africa and South America the figure is only ten percent. (South Pacific *Record*, 22 November, 2003). Further:

> Tithe receipted by the Church in the South Pacific has been declining for at least the past 25 years when compared with income.
> (South Pacific *Record*, 8 September, 2001).

Brother Rod Brady, South Pacific Division Treasurer, reported that,

> Mission offerings taken at our Camps have almost halved from more than $A145,000 in 1998 to about $A75,000 in 2002.
> (South Pacific *Record*, 13 December, 2003).

> In 1930 in the depth of the world economic depression, the worst of the twentieth century, offerings equaled 91 percent of tithe. In 2000 in the South Pacific we gave 45% of tithe in offerings. (*Ibid*).

If our church were a commercial business the stockholders would long ago have called an extraordinary meeting and voted out virtually every President and all members of the Executive Committees because of their gross dereliction of duty and failure to prosper the work of the church. But using strategies ingeniously designed by leadership, men who have failed the constituency – and more importantly, have failed their God – are re-elected to office even when the majority of delegates desire otherwise. This was evidenced in the re-election of the President of the Victorian Conference in 2003. It was also illustrated in the recent elections of the Iowa-Missouri Conference in the North American Division.

It surely hurts us to write these facts. But a failure to point these matters out would be a dereliction of our duty as ordained pastors. We are yet, as God commands, to

> bear a still more pointed message than was borne by John the Baptist.
> (*Testimonies for the Church*, Vol. 1, p. 321).

Even when the North American Division, in a rare admission of fearful failure, admitted at its Quinquennial Session at San Diego in 1991:

> There is grave danger that the precious Adventist message will not be passed on to the next generation. (*Adventist Review*, 7 March, 1991),

no effective remedial measures were taken. We simply continue to dare to give our God ticks and crosses and profess to marvel at the blindness and stupidity of God's church in the days of Israel and Judah, ignoring the statement of God's prophet:

> The same disobedience and failure which were seen in the Jewish church have characterized in a greater degree the people who have had this great light from heaven in the last messages of warning. (*Testimonies for the Church*, Vol. 5, p. 456).

No doubt many in our church today would place a cross against that inspired statement, which is now fully fulfilled, for any man or woman of integrity to see. There is one reason alone why the Seventh-day Adventist Church survives; it is the presence in its midst of the very small remnant.

> Except the LORD of hosts had left unto us a very small remnant, we should have been as Sodom, and we should have been like unto Gomorrah. (Isaiah 1:9).

Today that portion of God's church upon whom He places His blessing and who, under God's grace and power, alone, stand between the ultimate success of His church and its utter annihilation, are scorned by leadership. Nothing has been learned from Holy Writ. Nothing has been learned from the faithlessness of earlier generations. We, as a people are blind to the lessons of God's church of the Exodus. That church failed miserably when it ignored the words of God through His prophet, Moses. We do not see ourselves in the destruction of Jerusalem when the inspired words of the prophet Jeremiah were scorned. Perhaps his words were accorded ticks and crosses too. Nor do we cease from our worldly vocations and activities in order to ponder the lessons to be learnt from the failure of God's church to heed the words of the greatest prophet up to that time, John the Baptist.

And when the "prophet" without compare, Christ Himself, trod this earth, His success in arousing fidelity within His church was, in human evaluations, minimal. We should not in the least be surprised that Sister White, the prophet of the end time fared no better. And yet in our humanness we are surprised.

Surely it is time for the Elijah message to be proclaimed with unprecedented power in our midst, not with hearts filled with hate of our brethren and sisters, but with a sense of deep genuine Christian love for those who are now so deluded that they believe that in destroying the Spirit of Prophecy they are doing our God a service. Surely no one would wish the wrath of God to fall upon any man or woman.

Very frequently in our great confidence in today's scientists and their achievements, we contrast them with the "ignorance" of such men during Sister White's lifetime. Yet Sister White's lifetime (1827-1915), produced some of the most brilliant scientific minds of the Christian era. Let it be remembered that these men and women often labored alone in makeshift laboratories, creating their own equipment and without millions and millions of dollars of government and corporate grants.

We cite a few of these outstanding scientists. George Leopold Curvier (1769-1832) who, almost single-handed, established the sciences of comparative anatomy and paleontology, the study of fossils. He strongly opposed evolutionary concepts.

Michael Faraday (1791-1867) discovered benzene, invented the transformer, electro-magnetic rotation which led to the invention of the electric motor. He discovered that altering the magnetic field produced an electric current. This discovery made possible today's massive-electricity generators worldwide. He found the principles of electrolysis, the process of passing electric currents through solutions, which later led to the process of electroplating of metals. He elucidated the laws of electrochemistry. He coined the terms *anode*, *cathode* and *electrolyte*. He, further, conceived the concept of field theory. The unit of electrical capacitance, the farad, was named in his honor.

Samuel Finley Bruse Morse (1791-1872) invented the telegraph and the morse code. He built the first telegraphic line from Washington to Baltimore. It was along that line in the significant year, 1844 (May 24), that the now famous words "What hath God wrought?" were sent.

Charles Babbage (1791-1871), the third great scientist born in 1791, invented the difference engine which was a large calculator which calculated mathematical tables. In the 1830's Charles Babbage conceived the analytical engine which had a capacity to store mathematical memories. In 1831 he founded the British Association for the advancement of science and also the Statistical Society in 1834. Charles Babbage, in addition, compiled the first reliable actuarial tables. He invented the ophthalmoscope, used by physicians to view the retina and other parts of the eye, the speedometer and the cowcatcher on locomotives and numerous other articles of equipment.

Mathew Fontaine Muay (1806-1873) published *The Wind and Current Charts* in 1847. So helpful were these charts that sea-travel time between England and Australia was cut by over twenty-two percent and such travel time between New York and San Francisco via Cape Horn was reduced by over twenty-seven percent. Matthew Muay also sounded the depths of much of the Atlantic Ocean. This information was of inestimable value when Samuel Morse sought to lay the first transatlantic-telegraphic cable.

James Prescott Joule (1818-1889) demonstrated that the amount of heat produced in one second in a wire carrying an electric current equals the square of the current multiplied by the resistance. The heat produced measures the electric power lost. (Joule's Law). He also quantified the relationship between heat, electricity and mechanical work. Joule's discoveries gave rise to the science of thermodynamics. It was his work which established the First Law of Thermodynamics which states that energy can neither be created nor destroyed, but is simply changed from one form to another. This is a revelation of God's infinite power. The unit of energy is now called the Joule. He worked with William Thomson on many other projects.

Louis Pasteur (1822-1895) created the science of microbiology. He proved that fermentation occurred only when germs were present. He destroyed the theory of spontaneous generation of life and introduced pasteurization. Louis Pasteur invented a vaccine for the deadly disease of rabies. He demonstrated that if this vaccine was given soon after a bite from a rabid animal, the individual's life could be saved. In Southeast Asia Russell treated a number of such cases, using a refinement of Dr. Pasteur's discovery. All patients survived. None would have survived without the treatment.

Gregor Mendel (1822-1884) discovered the basic laws of genetics which determine our heredity. Mendel's First Law set out his discovery that traits in offspring are controlled by the composition of two cells – the male and the female reproductive cells. Mendel's Second Law stated that all characteristics in a species are quite independent and depend upon the genes present in the male and female reproductive cells.

William Thomson, later created by Queen Victoria the First Baron Kelvin of Largs (1824-1907) was a man of brilliance. Baron Kelvin introduced the absolute temperature scale. He found that when temperatures reached -273.15° Celsius (-459.67° Fahrenheit) all activity of molecules ceased and thus this was the absolute lowest temperature possible. Temperature measured from -273° Celsius use the Kelvin Scale. Thus 0° Celsius, the freezing point of water, is 273 K (no degree sign is used on the Kelvin Scale). One hundred degrees Celsius, the boiling point of water, is 373 K on the Kelvin Scale. Baron Kelvin strongly refuted evolution in his monograph, *The Doctrine of Uniformity in Geology Briefly Refuted*, published in 1865. He, in cooperation with James Joule, contributed many advances in science.

Sir Joseph Lister (Later Baron Lister) (1827-1912) has been called the father of modern surgery, for his introduction of the use of sterilization in operating theatres, greatly reducing wound infections, which not infrequently led to the post-operative deaths of the patients. It was a medical breakthrough of enormous magnitude. He received his knighthood in 1883 and was created First Baron Lister of Lyme Regis in 1897. Both awards were presented by Queen Victoria.

James Clerk Maxwell (1831-1879), Professor of Physics and Astronomy, King's College, London, discovered that the speed of electromagnetic waves was virtually identical to the speed of light. Today, radio, television, computers and radar find their ultimate origins in Dr. Maxwell's work. His theories also opened the way for Albert Einstein's (1879-1955) theories of relativity. Albert Einstein was another genius of Sister White's lifetime. He enunciated his theory of special relativity in 1905. He published the final draft of his theory of general relativity in 1916, the year following Sister White's death. James Maxwell introduced the field of statistical thermodynamics. He undertook valuable research on color blindness and color photography.

Sir Ambrose Fleming (1849-1945) was a consultant to the Edison Electric Light Company. He discovered, in the 1880's, practical solutions to problems involved in large-scale lighting, so valuable to us today. His thermionic valve (sometimes termed a vacuum diode) became an important component in Marconi's wireless.

George Washington Carver (1864-1943) was a genius in the field of agriculture. Much of his work was accomplished after Sister White's death. He did more than anyone in combating the boll weevil infestation of the cotton crops of the southern states of the United States and taught farmers' wives to prepare healthful meals. In later life he developed plastic from soya beans and also a multitude of uses for agricultural products in order to increase the profitability of farming. This is instanced by the fact that he developed approximately sixty products from the pecan nut alone. Dr. Carver set forth one hundred and eight ways to use sweet potatoes. He is probably best known for introducing peanut butter to the world. He also devised over one hundred ways to utilize peanuts.

Let it not be forgotten that heavier-than-air aircraft flight was introduced by Wilber (1867-1912) and Orville Wright (1871-1948) in Sister White's lifetime – in the year 1903.

There were a huge number of other brilliant scientists of the nineteenth and early twentieth centuries, such as the Russian physiologist, Ivan Petrovich Pavlov (1849-1936), Gugielmo Marconi, later created a Marchese (Marquis) (1874-1937), the inventor of radio, and Marja Skeodowska, better known as Madam Curie (1867-1934), who won two Nobel Prizes, one in physics with her husband, Pierre (1859-1906), in 1903 for the discovery of radium, and one alone in chemistry in 1911.

Some may question why we have taken this detour into nineteenth and early twentieth century science. The plain answer is that today many of our people cast aspersions upon Sister White's citing of material from health scientists of her day. They refer to the false concepts of nineteenth century health science. That false notions existed is undoubted. If Christ did not return for a further one hundred years, mankind would discover many deficiencies in today's science too. But we dare not overlook the many brilliant discoveries of the nineteenth century which have survived over a hundred years of scientific testing and careful scrutiny. When we step into an aeroplane we evidence faith in the results of numerous nineteenth and early twentieth century scientific discoveries.

Sister White always supported a scientific approach to health; this was evidenced when she set up such a school of medicine in 1905 at Loma Linda. Many other health forms, not based upon careful scientific research – faulty as this is on occasions – existed in Sister White's day, but she eschewed them.

We believe that the views of many of the non-Seventh-day Adventist health reformers of the nineteenth century have been undervalued by present day researchers. In some cases their research is still ahead of current generally accepted medical science. This is, no doubt, the reason why God inspired Sister White to use some of their material in her books.

Incidentally, all the scientists selected above professed the Christian faith except Albert Einstein and those in the last paragraph. Those Christian scientists did not accept the evolutionary theories so rampant in their day. (See Ann Lamont, *21 Great Scientists Who Believed the Bible*, Answers in Genesis, Brisbane, Australia, 2000). Seventh-day Adventist theologians, administrators and scientists would do well to emulate the example of these scientists.

Is it not time that all of us trembled as did Felix (Acts 24:25)? But let us not await a "convenient season" to return to the Lord as did Felix, for surely,

> Now is the accepted time: behold NOW is the day of salvation.
> (2 Corinthians 6:2 – emphasis added).

We sincerely plead with our fellow workers in the cause of God and our fellow believers to depart from the folly of the destruction of the Spirit of Prophecy. It is time for each one of us to value Christ's inestimable salvation as never before, for judgment day is nigh at hand. We write with no holier-than-thou spirit for we, daily, are seeking our own salvation, pleading with God to cleanse us of every defilement. Heaven and eternity are at stake. Let each reader recognize that:

> [27]Esaias also crieth concerning Israel, Though the number of the children of Israel be as the sand of the sea, a remnant shall be saved: [28]For he will finish the work, and cut it short in righteousness: because a short work will the Lord make upon the earth. [29]And as Esaias said before, Except the Lord of Sabaoth had left us a seed, we had been as Sodoma, and been made like unto Gomorrha.
> (Romans 9:27-29).

27 Self Abuse

Masturbation, which Sister White referred to, in her refined language, as self abuse (*Testimonies for the Church*, Vol. 2, p. 392), was addressed by God's servant. Sometimes she also used the term solitary vice (see later in this chapter). There is probably no counsel of the Spirit of Prophecy more ridiculed, with the exception of her writings upon the subject of the amalgamation of man and beast, than her presentation concerning the dire consequences of masturbation. We are prepared to address this matter openly.

Dr. Ronald Numbers, Professor of the History of Medicine and the History of Science at the University of Wisconsin, made several comments upon this matter. Dr. Numbers quoted a number of authors of the decades of the 1840's to the 1860's who wrote on the subject of

> masturbation, which was thought to cause a frightening array of pathological conditions ranging from dyspepsia and consumption [tuberculosis] to insanity and loss of spirituality. (Ronald Numbers, *op. cit.*, p. 150).

Health writers such as Sylvester Graham (1848), William A. Alcott (1855), Russell T. Trall (1862), and James C. Jackson (1862) were cited by Dr. Numbers. (see *op. cit.*, Endnote 35, p. 245). As we have documented in a previous chapter, the nineteenth century was an age of remarkable expansion of scientific knowledge. Despite many areas of ignorance, there was considerable truth also in the fields of health and surgery. Dr. Numbers appeared to place no value upon this fact. Rather, he presented these men as promoting ignorant guesswork.

Dr. Numbers' thesis was that Sister White's views were greatly influenced by the writings of such men, rather than by the guidance of divine inspiration. He referred to this by informing the reader that Sister White

> possessed both Trall's and Jackson's books on sex by late 1863.
> (Dr. Numbers, *op. cit.*, p. 150).

Dr. Numbers went on to state Sister White's views in the book, *Appeal to Mothers – Relative to the Great Cause of the Physical, Mental and Moral Ruin of Many of the Children of Our Time*, Steam Press, Battle Creek, 1864, so paralleled a number of eighteenth century health writers that,

> taking her word at face value, they [the publishers] asserted that "she had read nothing from these authors here quoted, and had read no other works on this subject, previous to putting into our hands what she had written. She is not therefore a copyist, although she has stated important truths to which men who are entitled to our highest confidence, have borne testimony." (*Ibid*, p. 154).

Here is presented an implied slight against Sister White's truthfulness. When Dr. Numbers cited a "parallel" between Sister White's writings of 1864 and those of Horace Mann, he admitted that she read Mann's book

> no later than 1865.   (Ibid, p. 155).

Such evidence does not satisfy his inference. Dr. Numbers' claim was not that she read those books by 1865, but that she read them before the publication of her book in 1864. Further, other "parallels" quoted are cited from writings of 1873, 1876, 1885, 1869 and 1870 respectively, well after Sister White gave the assurance of 1864 that she had read none of the books before writing her *Appeal to Mothers*. (See Dr. Numbers, *op. cit.*, pp. 155-157 and compare with pages 246, 247 Endnotes numbers 46, 49, 51, 52, 54. See dates above. These correspond with the respective endnotes).

Unless the reader bothered to check the endnotes he could be forgiven for concluding that Sister White had lied in 1864. It must not be forgotten that in his preface Ronald Numbers declared:

> I have parted company with those Adventist scholars who insist..."that as a sincere, dedicated Christian and a prophet, Ellen White would not and did not falsify." (*Ibid*, pp. xi, xii) – the statement within the quotation marks which is denied was made by Elder Arthur L. White.

Clearly Ronald Numbers was here attempting to confirm his belief that Sister White lied. We would expect that Dr. Numbers was presenting the strongest evidence of falsehood he had garnered. Assuming this, then we would find that Sister White would be utterly cleared of any conviction of falsehood in any nation with an unbiased judiciary. His evidence was not credible.

Dr. Numbers cited passages from Sister White's book, *Appeal to Mothers, The Great Cause of the Physical, Mental and Moral Ruin of Many of the Children of Our Time*, Steam Press, Battle Creek, 1864. In this book Sister White addressed physical, mental and spiritual consequences resulting from masturbation, which she there designated as "solitary vice."

Many professed Seventh-day Adventists disparage Sister White's comments concerning the mental illness which flowed from masturbation, despite the fact that Sister White gained this information from a vision she received from God on June 5, 1863.

The mistake which these Seventh-day Adventist critics are making is the very mistake they charge upon Sister White. They are relying upon widespread contemporary medical opinion. This is a failing of mankind through the ages, a fashion Sister White most assuredly did not follow.

Time and time again, medical science has found it necessary to catch up with the advanced medical science imparted to Sister White. In 1909 Sister White wrote:

> People are continually eating flesh that is filled with tuberculous and cancerous germs. (*Ministry of Healing*, p. 313).

None even then could deny that cattle were a source of bovine tuberculosis in humans. Robert Koch (1843-1910), a German bacteriologist, discovered the germ, *Mycobacterium tuberculosis*, in 1882. It is well proven that it may be transmitted in food through the intestinal tract as well as through the respiratory system and occasionally the skin. The germ, which is closely related to that of leprosy, *Mycobacterium leprae*, is difficult to eradicate from the body even today.

But Sister White's claim that germs were responsible, at least for some forms of cancers, was viewed as ludicrous a century ago. The evidence that germs played no part in the etiology (English spelling – aetiology) of cancer appeared self-evident. Physicians and nurses working in tuberculosis wards experienced a higher incidence of tuberculosis than the general public. This was understandable because of the contagious nature of the germs. But health workers serving in cancer wards experienced no incidence of cancer in excess of that in the general population. In the minds of medical scientists a century ago this was solid circumstantial evidence that Sister White was in error in this statement.

But none would dare to level such a charge in medical science today. It is well established that the viruses of Hepatitis B and C cause hepatomas, cancer of the liver. It is well attested that women infected with herpes genitalis virus possess a five-fold incidence of cancer of the cervix of the womb when compared to those women without infection of that virus. The Ebstein-Barr virus is now known to be a causative agent in Burkitt's tumor of the jaw in certain areas of Africa and nasopharyngiomas, cancers of the back of the nose and throat, in Chinese and certain other Asians. Also recent research has revealed that Karpose's sarcoma, a cancer of the skin, frequently affecting AIDS patients, is caused by a virus. It is not surprising that Sister White was well ahead of her time, for her comments were inspired by the Holy Spirit.

As late as the 1940's, one of the world's most prestigious medical journals, *JAMA – The Journal of the American Medical Association* – declared that there was no credible evidence of a relationship between cigarette smoking and lung cancer. When undertaking specialty training at the Royal Postgraduate Medical School in London in 1969, Russell had the privilege of listening to a lecture by Dr. Charles Fletcher, a pulmonologist, himself a cigarette smoker, who first suggested to the Royal College of Physicians of London that an investigation be undertaken to ascertain whether smoking was indeed a causative agent in lung cancer. That ten-year study, using the doctors of the United Kingdom as the subjects of the investigation, amply confirmed the relationship. Dr. Fletcher ceased his smoking.

At the time of writing this manuscript, the sad testimony of an important Australian politician, fifty-three-year old Jim Bacon, Premier of the Australian state of Tasmania, was heard by millions over national radio and television. Mr.

Bacon publicly declared himself to be an "idiot" after announcing his resignation from politics, upon the discovery of inoperable lung cancer. Mr. Bacon was a cigarette smoker. Had he known of and followed Sister White's counsel, he would have been saved an early death. Within four months of the diagnosis having been made, Mr. Bacon died on June 20, 2004 at fifty-four years of age.

In 1864, Sister White wrote:

> Tobacco is a poison of the most deceitful and malignant kind.
> (*Spiritual Gifts*, Vol. 4A, p. 128).

In 1886 she confirmed that,

> Tobacco is a slow, insidious, but most malignant poison.   (Manuscript 29, 1886).

Sister White repeated these words in 1909 in her book *Ministry of Healing*, p. 327.

In the late nineteenth century, physicians were prescribing smoking for asthma, bronchiectasis and emphysema patients because it initiated coughing and thus the expectoration of phlegm. They did not recognize its malignant potential.

Thus we discern the benefits of inspired writings. Folly they may be to the experts of the day, but how privileged Seventh-day Adventists are to have been privy to the counsels of the Lord all these years! The tragedy is that it is a rare life-long Seventh-day Adventist who has heeded, unfailingly throughout life, God's loving care in providing health principles for His children.

So in the matter of Sister White's counsels and warnings concerning masturbation, are we in a position to treat them with scorn and deny their validity?

Often today, masturbation is treated lightly. Frequently the counsel of Ellen White is ignored or even belittled in this age of all manner of sexual promiscuity. It has frequently been referred to as reflecting the false morality of the Victorian era. Many laugh with scorn at the counsel of Ellen White. But the Word of the Lord cannot be put aside.

> ...both mind and body were enfeebled through the habit of self abuse.
> (*Testimonies for the Church*, Vol. 5, p. 91).

> Your children have practiced self abuse until the draft upon the brain has been so great, ... their minds have been seriously injured. The brilliancy of youthful intellect is dimmed.   (*Testimonies for the Church*, Vol. 2, p. 392).

> If he continues in this vicious practice [masturbation] he will eventually become idiotic.   (*Testimonies for the Church*, Vol. 2, p. 402).

Today modern science is beginning to rethink the issue in the light of relatively recent discoveries. There is a growing concern that this "harmless exploration" does have serious emotional consequences. Dr. David Horrobin of Oxford University related the problem to zinc deficiency. He stated:

> The effect of zinc deficiency has particularly profound effects on the male, because extraordinary amounts of zinc are found in the testicles and the prostate gland... The amount of zinc in semen is such that one ejaculation may get rid of all the zinc that can be absorbed from the intestines in one day.
> (David Horrobin, M.D., Ph.D., *Zinc*, Vitabooks, Inc., 1981, p. 8).

Dr. Horrobin then made these striking statements:

> In humans, among the most consistent effects of zinc deficiency are changes in mood and behavior. There is depression, extreme irritability, apathy and even in some circumstances, behavior which looks like schizophrenia.... It is even possible, given the importance of zinc for the brain, that 19th century moralists were correct when they said that repeated masturbation could make one mad! Similarly, the high livers were also correct when they said that a diet rich in oysters was necessary to compensate for excessive sexual indulgence. [Oysters supply a high level of zinc]. (David Horrobin, *Ibid*).

Another authority, Dr. Carl Pfeiffer of Harvard University, reported research on this issue:

> We hate to say it but in a zinc-deficient adolescent, sexual excitement and excessive masturbation might precipitate insanity.
> (Carl Pfeiffer, Ph.D., M.D., *Zinc and other Micro-Nutrients*, Keats Publishing, Inc. 1978, p. 45).

But there is another issue. Few acts are more egocentric than masturbation and egocentricity is at the root of a vast array of mental illnesses. Some argue that they masturbated in their teenage years without experiencing any mental illnesses. This comment is meant to nullify Sister White's inspired warning. It is akin to a ninety-year-old smoker, who has indulged the addiction for more than seventy years, using his longevity as evidence of a lack of relationship between cigarette smoking and lung cancer.

Others contend that youth would be no more at risk of zinc depletion than married men who indulge in frequent acts of sexual intercourse with their wives. This, manifestly, is a reasonable assertion. Is there not a fearful level of mental illness in our community today? Psychiatrists, psychologists, counselors and psychiatric hospitals have never been busier. Could it be that some of these patients are zinc depleted?

There is, however, another factor related to masturbation. This act requires no consenting second individual, a factor which frequently limits the number of ejaculations among those who confine themselves to sexual intercourse. Masturbation involves the will of a single individual and thus frequently is indulged at shorter intervals than those who practice sexual intercourse.

Further, the teenage years frequently introduce an unsettled period in the lives of youth where their earlier dependence upon their parents is shed in their minds, but not in fact, and complex emotions are aroused as young lads take their first faltering strides towards manhood. Every nutritional element is essential for the mental and physical health of the emerging adult. Thus there is an increased vulnerability in this era of life. Many youth do not pass through this period unscathed. Mental illness and suicides during this period of life have reached alarming levels.

We do not propose that zinc depletion is the lone factor involved in mental disturbances produced by masturbation. The full verification of many of God's counsels both in Scripture and the Spirit of Prophecy will not be revealed until we sit in Christ's Seminars in His kingdom. In the meantime, wise is the individual who places his trust in God and not man. God's advice on this matter is plain:

> Cease ye from man, whose breath is in his nostrils: for wherein is he to be accounted of? (Isaiah 2:22).

> Thus saith the LORD; Cursed be the man that trusteth in man, and maketh flesh his arm, and whose heart departeth from the LORD. (Jeremiah 17:5).

28 The Amalgamation of Man and Beast

When Russell commenced his medical studies at the University of Sydney in the 1950's, the Chairman of the Zoology Department was Challis Professor L. G. Birch, B.Agr.Sc., D.Sc., a man who was highly regarded in his field of academic expertise. He was also a lay-preacher in the Methodist Church.

It should be understood that in the British tertiary system of education adopted by Australia, a Doctor of Science (D.Sc.) is a degree which is infrequently awarded, being regarded as a higher academic rank than the Doctor of Philosophy degree (Ph.D) in scientific studies.

In one of his first lectures, Professor Birch launched into a vitriolic attack upon Creationism. Posing a ridiculous caricature of creationists, he was able to demolish this view very effectively, to the satisfaction of the great majority of the six hundred first-year students commencing the six-year medical course. Professor Birch claimed that creationists taught that all creatures on earth with all their varieties were created by God during creation week. In this he suggested that we creationists claimed that every dog variety was created by God and preserved in Noah's Ark.

Such blatant misrepresentation of our belief astonished Russell. He expected much more difficult scientific "evidence" than that. Creationists well know that selective breeding of animals and plants can produce new varieties, for God placed a vast potential for biodiversity in our genes and in those of all His biological creations.

In the fourth year of his course Russell encountered the Chairman of the Bacteriology Department, Bosch Professor Patrick Macartney de Burgh. In one of his lectures the professor made a clearly illogical statement. He declared viruses to be an intermediate stage between inanimate matter and bacteria. Since viruses possess no ability to reproduce themselves, the theoretical first virus to "evolve" would have been the last. Viruses only multiply by infecting complex cells and causing them to reproduce the virus. Thus complex cells, including bacteria, had to pre-exist viruses or be created simultaneously in order for them to be reproduced.

Yet here were science lecturers at what was not only Australia's first university, but regarded worldwide at that time to be its most eminent, making absurd statements.

Before entering the medical course Russell had read Dr. Frank Lewis Marsh's book, *Creation, Evolution and Science*. Despite receiving his doctorate from the University of Nebraska, Dr. Marsh had maintained his faith in the Bible and the Spirit of Prophecy. Russell owes him, through the 1947 edition of his book, a deep debt of gratitude. It is still a prized book in his library. Russell's scientific studies at the University, included zoology, physics, chemistry, anatomy, physiology, embryology, bacteriology, histology and biochemistry. The study of these scientific disciplines increased his wonderment of the creative genius of the God of heaven. Never for a moment did his faith in creation waver.

Of course much more superficially credible arguments in favour of evolution are advanced by scientists who blindly refuse to recognize the God of heaven. God's infinite creative brilliance is to be seen in the physical world, even more in the field of biological science. (See our book, *The Big Bang Exploded*). Yet, many of our theologians and scientists dare to believe atheistic scientists and doubt Genesis.

On September 8, 1947, Dr. Frank Marsh and Dr. Harold W. Clark, both devout Seventh-day Adventists and both powerful and knowledgeable defenders of creation, met in debate before fifteen of the Seventh-day Adventist Church's leaders. The debate had been organized by the General Conference President, Elder James Lamar McElhany (1880-1959), President (1936-1950). The chairman of the debate was Elder Milton Earl Kern (1875-1961), President of the Seventh-day Adventist Seminary (1937-1943), who was a former Secretary of the General Conference. The subject of the debate was Sister White's statements concerning the amalgamation of man and beast.

Dr. Clark opened the debate. He asserted that Sister White meant precisely what she had written. It was a brave position to take in view of the absence of any scientific evidence that such was possible.

Dr. Marsh spoke second. His conclusion was that Sister White's statements referred to the intermarriage of followers of God with idolaters.

No vote was taken but those present felt that if the vote had been called for, twelve would have supported Dr. Marsh's position and three Dr. Clark's. Notwithstanding that likely result, Dr. Clark was correct, and Dr. Marsh, for once, was wrong.

Dr. Graeme Bradford's book, *Prophets Are Human*, claimed that:

> Mrs. White wrote that some races are a mixture of man and beast. (*op. cit.* p.13).

Did Sister White really make this assertion? Read her words carefully. Sister White wrote:

> But if there was one sin above another which called for the destruction of the race by the flood, it was the base crime of amalgamation of man and beast which defaced the image of God, and caused confusion everywhere. God purposed to destroy by a flood that powerful, long-lived race that had corrupted their ways before him. (*Spiritual Gifts*, Vol. 3, p.64).

Every species of animal which God had created were preserved in the ark. The confused species which God did not create, which were the result of amalgamation, were destroyed by the flood. Since the flood there has been

> amalgamation of man and beast, as may be seen in the almost endless varieties of species of animals, and in certain races of men. (*Ibid*, p.75).

Notice here that there is quite a difference between Dr. Bradford's assertion that Sister White "wrote that some races are a MIXTURE of man and beast" (emphasis added) and the words she actually wrote. She stated that "there had been an amalgamation of man and beast." Sister White's statement leaves open the possibility that there was an amalgamation between man and man and also amalgamation between beast and beast.

While we do not discount this conclusion, drawn from her words which are not absolutely precise, we believe that the most likely meaning of these two passages above is that she meant the amalgamation of man *with* beast. Notice the first passage in which the servant of the Lord described the amalgamation as defacing "the image of God." Man alone was created in God's image.

And God said, Let us make man in our image, after our likeness: (Genesis 1:26).

No beast was created in God's image. It is almost certain that the image of God in man was defiled by the amalgamation of man with beast and perhaps beast with man.

Not only before, but also after the flood, has amalgamation of men and beast occurred. (See *Spiritual Gifts*, p. 75 above). Sister White plainly stated that Satan undertook plant amalgamation. Writing in Australia in 1899 she stated:

> Not one noxious plant was placed in the Lord's great garden, but after Adam and Eve sinned, poisonous herbs sprang up. In the parable of the sower the question was asked the master, "Didst not thou sow good seed in thy field? from whence then hath it tares?" The master answered, "An enemy hath done this" (Matt. 13:27, 28). All tares are sown by the evil one. Every noxious herb is of his sowing, and by his ingenious methods of amalgamation he has corrupted the earth with tares.
>
> (*SDA Bible Commentary*, Vol. 1, p.1086; *Selected Messages*, Vol. 2, p.288).

These inspired statements of Sister White have been challenged repeatedly. It was well known that bestiality – sexual intercourse between humans and animals – produced no progeny. Thus Sister White's words were ridiculed.

One of the great acts of arrogance of mankind is that at any point in time we imagine that we know most of that which is to be known about science and nature. But repeatedly we have been proven incorrect in this assumption. Even during a large part of the first half of the twentieth century, astronomers believed that the entire universe consisted of a single galaxy – the Milky Way – of which our planetary system forms a part. Today the count of galaxies has increased from one to around one hundred billion (100,000,000,000), an enormous alteration. Yet how can we be certain that this count will not further increase as mortal man constructs even more powerful telescopes and devises more and more methods of detecting such cosmic objects?

In 1881 Sister White wrote that:

> God...upholds millions of worlds [planets].
> (*Testimonies for the Church*, Vol. 4, p. 653).

On May 15, 1896 Sister White declared that:

> God has unnumbered worlds [planets] that are obedient to His laws.
> (*Special Testimonies on Education* quoted in *Counsels to Parents, Teachers and Students*, p. 66).

In the nineteenth century not a single planet outside our solar system had been identified. Since the first such planet was confirmed in the 1990's, each year more have been identified. *Scientific American*, May, 2004 reported that one hundred and twenty planets have been identified outside our solar system. With new techniques now devised for detecting these planets, a large increase in the number of such planets discovered is expected. The same edition of *Scientific American* revealed the discovery of three new planets in our own solar system, one each in the years 2002 (Quaoar), 2003 (Sedna) and 2004 (not yet named, as we write, but designated 2004 WD).

Many times we have judged the inspiration of the Holy Spirit through the "wisdom" of our ignorance. Thirty years ago Russell conversed with a theologian who assured him that there were no health or biological reasons why cattle were classed as clean and horses unclean by Scripture. The distinction he suggested was cultic, based upon social beliefs during the era of the life of Moses.

Russell then possessed no knowledge concerning the difference in one's health if he ate cow's flesh or horse's flesh. Nor does he yet understand the basis for this divinely-inspired distinction which was present at the time of the Flood (Genesis 7:8). One day scientists may discover the reason. But as Russell responded to the theologian, "One matter is certain, when we sit down at the Master's feet in the kingdom He will assuredly supply our present ignorance with ample evidence of His wisdom. Until that day I will trust His word." It is on the basis of the vast ignorance of mankind that many arguments diminishing Sister White's inspired words falter.

The subject of the amalgamation of man and beast during the nineteenth and first half of the twentieth centuries was a matter of mystery. Even in the 1950's when Russell was studying Medicine at the University of Sydney, he was puzzled concerning this matter, but not daunted.

However, through the second half of the twentieth century as our knowledge of genetics has expanded "at the speed of light," following the discovery of the double-helix formation of the deoxyribo-nucleic acid (DNA) molecule by James Watson (born 1928) and Francis Crick (1916-2004), which they completed on

> Saturday, 7 March, 1953.
> (John Gribbin, *In Search of the Double Helix*, Corgi Books, London, 1988, p.239),

our understanding has grown in massive strides.

When Russell completed his specialty training in 1969 in London he felt he was knowledgeable concerning the subject of genetics. Yet when he sat at Andrews University in a class taught by his son, Timothy, who had received his Ph.D. in genetics in the early 1990's, Russell recognized just how little he had known in 1969.

Yet Timothy, himself, had received a rude shock. When, in 1993, he attended a large genetics convention in Houston, Texas, convened to celebrate the fortieth anniversary of Watson and Crick's discovery of the double-helix DNA molecule, he was astounded to learn how much more had been discovered only two years after he had completed his doctorate. He had scored A's in every Ph.D. course he had taken, yet in two years he felt out of date. Later he was able to have a chat with Professor Crick and expressed his amazement at the rapidity of advances in the science of genetics. Professor Crick, who received the Nobel Prize for his discovery, replied, "Don't worry Timothy, it's now largely beyond me, I just can't keep abreast of all the thousands of new discoveries myself."

We record the above family experiences in order to demonstrate the abject folly of judging any of Sister White's writings as false on the basis of current scientific knowledge, brilliant as many of these discoveries are. We would do well to observe the words of Sir Martin Rees (born 1942), Master of Trinity College, Cambridge University, England, the current holder of the prestigious title of Astronomer Royal and a former Professor of Astronomy. Sir Martin succinctly expressed the current state of scientific knowledge:

> If we learn anything from the pursuit of science, it is that even something as basic as an atom is quite difficult to understand.... This alone should induce skepticism about any [scientific] dogma or any claim to have achieved more than a very incomplete and metaphorical insight into any profound aspect of our existence.
>
> (*Scientific American*, July, 2004, p. 25).

We Seventh-day Adventists should possess an even greater humility than that expressed by Sir Martin Rees, for we possess a knowledge of the infinite God of the universe.

What Sister White – if she were not directly inspired by God – could not have possibly understood herself, today we do, for genetic engineering is advancing yearly by giant steps.

We must remember that prior to the Noachian Flood,

> There were giants in the earth in those days; and also after that, when the sons of God came in unto the daughters of men, and they bare children to them, the same became mighty men which were of old, men of renown. (Genesis 6:4).

There were not only men of massive physical strength but also "men of renown," possessing intellects far beyond ours. Further, this intellectual brilliance was combined with wickedness commensurate with their intellectual and physical powers, for we are told:

> ⁵And God saw that the wickedness of man was great in the earth, and that every imagination of the thoughts of his heart was only evil continually. ⁶And it repented the LORD that he had made man on the earth, and it grieved him at his heart. (Genesis 6:5, 6).

Their minds yielded to Satan, there is no doubt that Satan coached those vile and wicked men in all his evil arts. We must remember that these men, who lived for centuries, were able to develop their skills and knowledge over periods of nine generations and thus influence vast numbers of their descendants and contemporaries.

Adam was lofty and noble (*Great Controversy*, p.644; *Patriarchs and Prophets*, p.45; *Spiritual Gifts*, Volume 4-a, p.120). He was more than twice as tall as we are (*Spiritual Gifts*, Vol. 3, p.34; *Story of Redemption*, p.21). He possessed twenty times the vital force of that of today's men, no doubt even when in their mental and physical primes. (*Testimonies for the Church*, Vol. 3, pp.138, 139). Even though these Edenic characteristics were somewhat diminished by the principle of sin in the life, the fact that many of Adam's descendants lived nine centuries and more, including his great-great-great-great-great-great-great grandson, Noah, and even Noah's son Shem lived six centuries, there can be no shadow of doubt that such men would have been capable of the acquirement of vast stores of knowledge, building upon that which Adam undoubtedly conveyed to them from the knowledge he had acquired in Eden.

In a letter, written in 1898, Sister White stated:

> There perished in the Flood greater inventions of art and human skill than the world knows of today. The arts destroyed were more than the boasted arts of today (Letter 65, 1898). (*SDA Bible Commentary*, Vol. 1, p. 1089).

The loss of profound knowledge at the time of the Flood is often overlooked. In another letter written the following year, Sister White revealed that,

> More was lost in the Flood, in many ways, than men today know. Looking upon the world, God saw that the intellect He had given man was perverted, that the imagination of his heart was evil and that continually. God had given these men knowledge. He had given them valuable ideas, that they might carry out His plan. But the Lord saw that those whom He designed should possess wisdom, tact, and judgment, were using every quality of the mind to glorify self. By the waters of the Flood, He blotted this long-lived race from the earth, and with them perished the knowledge they had used only for evil. When the earth was repeopled, the Lord trusted His wisdom more sparingly to men, giving them only the ability they would need in carrying out His great plan (Letter 175, 1896). (*Ibid*).

That mankind carefully studied the beasts that God had created cannot be doubted.

> How did man gain his knowledge of how to devise?—From the Lord, by studying the formation and habits of different animals. Every animal is a lesson book, and

from the use they make of their bodies and the weapons provided them, men have learned to make apparatus for every kind of work. If men could only know how many arts have been lost to our world, they would not talk so fluently of the dark ages. Could they have seen how God once worked through His human subjects, they would speak with less confidence of the arts of the antediluvian world. (*Ibid*).

That these men, now bent on evil, had acquired the knowledge of the genetic code and possessed skills in manipulating it, need not be doubted. That this knowledge survived the Flood is a conjecture which bears credibility. We know the skills, many long since lost, of the long-lived post-deluvian races, who also lived several hundreds of years, as we view their architectural achievements in edifices such as the pyramids. In these we perceive their advanced astronomical knowledge also. They even corrected for the curvature of the earth in their construction.

Let it not be forgotten Shem lived to six hundred years of age. His son Arphaxad, lived 438 years; grandson, Salah, 433 years; great-grandson, Eber, 464 years. (See Genesis 11:10-17). During the life of Eber's son, Peleg, the earth was divided, almost certainly after the destruction of the Tower of Babel. Since Eber outlived his own son, Peleg, by 191 years, he was most certainly alive at the time of the destruction of the Tower of Babel. Peleg's grandfather, Salah, outlived him by 130 years; his great-grandfather, Arphaxad outlived Peleg by 100 years. Shem, Peleg's great-great grandfather, survived him by 162 years, while even his great-great-great grandfather, Noah, lived ten years beyond Peleg's death. Indeed, Noah did not die until two years prior to Abraham's birth and Shem and Abraham were contemporaries for 150 years, almost the entire life of Abraham.[1]

Even Isaac and Shem were alive contemporaneously for about fifty years. Thus the knowledge of the antediluvians was passed on to many generations.

We must remember also that sin and wickedness soon arose after the flood. Nimrod was a great-grandson of Noah. Thus Sister White wrote in a 1896 letter:

---

[1] In fact the lives of Abraham and Noah probably overlapped. We state this because the patriarchs counted their age of one from birth, as the Chinese still do today. This is confirmed in the account of Noah's life. Scripture states that Noah was six hundred years old when the Flood came. (Genesis 7:6). Yet later the Bible declares that the Flood commenced in Noah's six-hundredth year. (Genesis 7:11). Thus Noah was actually, by western calculations, 599 years old when the Flood came and was only in his "six hundredth and first" year, that is 600 years old by western calculations, when the floodwaters were dried up. (Genesis 8:13). Using the eastern reckoning of ages, Arphaxad was thirty-five when he begat his son Salah. (Genesis 11:12), but by western calculations he was thirty-four and an unspecified number of months when his son was born. This is true of each of the ten generations between Noah and Abraham. Since Scripture does not provide us with the number of months beyond their birthday that each patriarch was when his son was born we may make a rough approximation of an average of six months. This would reduce the number of years by five in western calculations. (Ten generations multiplied by $1/2$ a year = five years). Thus it is likely that Abraham was about three years old when Noah died.

> But no sooner was the earth repeopled than men resumed their hostility to God and heaven. They transmitted their enmity to their posterity, as though the art and device of misleading men, and causing them to continue the unnatural warfare, was a sacred legacy (Letter 4, 1896). (*Ibid*).

Writing in *The Review and Herald* of December 10, 1903, Sister White, speaking of the confederacy of the dwellers on the Plain of Shinar, revealed that:

> This confederacy was born of rebellion against God. The dwellers on the plain of Shinar established their kingdom for self-exaltation, not for the glory of God. Had they succeeded, a mighty power would have borne sway, banishing righteousness, and inaugurating a new religion. The world would have been demoralized. The mixture of religious ideas with erroneous theories would have resulted in closing the door to peace, happiness, and security.

Few Seventh-day Adventists have pondered the implications of a single sentence written by Sister White at the age of thirty in 1858. (See *Early Writings*, p. 184). In this sentence is encapsulated the qualities of the antediluvians and even those who lived after the flood to the days of Abraham. When we examine this sentence, none has any excuse to doubt that neither the inhabitants before the Noachian Flood, nor those after the Flood, had the skills and abilities to manipulate genes.

> I was informed that those who lived in the days of Noah and Abraham were more like the angels in form, in comeliness and strength. (*Spiritual Gifts*, Vol. 1, p. 70).

It was due to these mental and physical advantages that there was no need of the writing of Scripture until five hundred years after the birth of Abraham, for the history of the world and the plan of salvation were passed down by word of mouth to following generations, by men with superb memories.

In view of these facts there is now no excuse for Seventh-day Adventists to cast the least doubt upon Sister White's inspired revelations that genetic engineering in those days was undertaken, in which there was an amalgamation of man and beast.

How do we, the authors, ourselves know that the races we have discovered in our own ancestry – English, German, Irish, Scottish and very likely if we go back thirteen-hundred years, Slavic, (and who knows what other races make up our ancestry), have not been cursed by such genetic engineering? We know not if some evil scientist soon after the flood did not insert animal genes in one or more of our ancestors.

Today scientists, with their greatly limited minds as compared with the mental skills of those even living in the first few generations after the flood, are able to achieve the skills of genetic engineering. Why should we then stumble over Sister White's inspired revelations that such genetic tinkering occurred in an era when men were far more intellectually able to accomplish these feats of science? Shame on us as a people!

That their early post-deluvian minds were vastly more retentive of knowledge than we are today, may be judged from the fact that God found it unnecessary to commit the story of Creation and the early history of the world, together with His inestimable plan of salvation, to written form until over eight hundred years after the Flood.

> During the first twenty-five hundred years of human history, there was no written revelation. Those who had been taught of God, communicated their knowledge to others, and it was handed down from father to son, through successive generations. (*Great Controversy*, p. v).

"Dr. Harold Smithurst," a fictional character in *Prophets Are Human*, rightly conceded that,

> With scientific progress over recent years we can see it is possible to mix the genes of animals and humankind. So she [Sister White] wouldn't be out of harmony with science on that account. (*Prophets Are Human*, p.65).

Nevertheless, doubt was engendered by the words,

> However, [How often this word prefaces doubt], it's the statement made about the mixture giving us certain races that creates a problem. It was commonly believed in her day that certain races of people came into being as a result of the amalgamation between humans and animals – for instance, the wild Bushmen of Africa. (*Ibid*).

Here again, Dr. Bradford inferred the charge that Sister White was simply regurgitating the views of secular minds of her day. This was a most serious accusation for, if true, it seriously undermined Sister White's prophetic gift. Well we would ponder, "What else did she proclaim which was simply the conventional wisdom of her day?" "Did Sister White only present the conventional wisdom of faulted Protestant theologians when she set forth the plan of salvation?" This would be a valid question if Sister White's writings were sprinkled with error because she was dependent upon uninspired writers for her written concepts.

While Dr. Bradford does not accuse Sister White of identifying the "wild bushman of Africa" as an amalgamation of man and beast, to include it is to associate Sister White with this quite unsubstantiated claim, for Sister White identified no race of mankind blighted by amalgamation of man and beast. In March, 2003, during our visit to South Africa, we met a few African bushmen. They were, of course, ordinary human beings.

Our problem is that some of us in our naivety have been seeking races which appear half-human and half-beast. It seems that the ancients looked for such creatures as seen in their mythical mermaids and figures of beasts with human heads, shoulders and upper limbs but animal bodies such as the centaur, half human, half horse. Perhaps some early scientists in these cultures dreamed of a human with a fish-tail, who could swim the vast stretches of earth's oceans. Perhaps others hoped to use genetic engineering to design a work-horse with the mind of a man and capability of speech. Such a theoretical creature could be instructed to plough a field and be left to do so without human guidance during the day of work. Of course no such creature was ever designed.

Yet we well know that in many of our supermarkets and fruit and vegetable stalls today are tomatoes containing a fish gene which extends the shelf-life of these tomatoes. Do these genetic amalgams of fruit (as tomatoes rightly are classified) and fish appear like a tomato with a fish's tail protruding from it? Of course not!

> Scientists are able to splice together genetic material from humans and animals… Chinese experts made a hybrid embryo from a human and a rabbit last year.
> (Brisbane *Sunday Mail*, September 19, 2004)

As we were writing this chapter, one of the news reports on the Australian ABC Newsradio and also on the SBS Television News of February 17, 2004, revealed that by placing a new gene into mice and rats scientists have succeeded in doubling muscle bulk. The news item predicted that such genes could be used by athletes to improve dramatically their athletic performances. No blood or urine test could be useful in detecting this genetic alteration. Only an operation to remove muscle tissue for examination would lead to detection. Few athletes would countenance such tests.

A scientific journal included an article concerning this matter, entitled "Gene Doping." The journal stated:

> Gene therapy for restoring muscle lost to age or disease [for example, muscular dystrophy] is poised to enter the clinic, but elite athletes are eyeing it to enhance performance. Can it be long before gene doping changes the nature of sport?
> (*Scientific American*, July, 2004, pp. 36-43).

A synthetic gene has been developed to greatly enhance muscle strength and bulk.

It is quite possible that as antediluvian and postdiluvian men viewed the mighty strength of bulls, they could well have inserted such a muscle gene into men, thus maximizing mankind's strength. It is also possible that they could have synthesized a gene, similar to that already achieved by scientists today. What damage such defiling of God's genetic code does to the human system, originally perfectly designed by our Creator, we do not know.

It is time that we heeded the powerful admonition of King Jehoshaphat.

> …Jehoshaphat stood and said, Hear me, O Judah, and ye inhabitants of Jerusalem; Believe in the LORD your God, so shall ye be established; believe his prophets, so shall ye prosper. (2 Chronicles 20:20).

We possess no good reason to doubt this admonition today as we study the Spirit of Prophecy.

Part VI
An Ineffective Ministry

29 The Ministry and the Ellen White Reality Check

The impact of the destruction of faith in the Spirit of Prophecy upon ministerial training at Avondale College and subsequent ministerial performance has been evaluated. (See evidence below) The results are clear for all to see. Yet, rather than learning from the results of the attempted demolition of the Seventh-day Adventist faith, many in the church have deemed it appropriate to further degrade the one object of Christ's supreme regard. Many in the leadership of the church appear to be bent upon leading it deeper into the Omega of Apostasy which they have sponsored, by calling a Summit at Avondale College.

The preponderance of attendees and presenters at the Summit were, no doubt, selected to lead to an atmosphere of doubt in the Spirit of Prophecy. All details emerging indicate this fact.

Let us turn to a non-Seventh-day Adventist survey of Avondale's ministerial educational results and the consequences in the field after graduation.

Prior to March, 2002, the South Pacific Division sought the assistance of the Christian Research Association of Melbourne to provide information concerning various aspects of the training and ministry of the one hundred and seventy Avondale graduates who entered the ministry in the previous decade. That report was presented to the Division in May, 2002. It presented a disastrous state among these pastors, which in turn is reflected in the deplorable state of today's church. Eighty-five (fifty per cent) of the ministers responded to the survey; seventeen per cent of the responders had already departed from the ministry.

Of no surprise, but a matter of extreme concern, was the evaluation of these pastors of their training at Avondale College. Considering the perilous state of Avondale ministerial training, one matter of major concern is the revelation of the survey that,

> Those students for whom English was not their first language rated Avondale much more positively than did students for whom English was their first language.

Since the ethnic churches now constitute a large segment of our membership in Australia and New Zealand, this finding should challenge the thinking of ethnic church congregations, causing them to so stand by the principles of the faith, that their young people will discern the pitiful level of ministerial education offered by Avondale College. They would be well advised to seek genuine ministerial training elsewhere for their young men. This they will find in faithful self-supporting training schools.

In this report we can only quote a selection of the comments made by these pastors for the report extended for more than sixty pages. Of course, some of the pastors reported positively upon their education at Avondale and yet even among these were comments which will alarm and alert sincere Seventh-day Adventists. The clear message is that some of our young ministers revelled in the liberal teachings, pluralism and human opinions which pervaded their training. Two reported:

> "My understanding of the Bible and the gospel has evolved dramatically due to my training at college. This evolution has taken me toward the 'Liberal' end of the spectrum. A process I am thankful for."

> "All Biblical subjects maintained an openness to learning and voicing one's opinion. Diversity of opinion was excellent."

Disdain for the beliefs of faithful members in the pew was evident.

> "Avondale lecturers are of a high caliber both as academic professionals and practising Christians. Any concerns about the content of the theology curriculum usually assumes the inadequacy in doctrinal/Biblical teaching at the local church level (in my experience) – unprogressive and outdated theology."

It is also evident that "the old paths" are no longer acceptable.

We were surprised at the very crude language used by some pastors, language unbecoming to any Christian. The words of four pastors are cited:

> "…in spite of all the stuff ups…."

> "…I had no support from the gutless conference presidents…."

> "…not be gutless, but tell the truth and do what is right…."

> "It's a lot of crap…."

How this language is understood in other English-speaking nations we do not know, but in Australia and New Zealand it is only used by the crudest elements of society.

Examples of the evaluation of the pastors of their training at Avondale present a sorry state of affairs in this Division institution:

1. DESTRUCTION OF FAITH:

> "Avondale tried to teach us to think. Instead it tore down our faith and never taught us to rebuild it."

> "If anything Avondale almost crushed any confidence in Adventism and Christianity."

2. DEPLETION OF SPIRITUALITY:

> "They teach theology, that is their job. I found I lost a great deal of my 'experience with the Lord.'"

3. UNCERTAINTY ENGENDERED:

"Training at Avondale raised more questions then it gave answers or understandings."

"My experience with Jesus was strengthened due to the many theological conflicts I had in the classroom.... I also hold no personal grudges against the lecturers, but a number of them do not support the church or its mission in the way the church expects."

4. HIGHER CRITICISM TAUGHT:

"I often went to God pleading for help to answer higher critical attacks on God's Word."

"Many lecturers were involved in higher critical techniques to approach Scripture. A number of articles were introduced to the class that destroyed confidence in the Bible and especially Spirit of Prophecy. There were direct attacks on heavenly sanctuary doctrine, 1844, the Remnant concept, Ellen G White, Revelation 14:6-12."

5. LECTURERS DOUBTING INSPIRATION:

"Most teachers struggled to have a simple trust in Jesus and a confident faith in His infallible Word. This made it hard to be involved in that type of environment."

6. LACK OF TEACHING OF PROPHECY:

"We did not study the 27 Fundamentals in detail – especially Daniel and Revelation. We did not study these exegetically for prophetic meaning – only historical meaning.... I had people who knew more about our beliefs in the local church than I did! I was embarrassed many times and asked 'what did they teach you at Avondale?'"

7. LACK OF TRAINING IN TRUTH:

"I was very disappointed that we wasted so much time with the academic nonsense that was dished up. We should have spent more time studying the TRUTH instead of scholar's garbage."

8. SECULAR ATMOSPHERE:

"There is a pervasive worldly/secular atmosphere at Avondale that just seemed to be constantly sapping the spiritual life out of me – all under the guise of 'Christianity'. That part was awful."

9. FAILURE TO TEACH PRACTICAL MINISTRY:

"Avondale was the worst 2 years of my life. Avondale was an academic game. It should have been an 'experience'.... The volunteers I now employ after one year are more qualified than those who spend 2-4 years at Avondale – Why? Because they are taught practical ministry."

"There could have been more practical subjects in the course instead of mostly theory."

"The approach of Avondale College to ministry was impractical and highly scholastic leaving me with few learned skills for ministry."

"Avondale College did not prepare us for the role and function of a day to day pastor. Hopeless!!"

"I never recall a lecturer sharing how to lead a person to Jesus and go through the 'sinners' prayer with someone."

10. TRAINING LED TO SOME LEAVING THE MINISTRY:

"Distinctives were blurred not stressed. Fundamentals taken for granted. I have been in Ministry now for 10 years. Most of my class have dropped out. Most were new Adventists and college did not ground them."

11. DESTRUCTION OF DISTINCTIVES:

"Some lecturers spent more time tearing down Adventist distinctives than teaching them. I fear [for] any young person deciding to go to college to be trained as a minister."

We summarize the doctrines diminished; the numbers refer to the points above:
1. The Bible – 4, 5,
2. The Spirit of Prophecy – 4
3. Sanctuary doctrine – 4
4. 1844 – 4
5. The Remnant – 4
6. Sister White – 4
7. The Three Angels' Messages – 4
8. Prophecy – 6

A summary of other training defects:
1. Practical ministry – 9
2. Faith destroyed – 1, 2, 10, 11
3. Doubts engendered – 3, 5
4. Higher criticism taught – 4
5. Truth diminished – 7
6. Secularism dominated – 8

These sample responses expose the utter failure of Avondale College as a training ground for the ministry. If Avondale College were to close its doors this year, it would be to the great benefit of our church in the South Pacific. Nothing causes greater harm to a church than ministers steeped in error, unable to discern between sin and righteousness. The evaluations cited above must be considered in the light of the fact that many students entering Avondale are not stayed upon the truth. Such would not correctly perceive error as it is presented to them. That some have, indicates the dangerous situation at Avondale and as it continues to pursue university status (South Pacific *Record,* March, 2004), and the College Church continues to press for the return of Dr Ford to our pulpits, the situation can only deteriorate further.

What can we expect of our graduating pastors when a senior theology professor, Dr. Norman Young, dared to destroy our prophetic interpretation over national radio? He stated:

> "I think the biggest problem has been our eschatology [our understanding of end-time prophecies], in the way we have interpreted parts of Daniel. Yes and we have interpreted very much a 'them and us' mentality and 'them' is going to be against the 'us', and we have been, I think, less than charitable in the way we have interpreted the book of Revelation in particular, relative to the other Christian communities. We have been quite comfortable about sticking 'Babylon' kind of language on them which, I find, quite unpalatable and very poor exegesis [explanation of a passage of Scripture]."
>
> (Interview of Dr. Norman Young with Jon Cleary, Radio National [2BL Sydney], March 3, 2002).

The same professor, in 2001, presented a lecture at Macquarie University in Sydney, declaring that Antiochus Epiphanes fulfilled the prophecy of Daniel 9:27. The abomination of desolation cannot refer to Antiochus Epiphanes (215-163 BC) for Christ placed the abomination of desolation future to His days on earth, at the time of the destruction of Jerusalem and the final events on this sin-cursed earth, not back in the second century BC when Antiochus Epiphanes ruled.

> When ye therefore shall see the abomination of desolation, spoken of by Daniel the prophet, stand in the holy place, (whoso readeth, let him understand:)
>
> (Matthew 24:15).

The Christian Research Association report also painted a dismal account of intern supervision and care of newly-appointed pastors by their mentors and Conference Ministerial Secretaries.

What the South Pacific Division did with this survey is not yet evident. One major difficulty is that the present Division Secretary, Dr. Barry Oliver, was a Professor of Theology at Avondale College during most of the period in which these ministers undertook their training. Writing two years after the survey was undertaken, we discern no significant change in the training at Avondale. The Summit of February 2-5, 2004, re-evaluating Sister White provided proof beyond all dispute that the same destruction of faith prevails. The 2002 survey clearly did not cause sufficient alarm in the Division office to call a Summit inviting faithful laypeople and ministers to provide solutions to the obvious failure of Avondale.

There is an urgent need for Division accountability since the Division President is the College Board Chairman. Avondale College has shareholders – every church member in the South Pacific. With comments such as those cited above, it is perfectly understandable why the Division has not laid this report before the church membership during the more than two years since it was rendered. But nothing less is acceptable. The laity must be informed and consulted. By this suggestion we do not urge the formation of a select few chosen from the liberal wing of the church.

This report reveals a crisis of monumental proportions in the Seventh-day Adventist Church. The church organization in the South Pacific Division has failed God's people and, far more importantly, God Himself. The officers of the church organization are certainly not qualified themselves to restore that which they have destroyed. Avondale College was founded by God through Sister White, to be an example to the world church as God's paradigm for all other Seventh-day Adventist colleges. In its early days the Holy Spirit walked the grounds of the campus.

> We need to realize that the Holy Spirit, who is as much a person as God is a person, is walking through these grounds.
> (*Manuscript* 66, 1899, a talk given to the students at the Avondale School, see *Evangelism*, p. 616).

It is the duty of the Division to share this sixty-four-page report with every church member. Enormous changes to the staffing of the College must be undertaken. All professors unfaithful to their trust must be released. We dare not continue the present course, for God cannot bless the Seventh-day Adventist church in apostasy any more than He did Israel. Manifestly, men and women of the greatest spiritual attainments and fidelity to Scriptural truth and the inspired writings of Sister White, men and women filled with the Holy Ghost, should be called upon to rectify the disastrous state of our church.

Lay people, the remedy rests with you. The church organization has demonstrated a total incapacity to dispel the Omega of Apostasy now rampant in the South Pacific and on all inhabited continents. Letters of protest are required. To sit by in quietude without lifting our voices and pens in protest is to suffer God's strident condemnation.

> [10]His watchmen *are* blind: they are all ignorant, they *are* all dumb dogs, they cannot bark; sleeping, lying down, loving to slumber. [11]Yea, *they are* greedy dogs *which* can never have enough, and they *are* shepherds *that* cannot understand: they all look to their own way, every one for his gain, from his quarter. [12]Come ye, *say they*, I will fetch wine, and we will fill ourselves with strong drink; and tomorrow shall be as this day, *and* much more abundant.   (Isaiah 56:10-12).

Constituents at Local Conference, Union Conference and Division Constituency meetings should ensure that the agenda lists the matter of the Omega of Apostasy early in the proceedings, so that it may be fully discussed before delegates need to return home. This enables all delegates to speak to the issue. There can be no more pressing item for discussion. Faithful laity and ministry should not rest satisfied until positive answers to this evil in our midst are addressed and Biblical and Spirit of Prophecy solutions put in place. None should feel satisfied with pat answers. There should be an insistence upon the appointment of a commission to examine, recommend and implement the sweeping changes urgently needed. The church administration must not be permitted to stack such a commission with its own appointees. Humble, faithful laypeople are required – not those who are dependent upon the favour of church administrators for their preferment. Let us select those which Scripture counsels, those –

> Who are least esteemed in the church. (1 Corinthians 6:4).

Sweeping changes in how the College teachers are appointed must be implemented and all unfaithful teachers and college administrators terminated. Nothing short of these drastic actions will measure up to the critical situation in our Colleges. Only those who teach, believe, and in God's grace, practice Scriptural and Spirit of Prophecy counsels must be appointed.

Having provided the reader with that which is transpiring in the training of our ministers, we now turn to the consequences affecting their ministry in the various Conferences. Since the survey was conducted among those who had entered the ministry in the decade prior to the issuing of the report in 2002, it provided an up-to-date picture of the shameful state of ministerial preparation for the sacred duty of ministry in the South Pacific.

Only church members devoid of spirituality could remain unmoved by the current state of our ministers, which is fully reflected in the failure of most pastors in our midst. We can only conclude that Avondale College bears the major responsibility in this Division for the fact that Sister White evaluated the work of the ministry in these last days as a betrayal of ministerial duty.

> The ancient men, those to whom God had given great light and who had stood as guardians of the spiritual interests of the people, had betrayed their trust.
> *(Testimonies for the Church,* Vol. 5, p. 211).

Avondale College must also accept responsibility for the fact that, along with most of our Seventh-day Adventist Colleges and Universities on other continents,

> pride, avarice, selfishness and deceptions of almost every kind are in the church.
> *(Testimonies for the Church,* Vol. 5, p. 210).

Upon these institutions rest much of the responsibility that in our church,

> the servants of Satan triumph. God is dishonoured, the truth made of none effect.
> *(Testimonies for the Church,* Vol. 5, p. 211).

Avondale College appears to be wanting in its failure to warn those entering ministry that,

> No superiority of rank, dignity, or worldly wisdom, no position in sacred office, will preserve men from sacrificing principle when left to their own deceitful hearts. Those who have been regarded as worthy and righteous prove to be ringleaders in apostasy and examples in indifference and in the abuse of God's mercies. Their wicked course He will tolerate no longer, and in His wrath He deals with them without mercy. (*Testimonies for the* Church, Vol. 5, p. 212).

This is a warning which all we ministers must ponder, seeking the Holy Spirit's power to keep us loyal to our wonderful God, true watchmen on the walls of Zion, true shepherds of God's precious flock. It is in the hands – and is the first sacred duty – of each minister to study divine counsels for himself.

Professors hold a place of advantage. If they are not guided by the Holy Spirit, they can destroy their students – both as faithful ministers and in their personal walk with God. Students depend upon professors for their academic grades. This predisposes them to accept the professors' thoughts as truth. This situation is compounded by the fact that most young people entering Avondale to train for ministry would, no doubt, fail an elementary examination on the three angels' messages, Daniel and Revelation, the sanctuary message, the remnant church, end-time events, righteousness by faith, true Sabbath observance, even the state of the dead and other salient features of the faith.

Let our teachers at Avondale give full weight to the fact that in God's final judgment, the suffering of unfaithful pastors, themselves included, will be

> tenfold greater than that of their people. (*Early Writings*, p. 282)

Here is the personal tragedy for those young people destroyed by Avondale and of those bent upon their destruction. Here lies the responsibility of the South Pacific Division leadership at all levels. Here resides the culpability of pastors and laymen who remain in silence, fearing their own reputations would be destroyed should they vocally, and by pen, cry out against the rank abominations in our church. This was a fault evident among the spiritual leaders in Christ's day.

> The day of God's vengeance is just upon us. The seal of God will be placed upon the foreheads of those only who sigh and cry for the abominations done in the land. (*Testimonies for the Church*, Vol. 5, p. 212).

> [42]Nevertheless among the chief rulers also many believed on him; but because of the Pharisees they did not confess him, lest they should be put out of the synagogue: [43]For they loved the praise of men more than the praise of God.
> (John 12:42, 43).

The prevailing theme among our teachers and thus our people today is that the saints will continue to sin until Jesus comes. This view is unscriptural.

> Here is the patience of the saints: here *are* they that keep the commandments of God, and the faith of Jesus. (Revelation 14:12).

Others preach sermons ignoring the Words of God.

> Having therefore these promises, dearly beloved, let us cleanse ourselves from all filthiness of the flesh and spirit, perfecting holiness in the fear of God.
> (2 Corinthians 7:1).

Their sermons rather encourage their hearers to believe the very opposite. We quote below the tenor of these sermons, emphasising the errors in bold type, while comparing them with the truth:

> **Despite having** these promises dearly beloved, **we cannot** cleanse ourselves from all filthiness of the flesh and spirit and we cannot perfect holiness in the fear of God.

Still other preachers implicitly deny –

> ⁶Whosoever abideth in him sinneth not: whosoever sinneth hath not seen him, neither known him…. ⁹Whosoever is born of God doth not commit sin; for his seed remaineth in him: and he cannot sin, because he is born of God.
> (1 John 3:6, 9).

Rather, the tenor of their messages declares that:

> Whosoever abideth in him **continues to sin: whosoever sinneth has seen him and does know him if he so professeth….** Whosoever is born of God **continues to live a life of sin;** for his seed remaineth in him and he **cannot cease from sin despite being** born of God.

Other presentations from the pulpit appear to have totally dismissed the words below:

> That we henceforth be no more children, tossed to and fro, and carried about with every wind of doctrine, by the sleight of men, and cunning craftiness, whereby they lie in wait to deceive; (Ephesians 4:14).

Rather, the theme of the presentation is:

> **That we henceforth be children** tossed to and fro and carried about by every wind of doctrine, by the sleight of men, and cunning craftiness, **happily listening while** they lie in wait and deceive.

Finally, some ministers dare to ignore the following encouragement to their listeners.

> But we are bound to give thanks alway to God for you, brethren beloved of the Lord, because God hath from the beginning chosen you to salvation through sanctification of the Spirit and belief of the truth: (2 Thessalonians 2:13).

On the contrary, those present in the pews are left with the understanding that:

The Greatest of All the Prophets

> We are bound to give thanks always to God for you, brethren beloved of the Lord, because God hath from the beginning chosen you to salvation, **though unsanctified and believing heresy.**

The theme of most pastors today is as if Revelation 14:12 were,

> Here is the patience of the saints. Here are they that **cannot possibly** keep the commandments of God, **despite possessing** the faith of Jesus.

Salvation is at stake! Only those who *are* now holy will be holy still after the close of probation.

> He that is unjust, let him be unjust still: and he which is filthy, let him be filthy still: and he that is righteous, let him be righteous still: and he that is holy, let him be holy still. (Revelation 22:11).

> It is now that we must keep ourselves and our children unspotted from the world. It is now that we must wash our robes of character and make them white in the blood of the Lamb. It is now that we must overcome pride, passion, and spiritual slothfulness. It is now that we must awake and make determined effort for symmetry of character. (*Testimonies for the Church*, Vol. 5, pp. 215, 216).

30 The Current State of Our Ministry

The "Seventh-day Adventist Minister Survey" revealed a faulted interview system in selecting ministerial graduates for Conference appointment. The internship programme was, in most instances, a failure, and mentors, ministerial secretaries and Conference presidents, with some notable exceptions, were quite unhelpful in offering support for these fledglings in the ministry.

Below are quoted sample comments from the young pastors interviewed.

1. Interview process for selection for appointment:

   "It was a disaster!!! Judgmental and preconceptions!!! A non Christian experience!! It's a wonder I survived it!"

   "…I found the question offensive because at the time I was very genuine about being a minister and serving the church."

   "Very false and only judging the externals."

   "We weren't asked how we related to church fundamental beliefs. Many of my friends whom I knew did not share the church's basic beliefs. I slipped through the loophole of the interview process. The hardest question they asked any of us that year was "can you fit comfortably into the framework of the SDA church?" they all [*we assume this refers to his friends*] said yes. Too much "overbalance" on appearance and demeanor in the interview and not on genuineness of character."

   "Extremely poor. Uncertain of what was expected of me. I didn't even have an interview but got picked up in the last call up."

   "Left to the last possible moment. Other potential calls were blocked because of a dollar for dollar scheme. Not all 'carrots' offered were delivered leaving a not so good taste with regard to integrity. The process and calling structures need to be more transparent."

   "Jobs for the boys."

   "My family had special needs which were basically ignored. I felt pressured into accepting a call I did not want to take – I succumbed to the pressure applied. I was left with the distinct impression that administrative concerns in staffing a church were far more important than my personal situation in my family."

2. Experiences during period of internship.

   "It's a joke…. I'm out in the wilderness with no support from the church."

"The only intern program I received was a visit from the minister about 2-3 times a year. About once a year I travelled 400 km each way to visit him. Apart from a few hours chat at each meeting and going through parts of the intern manual, he listened to one of my sermons and made some suggestions. There were supposed to be the 6 monthly reports sent to the office. They were never completed or sent, nor did anyone enquire about the non-compliance. In other words nobody cared."

"Visit me! Seriously I was left to fend for myself. Only for a couple of mates in ministry I wouldn't still be in ministry today."

"Basically it stinks! I look at associates in the business world on how much in service support, assistance in professional development they get and I shake my head. Interns are left to sink or swim. If you don't fit the mould you die."

"Many ministers that the church needs are leaving when they shouldn't need to."

"What internship program? You are Joking. I have been given 3 Churches to look after and a mentor whom I don't even meet until I ring him for clarification of something that I wanted a second opinion on."

"My internship was a non event."

"The assignments in the folder were excellent that is prepared by the church. But as you can see the examples of my mentors and the quality of relationships that I had with them was less than adequate. Both were less than competent – the second couldn't even write a letter in English. The shallowness of my mentors did nothing but drain me of energy. It seems that often they were threatened by my energy and zeal."

"The internship was a joke. My mentor felt threatened by me and the church was against him, leaving me as the meat in the sandwich. He had many personal issues that were affecting his ministry and the church clung to the fresh new face they saw in me. Most of what I did would 'outshine' him and he didn't like that…."

"The first two years of my ministry was a very rough time for me and I hope no other intern would go through the same thing. Please do not place interns in churches that are fighting and arguing on different issues and hoping for them to survive. Please give them mentors who would sit down with them weekly and discuss the work not one like I had that he was."

"His negative example taught me how not to do ministry."

"It is not a program at all!! It is just an excuse to make the new guys toe the line anyway the bosses think."

The best comment by far was:

"Did not have a mentor. Thrown in at the 'deep end.' But it was GREAT to trust in the Lord as my mentor.

3. Assistance of Conference Ministerial Secretaries.

"He could have phoned or turned up! Never saw him personally in my entire first 4 years of ministry."

"Called once a year to see how I was going."

"Visited me – I had never had a visit in my first 4 years of ministry."

"As an intern – even a 5 minute phone call would be a start!"

"Monitor my mentors' training of me. Hear my cries for help – at least acknowledge."

Others did receive help. Clearly, some ministerial secretaries take their work seriously while others do not.

4. Conference Presidents.

"Questions were raised behind my back about my ability as a pastor. The president spoke to people behind my back and never spoke directly to me. This culture of secrecy and unwillingness to share constructively complaints received from church members allows no basis for conflict resolution."

"When people of my parish rang him about a complaint, he should not have immediately assumed I was wrong, but listened to my side of the story first."

"Be supportive. Not act on information from church members without first finding/enquiring if it is true."

"I was used as a method of covering 4 churches and two companies in a parish that required a huge amount of travel. This led to burn out in my first 2 years of ministry. The conference and president put me in a burnout situation before I even finished my (joke) internship."

"Not be gutless, but tell the truth and do what is right."

The author of the report stated that
"Seventh-day Adventist administration and organisations was cited by far the most frequently as causing them to feel disillusioned."

5. Decisions for ordination to the ministry.

"It's a lot of CRAP!. You should be automatically ordained after 5 years in ministry [*subject's emphasis*]. It is a boys club and you only get accepted if you are one of the boys. If you survive 4 years of Avondale, 5 years of ministry and people don't think you're good enough to be ordained??? They should have told you years ago so you can get a job doing something else and not waste people's time."

"My perception of the validation for my ordination was not about me, my gifts or abilities but about motivation when shifted to a new location. 'We want you to arrive there as an ordained minister and have the title *Pastor*'."

"I find it a very mysterious process. You never know where you stand in this regard. No one talks about it."

"It seems very subjective."

It is little wonder that we have a ministry suffering many frustrations. Below are listed only those frustrations which more than forty per-cent of the ministers reported. The figures cited are percentages of those ministers who felt either extreme or moderate frustration with each item.

1. Lack of time for me, my family, personal pursuits 73.0
2. Intolerance by some members 69.0
3. Negative attitudes of local church 67.9
4. Members' unwillingness for change of worship 65.5
5. Lack of visible results 64.3
6. Attitudes of church administrators 61.9
7. Congregation expectations I cannot meet 59.5
8. Casting/applying an appropriate vision 57.6
9. Conforming to a model of ministry that is not me 56.0
10. Little or no input into future career 55.1
11. Intolerance of differing theological interpretation 54.8
12. Being on call at all times 46.4
13. Difficulty in finding Bible study contacts 42.4
14. Gaining decisions for baptisms 42.4
15. Having to prepare sermons each week 40.5

These matters are worthy of consideration. Of course, some of the frustrations of the young ministers may have been generated themselves when the laity thwarted them from lowering God's standards of worship and faith. It is incredible how high on the frustration list is the failure to be able to introduce new forms of worship. Praise God there is still some resistance to celebration services. But as young people are isolated from faithful congregations by youth services, youth camps and other youth activities, they are beguiled by scheming Conference Youth Directors.

In the light of this report it is little surprise that the survey found that

> "Just over sixty per cent of respondents rated their relationship with their families excellent with only one in ten considering this to need improving. Over half expressed strong commitment to the Seventh-day Adventist organisation. Only half felt that their relationship with Jesus Christ was excellent."

Further, only 65.9 per cent of these ministers possessed a "Lifelong Commitment" to the Seventh-day Adventist Ministry. That more than a third of these pastors did not possess a life-long commitment to God's call to ministry, surely disqualified them.

Where does the Seventh-day Adventist Church in the South Pacific go from here? Many of the believers in this Division have lost all hope that the present organisation from the local church ministry through the Conferences, Unions and the Division, will ever enter into a process of reform. So entrenched are the proponents of the New Theology that they are in total control of administrative appointments. Virtually every feature of the Omega of Apostasy is promoted by the majority of church administrators. Let the reader once more be the judge.

> The enemy of souls has sought to bring in the supposition that a great reformation was to take place among Seventh-day Adventists, and that this reformation would consist in giving up the doctrines which stand as the pillars of our faith, and engaging in a process of reorganization. Were this reformation to take place, what would result? The principles of truth that God in His wisdom has given to the remnant church, would be discarded. Our religion would be changed. The fundamental principles that have sustained the work for the last fifty years would be accounted as error. A new organization would be established. Books of a new order would be written. A system of intellectual philosophy would be introduced. The founders of this system would go into the cities, and do a wonderful work. The Sabbath of course, would be lightly regarded, as also the God who created it. Nothing would be allowed to stand in the way of the new movement. The leaders would teach that virtue is better than vice, but God being removed, they would place their dependence on human power, which, without God, is worthless. Their foundation would be built on the sand, and storm and tempest would sweep away the structure. (*Selected Messages*, Vol. 1, pp. 204, 205).

Church members called to serve as delegates to Conference Constituency meetings must act wisely for today, leading church administrators at Division and Union levels have mastered the art of manipulating selection committees, nominating committees and constituency delegates to maximize the likelihood that the Division and Union choices are elected.

We cite two instances. In the 1980's Pastor Gordon Lee, who was a fellow student at Avondale College with us, undertook an effective work in raising the standards of the ministry in the Western Australian Conference of which he was the President. He found it necessary to warn some ministers to cease their consumption of alcohol and others to cease their attendance at movie theatres. Eventually he found it incumbent upon him to dismiss some of the young Avondale College graduates for their unfaithfulness to truth and principle.

These actions did not sit well with leadership. Yet there was good support among the laity. Serious charges were later laid by some of the members of the Nominating Committee. The following allegations arose from these charges. The members of the nominating committee decided, despite the fact that the Union President who chaired the meeting carefully advised otherwise, to recommend Pastor Lee's re-election.

Thwarted in his efforts, the chairman of the nominating committee pulled out his trump card. He informed the committee that in two weeks time the Victorian Conference Constituency would meet and it was all but certain that

Pastor Lee would be chosen to the Presidency of that Conference. Accepting his statement on its face value the Nominating Committee dropped their support for Pastor Lee and voted Pastor Peter J. Colquhoun, then President of the South New Zealand Conference to the post. No two Conferences are further apart in Australia and New Zealand than the Western Australian and the South New Zealand Conferences. It is doubtful if many of the members of the Nominating Committee possessed much knowledge of Pastor Colquhoun's capabilities and suitability at that time.

One member of the Nominating Committee of the Victorian Conference reported that during their deliberations two weeks later, Pastor Gordon Lee's name received no mention. Pastor Calvyn Townend was appointed President. During his Presidency, Pastor Townend sent letters to all churches in the Victorian Conference warning them to refrain attending a meeting in Melbourne in which Pastor George Burnside had been invited to preach. Pastor Burnside faithfully taught the truth. In his obituary the South Pacific *Record*, (April 30, 1994) conceded that Pastor Burnside

> was the South Pacific Division's most successful evangelist.

What is beyond dispute is the fact that Pastor Lee, now retired, was never again appointed to a Conference Presidency.

The Nominating Committee of the Western Australian Conference should have followed their convictions and recommended the re-appointment of Pastor Lee. They could have been recalled if Pastor Lee had been transferred to the Presidency of the Victorian Conference.

At the 2003 Victorian Conference Constituency Meeting many delegates generally believed that the President, Pastor Dennis Hankinson, would be replaced as he was judged by many in both the "conservative" and "liberal" elements of the church as unsuited for the post.

He had commenced his Presidency poorly by agreeing to pose in surf-riding gear with surfboard together with the head of the Victorian Satanist Church who held a chalice in his hand and was dressed in his evil robes which included upside-down scarlet crosses. This photograph, in full color, appeared on the front page of the *Melbourne Express*, March 30, 2001, taking up almost all of the page. Incredibly the South Pacific *Record*, April 21, 2001, followed the *Melbourne Express* with a full-front page photograph of the newspaper's front page accompanied by the words "President makes cover story." Then followed a full page report which once more depicted the newspaper front page in miniature, entitled "President's Testimony a Cover Story."

Not surprisingly the Victorian Conference monthly newsletter, *Intravic*, April 2001, reported this open disgrace to our faith under the headline "President's interview leads to Witness."

It surely did provide a witness! Letters were written to the Division leadership, even by some from other Conferences, but apparently their rightful, earnest concerns fell upon blind eyes.

During the 2003 Constituency Meeting of the Victorian Conference, more than twenty delegates, including at least four Conference pastors, appeared before the nominating committee to register their concerns at the proposal to re-elect Pastor Hankinson. Both the South Pacific Division President, Pastor Laurie Evans, and the Australian Union Conference President, Pastor Chester Stanley, were present.

Despite these facts, the nominating committee again returned Pastor Hankinson's name as its nominee. By a very slim margin he was re-elected. As usual, two factors brought success to the leaders' wishes.

1. Leadership had successfully outmaneuvered the constituency members;
2. Many delegates see it as an act of disloyalty to vote against the recommendation of the nominating committee which they, usually correctly, assume has leadership support.

Incredibly, not one of the more-than-two-hundred delegates moved a motion requesting that the concerns expressed by concerned delegates to the nominating committee be conveyed to the remainder of the delegates so that an informed vote could be made. Not one! Nor did anyone stand to request the exact count of the votes, or suggest a second count by representatives of the delegates. Once again, not one!

Delegates must remember that there is a growing tendency to appoint Conference Presidents with whom leadership feels comfortable. It is the constituency members' duty to vote for consecrated, capable men of fidelity to fill these posts. Otherwise the evil of what Australians designate as cronyism – the appointment of leaders' friends and supporters to high office – becomes entrenched.

PART VII
Was Sister White a Prophet?

31   A Perceptive Woman

As the efforts intensify to discredit Sister White's prophetic gift, claiming secretarial interference in her work, we again ask the question: If Sister White did not write these prophetic works, which prophet did? Let this alternative prophet be named! For undoubtedly only a prophet of God could have so accurately set forth today's contemporary events in the late nineteenth and early twentieth centuries. This chapter and the following two amply confirm this fact.

The year 1884, six years into Leo XIII's pontificate, a fifty-seven-year-old woman, Sister Ellen White published a book entitled *Spirit of Prophecy*, Volume 4, Pacific Press, Oakland, California. It was a book remarkable in many ways. Sister White was a diligent and careful student of the prophecies of Daniel and Revelation and also of the history of the Christian Church. She was not an alarmist, nor did she venture into flights of fancy as so many would-be prophetic exegetists have been prone to do. Hers was a prayerful daily study, comparing Scripture with Scripture under divine guidance and pursuing the study of the works of credible historians.

Sister White was a patriotic American, born in 1827 in Maine, one of the New England states, where most of the population was devoutly Protestant. She, herself, was raised in the home of a Methodist lay-preacher. Since our maternal ancestors were Methodists, we share an understanding of her spiritual background. Despite her loyalty to her nation, this woman correctly identified the second beast of Revelation 13 as her homeland, the United States. It was a painful realization and went contrary to her patriotic instincts.

Further, as she recognized that the prophecy was plainly indicating that the Papacy and the United States would unite in the last day persecution of Christ's flock, this concept ran totally contrary to the evidence of her day. While her Methodist background caused her no surprise in the specific prophesied deeds of Rome, the complicity of the United States was an entirely different matter. It tested her fidelity to Scripture, a test she withstood. There were numbers of reasons in 1884 for rejecting outright the declarations of the prophecy. We shall examine these.

Firstly, the United States was the bulwark of religious liberty. Her nation, in adding the First Amendment to its Constitution, had guaranteed not only religious liberty, but the separation of church and state. It was an example to the nations of the world. Our own nation, Australia, in 1901 when the states federated, adopted the very concepts of the United States' First Amendment as Article 116 of its constitution. This Article had incorporated both the non-establishment clause and the free-exercise clause from the First Amendment of the United States' Bill of Rights.

Richard Ely, Professor of History at the University of Tasmania, himself an ordained Presbyterian minister, recorded in his book *Unto God and Caesar*, pages 26, 42, 78, 122, 136, Sister Ellen White's efforts to promote the adoption of Article 116 in the Australian Constitution of 1901. Sister White resided in Australia from 1891 to 1900. Our grandmother once met her and heard her speak, just prior to Sister White's departure for the United States.

Roger Williams was the founder of the state of Rhode Island, which was the first state in history to specifically guarantee religious liberty in its constitution. Roger Williams had written in *The Bloody Tenet of Persecution*,

> [It is] a monstrous paradox, that God's children should persecute God's children, and then they hope to live together eternally with Christ Jesus in the heavens, should not suffer each other to live in this common air together.
> (Later published in 1848 by the Hanserd Knollys Society of London, p. 370, note 1).

It 1884, despite the apparent groundswell of support to impose Sunday laws by enactment of the United States Senate, the efforts of the leader of this movement, Senator William Henry Blair of New Hampshire, proved fruitless. Americans still valued their stand on religious freedom. Yet Sister White wrote,

> Protestantism will yet stretch her hand across the gulf to grasp the hand of Spiritualism; she will reach over the abyss to clasp hands with the Roman power; and under the influence of this threefold union, our country will follow in the steps of Rome in trampling on the rights of conscience.
> (*Spirit of Prophecy*, Vol. 4, p. 405).

Only a person absolutely true to Scripture and inspired by God could have written such a prediction concerning the United States 120 years ago. Without divine prophecy the claim would have been absurd. Here we see foretold a fourfold union, consisting of the three actors above – Apostate Protestantism, Spiritualism and Roman Catholicism – together with the political power of the United States.

We have already documented the "Holy Alliance" between the United States and the Vatican (see chapter "The Final Unholy Alliance" in our book *Two Beasts, Three Deadly Wounds, and Fourteen Popes*, Hartland Publications, Box 1, Rapidan, VA 22733, USA, 2001) and between Evangelical Protestants and conservative Roman Catholics (*Ibid*, chapter "The Religious Right"). The *Bakersfield Californian*, July 2, 1994, published a full-color cartoon of Uncle Sam stretching his hand across the "gulf" of the Atlantic Ocean to the Pope in Rome. It was an uncanny depiction of that which Sister White had written precisely 110 years earlier, seventeen years after the United States had broken off diplomatic relations with the Vatican in response to Pius IX's issuing his offending *Syllabus of Errors*.

In his book, *The Ambassador's Story*, published in 1994, Thomas P. Melady, the second United States Ambassador to the Vatican, 1989-1993, wrote that the long period of the breach in diplomatic relations between the United States and the Vatican, 1867-1984, a period of 117 years, coincided with "a period of strong anti-Catholicism in the United States." President Ronald Reagan (1910-2004) had resumed diplomatic relations with the appointment of William Wilson to the post in 1984.

In 1951 President Harry Truman failed in his effort to have the United States Senate affirm his appointment of General Mark Clark as Ambassador to the Vatican. The thirty-three years between Truman's abortive effort and Reagan's success included the pontificate of John XXIII. John successfully allayed Protestant fears concerning the Papacy.

Melady, a Roman Catholic as was also William Wilson, stated in his book that,

> Suspicion of the Vatican had significantly diminished largely as a result of positive interreligious relations involving the Catholic Church since the Second Vatican Council. (*The Bakersfield Californian, op. cit*).

It is not without significance that this review of Melady's book was written by Rabbi Rudin, National Interreligious Affairs Director of the American Jewish Committee. He noted the part played by Melady in the creation of diplomatic ties between Israel and the Vatican. After all, didn't Scripture foretell that *all* the world would wonder after the beast? (Revelation 13:3).

The long years of anti-Catholic sentiment in the United States make Mrs. White's predictions in 1884 all the more remarkable. In 1888 Sister White authored the book which she entitled *The Great Controversy*. There, quoting Revelation 13:3, she stated,

> The prophecy of Revelation 13 declares that the power represented by the beast with lamblike horns shall cause "the earth and them which dwell therein" to worship the papacy – there symbolized by the beast "like unto a leopard." The beast with two horns is also to say "to them that dwell on the earth, that they should make an image to the beast;" and, furthermore, it is to command all, "both small and great, rich and poor, free and bond," to receive "the mark of the beast." Revelation 13:11-16. It has been shown that the United States is the power represented by the beast with lamblike horns, and that this prophecy will be fulfilled when the United States shall enforce Sunday observance, which Rome claims as the special acknowledgment of her supremacy. But in this homage to [the] papacy the United States will not be alone. The influence of Rome in the countries that once acknowledged her dominion is still far from being destroyed. And prophecy foretells a restoration of her power.
> (*The Great Controversy*, pp. 578, 579, 1888 ed.).

It was a brave declaration, one indicative of the author's profound trust in the divine inspiration of Scripture, when it is considered that Protestant America seethed with anti-Catholic sentiment at the time she penned this conclusion.

In 1846, when Sister White was nineteen years old, Samuel J. Cassells, a Presbyterian minister of Norfolk, Virginia, published a book entitled *Christ and Antichrist*. The alternative name printed in the title page of the book was *Jesus of Nazareth Proved to be the Messiah and the Papacy Proved to be the Antichrist Predicted in the Holy Scriptures*. This book was published by the Presbyterian Board of Publications, Philadelphia. Leading clerics of the Presbyterian, Baptist, Methodist and Episcopalian churches gave the book their endorsement. This Protestant view of the Papacy extended throughout mainstream American Protestantism until the end of the nineteenth century and persisted to a considerable extent to the middle of the twentieth century. While American anti-Catholic sentiment prevailed, the future alliance of the United States and the Vatican was a chimera. Yet Sister White was not turned from Biblical pronouncements by this situation.

Secondly, in her 1884 book on this subject written only fourteen years after Pius IX proclaimed the dogma of Papal Infallibility, Sister White referred to the long tradition of this claim and wrote concerning future Protestant complacency, not as if writing in the nineteenth century, but rather in our century, the twenty-first. The ecumenical movement has led to Protestants becoming lulled into a sense of amnesia. They have, in general, lost all memory of Papal history. Even when John Paul II in 1998 threatened "whoever," – not just the Roman Catholic faithful – whoever did not abide by Roman Catholic dogma would be "punished as a heretic," (Apostolic Letter, *Ad tuendum fidem*) – we Protestants remained in a state of somnolence akin to a deep coma. Thus Sister White's words, so perceptive, rooted in her study of Revelation, are a wake-up call for us today. They, too, speak to the hearts of Roman Catholics and non-Christians. It is high time to heed the Apostle Paul's admonition.

> And that, knowing the time, that now it is high time to awake out of sleep: for now is our salvation nearer than when we believed. (Romans 13:11).

> Ye are all the children of light, and the children of the day: we are not of the night, nor of darkness. (1 Thessalonians 5:5).

Read Sister White's perceptive words with care.

> The defenders of popery declare that she has been maligned; and the Protestant world is inclined to accept the statement. Many urge that it is unjust to judge the Romish Church of today by the abominations and absurdities that marked her reign during the centuries of ignorance and darkness. They excuse her horrible cruelty as the result of the barbarism of the times, and plead that civilization has changed her sentiments. (*Spirit of Prophecy*, Vol. 4, p. 380).

Sister White's words are amply fulfilled today. Roman Catholic historians are excusing the cruelties and injustice of the Papacy. The Brisbane *Courier Mail* of November 2, 1998, reporting on the views of Roman Catholic historians, stated,

Modern scholars have for several decades been reappraising the Inquisition. Some now maintain that the justice it meted out, although brutal, was neither capricious nor unusual for the times.

What these scholars failed to declare was that the brutality of the times was the responsibility of the Roman Catholic Church which so dominated Europe that it set the trends, the standards and the atmosphere of the society. Even worse, it was this church which sanctioned such brutality as a service to God.

Sister White perceptively pointed to the Dogma of Papal Infallibility, proclaimed only fourteen years prior to authoring her book. She set forth the chilling implications of this dogma, implications which Scriptural prophecy in Revelation chapter 13 declares will be fulfilled just prior to Christ's Second Coming.

> Have these persons forgotten the claim of infallibility for eight hundred years put forth by this haughty power? So far from relinquishing this claim, the church in the nineteenth century has affirmed it with greater positiveness than ever before. As Rome asserts that she has never erred, and never can err, how can she renounce the principles which governed her course in past ages?
>
> The papal church will never relinquish her claim to infallibility. All that she has done in her persecution of those who reject her dogmas, she holds to be right; and would she not repeat the same acts, should the opportunity be presented? Let the restraints now imposed by secular governments be removed, and Rome be reinstated in her former power, and there would speedily be a revival of her tyranny and persecution. (*Spirit of Prophecy*, Vol. 4, p. 381).

When these words were written it seemed quite impossible that the Papacy would ever again muster such worldwide power, – unless one believed the prophecy of Revelation. And this Sister White manifestly did. In this she was encouraged by the many sacred visions concerning end-time events she received from the Holy Spirit. That the United States would unite in persecution with the Papal power seemed impossible, but in the years following 1980 we have seen the growing Vatican-American alliance. Even today it is inconceivable in the minds of many that Rome would persecute again – but she will; and the United States will provide the power and authority for her to do so and aid her in this work. This Scripture declares.

The revelations by the Red Cross in late 2003 and publicly in 2004 concerning American brutality towards prisoners of war in Afghanistan, Cuba and Iraq, are ominous portents of a new American concept of judicial "rights." The concurrence of many lawyers and citizens with this trend is alarming and full of forebodings for Seventh-day Adventists who evince faith in Scripture and the Spirit of Prophecy.

The United States in 1884 was a relatively weak nation as compared with the great European empires of Great Britain, Germany, France, Russia and Austria. Its foreign policy was dominated by the Monroe Doctrine. On

December 2, 1823, President James Monroe, (1758-1831 – President 1816-1824), America's fifth president – after whom Monrovia, the capital city of Liberia was named the previous year – issued the doctrine which bears his name. It led to an isolationist mentality in the United States.

Monroe simply codified that which, twenty-seven years earlier, George Washington (1731-1799 – President 1789-1797), stated in his farewell address, September 19, 1796. Monroe stated that,

> The American continents, by the free and independent condition which they have assumed and maintain, are henceforth not to be considered as subjects for future colonization by any European power.

In fact in 1823 much of North America was as yet unoccupied by western settlers, and other areas were in dispute. Britain, France and Spain all had their eyes on America, and in the Northwest the Tsar of Russia, who had claimed what is now Alaska, was thirsting for more American territory.

In 1845, President James Knox Polk (1795-1849 – President 1845-1849), invoked the Monroe Doctrine against Britain and France who were scheming to take the Yucatan province of Mexico. With the United States distracted by the Civil War of the 1860's, Spain seized the Dominican Republic and France set up a member of the Habsburg family, the Archduke Maximilian, as Emperor of Mexico.

By 1870, with Ulysses Simpson Grant (1822-1885 – President 1869-1877), as President, the Doctrine was immensely popular in the United States. The view that,

> Europe and the Americas constitute two separate and distinct spheres of political activity and, politically speaking, should have as little to do with each other as possible," (*Encyclopaedia Britannica*, 1963 edition, Vol. 15, p. 735),

dominated American thinking. It was a thinking which foresaw no American influence outside the Western Hemisphere. The NATO of the twenty-first century then appeared light-years away.

But God had spoken and Sister White believed. It was not until 1917, two years after Sister White's death, that the first breach in the Monroe Doctrine occurred. President Thomas Woodrow Wilson (1856-1924 – President 1913-1921), the last of America's eight presidents from Virginia, took the United States into the First World War as a belligerent.

But no sooner was the Treaty of Versailles signed, two years later in 1919, than America returned to her isolationist position, even refusing to join the League of Nations which was established at President Wilson's initiative. While in the inter-war period, the United States grew in population and military power, the crash of the stock market in 1929 kept it focused inward as first President Herbert Clark Hoover (1874-1964 – President 1929-1933), and then President Franklin Delano Roosevelt (1882-1945 – President 1933-1945), struggled to reestablish a vibrant economy. While initiatives of the administration and legislature made some progress in this direction, it took the Second World War to dispel the last vestiges of the Economic Depression.

That the United States did not envisage a major military engagement following the armistice of World War I is evidenced by the fact that the United States possessed only the seventeenth largest military force in the world at the time Adolf Hitler became Chancellor of Germany in February, 1933.

> By an act of February 12, 1925, the force of the regular [U.S.] army was set at 125,000 enlisted men and 7,953 enlisted men of the Philippine scouts.
> (*Encyclopaedia Britannica*, 1963 edition, Volume 22, p. 798).

Thus, even in 1941, when the United States entered World War II on December 7, following the Japanese bombing of Pearl Harbor, the United States was not envisaged as the lone military and economic superpower it has become in the six following decades.

32 A Turning Point in American History

December 7, 1941, was a turning point in American foreign policy and national thinking. The Japanese bombing of Pearl Harbor in Hawaii focused America outward. It had been attacked by an Asian nation and the United States has never forgotten this lesson. Ever since then it has grown to become the security officer of the world.

In the First World War, it was the sinking of the British passenger liner, the *Lusitania*, May 7, 1915, with the loss of 128 lives, by German U-boats which led to the United States' national psyche being conditioned for a breach of the Monroe Doctrine. In a decided sense the country had invited the attack by secretly concealing armaments destined for the Allies in passenger liners. The ill-fated passengers little dreamed they were traveling on a vessel which was, in fact, a huge bomb awaiting ignition. It took this tragic loss of life to permit the Monroe Doctrine to be temporarily ignored. The United States leadership had been forewarned by the German authorities that they were aware of the use of passenger vessels as armament carriers and that unless it ceased they would take action against those vessels.

Evidence has been put forth in support of some historians' views that the White House was well aware of the planned attack upon Pearl Harbor, but did nothing to thwart the attack in order that American opinion would become sympathetic to their nation's entry into World War II.

Whatever the truth of this theory, one matter is certain: America from this point on was launched into a policy course which would, exactly half a century later in 1991, lead President George Bush, Sr. (President, 1989-1993), to make the claim that the United States was then the lone superpower in the world. He was wrong. Revelation chapter 13 distinctly identifies, along with the United States, a second end-time superpower – the Vatican (also known as the Holy See).

President Bush's declaration, unchallengeable as it was in terms of military might, was a boast that exceeded reality. President Bush, Sr., had failed to factor in one nation whose military might was all but zero, whose sovereign territory extended a mere one-sixth of a square mile and whose resident population of about 1,000 was the least on earth – the Holy See. Scripture had foretold two last-day superpowers, not one. And in the crucial element of power – worldwide influence – the Vatican of the twenty-first century has no peer. Rome stands supreme, for its deadly wound has healed and all the world is wondering after it.

In 1990 Malachi Martin – an Irish Roman Catholic priest; a retired Professor of the Vatican's Gregorian University; an historian; and most importantly, a Vatican insider having been a close associate of the Jesuit

Cardinal Agostino Bea, a Vatican administrator – revealed the Vatican's self-assessment of its own political importance.

The title page of Dr. Martin's book, *The Keys of This Blood*, summarized its theme:

> The struggle for World dominion between Pope John Paul II, Mikhail Gorbachev [then President of the Soviet Union (U.S.S.R.)] and the Capitalist West [which is defined as the United States and Western Europe].

At first sight this competition appeared ludicrous. It was true that the United States and its allies in Western Europe were in fierce competition with the Soviet Union for world domination. That competition between two nations of massive military strength, determined political will, and lust for world dominion, was settled in favor of the United States in 1991 when the Soviet Union was dissolved and Mikhail Sergeyevich Gorbachev lost his power. Of the three competitors cited by Malachi Martin, only two, the Vatican and the United States, remained.

Although Russia was a nation of massive area, eventually expanding its territory to more than eight million square miles, and in 1884 was a significant and powerful empire, Sister White did not cite her as a player in the end-time scenario. In this she had a decided advantage over Malachi Martin who wrote more than a century later. That advantage was that although she was not a cleric and Dr. Martin was, she saw the end-time players through prophecy and visions, while Dr. Martin did not. The Bible speaks of just two end-time superpowers, not three.

Whereas Dr. Martin saw these three powers in competition, Sister White's Bible-based perspective saw two, the United States and the Vatican, in alliance. Indeed this cooperation was already in place as Communism crumbled in Eastern Europe at the time Dr. Martin wrote.

How could the Papacy be seen in the same league as the United States and the Soviet Union in the 1980's? Dr. Martin rightly summed it up:

> Pope John Paul II, the 264th successor of Peter the Apostle ... was himself the head of the most extensive and deeply experienced of the three global powers.
>
> (*Ibid*, p. 17).

By "extensive" Martin referred to the intelligence system of the Roman Catholic Church, composed of its hierarchical clerical operatives and its devout laity. Further, a state which is also a religious faith has a moral power which, when exerted over more than a billion spiritual subjects, carries a power which transcends armies, navies and air forces; it carries more fire power than guns, tanks, naval vessels, military aircraft and intercontinental missiles combined. Indeed, when backed by the weaponry of the North Atlantic Treaty Organization (NATO) it has all those too.

While looking through prophetic spectacles, Sister White saw this in vision, as did the Apostle John 1,800 years earlier.

Malachi Martin's years of association with the Vatican at close range made his revelations of Papal aims credible. He stated that,

> The chosen purpose of John Paul's pontificate, the engine that drives his papal grand policy, and that determines his day-to-day, year-to-year strategies – is to be victor in that competition, now well under way. For the fact is that the stakes John Paul has placed in the arena of geopolitical contention include everything – himself, his papal persona, the age old Petrine Office he now embodies, and his entire Church Universal, both as an institutional organization unparalleled in the world and as a body of believers united by a board of mystical communion.   (*Ibid*).

Clearly the present pontiff harbors no doubts that the deadly wound has been healed. For centuries Roman Catholics have been seeking a new Hildebrand (Pope Gregory VII, Pope 1073-1085), who could exert sufficient power to lord it over powerful rulers. In Pope John Paul II they have the "reincarnation" of their Hildebrand at last. It has taken them over nine centuries to find him, but find him they have. When John Paul spoke to President Reagan expressing his displeasure regarding American foreign aid for birth control in third world countries, Reagan ceased it (*Time*, February 24, 1992). When, in 1998, the man who imagined himself to be the most powerful man on earth, President Bill Clinton, breached papal protocol and sat before John Paul had taken his seat, the President was rebuked by papal aids for his *faux pas*. Clinton humbly apologized to the Pope. In matters of protocol it is the more powerful who imposes his will upon his inferior. Clinton may not have been compelled to stand in the snow for three days in order to render his apology as Hildebrand, Gregory VII, demanded of King Henry IV, but he had learned his place in the world pecking order.

In her 1884 volume Sister White surely wrote of the days in which we now live when she stated,

> The Roman Church is far-reaching in her plans and modes of operation. She is employing every device to extend her influence and increase her power in preparation for a fierce and determined conflict to regain control of the world, to re-establish persecution, and to undo all that Protestantism has done. Catholicism is gaining ground in our country upon every side. Look at the number of her churches and chapels. Look at her colleges and seminaries, so widely patronized by Protestants. These things should awaken the anxiety of all who prize the pure principles of the gospel.   (*Spirit of Prophecy*, Vol. 4, p. 382).

She also warned against the allurements of the Roman Catholic religion:

> Many suppose that the Catholic religion is unattractive, and that its worship is a dull, stupid round of ceremony. Here they mistake. While Romanism is based upon deception, it is not a coarse and clumsy imposture. The religious service of the Romish Church is a most impressive ceremonial. Its gorgeous display and solemn rites fascinate the senses of the people, and silence the voice of reason and

of conscience. The eye is charmed. Magnificent churches, imposing processions, golden altars, jeweled shrines, choice paintings, and exquisite sculpture appeal to the love of beauty. The ear also is captivated. There is nothing to excel the music. The rich notes of the deep-toned organ, blending with the melody of many voices as it swells through the lofty domes and pillared aisles of her grand cathedrals, cannot fail to impress the mind with awe and reverence. (*Ibid*, pp. 382, 383).

It is true that in March 2000, Pope John Paul II apologized for the past sins of Roman Catholics. The apology did not satisfy those who recognized that many of the Roman Catholic faithful who committed those sins were priests, prelates and popes. But even these papal apologies were correctly evaluated by Sister White in 1884.

> The Romish Church now presents a fair front to the world, covering with apologies her record of horrible cruelties. She has clothed herself in Christlike garments; but she is unchanged. Every principle of popery that existed in ages past exists today. The doctrines devised in the darkest ages are still held. Let none deceive themselves. The popery that Protestants are now so ready to embrace and honor is the same that ruled the world in the days of the Reformation, when men of God stood up at the peril of their lives to expose her iniquity. She possesses the same pride and arrogant assumption that lorded it over kings and princes, and claimed the prerogatives of God. Her spirit is no less cruel and despotic now than when she crushed out human liberty, and slew the saints of the Most High.
> (*Ibid*, pp. 387, 388).

The Papacy could not invoke worldwide persecution in the nineteenth century. In 1884 it appeared that the Papacy was in a state of feebleness. We marvel at Sister White's courage to defy the contemporary state of the Roman Catholic Church and to focus on its prophetically specified future. Listen as one Roman Catholic historian, a Fellow at Jesus' College, Cambridge University, described the seemingly almost insurmountable odds confronting the Papacy at the very period in which Sister White wrote:

> In Italy, processions and outdoor services were banned, communities of religious [orders] dispersed, church property confiscated, priests conscripted into the army. A catalogue of measures, understandably deemed anti-Catholic by the Holy See, streamed from the new capital [Rome]: divorce legislation, secularization of schools, the dissolution of numerous holy days.
> (John Cornwell, *Hitler's Pope*, Penguin Books, London, 1999, p. 14).

If Papal stocks were low at its own back door, Italy, they were no more promising elsewhere in Europe.

> In Germany partly in response to the divisive dogma of the infallibility, Bismark began his *Kulturkampf* ("cultural struggle"), a policy of persecution against Catholicism. Religious instruction came under state control and religious orders were forbidden to teach: the Jesuits were banished; seminaries were subjected to

state interference; church properties came under the control of lay committees; civil marriage was introduced in Prussia. Bishops and clergy resisting *Kulturkampf* legislation were fined, imprisoned, exiled. In many parts of Europe, it was the same"; in Belgium Catholics were ousted from the teaching profession; in Switzerland religious orders were banned; in Austria, traditionally a Catholic country, the state took over schools and passed legislation to secularize marriage; in France there was a new wave of anticlericalism. The conviction had been widely and confidently expressed by writers, thinkers, and politicians across Europe – Bovio in Italy, Balzac in France, Bismark in Germany, Gladstone in England – that the Papacy, and Catholicism with it, had had its day."

(*Ibid*, pp. 14, 15).

That this bleak outlook would be dramatically altered during the course of the twentieth century was hardly anticipated except in the writings of John, the Seer of Patmos and those of Sister White 1800 years later.

Sister White's heritage surely was her abiding trust in the Scriptures as a guide to the past, the present and the future. This, together with the visions she received, was the secret to her accurate portrayal of today's events over a century before their fulfillment. Her words were inscribed at a time when the Papacy was impotent and the United States weak and isolationist. The chapter entitled *The Scriptures a Safeguard* in her 1884 book could well serve as the motto of her life. Mrs. White's connection with the Apostle John was that she implicitly believed the inspired prophecies of the Apostle, despite contemporary evidence to the contrary. Her connection with John Paul II was that, believing prophecy, she saw the day when the Papacy of John Paul would achieve the completed healing of the deadly wound. Not only did Sister White believe prophecy, she received visions of the future from God. Current events certify her credentials as a genuine prophet of God, a reliable interpreter of Scripture.

33 SEPTEMBER 11

Approximately at 8:45am, September 11, 2001, American Airlines flight #11 from Boston, scheduled to land in Los Angeles with 92 passengers and crew, and carrying 30 tons of jet fuel, was deliberately aimed at the north tower of the World Trade Center in New York.

That impact caused violent destruction between the 96th and 103rd floors of the 110-story tower. The destruction of the floors above the site of impact could have been anticipated even by those with little or no engineering knowledge, but the fact that virtually the entire tower collapsed an hour and three quarters after the crash, came as a surprise to laypeople. At 9.03am on the same day United Airlines flight #175, carrying 65 people on board, also en route to Los Angeles from Boston, was deliberately flown into the south tower of the World Trade Center between the 80th and 91st floors. The tower collapsed at 10.29am.

The collapse resulted from the fireballs which generated heat beyond 1000 degrees Celsius. Such heat approached the melting point of steel, causing both towers to collapse upon themselves. Two other planes hijacked by terrorists were on similar missions. American Airlines flight #77 hit the Pentagon in Washington, D.C. after diverting from its planned flight path from Washington Dulles to Los Angeles. United Airlines flight #93 traveling from Newark to San Francisco crashed in Pennsylvania after an apparent failed attempt to disarm the terrorists. All 64 on board the American Airlines' plane and 45 on the United Airlines' plane perished.

That unprecedented terrorist attack shook far more than the buildings targeted. The shock waves extended throughout America and beyond, to shake the entire world. These terrorist attacks provoked the invasions of Afghanistan in 2001 and Iraq in 2003, and the catastrophic attacks on the American military and its allies in both countries together with the loss of lives of many Afghans and Iraqis. The coordinated attacks upon both towers of the World Trade Center and the Pentagon in Washington D.C., together with a fourth planned attack on an unknown target, which ended in the crash of United flight #93 from Newark in rural Pennsylvania, were an augury of worldwide preparation for war, economic ruin which has not yet resulted, unprecedented security measures, massive grief, growing fear, and doubt that this world would ever be the same again.

These evil terrorist attacks were carefully planned and orchestrated. In June 2004, it was revealed in the media worldwide that initially Osama bin Laden had planned ten simultaneous attacks on American targets, including nuclear facilities, but logistic difficulties led to a scaling down of his evil ambitious plans. Here we see God's hand. There is little doubt that neither the suicidal terrorists nor the masterminds behind them envisaged the wider implications of their action. If "success" is the correct word, then we suspect that these killers achieved "success" far beyond their expectations.

The dedicated student of Scripture will not rush into judgment as to the end-time implications of these terrorist attacks. It is quite impossible even now to present a thorough historical perspective. Further, we possess no prophetic gift, and thus the full consequences and implications of this tragic event remain beyond the scope of this chapter. Nevertheless, such defects of knowledge do not prevent some considered conclusions being drawn. In this effort Scripture can assist.

With certainty we can know that those seventy-five minutes of terrorism will be recited over and over again. They will stain the pages of history books as long as earth lasts. They will repeatedly be analyzed in magazine articles. Such articles will be read avidly, even by generations yet unborn, should God extend the period of probation for this old earth. Book after book will be written on the subject. Many already have been published. Television and radio programs will capture huge viewing and listening audiences, even among those who proclaim that they hated the study of history at school. September 11 was an event from which later history is already being dated. This event was of the greatest historical importance.

Our hearts went out to the bereaved. Many families were shattered by this vile act. No doubt many good people died, for evil does not discriminate. We saw heartache of massive proportions.

In this chapter we seek to place historical events in the context of divine prophecy. We make some tentative comments relevant to this objective in respect of the events of September 11, 2001 and the three years which have ensued.

Media reports around the world echoed and re-echoed. Armageddon-type language freely punctuated newspaper headlines. We refer to the coverage in our homeland, Australia.

The *Weekend Australian* newspaper, one of our homeland's most respected, in its September 22, 2001 edition included no less than 31 articles related to the events of September 11, 2001. This was typical of the coverage of this terrorist attack by news media in the nation. Not only the United States but the whole world was consumed with this event and the issues which it generated.

What was chilling was the rapidity with which the United States was initially able to form a worldwide coalition of nations against a foe – terrorism – which is as elusive as it is terrifying. Usually such decisions require careful governmental analysis and discussion, considerations of popular sentiment, national interests, economic impact, diplomatic issues, national consequences, and a plethora of matters impacting the welfare and interests of the nation. How different was this response from the tepid international response in 2003 when President Bush Jnr. called for war on Iraq.

Ignoring such a careful, wise, considered approach to decision-making, nation after nation rallied behind the American banner in its call for a prolonged war on terrorism, a war declared so rapidly that it cannot be doubted that American-decision makers possessed minimal information upon which to develop that course which would best serve its aim to defeat terrorism.

The Melbourne *Herald Sun* reported in its September 15, 2001 edition that in the

> US and NATO [then an organization of 19 nations] military planners make ready for what US President George Bush calls the first war of the 21st century.

Australia was among a great number of nations which offered military or other forms of assistance. On September 21, Lord George Robertson, the Secretary General of NATO, stated that all the other eighteen nations of the NATO alliance supported the United States. (*The Australian*, September 22, 2001).

It is probable that, apart from a few history buffs in the Bush Jnr. administration, knowledge of the Afghan nation's centuries-old ability to repel armed attacks was scant.

Understandably, many in the West associate Islamic people with Arabs. But, the overwhelming number of adherents to the faith of Islam are not Arabs. Indeed, most Muslims live in Indonesia, Bangladesh, Pakistan, and other Asian countries such as Malaysia and the Philippines as well as in Western, Northern and Eastern Africa. Westerners recall the Six-Day War of 1967 when Israel defeated a coalition of Arab nations in that many days. It may have been thought, "What resistance then, can this relatively small nation of Afghanistan, with its population of twenty-five million, mount against the might of the United States, NATO and the rest of the world?" History testified that the short answer was: "Considerable."

Afghans are not Arabs! They are men and women of mixed ethnic origins (chiefly Iranians, Mongols and Turks), raised in a daunting landscape. They are courageous, fierce defenders of their sovereignty, and well grounded in bearing hardship. Two-thirds of the nation consists of 39 per cent Pathans (Pushtun) of Iranian origin, 25 per cent Tajiks and 6 per cent Uzbeks. These latter two races are from the nations to Afghanistan's north, Tajikistan and Uzbekistan, both formerly republics of the Soviet Union. The remaining Afghans are spread among other races, chiefly the Hazaras (Mongols, 19 per cent). The Tajiks are related to Iranians and the Uzbeks to the Turks.

In recent times the Afghans have repulsed Iranian invasions backed by Russia in 1837. Then in the First Afghan War (1838-1842) the British were decimated by sickness, hardship and persistent guerrilla attacks – a form of encounter in which the Afghans excel. The British did not learn their lesson, for in 1878 they launched the Second Afghan War, the consequences of which were no less dire.

When the Soviet Union attacked Afghanistan (1979-1989) they left, utterly defeated. Reported in the Brisbane *Sunday Mail*, September 23, 2001, Colonel Uri Malishev, a Soviet military commander during the Soviet-Afghan

War, stated that, "the enemy and the unforgiving landscape made it an impossible battlefield." Malishev concluded that,

> The Afghans are an enemy that you rarely see and have little hope of beating. No invading force has ever tamed Afghanistan. (*Ibid*).

The difficulty which the coalition forces have found in locating the whereabouts of Osama bin Laden is proof positive of these difficulties, as also is the regrouping and reorganizing of the defeated Taliban forces.

The question is, Can the military might of the rest of the world fully quell the fierce spirit of this warrior nation? Present evidence is that they cannot. Military activity is still widespread in Afghanistan, even though the Taliban has been displaced from office.

Initially, the threat of war focused on Afghanistan many days before that country claimed, on September 30, 2001 to have taken bin Laden, prior to the coalition's attack on Afghanistan, into protective custody. (*Melbourne Age*, October 1, 2001). It was also declared, and preparation for military conflict made, before evidence of bin Laden's complicity was established. Words such as *suspicion* and *chief suspect* were freely used. Certainly bin Laden made no confession of guilt. In fact, he sent a denial to Pakistan. (*Australian*, September 16, 2001). While the word of a terrorist is unreliable, nevertheless, in this case, his guilt could not, prior to the assault on Afghanistan, be established on the basis of his own admission.

It was remarkable that Americans had so soon forgotten the lesson of Vietnam. Polls at the time suggested that more than seventy per cent had expressed support for war. (Sydney *Daily Telegraph*, September 19, 2001). The United States Congress supported the president with but one dissenting vote, that of a Californian congresswoman. In outlining his plans before the joint sitting of Congress, President Bush received an incredible twenty-four standing ovations. (*Weekend Australian*, September 22, 2001). Such bipartisan support emboldened his administration in its plans.

Americans would have done well to consider the words of a Russian veteran of the Soviet-Afghan War: "Americans would think Vietnam was a picnic compared with what they would face on the ground in Afghanistan." (*Ibid*). This has not yet proven correct in Afghanistan, but there is now a growing body of informed opinion which asserts that Iraq is looming as another Vietnam.

Russell visited Saigon and Long Bin in Vietnam a few weeks after the Tet offensive in 1968. He toured the American base in Saigon. Never had he seen such military armaments. He even sat in the American Commander, General Westmoreland's, helicopter. But all that equipment was no match for determined Vietnamese guerrillas who were seldom seen, but who effectively slaughtered more than 50,000 of the young manhood of America and large numbers of soldiers from other nations including Australia.

To measure the near impossibility of stamping out terrorism by military means, simply look at Israel – a nation occupying territory 3.5 per cent of the area of Afghanistan. The United States leaders are no doubt now measuring the lack of success of a first-class army such as Israel's in an arena of relatively easy terrain. In its efforts to prevent acts of suicide terrorism, it has failed. Would the United States and its allies succeed in far more daunting circumstances? That question was surely considered. Israel easily prevailed in a set war in 1967, but it is almost impotent to stem the tide of suicide terrorism.

Even more instructive is the war waged against terrorism by the British army – a first-class force – and the British police force in Northern Ireland. This territory is relatively small, about two per cent of the size of that covered by Afghanistan. It is a part of British sovereign territory, its terrain is relatively easy to encompass, and the IRA [Irish Republican Army] do not make a practice of the use of suicide terrorism. Yet after three decades the British have still to win the war against the terrorists. Similar comments could be offered concerning Spain and its Basque terrorists. America and the rest of the world *must* learn the lessons available in the histories of other nations.

We believe that every effort should be made to counter the vile terrorism which is now part and parcel of this world. But it makes little sense to shed the life-blood of the youth of America and its allies, and that of innocent citizens of Afghanistan and Iraq, with little hope of lasting success. The US administration was fearing retaliatory terrorist strikes (Melbourne *Herald-Sun*, October 1, 2001) before a shot had been fired in this war. Such a course will almost certainly be judged by some as degrading the United States and its supporters to the status of the terrorist nations. Already slogans are appearing in many lands, "American leaders in world terrorism."

This perception could not have been lessened by the statement of the US Secretary of State, General Colin Powell. He declared that

> everything including the ban on killing foreign leaders would be reviewed.
> (*Australian*, September 18, 2001).

In this thought there were bipartisan cries of support in Congress. Said Senator Graham [Democrat, Florida],

> We must have the authority to assassinate people before they can assassinate us.
> (*Ibid*).

In this call Senator Graham was joined by Republican Senator Richard Shelby.

President Bush's words to the other nations of the world, "Either you are with us or you are with the terrorists," brooks no neutrality. Does the United States have such a worldwide right to make this implied demand, having warned non-compliant nations of the consequences, should they be judged terrorist by the United States and its allies? Is there no place for conscientious neutrality? Such nations who eschew a potentially futile and bloody war may be in a position to achieve far more in curbing the rise of terrorism than the belligerents.

We stated that it is a chilling fact that the great majority of the world's nations, Islamic and non-Islamic, rushed with seemingly indecent haste to the American call to arms. Ill-considered commitments were made.

We stand amazed that nations such as China, Libya, United Arab Emirates, Russia, Saudi Arabia, Pakistan and vast numbers of the world's sovereign states supported America's cause in Afghanistan. This included the four most populous nations of the world – China, India, the United States and Indonesia. In these four nations reside almost 50 percent of the citizens of the world. Indonesia is the largest Islamic nation upon earth. When this war erupted, it was truly a world war, exceeding both the First and the Second World Wars in the numbers of national participants. It could rightly be designated a Third World War, for every continent was a participant in one manner or another. This was quite different from the general lack of support for the American war in Iraq in 2003. The Bali bombing on September 12, 2002 and the bombing outside the Australian Embassy in Jakarta in September, 2004 demonstrated the power of Moslem terrorism in Indonesia. Similar terrorist attacks in Iraq, Saudi Arabia, Pakistan, Turkey and Yemen demonstrated how widespread terrorism is today.

General Colin Powell, US Secretary of State, did state on the day following the terrorist attacks that,

> The administration intended a campaign of military action – rather than short-term retaliation – against the terrorists and their perpetrators.
> (*Australian*, September 13, 2001).

Speaking on September 16, President Bush stated,

> We're at war. There's been a war declared...."   (*Ibid*, September 17, 2001).

He urged his troops and the nation to be prepared for a long and difficult fight.

> You will be asked for your patience for the conflict will not be short ... the course of victory may be long.   (*Ibid*).

These words are proving "prophetic". Fortunately, as the shock of the terrorist strikes slowly abated, the administrators saw the fuller picture and the rhetoric became more realistic.

Could it be that Revelation 13 is on the verge of fulfillment? The Spirit of Prophecy plainly sets forth that the two great powers at the end of time, the Vatican and the United States, will lead the nations of the world – Afghanistan, Iraq, Iran, North Korea, and Sudan not excepted – into enforcing a universal death decree. This death decree will be aimed not against terrorists, but against humble followers of Scripture who desire to worship God in the beauty of holiness on His holy seventh-day Sabbath. This fact bears the credentials of inspired accuracy.

We dare not predict whether Revelation 13 is on the verge of fulfillment. But it is now demonstrated that it has been a simple matter, when economic ruin and massive loss of life are threatened, for America to command the support of the weaker nations of the earth; nations of all religious persuasions; some nations it formerly saw as its deadly enemies. Further, America and other nations have invoked serious breaches of civil liberties on the excuse that this assists in the fight against terrorism. That the citizens of these countries have largely accepted this restriction of their civil liberties, is ominous. The words of the Spirit of Prophecy are fulfilling with pin-point accuracy before our eyes. The fulfillment of Revelation 13 must be almost upon us.

While Pope John Paul II has been uncharacteristically silent, there are no grounds to conclude that he has not been consulted and his approval sought every step of the way. This was seen confirmed in a statement made by a senior Vatican spokesman Joaquin Navarro-Valls:

> It is certain that, if someone has done great harm to society, and there is a danger that if he remains free he may be able to do it again, you have the right to apply self-defense for the society which you lead, even though the means you may choose may be aggressive. (*Washington Post*, September 25, 2001).

The Brisbane *Courier Mail*, September 24, 2001 headlined an article setting forth the Pope's move at that time to form a worldwide coalition of the religions of the world. Such a move merited close attention in view of divine prophecy. And yet, in this time of peril, to what source are people looking for prophetic guidance? The Sydney *Sunday Telegraph*, September 16, 2001 reported that one of the most searched-for words on the Internet since the September 11, 2001 disaster was "Nostradamus." How tragic!

But it is scriptural prophecy which needs to be examined. We have found that one nineteenth-century woman, Sister White, illuminated by divine visions and her own study of the prophecies of Daniel and Revelation, outlined with great accuracy the events now taking place in the religio-political arena. We are, in general, quite skeptical of the myriad claims predicting future events from a study of the Bible, but her uncannily-accurate conclusions have been so remarkably confirmed in the twentieth and twenty-first centuries that they have focused our intense interest and confirmed her inspired status.

34 Sister White's Twenty-First Century Prophecy

Thus we searched, in retrospect, in order to determine if Sister White could possibly have prophesied any event even vaguely approaching that of Tuesday, September 11, 2001. To our astonishment, we discovered a statement which she wrote in 1909, six years prior to her death in 1915. The first New York *skyscraper* had been built in 1887. It was considered such a marvel that it was termed, *The Tower*. That building was *ten* stories high. By 1904 a building of over *twenty* stories was erected in that city. It was not until 1931 that the Empire State building was erected and we truly entered the era of skyscrapers.

We quote from Sister White's 1909 work, *Testimonies for the Church*, Vol. 9, pp. 12, 13:

> On one occasion, when in New York City, I was in the night season called upon to behold buildings rising story after story toward heaven. These buildings were warranted to be fireproof, and they were erected to glorify the owners and builders. Higher and still higher these buildings rose, and in them the most costly material was used.
>
> As these lofty buildings went up, the owners rejoiced with ambitious pride that they had money to use in gratifying self.... The time is coming when in their fraud and insolence men will reach a point that the Lord will not permit them to pass, and they will learn that there is a limit to the forbearance of Jehovah.
>
> The scene that next passed before me was an alarm of fire. Men looked at the lofty and supposedly fire-proof buildings and said: "They are perfectly safe." But these buildings were consumed as if made of pitch. The fire engines could do nothing to stay the destruction. The firemen were unable to operate the engines....
>
> No earthly power can stay the hand of God. No material can be used in the erection of buildings that will preserve them from destruction when God's appointed time comes to send retribution on men for their disregard of His law and for their selfish ambition.

It is an interesting coincidence that this prophecy commenced in Volume nine, page 11 – 9/11. This cannot be forgotten and makes it easy to remember the reference for this prophecy.

We note the emphasis on the claims that the buildings destroyed were "warranted to be fireproof" and it was claimed that "they are perfectly safe." After both these claims were shown to be false, engineering experts appeared on television screens, stating that the World Trade Center was constructed in such a manner specifically to be able to withstand an accidental aircraft crash into the body of the building. It was also stated that the building was made to the highest standard of fireproofing. These facts add weight to the accuracy of this remarkable prediction.

In the quoted passage we see some positive measures, unrelated to war and bloodshed, which can be taken in the war against terrorism; for surely no war, no assassination of political leaders as mooted, no schemes of man, can stay this terrorist plague. God, and God alone, can protect us. Until this principle is understood, the measures that man takes may only worsen terrorism. President Bush in speaking to Congress stood beneath an engraved promise in the House of Representatives – "In God We Trust." However, while resorting to biblical concepts such as "Be ready" and "The hour is coming," the President promoted material solutions, not divine ones. Therein lies terrible danger for the future.

The question being asked by many is, Why did God permit these terrorist acts? The better question would have been, Why had something like this not happened decades ago? The answer is, God's protecting mercy.

Once more Sister White is helpful in providing understanding. She had also carefully studied the prophecies of the end time presented by our Lord and Savior Jesus Christ which are recorded in Matthew 24, Mark 13 and Luke 21. We present her work not to uplift *her*, but to demonstrate how human beings who seek God can discern the meaning of the Bible, God's sure Word. Further, it presents solid evidence of the inspired nature of her writings. We again quote from her remarkable 1884 book, *Spirit of Prophecy*, Vol. 4, p. 407:

> Satan works through the elements also to garner his harvest of unprepared souls. He has studied the secrets of the laboratories of nature, and he uses all his power to control the elements as far as God allows. When he was suffered to afflict Job, how quickly flocks and herds, servants, houses, children, were swept away, one trouble succeeding another as in a moment. It is God that shields his creatures, and hedges them in from the power of the destroyer.

America's sole answer to calamity would be in true dedication to the One who alone can, and has, protected us.

Another question is proper. Why did not the terrorists use nuclear, and biological or chemical terrorism? These potential sources of devastation have been mentioned in newspapers worldwide. There is only one rational answer: God in His mighty love and great mercy has held back this terrible source of destruction. The more than two thousand in New York so cruelly deprived of life would have been multiplied many times had such methods been employed. Authorities have seen how easily crop-duster aircraft could have been harnessed for such a purpose. They have already verified that terrorists were working on this plan. For a period the US grounded all aircraft of this type. Investigators have seen that a considerable number of likely terrorists were seeking licenses to drive trucks containing hazardous materials such as could be used in chemical warfare against major cities.

God in His goodness has provided us with mercy. God has His angels holding back the worst of these winds of strife until His saints are sealed. The apostle John revealed this protection.

> ¹And after these things I saw four angels standing on the four corners of the earth, holding the four winds of the earth, that the wind should not blow on the earth, nor on the sea, nor on any tree. ²And I saw another angel ascending from the east, having the seal of the living God: and he cried with a loud voice to the four angels, to whom it was given to hurt the earth and the sea, ³Saying, Hurt not the earth, neither the sea, nor the trees, till we have sealed the servants of our God in their foreheads. (Revelation 7:1-3).

But avarice, immorality, hate and frivolity reign in most large cities around the world. God, now merciful, will not always forbear. In speaking of a time future to her own, Sister White wrote:

> ...he [Satan] will bring disease and disaster until populous cities are reduced to ruin and desolation. Even now he is at work.... He imparts to the air a deadly taint, and thousands perish by the pestilence. These visitations are to become more and more frequent and disastrous. Destruction will be upon the inhabitants of the world. (*Spirit of Prophecy*, Vol. 4, pp. 407, 408).

Far from creating fear in their hearts, our desire is to lead our readers to have faith *in* Jesus and to themselves possess the faith *of* Jesus. (Revelation 14:12). Let us believe the inspired words of our prophet. The prophecy just quoted could well foretell the use of biological warfare against the great cities; yet God has promised protection to all those who have fully surrendered to Him.

> The angel of the Lord encampeth round about them that fear him, and delivereth them. (Psalm 34:7).

> > ¹ He that dwelleth in the secret place of the most High shall abide under the shadow of the Almighty.
> >
> > ² I will say of the LORD, He is my refuge and my fortress: my God; in him will I trust.
> >
> > ³ Surely he shall deliver thee from the snare of the fowler, and from the noisome pestilence.
> >
> > ⁴ He shall cover thee with his feathers, and under his wings shalt thou trust: his truth shall be thy shield and buckler.
> >
> > ⁵ Thou shalt not be afraid for the terror by night; nor for the arrow that flieth by day;
> >
> > ⁶ Nor for the pestilence that walketh in darkness; nor for the destruction that wasteth at noonday.

> ⁷ A thousand shall fall at thy side, and ten thousand at thy right hand; but it shall not come nigh thee. (Psalm 91:1-7).

It is worth our consideration that Sister White, in the context of Revelation 13, perceptively asserted that these tragic disasters and terrorist acts will not turn the great majority of the citizens of the world to Christ, but rather will lead them to an unconverted Christianity. There is no man, no woman so deceived, so cruel as the individual who turns zealously to religion without asking God to transform his or her wicked heart. The terrorists of September 11, 2001 were full evidence of this dictum. They were moved by religious zeal, even to the point of being prepared to lay down their lives for their cause. But their acts demonstrated that they did not cherish the love of God in their hearts.

Christians fare no better than the followers of Islam if they possess a religious zeal without a humble yielding of their lives to God. The Bible must be the guide-book to teach us that Christ alone can purify our characters. It teaches us that those who seek virtuous characters will be motivated by the love of God and Christ, who alone has cared for us and demonstrated infinite love in the plan of salvation. It is the Holy Spirit who provides power to seek and live such a life. Christ underlined true love for Him.

> If ye love me, keep my commandments. (John 14:15).

Today, even most Christians eschew this directive. Many claim that the Ten Commandments were destroyed at Christ's death. Others categorically state that the Commandments cannot be obeyed. If these propositions are correct, then we implicitly charge Christ with mocking us in His charge to keep His Commandments, and we deny His promised power.

> Now unto him that is able to keep you from falling, and to present you faultless before the presence of his glory with exceeding joy (Jude 24).

Either God has such power and is able, or He does not possess such power and is impotent to provide mankind with strength to fulfill His commands. Further, to deny this offered power is to imply that God is a liar. Such is a matter of great peril to our eternal lives.

The large majority of professed Christians, including many Seventh-day Adventists, do not obey the Fourth Commandment, which will become a major issue at the end of time. Let us quote once more from this book which has proven to be so helpful to us as we authored this manuscript:

> And then the great deceiver will persuade men that those who serve God are causing these evils. The class that have provoked the displeasure of Heaven will charge all their troubles upon the faithful few whom the Lord has sent to them with messages of warning and reproof. It will be declared that the nation is offending God by the violation of the Sunday-Sabbath, that this sin has brought calamities which will not cease until Sunday observance shall be strictly enforced, and that those who present the claims of the fourth commandment, thus

> destroying reverence for Sunday, are troublers of the nation, preventing its restoration to divine favor and temporal prosperity. Thus the accusation urged of old against the servant of God will be repeated, and upon grounds equally well established. "And it came to pass when Ahab saw Elijah, that Ahab said unto him, Art thou he that troubleth Israel? And he answered, I have not troubled Israel, but thou and thy father's house, in that ye have forsaken the commandments of the Lord, and thou hast followed Baalim." [1 Kings 18:17,18.] As the wrath of the people shall be excited by false charges, they will pursue a course toward God's ambassadors very similar to that which apostate Israel pursued toward Elijah. (*Spirit of Prophecy*, Vol. 4, p. 408).

Calls for prayer were made all over the United States and beyond. The President called for prayer as did the Congress, state governors, city mayors, the media and the churches. But such calls are futile unless we possess purity of heart.

> If I regard iniquity in my heart, the Lord will not hear me. (Psalm 66:18).

Not only futile, such prayers will lead to dire persecution of the righteous.

> ¹⁵And he [the second beast of Revelation 13 – the United States] had power to give life unto the image of the beast [the first beast of Revelation 13 – the Papacy], that the image of the beast should both speak, and cause that as many as would not worship the image of the beast should be killed. ¹⁶And he causeth all, both small and great, rich and poor, free and bond, to receive a mark in their right hand, or in their foreheads: ¹⁷And that no man might buy or sell, save he that had the mark, or the name of the beast, or the number of his name.
> (Revelation 13:15-17).

Here the universal death decrees and economic boycott are prophesied.

Finally, let us learn from recent history. In the 1920's and early 1930's, Germany experienced ruinous economic inflation; a mere postage stamp of the era cost 20 billion marks. In this crisis the middle class lost their affluence. One man promised to reverse the national financial ruin at the price of the revocation of liberty. His name was Adolph Hitler (1889-1945). Many Germans willingly paid that price, and millions of innocent men, women and children lost liberty and life as a consequence.

Today around the world there are again cries for restoration of a departed prosperity. Some are crying that they know they may have to forfeit some of their liberties in order to restore security and earthly comforts.

> Americans are determined to try [to win the war against terrorism] even if it means sacrifice and loss of civil liberties. (Melbourne *Age*, September 19, 2001).

Perilous are such concessions! Liberty must be prized as an inalienable right accorded us by God. To forfeit it, is to ruin all the very best in our world. Unless these calls are withdrawn and the citizens of the world prize liberty as they ought, we will be plotting the course for the fulfillment of Revelation 13.

Already, as we have seen, there is a thirst for vengeance, a desire for blood under the guise of "infinite justice." We would do well to examine the words of the prophet Isaiah:

> Justice standeth afar off: for truth is fallen in the street, and equity cannot enter.
> (Isaiah 59:14).

God may view our cities as pits of injustice. We would do well to commence our efforts for "infinite justice" among the poor and helpless. "Operation Infinite Justice" was the name initially chosen for the war against terrorism; later this war was designated "Operation Enduring Freedom." The alteration was made because the term *Infinite Justice* offended Islamic people who rightly believed that infinite justice is provided only by God.

The vast majority of those who will suffer under the biblically-prophesied death decree will be men, women and children totally innocent of any act of terrorism or any crime. Already the President of the United States has issued an ultimatum, not to American institutions alone, but to the financial institutions of the world, that America will enforce sanctions against any that undertake transactions of which the United States does not approve. (Melbourne *Age* newspaper, September 27, 2001).

The Bush administration made a list of terrorists and terrorist organizations whom they proscribed. The groups were located in various nations – Afghanistan, Algeria, Egypt, Libya, Mauritania, Pakistan, Philippines, Saudi Arabia and Uzbekistan. Terrorists such as the Roman Catholic Irish Republican Army (IRA) and the Hindu Tamil Tigers in Sri Lanka received no mention, possibly because they were perceived as no threat to the United States.

Yet the United States surely would have taken a more noble stand if it had included the IRA which has tremendous financial support from Irish Americans, especially in the northeastern states. If it is good for other countries to crack down on financial sources of terrorism which lead to attacks on America, the US would do well to dry up the source of income from its own country in a sincere effort to quell terrorism in Britain also.

While President Bush's clamp-down on terrorist finances is not a fulfillment of the worldwide economic boycott upon faithful followers of Christ as foretold in Revelation 13:17 quoted earlier, it does demonstrate America's will and authority to implement such economic boycotts against those of its choosing. The Papacy has chosen its ally well!

In order for Revelation 13 to be fulfilled, America and the other nations of the world must be prepared to trample upon the inalienable rights of civil and religious liberties.

In the current crisis American citizens have demonstrated an alarming preparedness to yield some of their liberties in the face of challenges to their personal security and prosperity. *The Australian* (September 18, 2001) reported that "Attorney-General John Ashcroft said the Justice Department would ask Congress for greater power to detain non-US citizens [and] wire-tap telephone calls."

The WorldNet Daily (September 27, 2001) reported:

> With Congress hotly debating whether to grant sweeping police powers to federal law enforcement agencies in the name of combating terrorism, two attorneys who have studied presidential directive in depth are concerned that civil liberties will take a beating from the executive branch as well as the legislative – and no one would realize it until it was too late.
>
> On September 14 President Bush, responding to the terrorist attacks upon the World Trade Center and the Pentagon three days earlier, issued a proclamation declaring a state of national emergency and reinforced it the same day with an executive order (EO 13223) calling the Ready Reserves of the Armed Forces to active duty.
>
> For constitutional attorney William J. Olson, alarm bells started ringing.
>
> "This is just the beginning," he told *WorldNet Daily*. "I am certain that the proclamation and executive order by the president are the first of a series of executive orders that are likely to be issued as the administration identifies the powers it wants to invoke."
>
> What is even more serious appears to be the growing acquiescence of America and its western allies to accept encroachments upon their liberties as necessary to national survival. Too often we are hearing the false dictum – we can have liberty without security or we can yield some of our liberties and have security.
>
> Nations must seek security while maintaining the liberties of their citizens. Neither aim should be abrogated. As Attorney James Standish, Director of Legislative Affairs at the World Headquarters of Seventh-day Adventists stated,
>
> "While calling for the protection of religious freedom and understanding of minority religious groups during America's terrorist crisis ... in past conflicts, civil liberties in the United States have sometimes been suspended."
>
> He cited the decision to intern Japanese Americans during World War II. (*Adventist News Network*, September 25, 2001). Australia interned newly arrived Italian immigrants during the same period.

What the terrorist crisis has demonstrated is that four essential conditions necessary for the fulfillment of Revelation 13:15-17 have been put in place during this Afghan crisis:
1. A willingness to deprive citizens of some of their civil and religious liberties;
2. An ability of the United States to marshal worldwide support, cutting through religious divides, for its policy against those it deems to be responsible for disasters causing loss of both lives and economic prosperity. Only thus will its death decree (Revelation 13:15) become universal (*all, both small and great, rich and poor, free and bond* – Revelation 13:16);

3. A worldwide economic boycott (*no man might buy or sell* – Revelation 13:17) can only be implemented when other nations comply with America's wishes to deprive America's enemies of the means to buy and sell.
4. Many have believed that the United Nations would be the biggest player in enforcing the prophecies of Revelation 13, but in its war with Iraq, the United States demonstrated that it can ignore world opinion and the will of the United Nations. How did Sister White know one hundred and twenty years ago that the United States would grow from its relatively weak position to the position it holds today? The clear answer is – she was inspired of God.

In the Afghan and Iraqi crises, the United States demonstrated its capacity to meet these conditions.

We again emphasize that the current crisis is not the final crisis contemplated in Revelation 13. But we do see that America is well positioned to fulfill the role which God has foretold. The final events of this world's history, culminating in Christ's Second Coming, are imminent.

May our God provide wisdom to national leaders and to each citizen of the nations. What the immediate future holds may be uncertain, but the ultimate outcome is determined, for God revealed these events for our guidance. It is time for all to ignore the attacks on Sister White's inspired status and re-read *The Great Controversy* in faith-strengthening confirmation. May we, each one, in serving Christ whole-heartedly, make no move which will imperil the liberties and rights of ourselves and others. Let us fully yield our lives to Christ.

Most of all, may we meet in heaven, for God's grace is more than sufficient for the coming crisis. Let us be found among God's saints, remembering that –

> Here is the patience of the saints: here are they that keep the commandments of God, and the faith of Jesus. (Revelation 14:12).

Was Sister White a prophet of God? The evidence has been set before you. In the imparted wisdom of God, the reader has the right to judge this matter.

In the events of September 11, 2001, there is a solemn message for each one of us. We have explained that the only reason why all the wicked cities of the world, including Paris, London, Moscow, Tokyo, Rio de Janeiro, Sydney, Cape Town, Jakarta, Manila, Los Angeles, Chicago, Mexico City, and a host of others, have not been visited by similar terrorist attacks and worse, is the mercy of God in positioning four mighty angels to hold back the winds of strife, thus limiting Satan's evil designs. It is also the reason that even more devastating attacks on New York using chemical, biological or nuclear weapons did not transpire.

> And after these things I saw four angels standing on the four corners of the earth, holding the four winds of the earth, that the wind should not blow on the earth, nor on the sea, nor on any tree. (Revelation 7:1).

Thank God for His tender mercy to the inhabitants of our wicked and vile world.

For many years we were puzzled by the second and third verses of the above text. They state:

> ²And I saw another angel ascending from the east, having the seal of the living God: and he cried with a loud voice to the four angels, to whom it was given to hurt the earth and the sea, ³Saying, Hurt not the earth, neither the sea, nor the trees, till we have sealed the servants of our God in their foreheads.
>
> (Revelation 7:2, 3).

Of course, we understood God's protection of His people, providing them with sufficient probationary time in order that they might be sealed for everlasting life. This is our God who

> ... is longsuffering to us-ward, not willing that any should perish, but that all should come to repentance. (2 Peter 3:9).

But we wondered why it was necessary for God to command a fifth angel to explain to the four angels holding back the winds of strife, their duty. Did not each of these four angels know their obligation in this responsibility?

In this mode of thinking we had, incredibly, overlooked the fact that just as God has provided humanity with decision-making freedom, so too has He accorded angels this freedom.

In her 1851 book, *Experience and Views*, published when Sister White was a young woman of twenty-three, she reported a vision which perceptively explained the quandary which we harbored. This vision was quite short, but startling in its implications for us today.

> I saw four angels who had a work to do on the earth, and were on their way to accomplish it. Jesus was clothed with priestly garments. He gazed in pity on the remnant, then raised His hands, and with a voice of deep pity cried, "*My blood, Father, My blood, My blood, My blood!*" Then I saw an exceeding bright light come from God, who sat upon the great white throne, and was shed all about Jesus. Then I saw an angel with a commission from Jesus, swiftly flying to the four angels who had a work to do on the earth, and waving something up and down in his hand, and crying with a loud voice, "*Hold! Hold! Hold! Hold! until the servants of God are sealed in their foreheads.*" (*Early Writings*, p. 38 – italics in the original).

Not surprisingly, Sister White was perplexed by the vision and did not understand it. Fortunately, an angel of heaven provided a clear explanation for her.

> I asked my accompanying angel the meaning of what I heard, and what the four angels were about to do. He said to me that it was God that restrained the powers, and that He gave His angels charge over things on the earth; that the four angels had power from God to hold the four winds, and that they were about to let them

go; but while their hands were loosening, and the four winds were about to blow, the merciful eye of Jesus gazed on the remnant that were not sealed, and He raised His hands to the Father and pleaded with Him that He had spilled His blood for them. Then another angel was commissioned to fly swiftly to the four angels and bid them hold, until the servants of God were sealed with the seal of the living God in their foreheads. *(Ibid)*.

Could it be that on September 11, 2001, this heavenly intervention in affairs of earth transpired? It appears that the four angels had judged that the cup of earth's iniquity was full and were about to release the winds of strife. Since this event was of sufficient significance for God to reveal it to Sister White ninety-two years in advance of the catastrophe, describing the destruction of mighty skyscrapers "rising story after story toward heaven" (*Testimonies for the Church*, Vol. 9, p. 12), depicting these events, even naming the specific city involved, this conjecture is worthy of consideration. We remember that the Empire State Building, New York's first skyscraper was not completed until 1931, sixteen years after Sister White's death and that God specified New York, not any city, but the very city out of the multitude of other wicked cities in the world in which this destruction would take place. Let us not forget that the chapter appearing in volume 9, pages 11–17 is entitled THE LAST CRISIS!

What is indisputable is the evidence this event supplies of Christ's tender and protective care of us, and His infinite love for us. How we thank God that He looked down upon us and correctly judged that we required a little further probationary time to meet the character standards required for heaven. We pray that none of us will spurn or waste this sliver of extended probationary time.

We have searched inspiration and have discovered no second such extension of our preparatory time. The urgent plaintive plea of Christ, "My blood, Father, My blood, My blood, My blood!" is never far from our thoughts, nor is the loud voice of the fifth angel, "Hold! Hold! Hold! Hold! Until the servants of God are sealed in their foreheads."

Our prayer is that none, church administrators, theologians, college teachers, ministers, elders, deacons, laypersons, and ourselves and our loved ones, will fail to heed these cries.

35 Has Rome Changed?

The answer to the question posed by the title of this chapter is an emphatic YES!

This answer was provided by Dr. Reinder Bruinsma, then secretary of the Trans-European Division. This Division incorporates the territories of the United Kingdom, Ireland, Iceland, the Netherlands, Norway, Sweden, Denmark, Finland, Poland, Latvia, Estonia, Lithuania, Hungary, Serbia and Montenegro, Macedonia, Bosnia, Slovenia, Croatia, Israel, Albania, Greece, Afghanistan and Pakistan.

In words that cannot be misunderstood, Dr. Bruinsma had declared:

> Although Adventists must strongly disagree with many aspects of Roman Catholic teaching and practice, honesty demands an acknowledgment that in recent decades Roman Catholicism has changed in positive ways in most parts of the world. Now, Catholics are not only allowed to read their Bibles, but are encouraged to do so. There is much spirituality in the Roman Catholic Church of which Protestants can be envious. Furthermore, the Catholic Church has formally accepted the principle of religious freedom. It is not fair to suggest that these and other positive developments are just window dressing and must, in fact, be watched with suspicion, or that they should be seen as clever tactics to lull other Christians into sleep while Catholics await a fortuitous moment when they can wipe out other Christians, Adventists first and foremost.
>
> (*Spectrum*, Vol. 27, Issue 3, Summer 1999).

These were startling words from a Division Secretary. Pastor Bruinsma's writings are becoming widespread. Recently, Dr. Bruinsma was the senior contributor to the Senior *Sabbath School Quarterly*, July-September, 2004. Those who received the South Pacific *Record* of July 17, 1999 saw his book, *It's Time*, advertised. He had written articles in 1999 in *The Adventist Review*, and thus he was becoming a widely-read denominational leader. On August 28, 1999, Dr. Bruinsma was the featured speaker at Avondale College homecoming.

Every sincere Seventh-day Adventist will be alarmed that a church leader would dare to publish an article in *Spectrum* magazine. This magazine, which has been published now for thirty-two years, has a track record that is simple to discern. Every effort has been made over these thirty-two years to destroy the salient doctrines of the Bible and the Spirit of Prophecy. It is not a magazine which leads men and women to God's truth, but rather tears down the sanctuary message, creation, the Spirit of Prophecy, the Sabbath and other vital truths. To publish an article in such a magazine is tantamount to standing on the side of those who oppose the precious truths entrusted to the Seventh-day Adventist faith, unless one is invited to uphold precious truth.

We are well aware that when denominational workers publish articles in godly magazines such as *Our Firm Foundation* and *The Last Generation*, they frequently receive rebuke from leaders and they do so at the risk of their denominational employment.

Some may ask, who is Pastor Bruinsma? The *Spectrum* magazine produced a short curriculum vitae:

> Reinder Bruisnma is the secretary of the Trans-European Division. He received his B.D. Hons. And Ph.D. in theology from the University of London. An author in English and Dutch, he has published numerous articles and ten books. His most recent English book is *It's Time to Stop Rehearsing What We Believe and Start Looking at What Difference It Makes*, (Idaho: Pacific Press, 1998).

Pastor Bruinsma is presently (2004) President of the Netherlands Union Conference.

Dr. Bruinsma's theme was that Rome has changed in a positive way, and that Seventh-day Adventists must change their view of her accordingly. He charged Seventh-day Adventists with an evaluation of the Papacy based upon the nineteenth century.

> Most of what Ellen G. White wrote about Catholicism originated during this period [the nineteenth century], a time in which Adventists perceived that external events on the American scene corroborated earlier predictions. Her increasing authority within the Seventh-day Adventist Church greatly contributed to the general acceptance of an eschatological scenario that received its more-or-less final formulation in this unique late-nineteenth-century American setting. Acceptance of her statements in *The Great Controversy* and elsewhere as inspired pronouncements, prevented later Adventism from taking another look at contemporary Catholicism while other Protestants were increasingly prepared to do so. (*Ibid*).

Pastor Bruinsma placed emphasis upon Sister White's part in preventing Seventh-day Adventism from altering its position on Catholicism. This is another theme coursing through his article:

> Still, her [Sister White's] major writings about Roman Catholicism dated from the 1880s and 1890s, and thus originated in a climate of Adventist confidence about the reality of the Catholic threat and the imminence of events predicted for decades. Once she codified those views, it became virtually impossible to re-evaluate them critically without questioning her prophetic authority. (*Ibid*).

Dr. Bruinsma also charged Seventh-day Adventists that we have been unfair to the medieval history of the Roman Catholic Church:

> In criticizing Catholic history, Adventists should try to be more balanced than in the past and should avoid offering a simple extension of the often-biased and inaccurate picture that many past Protestants have offered of the medieval Church. Medieval Christianity also had positive and beautiful dimensions. Moreover, Adventists must be willing to acknowledge that modern Catholicism has changed in many ways. It bothers me, in particular, to see how modern Adventist publications still rely mainly on nineteenth-century sources to describe Catholic views and intentions. (*Ibid*).

Here we perceive that Dr. Bruinsma has mounted a very serious attack upon both Scripture and the Spirit of Prophecy. Now these are very serious and disturbing charges from a man who is a member of the General Conference Committee and raises his hand in decision-making for the World Church. The real question he is posing is: Have we followed cunningly devised fables?

The answer is, absolutely no! Dr. Bruinsma's charge that we have based our current understanding of Roman Catholicism upon nineteenth century events is absolutely false. Our view of the Papacy is not based upon nineteenth century Protestant bigotry against Roman Catholics. Indeed, it is based upon sixth century B.C. knowledge, and upon first century A.D. knowledge, for we have based our understanding of the Papacy in these last days on Daniel 7, 8 and 12, Matthew 24, 2 Thessalonians 2, 1 John 2 and 4, 2 John, Revelation 12, 13, 14, 17, 18 and 19. These passages of Scripture receive absolutely no mention in Dr. Bruinsma's article.

That Dr. Bruinsma should have written in the manner he had at a time when the veracity of that which is stated in Scripture and *The Great Controversy* had never been more specifically verified, indicated a tremendous peril that has entered our church. Seventh-day Adventists are becoming blind to the sophistries of Roman Catholicism. Furthermore, the ecumenical spirit, which originated with Satan, is becoming a dominant feature of our church. Very rightly, Dr. Bruinsma had stated:

> The church's attitude toward the Roman Catholic Church illustrates the dilemma most poignantly. When private individuals, or "independent ministries," mass-produced excerpts from *The Great Controversy* about the alleged anti-Christian nature of Roman Catholicism and then distributed them far and wide, and when some bought advertising space on large bill-boards and newspapers to warn Americans about the real intentions of "the Beast" – as happened a few years ago in Florida and Oregon and, more recently, during the Pope's visit to Missouri – Church leaders hastened to distance themselves and the Church. Yet, the sponsors of these campaigns had, in fact, quoted from a book that the Church officially publishes in dozens of languages and had, albeit selectively, used official Adventist teaching.
>
> Adventist church leaders anxiously emphasize that, while the future end-time scenario must be kept in mind, we should not be deterred from having friendly

relations with other Christian churches. Their critics, however, see this as a dangerous dilution of the Adventist task to call people out of "Babylon." Clearly, this issue is potential dynamite. Some time soon the Church must decide unequivocally whether it is a Christian church – with its own unique witness – amidst other Christian churches, or whether it must stand alone over and against all other Christian bodies. (*Ibid*).

At the time Dr. Bruinsma wrote the *Spectrum* article, the General Conference was pursuing a lawsuit against Pastor Rafael Perez and his church for using the name, Seventh-day Adventist, without their permission. Dr. Bruinsma's admission that the use of *The Great Controversy* statements in public advertisements represented the use of a book officially approved and published by the church organization, was proper. However, such a statement would not have assisted the General Conference lawsuit if it had been offered in evidence in the Federal Court in Florida in October, 1999. Dr. Bruinsma's statement that the issue was one of potential dynamite was maybe more telling than even he thought.

Dr. Bruinsma's complaint that we are basing our understanding of Catholicism upon a few articles from the nineteenth century must be declared to be false. We are basing it upon the prophecies of the Bible and Spirit of Prophecy and the clear evidence of contemporary events in the years 1998 and 1999! We cannot be much more contemporary than that.

In his letter, *Dies Domini*, completed on May 31, 1998 and released on July 7, 1998, the Pope introduced the matter of civil legislation to uphold Sunday observance.

> Therefore, also in the particular circumstance of our own time Christians will naturally strive to ensure that civil legislation respects their duty to keep Sunday holy.

It is not Seventh-day Adventists who need to return to the nineteenth century to support truth. It is the Pope who turned to that very century in order to uphold his error. He was the one whom Dr. Bruinsma would have done well to have charged with this use of nineteenth century material, for he referred to the encyclical *Rerum Novarum* which was issued in the nineteenth century by Pope Leo XIII who held the pontificate from 1878 to 1903. That encyclical also upheld the intervention of the state to uphold Sunday observance.

By quoting this papal encyclical, Pope John Paul II made it contemporary Roman Catholic doctrine. This is what Pope John Paul II wrote in his apostolic letter, *Dies Domini*:

> Pope Leo XIII in his encyclical, *Rerum Novarum*, spoke of Sunday rest as a worker's right which the state must guarantee.

You will notice that in the words of an earlier pontiff, Pope Leo XIII, he used the words "which the state must guarantee." What a fulfillment of the words of

The Great Controversy that Rome does not change! Praise God that the servant of the Lord *did* set forth our position on Rome, else we might be blinded by Rome's apparent changes of position. But in the Pope's letter, *Dies Domini*, the Roman Pontiff provided absolutely irrefutable evidence that Rome has not changed her desire to utilize the state to enforce its will in relation to the enforcement of the counterfeit Sabbath.

Furthermore, three days earlier on May 28, 1998, Pope John Paul II issued another apostolic letter, *Ad Tuendum Fidem* (To Protect the Faith). This apostolic letter was designed to insert new codes into Roman Catholic Canon Law. Let us look at one of these new Canon Laws, Canon 1436:

> No. 1: Whoever denies a truth which must be believed with divine and catholic faith, or who calls into doubt, or who totally repudiates the Christian faith, and does not retract after being legitimately warned, is to be punished as a heretic or as an apostate with a major excommunication, a cleric moreover can be punished with other penalties, not excluding deposition.
>
> No. 2: In addition to these cases, whoever obstinately rejects a teaching of the Roman Pontiff or the College of Bishops, exercising the authentic Magisterium, have set forth to be held definitively, or who affirm what they have condemned as erroneous, and does not retract after having been legitimately warned, is to be punished with an appropriate penalty.

We would be forgiven if we thought that these were the words of a papal encyclical of the fifteenth century; but we repeat, this encyclical was issued on May 28, 1998! There is nothing nineteenth century in that encyclical. As the servant of the Lord so correctly foretold,

> The papal church will never relinquish her claim to infallibility. All that she has done in her persecution of those who reject her dogmas she holds to be right; and would she not repeat the same acts, should the opportunity be presented?
>
> (*The Great Controversy*, p. 564).

Sister White's rhetorical question bears no contradiction.

Not only does the Spirit of Prophecy assert this fact but Scripture states it in terms that cannot be refuted.

> [15]And he had power to give life unto the image of the beast, that the image of the beast should both speak, and cause that as many as would not worship the image of the beast should be killed. [16]And he causeth all, both small and great, rich and poor, free and bond, to receive a mark in their right hand, or in their foreheads: [17]And that no man might buy or sell, save he that had the mark, or the name of the beast, or the number of his name. (Revelation 13:15-17).

And now the Pope dares to introduce new Canon Laws which state that "whoever" – not just members of the Roman Catholic faith – but "whoever" will not follow the papal dictates will be punished as a heretic. Or, as the second part of that Canon Law states, "By an appropriate punishment."

Since the Pope referred to the nineteenth century, we are sure we can be forgiven if we should seek to understand just a little more of the thinking of the Pope he quoted, Pope Leo XIII. In his papal encyclical on human liberty he stated:

> Let us examine that liberty in individuals which is so opposed to the virtue of religion, namely the liberty of worship, as it is called. This is based on the principle that every man is free to profess as he may choose any religion or none...a liberty such as we have described...is no liberty but degradation.
> (*The Great Encyclical Letters of Pope Leo XIII*, Third Edition, Benzinger, 1903, pp. 149, 150).

We may be charged here with having used nineteenth century evidence but let it never be forgotten that it was Pope John Paul II in 1998 who referred to Pope Leo XIII and his concept of the state upholding Sunday observance. Thus the present Pope has made this work of Leo XIII current by his support of the earlier Pope's encyclical.

The impression given by Dr. Bruinsma was that Sister White basically only reflected the concepts of her contemporaries. Anyone who believes that Sister White was a slave to the ideas of others should read her statements concerning the Holy Spirit's personage and the eternal equality of our Lord and Savior Jesus Christ with the Father. She unequivocally upheld these two concepts but they were certainly not the views of nineteenth century Seventh-day Adventist ministers. Sister White did not rely on others for her concepts. She relied upon divine guidance. When she quoted from other sources she did so because she was guided in that which was accurate.

Thus Pastor Bruinsma's statement,

> Ellen G. White's treatment of the history of the Catholic Church did not differ in essence from the approach of other Adventist writers. (*Spectrum*, op. cit.),

trivialized the inspiration of the servant of the Lord. His statement was,

> In the chapter entitled "Liberty of Conscience Threatened," we detect the same insistence as in other representative Adventist publications that Catholicism will never change and that one should not be fooled by "the fair front" it presents to the world. "Every principle of the papacy that existed in ages past exists today," she wrote (571). (*Ibid*).

This statement concerning "Liberty of Conscience Threatened" did great injustice to the prophetic gift God bestowed upon Sister White. Dr. Bruinsma seemed to be concerned that Sister White's writings are accepted as truth. Notice on three occasions where he referred to her writings on Catholicism, he inferred that they were holding back progress of the Seventh-day Adventist Church's attitude to Catholicism:

1. Acceptance of her [Sister White's] statements in *The Great Controversy* and elsewhere as inspired pronouncements prevented later Adventism from taking another look at contemporary Catholicism while other Protestants were increasingly prepared to do so. (*Ibid*).
2. Still, her major writings about Roman Catholicism date from the 1880s and 1890s, and thus originated in a climate of Adventist confidence about the reality of the Catholic threat and the imminence of events predicted for decades. Once she codified those views, it became virtually impossible to re-evaluate them critically without questioning her prophetic authority. (*Ibid*).
3. One of the most central reasons for sustained anti-Catholicism, however, was that Ellen G. White had codified these views in her writings. Thus, it would be virtually impossible to re-evaluate them critically without questioning her prophetic authority. (*Ibid*).

We would say, praise God that she codified these matters for today, unlike Pastor Bruinsma's suggestions, they are being fulfilled precisely and they provide a wonderful warning to every loyal Seventh-day Adventist.

That Rome has not changed is plainly evidenced by the fact that the Pope issued "the most solemn form of papal document" (Reuters News, November 30, 1998) – a Papal Bull entitled "Incarnationis Mysterium" on November 29, 1998.

The Papal Bull offered to all Christians, indulgences "that will eliminate time in purgatory" (*International Herald-Tribune*, November 29, 1998) for certain duties from December 25, 1999 to January 6, 2001. Thus the disgraceful doctrines of indulgences and purgatory were re-affirmed. The Great Schism in the Christian church in the sixteenth century was caused by indulgences.

Now the Pope hoped to use this same unscriptural doctrine as an ecumenical feature:

> But by broadening the ways believers can earn an indulgence beyond Catholic rituals, the Pope is also trying to imbue the indulgences with some of the ecumenical spirit he wants to lend the celebrations [of the new millennium].
>
> (*Ibid*).

Has Rome changed? Certainly not!

Furthermore, in his post-synodal apostolic *Exhortation Ecclesia in America*, the Pope, in writing to American priests and laity, stated that,

> the Gospel was proclaimed by presenting the Virgin Mary as its highest realization.

What a disgraceful destruction of the gospel of our Lord and Savior Jesus Christ!

The Pope encouraged the American people to regard the Virgin of Guadalupe as the

"Patroness of all America and the star of the first and new evangelization." In addition he urged that the Virgin be acknowledged as "Queen of all America."

Again we ask, Has Rome changed? Again we reply, Absolutely no! Is *The Great Controversy* being fulfilled before our very eyes? Our answer is, Most certainly it is!

On May 13, 1999 the *London Daily Telegraph* revealed some of the details of the Anglican/Roman Catholic Commission findings. We quote just four pronouncements for Seventh-day Adventists to evaluate. Let each decide whether or not Sister White wrote under inspiration. Let each judge whether her writings are being precisely fulfilled today. Notice these extracts from the Commission's report.

1. The Bishop of Rome has "a specific ministry concerning the discernment of truth."
2. "The Primacy of the Pope is a gift to be shared."
3. The Bishop of Rome "would exercise a universal primacy."
4. The Pope is "a gift to be received by all the churches."

To state that Rome has changed is to ignore totally the evidence of that which is transpiring in our present time.

Dr. Bruinsma also stated:

> Adventists basically believe that they have much to teach and little to learn. They want respect from other churches, yet they avoid closeness to them. (*Ibid*).

We would confirm that Seventh-day Adventists have much to teach and little to learn from apostate Christianity. We still have much to learn, but that is from inspiration, and God has entrusted to us the mighty three angels' messages that they might be proclaimed world-wide.

Furthermore, we must take issue with the implied implications of Dr. Bruinsma's statement:

> Sometime soon the Church must decide unequivocally whether it is a Christian church – with its own unique witness – amidst other Christian churches, or whether it must stand alone over and against all other Christian bodies. (*Ibid*).

Here we see the ecumenical spirit being promoted. Never must Seventh-day Adventists become just another Christian church with its own unique witness. We are a movement called out to finish God's work on earth and to expose the apostasy of all the churches of Babylon.

We cannot understand Pastor Bruinsma's complaint:

> In criticizing Catholic history, Adventists should try to be more balanced than in the past and should avoid offering a simple extension of the often biased and inaccurate picture that many past Protestants have offered of the medieval Church. Medieval Christianity also had positive and beautiful dimensions. (*Ibid*)

Has Dr. Bruinsma not read the medieval record of the papacy? Let us not look to Seventh-day Adventist or even Protestant authors. Let us look to the assessment of highly educated Roman Catholic authors concerning that era. We recall back in 1955 when we were studying our History major at the University of Sydney, the Professor instructing us, Professor Bruce Mansfield, in front of a large class, including numbers of Roman Catholic teaching brothers, stated that during the sixteenth century the papacy was a disgrace. He confirmed his statement by quoting from numerous Roman Catholic historians. The facts of history cannot be controverted – and must not be – by Seventh-day Adventists. It was this period that was incorporated into the important 1260-year prophecy of Daniel 7 and 12, and Revelation 11, 12 and 13.

Dr. Peter de Rosa, a Jesuit priest holding a doctorate from the Gregorian University of Rome, a former professor of ethics at the Westminster Seminary – the chief Roman Catholic training school for priests in Britain – and also a professor of theology at Corpus Christi College, stated in his book *Vicars of Christ*, published 1989 by Corgi Books, London, that in the *Libro Nero* (Black Book), which was a guide to Inquisitors and which was still on display in the Vatican last century, the Inquisitors were admonished,

> Either the person confesses and he is proved guilty from his own confession, or he does not confess and is equally guilty on the evidence of witnesses [many of whom were unreliable]. If a person confesses the whole of what he is accused of, he is unquestionably guilty of the whole; but if he confesses only a part, he ought still to be regarded as guilty of the whole, since what he has confessed proves him to be capable of guilt as to the other points of accusation.
>
> (*Vicars of Christ*, page 228, square brackets in original).

Dr. de Rosa claimed that,

> 80 successive popes invoked the inquisition over a period spanning six centuries.
> (*Ibid*, p. 244).

Furthermore, Dr. de Rosa described the appalling condition of the papacy at the time John Huss was burnt at the stake. Three popes, as we have seen previously, were ruling simultaneously, Popes John XXIII, Gregory XII and Benedict XIII. John XXIII had attained to the papal office by murdering his predecessor, Pope Alexander V, and bribing the other cardinals to vote for him in the papal conclave. Eventually his crimes became so gross that he was brought before the Catholic Council at Constance. There he was charged with over seventy crimes. Quoting Gibbon in his book *The Decline and Fall* de Rosa stated (We repeat a little material quoted already in this book),

> The most scandalous charges were suppressed; the Vicar of Christ was only accused of piracy, murder, rape, sodomy and incest.

Dr. de Rosa went on to say:

It is significant that John XXIII was absolved from heresy, probably because he had never evinced sufficient interest in religion to be classed as heterodox.

(*Vicars of Christ*, p. 132).

For these crimes John XXIII was sentenced to three years jail. He and Huss were contemporary prisoners in the same jail. Notice Dr. de Rosa's insight into the treatment of Huss as compared with John XXIII:

> Huss – brave, chaste, incorruptible, stern opponent of simony [bribery to obtain religious office] and clerical concubinage, met a harsher fate [than John XXIII], forbidden counsel, tried on a trumped-up charge, interrogated by Dominicans who had not read his books even in translation – he was sentenced to death. Wearing a high hat with three dancing devils on it, flanked by Count Palatine's swordsmen, he was led out of prison on a glorious summer's day in 1415. Practically the entire town followed as the procession made its way to where Huss's books were being burned in a bright green meadow. He prayed for his persecutors as the fire was lit. Three times he was heard to say, "Christ, thou Son of the Living God, have mercy on me," before the wind blew flames into his face. His lips were still moving in prayer as he expired with a groan. To prevent his being honoured as a martyr, his ashes were scattered on the Rhine. It was clearly more sinful to say, as did Huss and the New Testament, that after the blessing the Eucharist should still be called "bread," than to be a greedy, murderous pope who misled the church on almost everything. (*Vicars of Christ*, pp. 132, 133).

Dr. de Rosa also documented the fact that there were some apparently sincere bishops. These bishops called the Council in Basle, Switzerland in 1432. This group of earnest bishops issued the following declaration:

> From now on, all ecclesiastical appointments shall be made according to the Canons of the Church. All simony [the purchase of holy offices] shall cease. From now on, all priests whether of the highest or lowest rank, shall put away their concubines, and whoever within two months of this decree neglects its demands shall be deprived of his office though he be the Bishop of Rome. From now on, the ecclesiastical administration of each country shall cease to depend on papal caprice.... The abuse of ban and anathema by the Pope shall cease.... From now on, the Roman Curia, that is, the popes, shall neither demand or receive any fees for ecclesiastical offices. From now on, a pope should think not of this world's treasures, but only of the world to come. (*Vicars of Christ*, p. 138).

It is interesting to observe the result of this righteous declaration. Dr. de Rosa stated:

> This was strong meat. Too strong. The ruling pope, Eugene IV, summoned his own council at Florence. Basle he labelled "a beggarly mob, mere vulgar fellows from the lowest ranks of the clergy, apostates, blaspheming rebels, men guilty of sacrilege, gaolbirds [jailbirds], men who without exception deserve only to be hunted back to the devil from whence they came." The papacy had squandered its

chances; there was to be no more. The same century that saw Eugene IV censuring the best efforts of Basle reform was to end with the pope who, above all, had come from the devil: Alexander Borgia. (*Vicars of Christ*, p. 138).

Russell has stood before the coffin of Alexander Borgia, Pope Alexander VI, in the Church of Mary Major in Rome. As he did so, Russell pondered the ultimate fate of this "devil."

Thus we see that which is written concerning the papacy in *The Great Controversy* is tempered with Christian love and courtesy. Papists themselves are not in any doubt concerning the vileness of the papacy in the Middle Ages. It is time that no Seventh-day Adventist leader attempted to re-write papal history. It is a history of a church led by Satan himself.

God's people deserved an explanation from Dr. Bruinsma concerning the first and second beasts of Revelation 13. He could not possibly hold the view that Rome had changed if he understood aright the identification of these two beastly powers. Dr. Bruinsma would do well to contemplate the words of inspiration:

> There has been a change; but the change is not in the papacy. Catholicism indeed resembles much of the Protestantism that now exists, because Protestantism has so greatly degenerated since the days of the Reformers. (*The Great Controversy*, p. 571).

The evil of the papacy today should be well understood:

> Every principle of the papacy that existed in past ages exists today. The doctrines devised in the darkest ages are still held. Let none deceive themselves. The papacy that Protestants are now so ready to honor is the same that ruled the world in the days of the Reformation, when men of God stood up, at the peril of their lives, to expose her iniquity. She possesses the same pride and arrogant assumption that lorded it over kings and princes, and claimed the prerogatives of God. Her spirit is no less cruel and despotic now than when she crushed out human liberty and slew the saints of the Most High. (*Ibid*).

We have a burden for Roman Catholics and apostate Protestants. We take seriously God's plaintive plea to call these people out of Babylon. If we re-write the history of the papacy, and if we are blind to that which is happening before our very eyes, we will never please our Lord, and souls will be imperilled. It is a sad reflection on the Seventh-day Adventist church of today that it is necessary to uphold these truths and document the errors now being perpetrated by ordained, credentialed leaders within our ranks. Dr. Bruinsma is currently a member of the General Conference Executive Committee. Whoever could have thought this necessary, when decades ago Seventh-day Adventists were united upon the platform of Bible and Spirit of Prophecy truth?

Part VIII
The Remnant Church

36 The Remnant

Today most Seventh-day Adventists appear to believe that the great majority of those of our faith will enjoy the glories of heaven. Many even believe that at the close of probation those sealed will include many Sunday-keepers. This false position has been largely established upon two errors which some in leadership have introduced into our midst.

The first of these is the key-doctrinal focus of the New Theology – the unscriptural claim that God's redeemed will be sinning until Jesus comes. Scripture plainly states otherwise.

> ³And hereby we do know that we know him, if we keep his commandments. ⁴He that saith, I know him, and keepeth not his commandments, is a liar, and the truth is not in him. ⁵But whoso keepeth his word, in him verily is the love of God perfected: hereby know we that we are in him. ⁶He that saith he abideth in him ought himself also so to walk, even as he walked.   (1 John 2:3-6).

> ²Beloved, now are we the sons of God, and it doth not yet appear what we shall be: but we know that, when he shall appear, we shall be like him; for we shall see him as he is. ³And every man that hath this hope in him purifieth himself, even as he is pure. ⁴Whosoever committeth sin transgresseth also the law: for sin is the transgression of the law. ⁵And ye know that he was manifested to take away our sins; and in him is no sin. ⁶Whosoever abideth in him sinneth not: whosoever sinneth hath not seen him, neither known him. ⁷Little children, let no man deceive you: he that doeth righteousness is righteous, even as he is righteous. ⁸He that committeth sin is of the devil; for the devil sinneth from the beginning. For this purpose the Son of God was manifested, that he might destroy the works of the devil. ⁹Whosoever is born of God doth not commit sin; for his seed remaineth in him: and he cannot sin, because he is born of God.   (1 John 3:2-9).

These words brook no two meanings. If these two passages were alone the counsel of Scripture, they would more than suffice to expose the New Theology as a crude and none-too-subtle attempt to deprive God's people of salvation.

The second faulted principle promoted by denominational leadership, which encourages many to believe that God's mercy will be extended to those who breach God's commandments, is the favour now shown to the ecumenical movement, inspired by Satan. For instance, in Europe, all the Seventh-day Adventist churches in some nations have signed the Charta Oecumenica. For instance, we cite the fact that the leaders on behalf of their Seventh-day Adventist Union (Netherlands) and Conferences (Northern and Southern French and the Belgium) in Belgium, France and the Netherlands have already signed this Charta, which includes the Roman Catholic, Protestant, Anglican, Eastern Orthodox and Old Catholic churches. The two principle signatories to the Charta are Cardinal Vlk, the Roman Catholic Cardinal-Archbishop of Prague, who signed on behalf of the Roman Catholic European Bishops' Conference and Jeremie, an Eastern Orthodox Metropolitan on behalf of all the Orthodox, Anglican, Protestant and Old Catholic churches in Europe.

In Germany both the North and the South German Unions of Seventh-day Adventists have joined the German Council of Churches. In the Pacific, the Solomon Islands Church is a member of SICA, the Solomon Islands Christian Association. Pastor Robert Folkenburg, when General Conference President, provided unspoken support for this membership when he attended a dinner hosted in his honor by SICA. In another South Pacific nation, Vanuatu, our church holds membership in the VCCC, the Vanuatu Council of Christian Churches. In the 1990's, the Secretary of the Vanuatu Mission of Seventh-day Adventists was also Secretary of the VCCC. These are but a few illustrations of the rapid inroads of the ecumenical movement into our church.

The ecumenical spirit which today dominates the thinking of many church administrators, theologians and pastors, disqualifies them from their calling as watchmen on the walls of Zion. The Lord solemnly warned against such unholy confederations:

> [12]Say ye not, A confederacy, to all them to whom this people shall say, A confederacy; neither fear ye their fear, nor be afraid. [13]Sanctify the LORD of hosts himself; and let him be your fear, and let him be your dread. (Isaiah 8:12, 13).

The Servant of the Lord, referring to this prophecy, focused it upon our day:

> Let the watchmen on the walls of Zion not join with those who are making of none effect the truth as it is in Christ. Let them not join the confederacy of infidelity, popery, and Protestantism in exalting tradition above Scripture, reason above revelation, and human talent above the divine influence and the vital power of godliness. (SDA Bible Commentary, Vol. 4, pp. 1141, 1142).

> You are not to look to the world in order to learn what you shall write and publish or what you shall speak. (Selected Messages, Vol. 2, p. 371).

Yet Scripture plainly attests to the awesome fact that the remnant, those who will be saved, will be few in number. The prophet Isaiah revealed this fact about 2,700 years ago.

> For though thy people Israel be as the sand of the sea, yet a remnant of them shall return: the consumption decreed shall overflow with righteousness.
> (Isaiah 10:22).

> Except the LORD of hosts had left unto us a very small remnant, we should have been as Sodom, *and* we should have been like unto Gomorrah. (Isaiah 1:9).

The prophet Paul synthesized these two ancient prophecies in applying them to the end time.

> [27]Esaias also crieth concerning Israel, Though the number of the children of Israel be as the sand of the sea, a remnant shall be saved: [28]For he will finish the work, and cut it short in righteousness: because a short work will the Lord make upon the earth. [29]And as Esaias said before, Except the Lord of Sabaoth had left us a seed, we had been as Sodoma, and been made like unto Gomorrha.
>
> (Romans 9:27-29).

While salvation is freely offered to all, only a very small remnant will accept it. Why is such a fearful situation so? It is because the great majority of us will falter over a stumblingstone. Once more the prophet Isaiah reminds us of this fact.

> [13]Sanctify the LORD of hosts himself; and let him be your fear, and let him be your dread. [14]And he shall be for a sanctuary; but for a stone of stumbling and for a rock of offence to both the houses of Israel, for a gin and for a snare to the inhabitants of Jerusalem. [15]And many among them shall stumble, and fall, and be broken, and be snared, and be taken. (Isaiah 8:13-15).

What is this stumblingstone? Again God enlightens us through His ancient prophet in the following verse:

> Bind up the testimony, seal the law among my disciples. (Isaiah 8:16).

Here we see that the Law of God, Christ's character, is the stumblingblock. It is this law which the proponents of the New Theology demean. If, in God's power we cannot obey it, the law of God is an abject redundancy for the citizens of this earth. If we can receive salvation while in breach of the law, unrepentant, then Satan and his angelic followers surely possess that salvation. That they do not, bears testimony to the fact that unrepented and unforsaken sin is an absolute barrier to salvation.

Some proponents of the New Theology deny that they believe they can reach heaven with unrepented sin in their hearts. We make some comments upon this claim. Firstly, if we sin until Jesus comes then we will have unrepented sin in our lives, for our Mediator ceases His mediatorial work at the close of probation. Secondly, the desecration of God's law approved in our church, as a result of this teaching, has given rise to untold woes.

Both the New Testament prophets, Paul and Peter, grasped Isaiah's words and related them to our day:

> [30]What shall we say then? That the Gentiles, which followed not after righteousness, have attained to righteousness, even the righteousness which is of faith. [31]But Israel, which followed after the law of righteousness, hath not attained to the law of righteousness. [32]Wherefore? Because they sought it not by faith, but as it were by the works of the law. For they stumbled at that stumblingstone; [33]As

it is written, Behold, I lay in Sion a stumblingstone and rock of offence: and whosoever believeth on him shall not be (confounded).

(Romans 9:30-33, margin).

Verse 30 above plainly disputes the fact that those who do not keep the law in Christ's power will be saved. Verse 32 also destroys the comfort of those who believe they can keep the law in their own power and not through Christ's power and righteousness.

Peter pointedly united his reference to Isaiah 8:13-15 to another passage of the prophet's writings:

> [15]Because ye have said, We have made a covenant with death, and with hell are we at agreement; when the overflowing scourge shall pass through, it shall not come unto us: for we have made lies our refuge, and under falsehood have we hid ourselves: [16]Therefore thus saith the Lord GOD, Behold, I lay in Zion for a foundation a stone, a tried stone, a precious corner stone, a sure foundation: he that believeth shall not make haste. [17]Judgment also will I lay to the line, and righteousness to the plummet: and the hail shall sweep away the refuge of lies, and the waters shall overflow the hiding place. [18]And your covenant with death shall be disannulled, and your agreement with hell shall not stand; when the overflowing scourge shall pass through, then ye shall be trodden down by it.
>
> (Isaiah 28:15-18).

This passage merits study and meditation under the guidance of the Holy Spirit. It is a warning to each of us who have made lies our refuge and contented ourselves with falsehoods. Notice that Christ, the Corner Stone, will measure each of us with exactitude by the plumbline of righteousness. Peter plainly declared that the Corner Stone, Christ, is also the Stumblingblock. This comes as no surprise for the law is the transcript of His character.

> [6]Wherefore also it is contained in the scripture, Behold, I lay in Sion a chief corner stone, elect, precious: and he that believeth on him shall not be confounded. [7]Unto you therefore which believe he is precious: but unto them which be disobedient, the stone which the builders disallowed, the same is made the head of the corner, [8]And a stone of stumbling, and a rock of offence, even to them which stumble at the word, being disobedient: whereunto also they were appointed.
>
> (1 Peter 2:6-8).

The New Theology is finding our Savior to be its stumblingblock. God has called His last-day people to righteousness. Peter continued, contrasting those who trust the falsehoods of the New Theology with those who "in the day of visitation", in Christ's power, "abstain from fleshly lusts":

> [9]But ye are a chosen generation, a royal priesthood, an holy nation, a peculiar people; that ye should show forth the praises of him who hath called you out of darkness into his marvellous light: [10]Which in time past were not a people, but are now the people of God: which had not obtained mercy, but now have obtained

mercy. [11]Dearly beloved, I beseech you as strangers and pilgrims, abstain from fleshly lusts, which war against the soul; [12]Having your conversation honest among the Gentiles: that, whereas they speak against you as evildoers, they may by your good works, which they shall behold, glorify God in the day of visitation.
(1 Peter 2:9-12).

If we had been required to list the criteria of the remnant church, our list may have been lengthy, even perhaps extending beyond twenty-seven or the twenty-eight proposed to be voted at the General Conference in St. Louis, Missouri in 2005. But our God makes matters very simple for us. The easiest words to understand in Scripture are those which He wrote with His own finger. Let us take just one four-word sentence which God wrote:

Thou shalt not kill. (Exodus 20:13).

This is so simple that a pre-school child could understand it, and understand it well.

Thus when God wished mankind to know with absolute certainty which church, among the thousands of Christian churches today, is His church, He provided us with just two criteria:

And the dragon was wroth with the woman, and went to make war with the remnant of her seed, which keep the commandments of God, and have the testimony of Jesus Christ. (Revelation 12:17).

Prior to examining these two criteria, we would draw the attention of God's people to a number of matters. No one can be in doubt concerning the identity of the dragon. So we may possess absolute certainty, three synonyms are provided – serpent, devil, Satan.

And the great dragon was cast out, that old serpent, called the Devil, and Satan, which deceiveth the whole world: he was cast out into the earth, and his angels were cast out with him. (Revelation 12:9).

And he laid hold on the dragon, that old serpent, which is the Devil, and Satan, and bound him a thousand years. (Revelation 20:2).

The woman represents a church. If in apostasy, it is a harlot; if a pure church, it is set forth as a virgin.

They say, If a man put away his wife, and she go from him, and become another man's, shall he return unto her again? shall not that land be greatly polluted? but thou hast played the harlot with many lovers; yet return again to me, saith the LORD. (Jeremiah 3:1).

For I am jealous over you with godly jealousy: for I have espoused you to one husband, that I may present you as a chaste virgin to Christ.(2 Corinthians 11:2).

Which category of church is the woman of Revelation 12:17? Manifestly it is a virgin church, one which professes a pure faith. Satan is never wroth with a harlot church, for it is already in his army.

However, we notice with alarm that even in this virgin church, Satan does not go to war with the church as a whole. We use the word "alarm" because if all the members of the church were pure he most certainly would attack it from top to bottom. But Scripture is precise. Satan makes war upon the remnant seed of the church alone. This provides evidence beyond any dispute that the church in general, which has been accorded a pure faith, is in apostasy, for Satan is too wise to war against his own warriors.

This raises the question of defining those who are the remnant who are so near to Christ that they keep the pure faith and thus engender Satan's rage. With two criteria these souls are defined and thus distinguished from every other professing Christian in the entire world.

The first criterion is that they "keep the commandments of God." Even if we confine this criterion to those who profess to keep all the commandments, this reduces the number of the remnant to less than one percent of all Christians, for the great majority of professing Christians are actually taught to disobey the fourth commandment, and thus they breach the entire ten.

> For whosoever shall keep the whole law, and yet offend in one point, he is guilty of all. (James 2:10).

But there are still some Christians, in addition to Seventh-day Adventists, who profess to keep all the commandments. These include Seventh Day Baptists, the Church of God Seventh Day, some remnants of the World-Wide Church of God and some groups of Seventh Day Pentecostals. Thus Christ provided a second criterion so that we may discern His remnant church among these – His remnant people "have the testimony of Jesus."

In order that we possess a divine definition of the term "testimony of Jesus," God, in Revelation, provided it.

> ...for the testimony of Jesus is the spirit of prophecy. (Revelation 19:10, last part).

It is no coincidence that the Seventh-day Adventist Movement commenced as a prophetic one. There was no mistake that this Movement, under the guidance of the Holy Spirit, obtained an understanding of the end-time prophecies of Daniel and John beyond any such previous knowledge. Seventh-day Adventism was founded by men and women who valued all prophecy found both in the Old and New Testaments. They firmly believed:

> [16]For we have not followed cunningly devised fables, when we made known unto you the power and coming of our Lord Jesus Christ, but were eyewitnesses of his majesty. [17]For he received from God the Father honour and glory, when there came such a voice to him from the excellent glory, This is my beloved Son, in whom I am well pleased. [18]And this voice which came from heaven we heard,

when we were with him in the holy mount. [19]We have also a more sure word of prophecy; whereunto ye do well that ye take heed, as unto a light that shineth in a dark place, until the day dawn, and the day star arise in your hearts: [20]Knowing this first, that no prophecy of the scripture is of any private interpretation. [21]For the prophecy came not in old time by the will of man: but holy men of God spake as they were moved by the Holy Ghost. (2 Peter 1:16-21).

To what does the term spirit of prophecy refer? Well, of course, it refers to every holy prophet in history, from Adam to whom Christ revealed the entire plan of salvation, to Sister White.

> To Adam were revealed future important events, from his expulsion from Eden to the Flood, and onward to the first advent of Christ upon the earth;
> (*Story of Redemption*, p. 48).

Luminaries such as Enoch, Noah, Abraham, Moses, David, Nathan, Elijah, Elisha, Huldah, Isaiah, Jeremiah, Ezekiel, Daniel, Nahum, Malachi, Zechariah and John the Baptist, and the apostle John, many of whom wrote not a single word of Scripture, come to mind as do many others.

> It is the voice of Christ that speaks to us through the Old Testament. "The testimony of Jesus is the spirit of prophecy." Revelation 19:10.
> (*Patriarchs & Prophets*, p. 366).

We repeat, it is no coincidence that Seventh-day Adventists are a people of prophecy. No other faith of Christendom has explored the end-time prophecies of Daniel and Revelation more accurately than we have. We trust the Testimony of Jesus, the Spirit of Prophecy, found in the various eras of earth's history.

But there are two other features of the Spirit of Prophecy. The first is that we are to present the message of the prophet, Elijah, in these last days.

> [1]Comfort ye, comfort ye my people, saith your God. [2]Speak ye comfortably to Jerusalem, and cry unto her, that her warfare is accomplished, that her iniquity is pardoned: for she hath received of the LORD'S hand double for all her sins. [3]The voice of him that crieth in the wilderness, Prepare ye the way of the LORD, make straight in the desert a highway for our God. [4]Every valley shall be exalted, and every mountain and hill shall be made low: and the crooked shall be made straight, and the rough places plain: [5]And the glory of the LORD shall be revealed, and all flesh shall see it together: for the mouth of the LORD hath spoken it. (Isaiah 40:1-5).

The second is that God's people would possess a prophet of the last days in their midst. They *have* the testimony of Jesus Christ, the Spirit of Prophecy. Revelation 12:17 is written in the context of the time of the end, following the completion of the 1260-year prophecy as certified in verse 14:

> And to the woman were given two wings of a great eagle, that she might fly into the wilderness, into her place, where she is nourished for a time, and times, and half a time, from the face of the serpent. (Revelation 12:14).

Not one of the Sabbath-keeping faiths, apart from the Seventh-day Adventist Church, even claims to possess a prophet. Thus the Seventh-day Adventist church alone stands as God's chosen Remnant Church. But even here, the vast, vast majority of its professed members will despise both the commandments of God and the Spirit of Prophecy, for only a remnant will be saved.

It is noteworthy that three other nineteenth-century churches profess to possess a prophet – Mormons (Joseph Smith), Christian Scientists (Mary Baker Eddy) and the Jehovah's Witnesses (Charles Russell). These three churches exclude themselves as the Remnant Church, for none keeps the commandments. The Jehovah Witnesses promote the absurd position that every day is a Sabbath, despite the fact that God wrote,

> [9]Six days shalt thou labour, and do all thy work: [10]But the seventh day is the sabbath of the LORD thy God:... (Exodus 20:9, 10).

God would be a cruel God if he designated every day as a Sabbath for none could ever work and even if they were on social security, they could die of starvation unless others provided them with food, for they could not buy anything.

> [15]In those days saw I in Judah some treading wine presses on the sabbath, and bringing in sheaves, and lading asses; as also wine, grapes, and figs, and all manner of burdens, which they brought into Jerusalem on the sabbath day: and I testified against them in the day wherein they sold victuals. [16]There dwelt men of Tyre also therein, which brought fish, and all manner of ware, and sold on the sabbath unto the children of Judah, and in Jerusalem. [17]Then I contended with the nobles of Judah, and said unto them, What evil thing is this that ye do, and profane the sabbath day? (Nehemiah 13:15-17).

Thus, those who, in God's grace and power, keep His commandments and honor the Spirit of Prophecy within their midst constitute the remnant of the Seventh-day Adventist Church. There is absolutely no other candidate. We state this not from a sense of denominational egotism, nor from a rush of triumphalism, but simply as a matter of indisputable fact.

Seventh-day Adventism alone remains as the one candidate for the remnant church. Our evangelists of old have long convinced thousands of honest-hearted seekers of truth of this fact. It is an indisputable fact, a fact which is impossible to challenge validly. We once more remind each reader that the few present-day churches claiming the presence of prophets in their midst do not keep the Commandments and the few other Sabbath-keeping churches despise the Spirit of Prophecy.

No one understands this fact more clearly than Satan. Thus he has launched violent attacks within our church upon both criteria of the remnant. Most Seventh-day Adventist pastors in the west today attack the first criterion, claiming that the keeping of the Commandments is an impossibility. They effectively deny God's promise through Jude:

> Now unto him that is able to keep you from falling, and to present you faultless before the presence of his glory with exceeding joy... (Jude 1:24).

Similarly in God's precious church most pastors in the west and many elsewhere now challenge the doctrine of the Spirit of Prophecy and Sister White's office as a prophet —both in subtle covert ways and, in the case of the South Pacific Division in 2004, in bolder, overt declarations.

Satan, of course, well understands this fact. Is it any wonder that he fires mighty rockets against these two doctrines? That he is doing so is not a matter of the least surprise. That church administrators, ministers, theologians, college professors and laity are aiding and abetting him in this work, is a matter of the deepest concern. Those who teach that we will sin until Jesus returns will most certainly demonstrate the teaching in their own lives. Of this we may be sure; but they will suffer eternal annihilation. Scripture is perfectly clear on this point.

> He that is unjust, let him be unjust still: and he which is filthy, let him be filthy still: and he that is righteous, let him be righteous still: and he that is holy, let him be holy still. (Revelation 22:11).

The same is true of the failure to support the presence of the Spirit of Prophecy in our midst.

> If you lose confidence in the testimonies you will drift away from Bible truth.
> (*Testimonies for the Church*, Vol. 5, p. 98).

37 The Sabbath and the Seal of God

The questioning of the Genesis account of origins and the inevitable desecration of the Sabbath, robs our people of the priceless gift of the seal of the living God.

> ²And I saw another angel ascending from the east, having the seal of the living God: and he cried with a loud voice to the four angels, to whom it was given to hurt the earth and the sea, ³Saying, Hurt not the earth, neither the sea, nor the trees, till we have sealed the servants of our God in their foreheads.
>
> (Revelation 7:2, 3).

That the Sabbath alone of the ten precepts of the Decalogue contains the seal of the living God cannot be disputed because the fourth commandment contains the three mandatory features of the seal – the name of the Ruler, His authority and the dominion over which His authority prevails.

On three occasions the name of God is recorded in the fourth commandment – the Lord thy God (Exodus 20:10); the Lord (twice in Exodus 20:11). His authority is clearly set forth – the Lord made [created] and God's territory over which He rules is specifically stated, "heaven and earth, the sea and all that in them is" (Exodus 20:11), is set forth. God did not permit Scripture to proceed beyond the first verse before offering man the seal of the living God, so important is it.

> In the beginning God [His name] created [His authority] the heaven and the earth [the territory over which He rules]. (Genesis 1:1).

God does not close His work of salvation before offering for the last time the inestimable gift of His seal.

> Saying with a loud voice, Fear God [His name], and give glory to Him; for the hour of His judgment is come: and worship Him that made [His authority] heaven, and earth, and the sea, and the fountains of waters [His domain].
>
> (Revelation 14:7).

The Sabbath, as we demonstrate in the chapter entitled *No Coherent Corpus of Belief*, bears the seal of the living God for it is the commandment of character perfection – holiness.

> Remember the sabbath day, to keep it holy. (Exodus 20:8).

> But in order to keep the Sabbath holy, men must themselves be holy.
>
> (*Desire of Ages*, p. 283).

The constant attacks upon the divinely inspired Scriptural account of creation are bound to destroy the sanctity of the Sabbath. We illustrate this fact with documented recent attitudes to Sabbath observance.

> The Sabbath will be lightly regarded.　　　(*Selected Messages*, Vol. 1, p. 205).

Thus wrote Sister White in describing the Omega of Apostasy.

September 15, 2000, the Opening Ceremony of the Sydney Olympic Games was held. It was a Friday evening during the Sabbath hours.

> North New South Wales Conference Youth Director Wayne French brought together an unprecedented number of Christians from throughout Newcastle and the Hunter Valley to put on what could be the biggest single Christian event in Newcastle's history so far – the *Games Opening Family Fun Day* on 15 September.
>
> Approximately 8000 Novocastrians [citizens of Newcastle] passed through the gates of the Newcastle Entertainment Centre from 12.00 pm [noon] through until 11.30 pm. Some of the performers included Superhubert, the Waratah Girls Choir, Dennis Clare & Tony Williams [famous mime artists], Living Proof – Disabled Talent School, Francine Bell, Tony Bentley (from Newcastle Herald). Continuous Christian presentations went for 7 hours before the live Opening Ceremony which was simulcast onto an [sic] 6 metre screen.
>
> Over 400 volunteer helpers were there throughout the day, with more than 150 Adventist Youth from Greater Sydney and NNSW Conferences. Other attractions included, horizontal bungy, a skate park, huge slide, jumping castles, ferris wheel, 45 exhibitions for charities and churches, games such as giant chess, giant drafts [sic], giant jigsaws, giant snakes and ladders, box hockey, 5 hole mini golf course, youth stage, Hang Out Café and much more. Pirates were there to welcome children with a showbag and give them a treasure map of the area where they could find different events which finally led to the Treasure Chest containing Peters Ice-creams and the wonderbook (a Christian portrayal of the gospel for children). Feedback from the public was extremely positive with many expressing disbelief that the Christian church could stage such a successful large scale event in Newcastle and all for a service to the community. Many bridges to other churches in the region were built. Roger Heft, [Anglican] Bishop of Newcastle, commented that *"good will and the desire for common witness was prevalent enabling the event to take place with a great deal of joy."*
>
> 　　　　(*NNSW [North New South Wales] Conference News* No. 193,
> 　　　　　　October 2000 – italics in the original).

This is the Conference into which we were born. This disgraceful event occurred in Newcastle, the city of our birth. Contrary to the false information dispersed about self-supporting workers, many of us care deeply for our church. We call it "our" church because we refuse to concede that the Seventh-day Adventist church belongs to the liberal, apostate element of the church. This is our church, weak and defective, in need of a mighty reformation and which now, we believe, can only be purified through the shaking process when those who demonstrate no love for God and His truth will be shaken out. Make no mistake, when dire penalties come for true Sabbath-keeping, only those who love God wholeheartedly, who obey Him in His strength, will dare to be known as *Seventh-day* Adventists. Then God will bring to His fold, the Seventh-day Adventist church, purified of all the dross, all His faithful flock who have been cast out by unfaithful church leaders. These Sabbath-breaking church leaders – unless, as we earnestly pray, they become re-converted – will have no part in the Seventh-day Adventist church after the sealing process is completed.

The activities of the 15th of September, 2000 were thought so newsworthy that they were placed on the front page of the North NSW Conference Newsletter. Unashamed, this defiance of divine directives was boasted as a wonderful event. Of course the Anglican Bishop of Newcastle praised the activities of that day and evening. At least he was not breaching *his* day of worship, nor the entertainment standards of *his* church.

But *we* were! It would be incredible if the Conference President and the Conference Youth Director were unacquainted with God's demands in respect of these matters. Undoubtedly we did build bridges to other churches. But the burning question is, In what direction are our people crossing that bridge?

We happily admit that we did not view the opening ceremony of the Olympic Games. But news reports of the event have left us with the profound impression that paganism prevails in Australia. The Olympic Torch was taken to "sacred" aboriginal sites, used for pagan ceremonies. The Torch was taken to the Melbourne Cricket Ground which served as the main stadium for the 1956 Olympic Games. It was stated that the torch had returned to the "hallowed turf" of the M.C.G. – what blasphemy when one knows what occurs there when cricket and football matches are in progress! The Torch was also taken to a Roman Catholic church where a requiem mass had been said for a poor young Italian Olympic cyclist who had been killed in a road accident as he prepared to participate in the 1956 Olympics. The priest in 2000 asked all to pray for the soul of the cyclist. Poor cyclist, was he still in purgatory after the passage of forty-four years and requiring prayers for his soul?

The flame had been lit in a pagan ceremony in Greece where Greek priestesses of the daughter of the Greek sun-god, Zeus, danced about the mirror which caught the "sacred" rays of the sun from which the torch was ignited. In the closing ceremony of the Olympic Games, it was reported, there were Greek priestesses present. The Australian transvestite dancing group disgraced our nation and surely told the world the level of our moral fibre as a nation today.

Yet Seventh-day Adventist leaders dared to defy Sabbath observance and godly entertainment standards to "witness" during this utterly pagan Olympic Festival. Further, they recruited Seventh-day Adventists from both the North New South Wales Conference and the adjoining Greater Sydney Conference to defile themselves in this debased program. After reading that report, we lost much sleep agonizing over our church. Is there not a currently-serving pastor who would risk his ministerial post by publicly and courageously rebuking this open sin? Will the Australian Union President, yet speak out? Will the South Pacific Division watchmen on the walls of Zion, warn God's people and our youth of the eternal consequences of such programs? Indeed, will any pastor, not yet retired, place integrity for Christ and love for Him above fear of dismissal? Such urgent warnings need to be public and widespread for thousands of souls are imperiled. Or will we "REVOLT MORE AND MORE"? (Isaiah 1:5, emphasis added).

April 15, 2000, was a holy Sabbath day. Churches in the North New South Wales Conference together with Macquarie College – which is a Seventh-day Adventist elementary and secondary school – took part in the Family Funday Festival. We quote from the *NNSW Conference News* of April, 2000:

> Macquarie College recently hosted a special training day. The NNSW Youth Department is involved in a program with the Combined Churches Commission to hold two 'festivals' in Newcastle and Lake Macquarie. The first festival on 15 April at Speers Point Park will feature such events as story telling, egg and spoon races, clowning, balloon sculpting, face painting, stilt walking, music. The Family Funday Festivals are free – provided as a community service to the people of the region. A visit from the Mayor and representatives from other community groups provided positive affirmation for the organizing team. Volunteers from Lake Macquarie and Newcastle churches are being involved. A further training day is scheduled at Warners Bay High School. Details and application forms are available from the Conference Youth Department.

April 15, 2000, we repeat, was a holy Sabbath day.

The article was accompanied by a photograph of a Seventh-day Adventist sister offering an apple to the Lord Mayor while the Quest Festival's mascot, Pepi the penguin, and Clarence the clown looked on. Quest 2000 is an Australia-wide ecumenical group which promotes "Christianity" by using drama, puppets, magic, clowns, and other most inappropriate means. How we pray for God's church when Conference Youth Departments are so deluded that they will be part of such ecumenical outreaches. Furthermore, they are prepared to desecrate the holy Sabbath day in order to win popularity with the churches of Babylon. It is time that a halt was called!

The 1993 General Conference Annual Council, held in Bangalore, India, voted to approve the use of prohibited worship forms in our churches. Thus our church world headquarters had opened the way for the desecration of worship. The report of this Council rendered by the Youth Commission of our church stated:

> Friday night and Sabbath afternoon programs should involve new approaches such as seminars, forums, agapé suppers, youth theater, mime, drama, radio programming, puppetry, weekends, campouts, outreach activities and more opportunities for fellowship....With the approval of the Annual Council, the General Conference's youth leaders are now formulating plans to implement the recommendations. (*Adventist Review*, November 4, 1993).

We praise the Lord that the Cessnock Church in the North New South Wales Conference sent a letter of protest to the Conference pleading that this type of activity cease. That church understood the high and holy call that God has given to His people. Today we are raising up a body of dilettantes.

Australia is not alone in blatant desecration of the Sabbath. An American church in the Southeastern California Conference felt it proper to defile holy Sabbath-keeping with hilarity substituting for holiness.

The Riverside Community Church, a regular Seventh-day Adventist Church, invited the Community to its Sabbath Easter Services. Below are details from its brochure:

> 'Celebrate Easter. Let the power of Easter change your life today.' *Saturday*, March 30 [2002] – Two Easter Services at 11am and 5pm, Life Changing Message, Music with Bobby G and the Band. Xtreme Children's Church and nursery. Just 4 the KIDS – Easter Egg Hunt and more. 3.00 – 5.00pm. Hot Air Balloon. Pony Rides. FREE hot dogs and soft drinks for everyone. Petting Zoo, Face Painting, a Bounce House. IT'S ALL FREE!

If this event was shameful in its desecration of the Sabbath, the advertisement went on to further uplift shameful standards by advertising an Easter Sunday Sunrise Service:

> Sunrise on MT. RUBIDOUX. INTERFAITH SUNRISE SERVICE – 6.30 Sunday, March 31.... Baptism – if you wish to commit your life to Jesus, you can be baptized. Bring swimming suit and a towel!

The article did not state whether the Riverside Community Church organized the program on Mt. Rubidoux or it was just one of the participants. This is an act of sun worship, for Christ rose before sunrise.

> The first day of the week cometh Mary Magdalene early, when it was yet dark, unto the sepulchre, and seeth the stone taken away from the sepulchre.
>
> (John 20:1).

This sunrise service had nothing to do with Christ's resurrection.

The baptism offer was an utter disgrace. No requirement for study of the Word was promoted. God is disgraced and the angels weep. The pastor of this church was a woman.

Sabbath defilement organized by various churches and Conferences – and apparently condoned by those higher in leadership, for no word of warning to God's flock was issued in the great majority of instances – is now escalating at an alarming rate. May God save His precious remnant and prepare them to receive the seal of the living God.

Here we see that disregard for the counsels of the Spirit of Prophecy has been paralleled by disregard for Scriptural truths including holy Sabbath-keeping. None who are deluded by these Sabbath desecrations will be included in the final composition of God's remnant who do KEEP the commandments of

God. None will receive the seal of the living God. All will be lost. How tragic! May God's professing people repent while Christ's mediatorial work is still available, for the close of probation is surely nigh at hand. This is our earnest prayer.

38 Sister White's Claims

Sister White was too modest to make bold claims on behalf of herself concerning her role in the Seventh-day Adventist Church, but she did write,

> We have the commandments of God and the testimony of Jesus Christ, which is the spirit of prophecy. (*Testimonies to Ministers*, p. 114).

Also in two letters, both written in 1906, Sister White wrote:

> Elder _____ enters into no controversy with opponents. He presents the Bible so clearly that it is evident that anyone who differs must do so in opposition to the Word of God.
>
> Friday evening and Sabbath forenoon he spoke upon the subject of spiritual gifts, dwelling especially upon the Spirit of prophecy. Those who were present at these discourses say that he treated the subject in a clear, forceful manner.
>
> In his teaching Elder _____ showed that the Spirit of prophecy has an important part to act in the establishment of the truth. When binding off his work, he called for me ... to speak to the people.
> (*Evangelism*, p. 257 – name of evangelist omitted in original).

What an awesome day in which we live! Many in our church are finding Christ a stumblingblock to their world-centered lives. If ever there was a day to seek our God to empower obedience to His law and to follow, in His grace, the counsels of Scripture and the Spirit of Prophecy, it is now! Destroy the Spirit of Prophecy and there will be no remnant. Satan's cup of joy would overflow. It is time that every faithful Seventh-day Adventist stood in defense of this vital prophetic gift.

The sights of the spiritual artillery of the Seventh-day Adventist Church have been turned from the churches of Babylon and the pagan and atheistic worlds to the most faithful elements in the church. While God's true remnant bear these trials, difficulties and great disappointments patiently, they nevertheless weep for the destruction of the church they love. Designedly, many in church leadership have hijacked God's church and delivered all but the remnant to the enemy.

But the Seventh-day Adventist Church will not be destroyed, although its structure, the organization, will. We remind our readership of this fact.

> The leaders would teach that virtue is better than vice, but God being removed, they would place their dependence on human power, which, without God, is

> worthless. Their foundation would be built on the sand, and storm and tempest would sweep away the structure. (*Selected Messages*, Vol. 1, p. 205).

> Under the showers of the latter rain the inventions of man, the human machinery, will at times be swept away, the boundary of man's authority will be as broken reeds, and the Holy Spirit will speak through the living, human agent, with convincing power. No one then will watch to see if the sentences are well rounded off, if the grammar is faultless. The living water will flow in God's own channels. (*Selected Messages*, Vol. 2, pp. 58, 59).

The very small remnant, alone, are the surety of this fact. Judgment Day is almost upon us. Those in the ascendancy of apostasy today may possess a sense of smugness, they may bathe in the plaudits of an unconsecrated laity, they may cast aspersions against noble dissentients who oppose their evil designs against God's truth, but a day is close at hand where fearful retribution is to be meted out to such unfaithful ones. Then it will be seen that God will judge the opposition to error by sincere Seventh-day Adventists who know the value of a soul and seek to save their brethren and sisters from deception, as admonitory benignity rather than a reposte.

> The people turned upon their ministers with bitter hate and reproached them, saying, "You have not warned us. You told us that all the world was to be converted, and cried, Peace, peace, to quiet every fear that was aroused. You have not told us of this hour; and those who warned us of it you declared to be fanatics and evil men, who would ruin us." But I saw that the ministers did not escape the wrath of God. Their suffering was tenfold greater than that of their people.
> (*Early Writings*, p. 282).

Today numerous ordained, credentialed ministers of the Seventh-day Adventist Church treat the Spirit of Prophecy as the European infidels of the eighteenth and nineteenth century treated Scripture. These infidels provided "evidence" after "evidence" of "mistakes" in Scripture: many claims of infidels appeared to the superficial reader of Scripture to be valid. The great majority of these objections have been rebutted by diligent searchers for truth, others will be explained in heaven. We possess a book authored by Dr. Gleason L. Archer (born 1916), *Encyclopedia of Bible Difficulties*, in which 283 objections are examined. In the great majority of cases Dr. Archer successfully refutes these doubting assertions.

In genuinely believing and living the precepts of Scripture and the Spirit of Prophecy, not a single soul has ever been led away from salvation. In contrast, the inevitable result of the effective destruction of these sources of truth is that the souls of the perpetrators are destroyed.

Our hearts are truly sorrowful as we write. The terror of the Day of Judgment is such that we fear for those whom we know and love in the faith, those who have launched themselves into this fearful attack. They intellectually know

Scripture. They surely recognize that the most severe punishment will descend upon those who were privileged to know God's truth and failed to stand by it.

> ⁴⁶The lord of that servant will come in a day when he looketh not for him, and at an hour when he is not aware, and will cut him in sunder, and will appoint him his portion with the unbelievers. ⁴⁷And that servant, which knew his lord's will, and prepared not himself, neither did according to his will, shall be beaten with many stripes. ⁴⁸But he that knew not, and did commit things worthy of stripes, shall be beaten with few stripes. For unto whomsoever much is given, of him shall be much required: and to whom men have committed much, of him they will ask the more. (Luke 12:46-48).

We, too, will be punished no less if we are unfaithful to our ordination vows:

> ¹I charge thee therefore before God, and the Lord Jesus Christ, who shall judge the quick and the dead at his appearing and his kingdom; ²Preach the word; be instant in season, out of season; reprove, rebuke, exhort with all longsuffering and doctrine. ³For the time will come when they will not endure sound doctrine; but after their own lusts shall they heap to themselves teachers, having itching ears; ⁴And they shall turn away their ears from the truth, and shall be turned unto fables. ⁵But watch thou in all things, endure afflictions, do the work of an evangelist, make full proof of thy ministry. (1 Timothy 4:1-5).

Today our earnest prayers ascend not only for ourselves and our dear ones, but for those who are heedlessly promoting the denial of God's precious faith. Let us all turn to the One who promised,

> Wherefore he is able also to save them to the uttermost that come unto God by him, seeing he ever liveth to make intercession for them. (Hebrews 7:25).

> The doctrines must be plainly understood. The men accepted to teach the truth must be anchored; then their vessel will hold against storm and tempest, because the anchor holds them firmly. The deceptions will increase.

> Satan is now more earnestly engaged in playing the game of life for souls than at any previous time; and unless we are constantly on our guard, he will establish in our hearts, pride, love of self, love of the world, and many other evil traits. He will also use every possible device to unsettle our faith in God and in the truths of His Word. (*Selected Messages*, Vol. 2, p. 58).

Part IX
From Doubt to Trust

39 Dispelling False Accusations

Scripture has been assiduously studied by infidel detractors in search of its supposed errors. A long list has been asserted by these faithless individuals. It is proper to state that there are puzzling matters recorded in the Bible. They fall into three categories:
1. Those for which valid answers are readily available;
2. Those for which possible explanations have been put forth;
3. Those for which, unless future insights are revealed, we will await heaven's explanation.

We provide one example of each. Some unthinking and ill-informed skeptics have stated that while two gospel writers spoke of five thousand people being fed by Christ (Mark 6:44; Luke 9:14), another spoke of four thousand (Matthew 15:38). Such an accusation of error is careless. The account in Matthew 15 is an entirely different occasion. This may be plainly documented by the fact that Matthew, like Mark and Luke, also recorded the feeding of the five thousand (Matthew 14:26), one chapter prior to his record of the feeding of the four thousand.

The second category cited above we illustrate:

> ...Thou shalt not seethe a kid in his mother's milk. (Exodus 23:19).

Strict observers of the Jewish faith observe this prohibition beyond the letter of the law unto our day. When Colin, in the 1950's, taught at the Mount Moriah War Memorial College, an orthodox Jewish educational institution, the young pupils were each provided with free milk on a daily basis. However, some of the pupils did not enjoy milk. They subverted the requirement to drink the milk by eating a kosher-meat sandwich prior to the issuing of the milk and thus excused themselves from the obligatory milk on the grounds that the Mosaic law forbade the presence of meat and milk simultaneously in their stomachs.

We were told that the reason that Moses set forth the above strange requirement was that God prohibited any pagan practice. The idolaters of Canaan, we were informed, entertained a practice in which they boiled a kid in the milk of its mother. It is a likely explanation, but we have been unable to confirm it from any authoritative source.

We have already confirmed that we know of no biological or nutritional reason for cattle being designated by God as clean meat and horse flesh as unclean meat. It is important in such matters that we recognize our limitations in knowing the mind of our omniscient God. Humility of heart certainly dictates that we believe His Word and await His heavenly explanations, knowing that God never provides regulations on the basis of caprice, but upon His infinite knowledge and His love for us.

The same principle must be our guide in our study of the Spirit of Prophecy. We propose, however, to comment briefly upon some accusations which have been leveled against the Spirit of Prophecy in Dr. Bradford's book for which information is available which enlightens our minds. In the scope of this book we will address the few which were raised in February, 2004, by the launching of this book.

Wigs Cause Insanity.
(See *Prophets Are Human*, p. 13)

Did Sister White really assert this proposition? Yes, she did!

> The artificial hair and pads covering the base of the brain, heat and excite the spinal nerves centering in the brain. The head should ever be kept cool. The heat caused by these artificials induces the blood to the brain. The action of the blood upon the lower or animal organs of the brain, causes unnatural activity, tends to recklessness in morals, and the mind and heart is in danger of being corrupted. As the animal organs are excited and strengthened, the morals are enfeebled. The moral and intellectual powers of the mind become servants to the animal.
>
> In consequence of the brain being congested its nerves lose their healthy action, and take on morbid conditions, making it almost impossible to arouse the moral sensibilities. Such lose their power to discern sacred things. The unnatural heat caused by these artificial deformities about the head, induces the blood to the brain, producing congestion, and causing the natural hair to fall off, producing baldness. Thus the natural is sacrificed to the artificial.
>
> Many have lost their reason, and become hopelessly insane, by following this deforming fashion. (*The Health Reformer*, October 1, 1871).

Sister White, four years earlier, had described the type of wigs to which she referred. They were:

> monstrous bunches of curled hair, cotton, seagrass, wool, Spanish moss.
> (*Ibid*, July, 1867).

One description of the eighteenth-century wigs described them as

> covering the back and shoulders and floating down over the chest. Smaller less pretentious wigs, custom-ordered from London, were also worn in the American colonies. (*Encyclopaedia Britannica*, 1963 edition, Vol. 23, p. 592).

Thus we must understand that the wigs to which Sister White referred were quite different from those worn today.

The Health Reformer, January, 1871, quoted two secular newspapers – *The Springfield Republican* and the *Marshall Statesman*, which described wigs which were made from fibrous bark which contained parasites.

Perhaps the most dangerous practice was the free use of lead-based powders in the wigs. Lead salts found in these powders can be absorbed into the blood stream through the skin. Today we are well aware of the absorption of chemicals through the skin. Many smokers wear nicotine patches on their skin in order to absorb the drug to enable them to tolerate the long-distance flights on non-smoking aircraft. Women during menopause now often use hormone skin patches to control their hot flushes. Many angina sufferers are relieved by the absorption of the medication nitroglycerine, embedded in a skin patch.

Such processes are enhanced when perspiration is present, as in the wearing of large wigs such as those described above, in hot weather. Science has demonstrated that:

> The [lead] poison affects the entire body but especially the nervous system [of which the brain is the control center], the gastrointestinal tract and the blood-forming tissues.... [It] is often manifested by severe cerebral [brain] involvement ("lead encephalopathy"). (*Ibid*, Vol. 13, p. 824, round brackets in the original).

Most educated people today are well aware that the presence of significant doses of any heavy metal, such as lead or mercury, destroys bodily organs, including the brain. Sister White also spoke of the effect of long wigs covering the back of the neck. She was clearly referring to periods of hot, humid weather. This, of course, can lead to sunstroke. In hot conditions the heat of the body is reduced by

> Evaporation of sweat from the skin.
> (*Encyclopaedia Britannica*, 1963 edition, Vol. 21, p. 571).

Covering the nape of the neck impairs the evaporation of the sweat from that region and thus can seriously damage the brain. Most readers will be aware that sunstroke can cause unconsciousness and even death.

Thus God's counsel, through His servant Sister White, was, of course, sound and rational, and certainly not absurd as her detractors have charged. Sister White may not have been personally aware of the mechanism of these dangers any more than Moses' inspired words prohibiting the eating of fat (see Leviticus 3:17) explained that a significant danger of eating that prohibited food is the higher levels of cholesterol in the blood. But those who in faith followed the counsel were spared impaired health. God's love is evident in all His counsels to His people.

The Closed Door
(See *Prophets Are Human*, p. 13)

After the disappointment of October 22, 1844, many of the Adventist believers accepted the false view that the door of mercy for the rest of the world closed on that day. Sister White also adopted this error. We often forget that Sister Harmon, as she was then, was a young teenager of sixteen years of age in October, 1844. She reached her seventeenth birthday a month later on November 26. Even more importantly, Sister Ellen Harmon had not been called to her prophetic ministry at the time of the disappointment. As an individual without the direct benefit of divine visions she was as liable to accept false beliefs as anyone else. Sister White in later life made no secret that she held this false view at that time.

Dr. Bradford, through one of his fictional characters, Dr. Harold Smithurst, went further than the facts when he claimed

> Ellen White did have a vision and she interpreted it to mean that no one could be converted to Christ after 1844. (*Prophets Are Human*, p. 58).

If this statement is correct then Sister White's claim that "I never had a vision that no more sinners would be converted" (*Selected Messages*, Vol. 1, p. 63), was manifestly false. So let us examine the evidence.

> For a time after the disappointment in 1844, I did hold, in common with the advent body, that the door of mercy was then forever closed to the world. This position was taken before my first vision was given me. It was the light given me of God that corrected our error, and enabled us to see the true position.
> (*Selected Messages*, Vol. 1, p. 63).

> With my brethren and sisters, after the time passed in forty-four I did believe no more sinners would be converted. But I never had a vision that no more sinners would be converted. (*Ibid*, p. 74).

These statements were written almost forty years later, in 1883, in an answer to a challenge. (See *Selected Messages*, Vol. 1, pp. 59-73 and a letter to Elder Loughborough, August 24, 1874, respectively).

Much has been made of the following statement:

> "It was just as impossible for them {those that gave up their faith in the '44 movement} to get on the path again and go to the city, as all the wicked world which God had rejected. They fell all the way along the path one after another."
> (*Selected Messages*, Vol. 1, p.62 – parenthesis in the original).

Sister White properly stated, referring to this statement,

> It is claimed that these expressions prove the shut-door doctrine, and that this is the reason of their omission in later editions. But in fact they teach only that which has been and is still held by us as a people, as I shall show. (*Ibid*).

In fact there is not a single reference in Sister White's writings, nor is there any documented evidence that following her call to the prophetic office in December, 1844, when she received her first vision, that Sister White supported the version of the closed-door doctrine which proclaimed that the door of mercy was closed for all the inhabitants of the world.

Sister White quite properly discarded the shut-door view of early Adventists after December 1844. Yet she spoke of other shut doors – when Noah entered the ark; when Sodom rejected the witness of the angels; in Christ's day when the great majority of God's church rejected His salvation. (See *Ibid*, p. 63).

Then Sister White clearly stated:

> I was shown in vision, and I still believe, that there was a shut door in 1844. All who saw the light of the first and second angels' messages and rejected that light, were left in darkness. And those who accepted it and received the Holy Spirit which attended the proclamation of the message from heaven, and who afterward renounced their faith and pronounced their experience a delusion, thereby rejected the Spirit of God, and it no longer pleaded with them. (*Ibid*).

Notice the door of mercy did not close upon those who had never been presented with the light. Sister White plainly stated that the door of mercy only shut upon those who had received the light and had subsequently rejected it.

> Those who did not see the light, had not the guilt of its rejection. It was only the class who had despised the light from heaven that the Spirit of God could not reach. And this class included, as I have stated, both those who refused to accept the message when it was presented to them, and also those who, having received it, afterward renounced their faith. These might have a form of godliness, and profess to be followers of Christ; but having no living connection with God, they would be taken captive by the delusions of Satan. These two classes are brought to view in the vision – those who declared the light which they had followed a delusion, and the wicked of the world who, having rejected the light, had been rejected of God. No reference is made to those who had not seen the light, and therefore were not guilty of its rejection. (*Ibid*, pp. 63, 64).

Sister White wrote an article in the *Review and Herald* of June 11, 1861, which has also been cited as evidence that she supported, even then, the shut-door theory of William Miller. Any reader of the passage will see that such an interpretation demonstrates a determined effort to pin error upon Sister White, without proper evidence.

> Our views of the work before us were then mostly vague and indefinite, some still retaining the idea adopted by the body of advent believers in 1844, with William Miller at their head, that our work for 'the world' was finished, and that the message was confined to those of the original advent faith. So firmly was this believed that one of our number was nearly refused the message, the individual presenting it having doubts of the possibility of his salvation because he was not in 'the '44 movement. (*Review and Herald*, June 11, 1861).

Sister White's comments on this passage are appropriate:

> To this I need only to add, that in the same meeting in which it was urged that the message could not be given to this brother, a testimony was given me through vision to encourage him to hope in God and to give his heart fully to Jesus, which he did then and there. (*Selected Messages*, Vol. 1, p. 64).

Sister White referred to yet another shut door in 1844 – the closing of the entrance to the holy place of the heavenly sanctuary, with the simultaneous opening of the door into the most holy place. (See *Early Writings* p. 42).

There is yet another shut door ahead – the close of human probation. Those who declare both Scripture and the Spirit of Prophecy to be guilty of including errors need to fear lest, having the light, they too will be shut out of God's kingdom when that door is forever closed.

Plagiarism
(*Prophets Are Human*, p. 13).

This matter is discussed in the chapter entitled "The Doubts Mount."

However, we will here present material which firmly demonstrates that Sister White made no secret of the use of the words of other writers, to whose works God had directed her mind. The passages she used accorded with divine knowledge.

Sister White was a woman whose conduct in the use of sources was perfectly transparent. When a prophet writes under divine guidance there is no place for covert or questionable practices for the God of heaven is not the originator of deceit. One of the reasons that Sister White's detractors possessed so much information concerning her use of sources is that she made no secret of the fact that God guided her to use these materials when they accurately represented matters related to history or health. All the books in Sister White's library were retained including the notes which she had written in them. There was no effort to discard them for she had openly referred to her sources. She had benefited from divine guidance in the volumes from which she selected accurate quotations.

Sister White did not set before God's people the claim to be a litterateur, but rather evidenced a humble spirit, acknowledging herself to be God's handmaiden. She admitted that she, in her own wisdom, contributed scant input in the early days of the Advent movement when sincere brethren and sisters searched for precious truth. It was only when God's power came upon her, that in vision He revealed to her the answers to perplexing issues for which those searchers for truth found no agreed solution.

There is much evidence that Sister White did not conceal the sources which she used in her work, nor did she keep the tomes in her library a matter of secrecy. Two examples will serve to document this fact.

In December, 1882, Sister White advocated the reading of the book, *The History of the Reformation*, written by J. H. Merle D'Aubigne, despite the fact that she quoted extensively from this masterpiece in her 1884 and 1888 editions of *Great Controversy*. Notice her published recommendation:

> Provide something to be read during these long winter evenings. For those who can procure it, D'Aubigne's *History of the Reformation* will be both interesting and profitable. From this work we may gain some knowledge of what has been

accomplished in the past in the great work of reform.

(Review & Herald, December 26, 1882).

We also are aware that at the time she was about to publish her book *Sketches from the Life of Paul*, in 1883, Sister White wrote:

> The Life of St. Paul, by Conybeare and Howson, I regard as a book of great merit, and one of rare usefulness to the earnest student of the New Testament history.
>
> <div style="text-align: right;">(<i>Signs of the Times</i>, February 22, 1883).</div>

Sister White, under God's inspired guidance, quoted some passages of Conybeare and Howsen's book, *Life and Epistles of St. Paul*, in her book, *Sketches from the Life of Paul*. Her book was already in manuscript form when she gave this recommendation. Sister White's critics stand exposed.

The Mixture of Man and Beast
(Prophets Are Human, p. 13).

See chapter entitled "The Amalgamation of Man and Beast."

Copied "I was shown" visions from others
(Prophets Are Human, p. 13).

See chapter entitled "Stratagem IV – Understanding the Gift."

40 Sister White's Health Practices and Her Translation

Unclean Food
(*Prophets Are Human*, p. 13).

Ronald Numbers, cited a Dr. Stewart as claiming that during

> the period between 1868 and 1894 [Sister White] ate meat and oysters and served meat on [her] table. (*Prophetess of Health*, op. cit., p. 194).

We would point out that nowhere in her inspired writings did Sister White advocate the eating of oysters. Further, no Seventh-day Adventist has claimed that Sister White's personal life was free of mistakes.

We do not discount the inspired words of the Psalms, Proverbs, Ecclesiastes or Song of Solomon, because of the fearful known breaches of God's law by the authors of these Biblical books. If Sister White sinned by eating oysters after learning of God's prohibition, this would in no wise invalidate God's inspired words revealed to her.

Speaking of a student at Battle Creek College Sister White stated disapprovingly:

> He is invited to accompany them for a walk, and they lead him to a saloon. Oysters or other refreshments are called for, and he is ashamed to draw away and refuse the treat. (*Testimonies for the Church*, Vol. 4, p. 435).

Similarly she wrote in the *Signs of the Times*, March 2, 1882, in a negative context that

> The sons of religious parents venture into the saloons for an oyster supper....
> (*Fundamentals of Christian Education*, p. 63).

Here are presented Sister White's inspired views. These we need to heed. Who was Dr. Stewart and in what atmosphere were his accusations framed? These are significant questions. We must not overlook the Biblical prohibition upon the ingestion of shell-foods.

> And all that have not fins and scales in the seas, and in the rivers, of all that move in the waters, and of any living thing which is in the waters, they shall be an abomination unto you: (Leviticus 11:10).

Dr. Numbers provided an endnote reference for Dr. Stewart's claim. It is an article in the *Review and Herald*, June 14, 1906. The article provided absolutely no elucidation on the matter asserted. The lone reference to eating stated:

> Our train into Los Angeles was a few minutes late, and we could not make close connections with the train for Loma Linda, so we spent a pleasant hour at the vegetarian restaurant, on the corner of Third and Hill Streets. This restaurant is now conducted by the medical missionary department of the Southern California Conference....

Elder Arthur White provided a little more detail concerning Dr. Stewart.

> Emissaries of Dr. Kellogg were sent out to hold a line of allegiance to him and the policies for which he stood. One such prominent physician, Dr. C. E. Stewart, was sent to the Pacific Coast. (*Ellen White*, Vol. 6, p. 60).

Sister White also sent a response to Dr. Stewart answering his doubting questions concerning the level of contribution of her literary assistants to her writings. (Letter 170, 1906, reported in *Ibid*, p. 93).

We must remember that the year 1906 was a year in which two powerful Seventh-day Adventists were using all their intellectual resources to destroy truth, including the witness of the Spirit of Prophecy. These were Dr. John Harvey Kellogg – pantheism – and Elder Albion Ballenger – the New Theology. Without doubt, Dr. Stewart was influenced by the false teachings of these men.

Thus we have to weigh the credibility of Dr. Stewart's evidence as an antagonist of Sister White. Sister White has always been a prime target of New Theology proponents.

The Eating of Pork
(Prophets Are Human, p. 14)

On October 21, 1858, Sister White wrote a letter to a man and his wife who were consuming a diet deficient in elements vital to health. Their professed purpose in this was to conserve funds for the work of God. Sister White demonstrated a balanced counsel in stating that:

> I saw that God does not require anyone to take a course of such rigid economy as to weaken or injure the temple of God. (*Testimonies for the Church*, Vol. 1, p. 205).

In this testimony Sister White took up the issue of eating swine's flesh from which this couple refrained.

> I saw that your views concerning swine's flesh would prove no injury if you have them to yourselves; but in your judgment and opinion you have made this question a test, and your actions have plainly shown your faith in this matter. If God requires His people to abstain from swine's flesh, He will convict them on the matter. He is just as willing to show His honest children their duty, as to show their duty to individuals upon whom He has not laid the burden of His work. If it is the duty of the church to abstain from swine's flesh, God will discover it to more than two or three. He will teach His *church* their duty. (*Ibid*, pp. 206, 207).

We observe that twice Sister White reminded this abstemious couple that God would convict His people of health principles in His own good time and not before.

At first reading this is puzzling counsel. It conflicts with Sister White's later counsel on this matter. In a testimony, written in 1868, five years after she had received her health reform vision, the servant of the Lord stated:

> You know that the use of swine's flesh is contrary to His express command, given not because He wished to especially show His authority, but because it would be injurious to those who should eat it. Its use would cause the blood to become impure, so that scrofula [tuberculosis] and other humors would corrupt the system, and the whole organism would suffer. Especially would the fine, sensitive nerves of the brain become enfeebled and so beclouded that sacred things would not be discerned, but be placed upon the low level with common things. Light showing that disease is caused by using this gross article of food has come just as soon as God's people could bear it. (*Testimonies for the Church*, Vol. 2, p. 96).

Many, in charging Sister White with providing inconsistent – and, in the case of the first letter, erroneous advice – often overlook the last words quoted above – "Light showing that disease is caused by using this gross article [swine's flesh] has come just as soon as God's people could bear it." Here we discern God's wisdom.

> ⁸For my thoughts are not your thoughts, neither are your ways my ways, saith the LORD. ⁹For as the heavens are higher than the earth, so are my ways higher than your ways, and my thoughts than your thoughts. (Isaiah 55:8, 9).

God waited to bring this dietary counsel before His people until the timing was right. He did not desire to confuse His people into believing that the health counsels contained in the Mosaic Law, which are applicable to all Christians, were grounds for us to continue all aspects of the Mosaic Law. God's people needed to recognize that, for example:

> The ceremonies connected with the services of the temple, prefiguring Christ in types and shadows, were taken away at the time of the crucifixion, because on the cross type met antitype in the death of the true and perfect offering, the Lamb of God. (*SDA Bible Commentary*, Vol. 6, pp. 1115, 1116).

> It was Christ's desire to leave to His disciples an ordinance that would do for them the very thing they needed—that would serve to disentangle them from the rites and ceremonies which they had hitherto engaged in as essential, and which the reception of the gospel made no longer of any force. To continue these rites would be an insult to Jehovah. (*SDA Bible Commentary*, Vol. 5, pp. 1139, 1140).

In contrast to the feast days prefiguring Christ's work for our salvation, the principles of health enunciated in the same law were timeless and thus applicable in the Christian era. Sister White was a faithful servant of God. She did not run ahead of God but patiently awaited God's own timing in bringing forth His counsels on this and other matters of truth. Thus she had correctly explained:

> If it is the duty of the church to abstain from swine's flesh, God will discover it to more than two or three. He will teach His church their duty.
> (*Testimonies for the Church*, Vol. 1, p. 207).

As we trace the growing body of truth revealed to God's people after 1844, we may recognize that our God did not rush us with the entire body of faith from the inception of the Seventh-day Adventist Movement, but little by little as God's people could absorb it. Even the time of Sabbath keeping, the parameters of the Sabbath day, were not revealed at first. For about ten years most Seventh-day Adventists kept the Sabbath from 6pm Friday to 6pm Sabbath. (See *Testimonies for the Church*, Vol. 1, p. 713).

It was not until 1855 that:

> I saw that it is even so: "From even unto even, shall ye celebrate your Sabbath." Said the angel: "Take the word of God, read it, understand, and ye cannot err. Read carefully, and ye shall there find what even is, and when it is. I asked the angel if the frown of God had been upon His people for commencing the Sabbath as they had. I was directed back to the first rise of the Sabbath, and followed the people of God up to this time, but did not see that the Lord was displeased, or frowned upon them. I inquired why it had been thus, that at this late day we must change the time of commencing the Sabbath. Said the angel: "Ye shall understand, but not yet, not yet." Said the angel: "If light come, and that light is set aside or rejected, then comes condemnation and the frown of God; but before the light comes, there is no sin, for there is no light for them to reject." I saw that it was in the minds of some that the Lord had shown that the Sabbath commenced at six o'clock, when I had only seen that it commenced at "even," and it was inferred that even was at six. I saw that the servants of God must draw together, press together. (*Testimonies for the Church*, Vol. 1, p. 116).

Let us remember that God's plans for us know no haste and no delay.

The Time of Jesus Coming
(See *Prophets Are Human*, p. 14)

Dr. Bradford (*Ibid*) stated that Sister White

> said in the 1850s that Jesus would come in a few months.

Since Dr. Bradford did not provide his documentation for this assertion this presents us with some difficulty. He was possibly influenced to write these words by Ronald Numbers' assertion:

> Early in 1849 Ellen had warned against thinking that time might "continue for a few years more" and in June of the following year her angel informed her that

"Time is almost finished." The doctrines that she and James had thoughtfully studied out over the past several years would now have to be learned by others "in a few months." (Ronald Numbers, *op. cit.*, p. 27).

Let us quote the words cited by Dr. Numbers:

> I saw some, looking too far off for the coming of the Lord. Time has continued on a few years longer than they expected, therefore they think it may continue a few years more, and in this way their minds are being led from present truth, out after the world. In these things I saw great danger; for if the mind is filled with other things, present truth is shut out, and there is no place in our foreheads for the seal of the living God. This seal is the Sabbath. I saw that the time for Jesus to be in the most holy place was nearly finished, and that time can last but a very little longer; and what leisure time we have should be spent in searching the Bible, which is to judge us in the last day.   (*Broadside*, January 31, 1849, Paragraph 11).

> In a view given June 27, 1850, my accompanying angel said, "Time is almost finished.... But now time is almost finished.... But time is now almost finished and what we have been years learning, they will have to learn in a few months. They will also have much to unlearn and much to learn again.
> (*Early Writings*, pp. 64, 67).

It must be understood that God was prepared to return any time after 1844 when a body of believers fully reflecting His character had been established.

> When the character of Christ shall be perfectly reproduced in His people, then He will come to claim them as His own.   (*Christ's Object Lessons*, p. 69).

Writing as early as 1851, a mere seven years after Christ entered the Most Holy Place of the Heavenly Sanctuary, Sister White declared:

> Had Adventists, after the great disappointment in 1844, held fast their faith, and followed on unitedly in the opening providence of God, receiving the message of the third angel and in the power of the Holy Spirit proclaiming it to the world, they would have seen the salvation of God, the Lord would have wrought mightily with their efforts, the work would have been completed, and Christ would have come ere this to receive His people to their reward.
> (*Selected Messages*, Vol. 1, p. 68).

That which Sister White wrote in 1849 and 1850, as quoted above, was God's plan. This plan, through Sister White, God set forth. The true Seventh-day Adventists of that era, Sister White included, could have then received the seal of the living God and the inestimable privilege of constituting the 144,000. But insufficient reached God's high and holy standard.

Writing in 1904 the servant of the Lord reflected upon those early days of great promise:

> In the great disappointment of 1844 the faith of His people was tested as was that of the Hebrews at the Red Sea. Had the Adventists in the early days still trusted to the guiding Hand that had been with them in their past experience, they would have seen of the salvation of God. If all who had labored unitedly in the work of 1844 had received the third angel's message and proclaimed it in the power of the Holy Spirit, the Lord would have wrought mightily with their efforts. A flood of light would have been shed upon the world. Years ago the inhabitants of the earth would have been warned, the closing work would have been completed, and Christ would have come for the redemption of His people.
> (*Testimonies for the Church*, Vol. 8, pp. 115, 116).

Another opportunity arose in 1888. Had that message been received, Christ would rapidly have completed His work on earth. But that opportunity passed because of unbelief. In 1900 Sister White wrote:

> Had the purpose of God been carried out by His people in giving to the world the message of mercy, Christ would, ere this, have come to the earth, and the saints would have received their welcome into the city of God.
> (*Testimonies for the Church*, Vol. 6, p. 450).

In 1909 the servant of the Lord wistfully stated:

> If every soldier of Christ had done his duty, if every watchman on the walls of Zion had given the trumpet a certain sound, the world might ere this have heard the message of warning. But the work is years behind. While men have slept, Satan has stolen a march upon us. (*Testimonies for the Church*, Vol. 9, p. 29).

We are impressed that God is once more rallying His people to follow Him with perfect hearts and minds desiring only that which consumed the thinking of the believers in apostolic times and which led to every being on earth hearing the gospel message prior to the fall of Jerusalem.

> Then the glad tidings of a risen Saviour were carried to the uttermost bounds of the inhabited world. The church beheld converts flocking to her from all directions. Believers were reconverted. Sinners united with Christians in seeking the pearl of great price.... The Spirit of Christ animated the whole congregation; for they had found the pearl of great price. (*Christ's Object Lessons*, p. 120).

Thus,

> To every nation was the gospel carried in a single generation.
> (*Acts of the Apostles*, p. 593).

> Thousands were converted in a day. In a single generation the gospel was carried to every nation under heaven. (*Testimonies for the Church*, Vol. 8, p. 26).

Paul declared about 64 AD that the gospel message had then reached all.

> If ye continue in the faith grounded and settled, and be not moved away from the hope of the gospel, which ye have heard, and which was preached to every creature which is under heaven; (Colossians 1:23).

> ⁵For the hope which is laid up for you in heaven, whereof ye heard before in the word of the truth of the gospel; ⁶Which is come unto you, as it is in all the world; and bringeth forth fruit, as it doth also in you, since the day ye heard of it, and knew the grace of God in truth: (Colossians 1:5, 6).

What a challenge this is to us today! This is no time to cast away our faith, replacing it with the New Theology designs. This is a time to draw near to God, seeking His justifying and sanctifying grace and pleading His blood on our behalf. We must not be culpable for contributing to yet another generation passing without calling upon the Lord to empower them to undertake a faithful work for Him under the power of the Latter Rain.

Sister White Said She Would Be Alive When Jesus Returns
(Prophets Are Human, p. 14)

Sister White wrote in 1856:

> I was shown the company present at the Conference. Said the angel: "Some food for worms, some subjects of the seven last plagues, some will be alive and remain upon the earth to be translated at the coming of Jesus."
> (*Testimonies for the Church*, Vol. 1, pp. 131, 132).

Sister White certainly did declare that in 1856 some present at a convention would receive various fates. Some would be "food for worms;" others would be unfaithful and thus endure the seven last plagues; some would be translated. Clearly *all*, including Sister White, have been "food for worms."

We have seen in the previous section of this chapter that in matters related to the Second Coming, Sister White received conditional prophecies. Had the full message of Christ our Righteousness been accepted into the hearts and lives of His people, the Latter Rain would have been poured out, the world would have been warned and Christ would have returned shortly after 1844, and failing that, after 1888.

The Bible contains many conditional prophecies:

> ¹And it shall come to pass, if thou shalt hearken diligently unto the voice of the LORD thy God, to observe and to do all his commandments which I command thee this day, that the LORD thy God will set thee on high above all nations of the earth:... ⁷The LORD shall cause thine enemies that rise up against thee to be smitten before thy face: they shall come out against thee one way, and flee before thee seven ways.... ¹⁵But it shall come to pass, if thou wilt not hearken unto the voice of the LORD thy God, to observe to do all his commandments and his statutes which I command thee this day; that all these curses shall come upon thee, and overtake thee:... ²⁵The LORD shall cause thee to be smitten before

thine enemies: thou shalt go out one way against them, and flee seven ways before them: and shalt be removed into all the kingdoms of the earth.

(Deuteronomy 28:1, 7, 15, 25).

This is but one example. The fulfilment of the prophecy of 1856 quoted above was dependent upon the acceptance of God's will for His people in 1844 and 1888. That acceptance failed to eventuate and thus that wonderful prophecy was delayed in its fulfillment. The question is, "Will we further delay it reaching its fruition?" That Satan is diligently urging us to spiritual indolence through unbelief has been amply documented in this book. But we believe that the sealing is now nigh at hand and that prophecy will be fulfilled in every detail. Let each seek to be a part of those privileged humans who will be translated.

Let none be discouraged when a conditional prophecy is not fulfilled at the time specified. The most quoted conditional prophecy, that of Jonah in respect of the destruction of Nineveh, in God's love, was not fulfilled at the time specified. But later when Nineveh returned to unabated wickedness it was fulfilled. (See Nahum 3:7; Zephaniah 2:13).

> In 612 BC, the men of Nineveh were defeated by the Medes and the city was looted and destroyed.   (*Encyclopaedia Britannica*, 1963 edition, Vol. 16, p. 459).

It is true that Sister White did rarely use the word "we" in relation to those who would be translated, but it is clear she was using this word in the corporate sense of faithful believers. Paul used the same concept.

> Then we which are alive and remain shall be caught up together with them in the clouds, to meet the Lord in the air: and so shall we ever be with the Lord.
>
> (1 Thessalonians 4:17).

Clearly none who received Paul's letter lived to the Second Coming. Paul also was in this group. Yet all of like faith living in the day of the Second Coming will be those whom Paul designated as "we who are alive and remain."

Had God's people remained faithful and noble, Sister White, if she had retained her faith, too, would have been included among the translated souls.

We have only dealt with a few of the prominent asserted "mistakes" in Sister White's writings. Satan will see that there will never be any absence of doubts either concerning Scripture or the Spirit of Prophecy. But happy are those souls who are guided by the Counsels of these two sources of inspiration. As for ourselves, we do not intend to write exhaustive defenses of the wonderful accuracy of the Bible and Spirit of Prophecy, chasing every doubt raised, for we have read Scripture and the Spirit of Prophecy extensively and we know the impact upon our lives. No material consisting of the Satanic compound of truth mixed with error ever stirs an individual to repentance. It never humbles his heart. It fails to lead him to Jesus. Scripture and the Spirit of Prophecy do.

41 If They Hear Not Moses

Concluding his parable of the rich man and Lazarus, Christ pointedly stated:

> If they hear not Moses and the prophets, neither will they be persuaded, though one rose from the dead. (Luke 16:31).

These words ring down through the ages to our day. Today the words of Moses, inspired of God, are under severe attack at the hands of many theologians and scientists in our church. These men continue to be employed in our denominational Colleges, ensuring that a great number of our ministerial and teaching graduates will be defiled by their teachings. Such are in grave risk of placing themselves in a position where they will become impervious to all truth.

For over three decades now, denominational workers have been writing faith-destroying articles in *Spectrum* magazine and, for a briefer period of time, in *Adventist Today*, without apparent penalty. For quite a number of years Elder Neal Wilson, then President of the North American Division, consented to his name being included as a consulting editor of *Spectrum*. Yet faithful servants of God, standing against error in this terrible crisis, have been dismissed from denominational service or otherwise penalized for their fidelity to the faith. Many denominational workers have found ready access for their faithless articles in official denominational publications. This we have abundantly documented in this book.

Sister White pointed us to Scriptural evidence.

> If rational beings really desire the truth, God will give them sufficient light to enable them to decide what is truth. If they have a heart to obey, they will see sufficient evidence to walk in the light. (*Review & Herald*, January 5, 1886).

No one should dare enter ministerial-teacher training unless, in God's grace, he is ready to follow this counsel. There devolves upon those who accept the sacred trust of training men and women for the ministerial and teaching service, the obligation to train these young people to trust implicitly God's Word and the Spirit of Prophecy. A fearful punishment awaits those who accept such responsibility and seek to undermine the faith of those entrusted to their care.

Such rabbis predominated in God's church at the time of the First Advent. As a consequence of this fact Sister White recorded that

> In the natural order of things, the son of Zacharias [John the Baptist] would have been educated for the priesthood. But the training of the rabbinical schools would

have unfitted him for his work. God did not send him to the teachers of theology to learn how to interpret the Scriptures. (*Desire of Ages*, p. 101).

What a lesson the experience of John the Baptist is for those who would train to be last-day messengers, preachers of the Elijah message today! Yet many reason that they can attend our denominational Colleges and study error and then graduate as preachers of truth. Few appear to understand that the training such young people receive fits them rather to pervert the truth. Very few remain faithful after years of imbibing error. Our book, *Keepers of the Faith*, in its first chapter, reveals how this process operates.

We illustrate the insidious influence of Avondale College by citing the experience of one young New Zealand man who decided to train there in 2002. Early in the academic year, March 28, 2002, this young man sent an e-mail to a friend in New Zealand. Again we remind our Northern Hemisphere readers that Australian academic years commence in the early part of the year. Notice this young man's early assessment of his College training.

> Well on the eve of a long weekend I write you this email! I often write that I think through certain thoughts and establish where I am so far that I am to a certain degree actively opposing much of this very dangerous doctrine.
>
> The most dangerous I believe, I will try and give some info[rmation] on now, it also explains largely why the college is producing a lack of power!
>
> It's called the 'historical critical method' and it's basically how to study the Bible; it's not a doctrine but affects every doctrine. There are three points in approaching the Bible: 1) They (the users) are not allowed to believe in the miracles of the Bible! 2) They use modern humanistic theories to get insight into what it must have been like, e.g. 'Well, since no one lives today without constantly sinning, when the Bible spoke of upright or perfect it can't really mean it. So they were really like us – indulgent sinners. Therefore don't worry if you sin then.' 3) They doubt the Bible and can't establish anything for sure because new light can come at any time, e.g. 'I kind of believe in the prophecy of Daniel seven but since the scholars are disagreeing I'd better not preach it because our old view may not be trustworthy'! I believe that this is why many of our ministers are leaving the work and are not tapping into power source of the Word of God!
>
> Please pray for me! At Avondale they don't accept that the miracles are to be done away with but they do accept everything else, and almost all the students accept this demonic delusion: In "Education" she [Sister White] speaks that one of the first steps of the first sin was doubt and Satan is using it here! Well praise God because everytime I run into a delusion or false doctrine our Lord sends His truth and although I am busy I must settle the truth and study to do so!
>
> Well I believe this is the root of the apostasy, Ford's debacle has truly been answered by groups such as ATS [Adventist Theological Society] the Biblical Research Institute, but most of those who liked what was taught (by Ford *et al*)

have gone to 'higher education' and if you ask me it's disgusting. Some in the Advent church don't even believe Homosexuality is bad. Some scholars say if Moses were around in our day, because we have condoms, he would accept premarital sex! And there's much, much more. Statements regarding Adventism being built on a false foundation are common. All of this must stop! And God will stop it. Please pray for our church: there is such a big work to do here but through God's power I believe there will be a reformation! Well I pray this gives you more light on what is going on.

PS. They are trying to get Dr Ford to teach seminars and a few classes here. It's interesting because the Conference [men] are saying no! But Avondale wants to become a university 'asap' [as soon as possible] and therefore will not be dependent on the Conference for the 4-6 million [dollars] a year they get, and Avondale can then make its own decisions without worrying about the frown of the Conference!

PPS. You know it's amazing how I get all of this info[rmation]!

This email was sent to twenty-two email addresses.

The young man returned home to New Zealand for the year-end vacation in November, 2002. In those eight short months his assessment of Avondale had totally altered. He had adopted the very concepts which had appalled him in March. Further, he was actively advocating enrollment in the College. Herein lies the danger of studying at the feet of unfaithful professors, some of whom are well acquainted with the techniques of neurolinguistic programming (NLP) which incorporates subtle Ericssonian hypnosis. It is time for our young people to be aroused to the dangers of studying in our apostate Colleges.

In the tragic experience of this once promising young man is illustrated the extreme peril of studying at Avondale College and similar training institutions on every continent. If mature, truth-loving believers could be beguiled in a single five-hour presentation by Avondale College professors at Elders' Summits, we cannot be surprised if young men and women who sit at the feet of these same professors day after day are led astray. This is the basis of the fearful impotence of our ministers today. We cannot find words to emphasize the alarming state of our college training. Our prayers, of deep earnestness must arise before our Lord to deliver His church from a situation far worse than even that in the schools of the rabbis during Christ's first advent.

Notice Sister White's warning concerning such "believers."

> But if they in heart desire to evade the truth, He will not work a miracle to gratify their unbelief. He will never remove every chance or occasion to doubt. If they honestly, sincerely grasp the light, and walk in it, that light will increase until lingering doubts will be dispelled. But if they choose darkness, their questioning and caviling over the truth will increase, their unbelief will be strengthened, and the light which they would not accept will become to them darkness, and how great will be that darkness! (*Review & Herald*, Jan. 5, 1886).

Today this prophesied condition of utter darkness largely prevails in our academic institutions. Instead of standing in the light of the glorious truths of inspired writings and rejoicing in this illumination, large numbers are wallowing in doubt and darkness. Speaking of this darkness the Servant of the Lord went on to warn:

> It will be as much greater than before the light came, as the light which was rejected was clearer and more abundant than the light which first shone upon them. (*Ibid.*)

These words are now fulfilled for all lovers of the truth to behold. To scorn the Spirit of Prophecy does not avail in removing the pointed truth of the inspired words written.

In the monthly edition of the *Adventist Review*, March, 2003, the question was asked, "Why did the Lord kill Uzzah? Apparently he was trying to help." Some of the information provided by Dr. Angel Manuel Rodriguez, Director of the Biblical Research Institute of the General Conference, was helpful.

However, this answer suffered from the expression of doubts.

Doubt 1:

> *The Incident.* The biblical text is not clear about the exact nature of the accident that led Uzzah to touch the ark. The text suggests that something happened to the oxen. Perhaps they stumbled or became unyoked (the meaning of the Hebrew term *shamat* is uncertain) – and apparently the ark moved. Uzzah immediately reached out and took hold of the ark. God reacted, striking down Uzzah and he died. The text gives a reason for God's drastic action: "The Lord's anger burned against Uzzah because of his irreverent act" (2 Samuel 6:7 – parenthesis in the original). (*Adventist Review*, March, 2003).

If Dr. Rodriguez had quoted from the King James Version he would not have been in doubt. It was not "something [that] happened to the oxen." The King James Version plainly states in verse 6:

> For the oxen shook it. (2 Samuel 6:6)

and the marginal reading states that they "stumbled."

Doubt 2:

> The Hebrew noun translated "irreverent act" (*shal*) appears only here in the Old Testament; its exact meaning is unknown. This has caused some scholars to argue that we probably have here a textual corruption. They prefer to follow the reason given in the parallel narrative in 1 Chronicles 13:10, that "he had put his hand on the ark." Based on comparative linguistics, scholars have suggested that the Hebrew noun *shal* expressed the ideas of disdain, impudence, and slander. In the context it indicates that Uzzah showed disrespect to God by improperly handling a symbol of His holy presence. (*Adventist Review*, March, 2003).

The King James Version states that God was angry with Uzzah because of his error. The marginal reading states "rashness." We may know the exact meaning of the Hebrew word *Shal*. Sister White confirmed the King James Version was not a textual corruption, for she quoted the passage, confirming its truth.

> But "when they came to Nachon's threshing floor, Uzzah put forth his hand to the ark of God, and took hold of it; for the oxen shook it. And the anger of the Lord was kindled against Uzzah, and God smote him there for his rashness; [marginal reading] and there he died by the ark of God." (*Patriarchs and Prophets*, p. 705).

Doubt 3:

> It is impossible to know the mental state of Uzzah as he reached out to seize the ark. One could argue that he was sincerely interested in protecting it. In that case the Lord was revealing to the people that the ends do not justify the means, that He can protect His holiness without our disrespectful assistance (cf. 2 Sam. 6:1, 2, 7-9). It could also be that since the ark had been in his house for several years, Uzzah was too familiar with it and lost some of the deference he should have had for its holiness. In any case his action was an act of desecration.
>
> (*Adventist Review*, March, 2003).

It is not "impossible to know the mental state of Uzzah." Sister White precisely informed of his state of mind:

> The Philistines, who had not a knowledge of God's law, had placed the ark upon a cart when they returned it to Israel, and the Lord accepted the effort which they made. But the Israelites had in their hands a plain statement of the will of God in all these matters, and their neglect of these instructions was dishonoring to God. Upon Uzzah rested the greater guilt of presumption. Transgression of God's law had lessened his sense of its sacredness, and with unconfessed sins upon him he had, in face of the divine prohibition, presumed to touch the symbol of God's presence. God can accept no partial obedience, no lax way of treating His commandments. By the judgment upon Uzzah He designed to impress upon all Israel the importance of giving strict heed to His requirements.
>
> (*Patriarchs and Prophets*, p. 706).

Here Sister White revealed the mental state of Uzzah:
1. He was presumptuous;
2. He had a reduced sense of the sacredness of the ark;
3. He had unconfessed sin in his heart.

Dr. Rodriguez has, in this article, adopted the mind-set of a great number of our theologians. He was a theologian at the Southwestern Adventist University in Keene, Texas, prior to accepting a position in the Biblical Research Institute of the General Conference. He had also served as President of the Antillian Adventist University in Puerto Rico, 1982-1987. The unnecessary doubts expressed by Dr. Rodriguez in his answer suffer from three defects:

1. He used the New International Version of Scripture, which does not demonstrate the same care as was taken by the sixteenth and seventeenth century English translators;
2. He appears to be overly impressed by "scholars."
3. He has ignored Sister White's inspired commentary upon Uzzah's death. It seems today that while many Seventh-day Adventist theologians happily quote the guess-work of Biblical scholars, according them an unwanted level of authority, they often diminish or ignore the inspired authority which accompanies the Spirit of Prophecy.

In these days of uncertainty, our people deserve to have the certainty of Scripture and the Spirit of Prophecy to be uplifted before them. Let the fallen churches major in uncertainty, destroying the faith of their adherents, but let us glory in the plain certainty of inspired writings.

If they hear not Moses, God's unfaithful people will be impervious to every form of evidence God presents. As prophesied by our Savior we are following the footsteps of the antediluvian world. Neither the evidence of the animals' orderly entry into the ark and the visible presence of the angel of God arrayed in glory, was sufficient to alter their sin-hardened hearts. They continued to celebrate in the seven remaining days of their lives.

> Notwithstanding the solemn exhibition they had witnessed of God's power—of the unnatural occurrence of the beasts' leaving the forests and fields, and going into the ark, and the angel of God clothed with brightness and terrible in majesty descending from heaven and closing the door; yet they hardened their hearts and continued to revel and sport over the signal manifestations of divine power.
> (*Story of Redemption*, p. 66).

The current spurning of Moses' account of Creation Week is a matter of the utmost significance. Continued, those supporting it will find that they themselves will be as verily lost as were the antediluvian host. It is this knowledge and our love for God's professed people which spurs us on to stand by the faith which God has delivered to His saints.

We possess the lessons of Israel, yet we ignore these lessons which would rouse us to our own peril.

> Thus it was with the Jewish nation; thus it will be with the Christian world in every generation. The rejectors of light treasure up to themselves wrath against the day of wrath. (*Review & Herald*, Jan. 5, 1886).

It is this certainty which urges our thoughts, praying that some will turn humbly to God so that He may rescue His people from this wrath. Our hearts genuinely are burdened by the knowledge that such men so cheaply sell the eternal heritage God is offering them. Thus we have addressed these matters in trenchant words.

Many major today in Biblical doubt and also concentrate on skeptical attacks upon the Spirit of Prophecy. Sister White saw such professing "believers" in prophetic vision.

> There are those who walk amid perpetual doubts. They feed on doubts, enjoy doubts, talk doubts, and question everything that it is for their interest to believe. To those who thus trifle with the plain testimonies of God's word, and who refuse to believe because it is inconvenient and unpopular to do so, the light will finally become darkness; truth will appear to the darkened understanding as error, and error will be accepted as truth. When thus shrouded in error, they will find it perfectly natural and convenient to believe what is false, and will become strong in their faith. (Ibid).

Sister White's words became more strident in her remarks upon this situation:

> There are men who have so long rejected light and truth that, like Pharaoh, they have become hardened in heart and fastened in unbelief. They crave error; their appetite is for falsehood. They drink up scandal against those who believe the truth as an ox drinketh up water, while they reject, with demonstrations of anger, the truth, pure Bible truth, which would give health and vigor to the soul. (Ibid).

These inspired words must strike our hearts for none of us is exempt from such a course unless we fully give our hearts to the control of the Holy Spirit. God's counsel to His flock today is:

> When there are so many false teachers, who lead men away from the path of obedience into that of transgression, we need to pray constantly that we may be led into all truth, and that we may not hesitate to stand in defense of the truth. (Ibid).

Yet so few are prepared to stand in defense of the truth. Praise God for those who do. Many, on the other hand, excuse every defilement of truth if it is supported by leadership. Such endanger their salvation. They have learned no lessons from the experience of the Jews in Christ's day.

Sister White surely issued a warning from God when she wrote:

> Those who transgress God's law will have much to say about charity; and when the truth is spoken they talk of the liberality and license given in God's word. But love for Christ and for the souls for whom he died, will lead to the utterance of faithful warnings and appeals by the servants of God. (Ibid).

With these words ringing in our ears, dare any of us despise the words of Moses, the one chosen to record Creation Week, and God's other chosen prophets?

42 Drifting Away from Bible Truth

The dire consequence of loss of confidence in the accuracy of Sister White's writings has been plainly declared:

> If you lose confidence in the testimonies you will drift away from Bible truth.
> (*Testimonies for the Church*, Vol. 5, p. 98).

> Many who have backslidden from the truth assign as a reason for their course that they do not have faith in the testimonies. (*Ibid*, p. 675).

Satan is the greatest fool in the history of eternity. He chose rebellion and ultimate oblivion rather than contentment as the most honored created being in the entire universe. But that fact does not equate with a lack of intellectual brilliance and perception. He well knows that God is about to pour out the Latter Rain so that the greatest and most appealing message of love, the Three Angels' Message, may be broadcast worldwide. Disparaging the Spirit of Prophecy, Satan well knows is a key to delaying the Latter Rain.

> As the end draws near and the work of giving the last warning to the world extends, it becomes more important for those who accept present truth to have a clear understanding of the nature and influence of the Testimonies....
> (*Ibid*, p. 654).

In his "defense" of Sister White, Graeme Bradford in his book, *Prophets Are Human*, compared the servant of the Lord with Biblical prophets. Such a course is proper provided there is no diminution of the words of the Biblical prophets. There are parallels between Sister White and those holy prophets of ancient times whom Scripture has so well described.

> [19]We have also a more sure word of prophecy; whereunto ye do well that ye take heed, as unto a light that shineth in a dark place, until the day dawn, and the day star arise in your hearts: [20]Knowing this first, that no prophecy of the scripture is of any private interpretation. [21]For the prophecy came not in old time by the will of man: but holy men of God spake as they were moved by the Holy Ghost.
> (2 Peter 1:19-21).

Now if these prophetic utterances are riddled with the confused ideas and erroneous concepts of the secular thinkers of their era, how could they present "a more sure word of prophecy"? It would be, rather, an unsure word. It would not be a "light that shineth," but cultural darkness with which we are confronted. And if, as Peter declared, prophecy "came not in old time by the will of man," is correct, it does not come to us polluted by the contemporary human errors of the day. If these prophets were truly moved by the Holy Spirit, how could they be led to pervert truth by inlcuding error? Did not our Savior, Himself assure us that,

> Howbeit when he, the Spirit of truth, is come, he will guide you into all truth: for he shall not speak of himself; but whatsoever he shall hear, that shall he speak: and he will show you things to come. (John 16:13)?

Either Christ here was speaking the truth or He was not. No follower of Christ surely would dare to accuse our Redeemer of misleading us.

In his fictional account Dr. Bradford represented Pastor Jared Downton offering the services of Dr. Harold Smithurst to help Doug and Jean with their questions concerning Sister White's ministry. He suggested:

> However, I do know someone I think can help. If you will allow me I will ask him to call and go over some of these things with you. He teaches at one of our colleges and has given a lot of time to finding answers to these questions. I believe he can help. (Graeme Bradford, *op. cit.*, pp. 21, 22).

Whether Dr. Graeme Bradford saw himself as Dr. Smithurst is unclear. Certainly he is a College professor of theology who has "given a lot of time to finding answers to these questions."

In the Introduction to his book, Dr. Bradford stated:

> I am deeply indebted to Robert Olson, Ron Graybill and Arthur Patrick who, while attached to the White Estate in the 1980's, first opened my eyes to some of the material I will share. (*Ibid*, p. 10).

Here Dr. Bradford stated that the material he proposed to present in the book through the voice of the mythical Dr. Smithurst is "material I will share." We notice that Dr. Bradford admitted to having been dependent upon others who had been entrusted with the sacred work of preserving and uplifting the prophetic ministry of Sister White. Let others judge whether these men were true to their trust.

Russell well remembers standing behind Dr. Ron Graybill at one of the two General Conference Sessions to which he was a delegate (1990, Indianapolis), well aware that the man to precede him in speaking had – in his Ph.D. thesis – provided Sister White with little greater status than that of Mary Baker Eddy, the founder of the Christian Science faith.

Dr. Bradford also wrote:

> I am also grateful to [Dr.] Ray Roennfeldt, Dean of the Faculty at Avondale College, for reading the manuscript [*Prophets Are Human*] and his helpful advice. (*Ibid*, p. 10).

When Pope John Paul II issued his Apostolic letter *Dies Domini* (The Lord's Day) in May 1998, a document which called for

Christians [who] will naturally strive to ensure that civil legislation respects their duty to keep Sunday holy, (John Paul II, *Dies Domini*, 31 May, 1998),

Dr. Roennfeldt declared:

> John Paul II's Sabbath theology is thoroughly salvation or Christ-centred.
> (*South Pacific Record*, 15 August, 1998).

We, to the contrary, judged the Pope's apostolic letter to be damnation and antichrist centered.

After the events of September 11, 2001, Dr. Roennfeldt expressed the view:

> I'm not sure that Ellen White's description of tall buildings of New York and their destruction by fire is a specific reference to the attack on the world Trade Centre (read *Testimonies for the Church*, Vol. 9, pp. 11-17 for yourself). The chapter referred to is entitled 'The Last Crisis.'
>
> Ellen White's focus doesn't appear to be on specific fires in New York as being signs of Christ's soon return. Rather, it's the injustice, the arrogance and selfishness of the advantaged that causes her to say, 'The condition of things in the world shows that troublous times are right upon us.'
> (*The Edge*, 5 November, 2001 – parenthesis in the original).

If we do use human counsellors to review our writings we must choose them with great care.

In the story-line of *Prophets Are Human*, Dr. Smithurst opened his comparison of his assessment of Sister White's writings with those of Biblical prophets thus:

> I found I had been unbiblical in my expectations of how the gift should operate, I found I'd been asking more of Ellen White than I would for biblical writers and prophets. (Dr. Bradford, *op. cit.*, p. 24).

Dr. Smithurst's first careful diminution of Scripture was his comment that,

> Despite all the evidence that this is a book [the Bible] from God, there are things found in the Bible which puzzle us at times. For instance, there is the brutality of the Israelites toward the Canaanites. They did this at the command of God. And there are some puzzling things found in the Psalms where the psalmist asks God to do some terrible things to their enemies. (*Ibid*, p. 26).

In his endnotes for this chapter Dr. Bradford cited two passages of Scripture to support his assertion through the lips of Dr. Smithurst.

> And they utterly destroyed all that was in the city [Jericho], both man and woman, young and old, and ox, and sheep, and ass, with the edge of the sword.
> (Joshua 6:21)
>
> [8] O daughter of Babylon, who art to be destroyed; happy shall he be, that rewardeth thee as thou hast served us.

> ⁹ Happy shall he be, that taketh and dasheth thy little ones against the stones.
> (Psalm 137:8, 9).

Dr. Smithurst did not provide an adequate explanation for these passages which demonstrate God's love to those who have rejected this mercy. Could it be that God destroyed them before they lived further to add sin to sin and thus suffer more punishment in the judgment? What is certain is that after a long period suffering the ingratitude and wicked acts of these nations, providing them ceaselessly with the evidence of His love and mercy, reluctantly God had to remove these nations of incurable reprobates for the greater good of His people and the ultimate success of His inestimable plan of salvation. Dr. Smithurst simply explained,

> I personally think God was working with people who were living in a culture that was less than ideal, and was trying to lift them to a higher plane. (*Ibid*).

Sister White elucidates the details of the fall of Jericho cited by Dr. Smithurst. Writing in the *Review and Herald*, October 16, 1900, she revealed no dependence on culture for this event.

> At the taking of Jericho the mighty General of armies planned the battle in such simplicity that no human being could take the glory to himself. No human hand must cast down the walls of the city, lest man should take to himself the glory of victory.

We do well to heed Sister White's words written in *The Signs of the Times*, April 14, 1881:

> There are deep mysteries in the Word of God, there are mysteries in His providences, and there are mysteries in the plan of salvation, that man cannot fathom. But the finite mind, strong in its desire to satisfy curiosity, and solve the problems of infinity, neglects to follow the plain course indicated by the revealed will of God, and pries into the secrets hidden since the foundation of the world. Man builds his theories, loses the simplicity of true faith, becomes too self-important to believe the declarations of the Lord, and hedges himself in with his own conceits. (*SDA Bible Commentary*, Vol 2, p. 995).

The very prophet whose work was diminished by Dr. Smithurst, would have elucidated God's perfect reasons for destroying Jericho, had he consulted her writings. Please ponder the last sentence in this quotation.

> To many these commands seem to be contrary to the spirit of love and mercy enjoined in other portions of the Bible, but they were in truth the dictates of infinite wisdom and goodness. God was about to establish Israel in Canaan, to develop among them a nation and government that should be a manifestation of His kingdom upon the earth. They were not only to be inheritors of the true religion, but to disseminate its principles throughout the world. The Canaanites had abandoned themselves to the foulest and most debasing heathenism, and it

was necessary that the land should be cleared of what would so surely prevent the fulfillment of God's gracious purposes. The inhabitants of Canaan had been granted ample opportunity for repentance. (*Patriarchs & Prophets*, p. 492).

To assign the destruction of the inhabitants of Jericho to cultural factors degrades Scripture and its Author.

On pages 29-34 of Dr. Bradford's book is a section entitled "The Bible a Mixture of the Human and the Divine." This heading surely contradicted Scripture.

> **All** scripture is given by inspiration of God, and is profitable for doctrine, for reproof, for correction, for instruction in righteousness:
> (2 Timothy 3:16, emphasis added).

Dr. Smithurst quoted the following passage of Scripture (see page 32).

> [14]I thank God that I baptized none of you, but Crispus and Gaius; [15]Lest any should say that I had baptized in mine own name. [16]And I baptized also the household of Stephanas: besides, I know not whether I baptized any other.
> (1 Corinthians 1:14-16).

Dr. Smithurst first quoted verses 14, 15 only. And then he dared to state:

> Now that isn't true. (Dr. Bradford, *op. cit.*, p. 32).

Here the author chose to lay the charge that Paul under inspiration wrote falsehood. Apparently Dr. Smithurst overlooked the fact that Paul was here writing a letter. If he had made a mistake and recognised this fact prior to sending the epistle, it would have been a simple matter to correct it. We handwrite family letters of eight pages almost every week. The recipients would be unable to count the number of corrections we have made over the years.

Paul, speaking to the Corinthian believers, stated, "I thank God that I baptized none of YOU," (emphasis added). Where does Scripture state that Stephanas was a Corinthian? The Biblical evidence is clear that he was not. Stephanas is mentioned on three further occasions in Scripture. We cite these references:

> I beseech you, brethren, (ye know the house of Stephanas, that it is the firstfruits of Achaia, and that they have addicted themselves to the ministry of the saints,)
> (1 Corinthians 16:15 – parenthesis in the text).

> I am glad of the coming of Stephanas and Fortunatus and Achaicus: for that which was lacking on your part they have supplied. (1 Corinthians 16:17).

> The first *epistle* to the Corinthians was written from Philippi by Stephanas, and Fortunatus, and Achaicus, and Timotheus.
> (Statement at end of 1 Corinthians chapter 16).

Here we see that Stephanas lived in Achaia, a large region of southern Greece which included both Athens and Corinth. It is clear from verse 15 above that Stephanas came from an area of Achaia other than Corinth. It is a sad matter that Paul's first epistle to the Corinthian believers has been used, devoid of evidence, to assert that Paul included untruths in his inspired letters.

One is discomforted by the innuendo in one of Jean's comments which Dr. Smithurst declared to be

> a wonderful summary of what I am saying. (Dr Bradford, *op. cit.*, p. 34).

Jean's statement was:

> Maybe we'll have to keep in mind the primary reason she [Sister White] wrote and not allow minor items to distract us." (*ibid*).

Is error ever minor? Is inspiration confirmed by the presence of error? There is no denial that Scriptural authors wrote in their own style and language – some in Hebrew, some in Aramaic, some in Greek. Peter's style was different from John's. Paul's was distinct from James' for the same truth can be expressed in different words. If someone stated, "Yesterday I bought a car," and later remarked to someone else, "Twenty-four hours ago I purchased an automobile," both statements would be equally correct but the words used would be totally unrelated in their etymologies.

Such differing expressions of truth must never be misconstrued to suggest error in Scripture.

Throughout *Prophets Are Human* there was an overuse of someone smiling. Just citing pages 32-34 we find:

> With a half-smile Dr. Smithurst asks… (p. 32)
>
> Dr. Smithurst puts down his Bible and laughs. (p. 32)
>
> The group chuckle together. (p. 32)
>
> Dr. Smithurst smiles. (p. 34)
>
> See also pages 25, 41 (twice), 44, 78 and 84.

Smiling is a gift of God. But there are times when a smile is derived from another source. It is no smiling matter to charge Scripture with error.

Further, throughout the book, Dr. Smithurst assumed a patronizing manner. On each of pages 32, 33, 34 Dr. Smithurst compliments the laypeople when they adopt his point of view. "Well said." See also page 38 "Well done Jean," "Well said Doug." (page 73). There has grown up among us as a people a sense that theologians, by bent of their theological training, have a big advantage over the laity. Often the reverse situation prevails. In the acquisition of truth, those who under God's guiding Spirit study Scripture, are well ahead of those who confine themselves to the study of academic theology. It is time that we as a people ceased to excuse our ignorance of truth with the explanation, "Well

I'm not a theologian." Grasp that advantage and study Scripture after earnest prayer for the guidance of the Holy Spirit. After all, it is laypeople untainted by theological study who will enlighten the world with God's glory.

> Thus the message of the third angel will be proclaimed. As the time comes for it to be given with greatest power, the Lord will work through humble instruments, leading the minds of those who consecrate themselves to His service. The laborers will be qualified rather by the unction of His Spirit than by the training of literary institutions. Men of faith and prayer will be constrained to go forth with holy zeal, declaring the words which God gives them. The sins of Babylon will be laid open. The fearful results of enforcing the observances of the church by civil authority, the inroads of spiritualism, the stealthy but rapid progress of the papal power—all will be unmasked. By these solemn warnings the people will be stirred. Thousands upon thousands will listen who have never heard words like these.
> <div align="right">(<i>Great Controversy</i>, p. 606).</div>

It is correctly stated that,

> Paul's statements taken from pagan scholars are well known.
> <div align="right">(Dr. Bradford, <i>op. cit.</i>, p. 43).</div>

The endnote cites Greek pagan philosophers Aratas (Acts 17:28), Epimendes (Titus 1:12) and Menander (1 Corinthians 15:33) (*Ibid.* – see page 53).

While these words are correct, no emphasis is placed upon the truth expressed by these pagan scholars. Even pagans are aware of some divine truths, although they rarely recognize these as heavenly truth.

Scripture is also distorted in the book.

> We know now that these Magi were very likely Eastern Astrologers. In the ancient world it was believed that the stars were gods who lived in the heavens above the clouds. The Magi accepted that this star-god could move through the sky and guide them as they sought a specific house in Bethlehem.
> <div align="right">(Dr. Bradford, <i>op. cit.</i>, p. 60).</div>

Where Dr. Smithurst obtained this information we are not informed: that it was not from inspiration is an absolute certainty. Sister White elucidated the beliefs of these men. They were very different from those views attributed to the Magi by Dr. Bradford.

> Others were upright men who studied the indications of Providence in nature, and who were honored for their integrity and wisdom. Of this character were the wise men who came to Jesus.

> The light of God is ever shining amid the darkness of heathenism. As these magi studied the starry heavens, and sought to fathom the mystery hidden in their bright paths, they beheld the glory of the Creator. Seeking clearer knowledge, they turned to the Hebrew Scriptures. In their own land were treasured prophetic

writings that predicted the coming of a divine teacher. Balaam belonged to the magicians, though at one time a prophet of God; by the Holy Spirit he had foretold the prosperity of Israel and the appearing of the Messiah; and his prophecies had been handed down by tradition from century to century. But in the Old Testament the Saviour's advent was more clearly revealed. The magi learned with joy that His coming was near, and that the whole world was to be filled with a knowledge of the glory of the Lord. (*Desire of Ages*, pp. 59, 60).

What a different picture of the wise men Sister White was inspired to write! Dr. Smithurst's comments suffer from a disregard for the inspired insights of the Spirit of Prophecy. Many of our theologians today are adrift upon the polluted oceans of theological guesswork.

Dr. Smithurst emphasised the faults of Abraham, Samuel, David, Jeremiah, Moses, Elijah, Peter, Paul and Barnabas. In this his remarks were truthful but in the context of this book they tended to cast aspersions on Scripture. The issue at stake is not the personal lives of these prophets but the messages that God inspired Biblical prophets to write.

Pr. Bruce Manners, Editor for over a decade at the *Signs Publishing Company*, proposed a low form of inspiration fraught with spiritual dangers, a fallible inspiration which, if correct, would open to all the right to use their own opinions to judge those inspired words which are correct and those which are false. In the variety of material Pastor Manners has placed before the readership of the denominational magazines he edited for more than a decade, largely in the 1990's, he provided many articles which disregarded God's prohibitions through the Spirit of Prophecy. Such a position would accord the reader the right to accept those areas with which he is in agreement and reject Sister White's counsels if one disagrees.

That Pr. Manners practices what he asserts cannot be denied. In the South Pacific Division Youth Magazine which he has edited, *The Edge*, he has clearly followed a policy of rejecting God's counsel concerning novel reading.

> We need to draw fresh supplies daily from the great storehouse of God's Word. This will give no time for novel reading, or for anything else that does not edify and strengthen for every good work. (*Sons and Daughters of God*, p. 325).

> Before accepting the present truth, some had formed the habit of novel reading. Upon uniting with the church, they made an effort to overcome this habit. To place before this class reading similar to that which they have discarded is like offering intoxicants to the inebriate. (*Testimonies for the Church*, Vol. 7, p. 203).

> I am acquainted with a number of women who have thought their marriage a misfortune. They have read novels until their imaginations have become diseased, and they live in a world of their own creating.
> (*Testimonies for the Church*, Vol. 2, p. 462).

> In the education of children and youth, fairy tales, myths, and fictitious stories are now given a large place. Books of this character are used in the schools, and they are to be found in many homes. How can Christian parents permit their children to use books so filled with falsehood? (*Ministry of Healing*, p. 446).

In *The Edge* novels are reviewed for the "benefit" of young people, one even receiving praise which included two "bloody murders." Pr. Manners has also ignored Sister White's counsel on music.

> Some think that the louder they sing the more music they make; but noise is not music. Good singing is like the music of the birds—subdued and melodious. In some of our churches I have heard solos that were altogether unsuitable for the service of the Lord's house. The long-drawn-out notes and the peculiar sounds common in operatic singing are not pleasing to the angels. They delight to hear the simple songs of praise sung in a natural tone. (*Evangelism*, p. 510).

> Their minds are filled with nonsense. Their conversation is only empty, vain talk. They have a keen ear for music, and Satan knows what organs to excite to animate, engross, and charm the mind so that Christ is not desired. The spiritual longings of the soul for divine knowledge, for a growth in grace, are wanting. (*Testimonies for the Church*, Vol. 1, pp. 496, 497).

> It is impossible to estimate too largely the work that the Lord will accomplish through His proposed vessels in carrying out His mind and purpose. The things you have described as taking place in Indiana, the Lord has shown me would take place just before the close of probation. Every uncouth thing will be demonstrated. There will be shouting, with drums, music, and dancing. The senses of rational beings will become so confused that they cannot be trusted to make right decisions. And this is called the moving of the Holy Spirit.

> The Holy Spirit never reveals itself in such methods, in such a bedlam of noise. This is an invention of Satan to cover up his ingenious methods for making of none effect the pure, sincere, elevating, ennobling, sanctifying truth for this time. Better never have the worship of God blended with music than to use musical instruments to do the work which last January was represented to me would be brought into our camp meetings. The truth for this time needs nothing of this kind in its work of converting souls. A bedlam of noise shocks the senses and perverts that which if conducted aright might be a blessing. The powers of satanic agencies blend with the din and noise, to have a carnival, and this is termed the Holy Spirit's working. (*Selected Messages*, Vol. 2, p. 36).

Month after month *The Edge*, for years has reviewed four rock music tapes or CD's, (example every issue of 2001, 2002, 2003) according them one to five stars depending upon the assessment of the reviewer. The type of music evaluated may be judged by the reviewer's estimate of some of its sound styles (mod-pop rockers – 4 stars – 29 September, 2001; sweet apple-pie pop – 3 stars –

ibid; rage against the machine – 4 stars – May 12, 2001; Queensland pop-rock – 3 stars – November 10, 2001; passionate American pop – 3 stars – 21 February, 2004; soul-searching heavy guitar pop – 4 stars – November 25, 2000; stadium-sized rock 'n' worship – 4 stars – *ibid*.

At the date of writing this manuscript Pr. Manners has been transferred to the post of senior pastor of the Avondale College Church and his appointed successor as editor of the South Pacific *Record*, the *Signs* and *The Edge* is Brother Nathan Brown, a 29-year-old who regularly reviewed novels in *The Edge*. *The Edge* also reviews television soap operas from time to time. (12 May, 2001).

Also the *Signs* editor clearly indicated that he believed that Sister White was in error when she counselled that:

> Cheap, worthless stories should find no place [in our periodicals].
> (*Counsels to Writers and Editors*, p. 17).

> It is not the business of any of God's stewards to extol any human being, be he living or dead. (*Ibid*, p. 19).

> It is not the business of the householder, whom God has appointed, to bring before the people subjects that may be found in the publications of the world.
> (*Ibid*, p. 20).

> All these common things are very cheap, and often are but stale food to those who are starving for the heavenly manna. (*Ibid*, p. 21).

Yet the cover stories of the *Signs* almost always deal with the lives of worldly men and women, sportsmen (Andre Agassi, champion tennis player – *Signs*, Jan-Feb, 2004; cricketers, rugby players), singers (Beatle, Paul McCartney – May, 2003), television stars, opera singers, movie stars and like entertainers.

Here we see the fruits of Pr. Manners claim that

> there has always been the suspicion that God would somehow protect his writers from even the simplest mistakes.... We now face the reality that this is not so.... With Ellen White two extremes are to be avoided. The first takes such a high view of her inspiration that is unrealistic, unworkable and unbiblical.
> (South Pacific *Record*, February 7, 2004).

In answering Pr. Manners' questions

> But you seem to put limits on that [God's] guidance [of Sister White]? (Dr. Patrick replied), Definitely. (*Ibid*, February 28, 2004).

Further, in response to Pr. Manners' more general question which included Biblical inspiration:

> So even an inspired person can be partly right and partly wrong? [Dr. Patrick replied] You've got it! (*Ibid*).

Tragically the South Pacific Division leadership, by its failure to make a public protest, has prepared the soil to "advance" from lack of faith in the Spirit of Prophecy to a similar lack of regard for Biblical inspiration. In this is being fulfilled the inspired words of the very one whose writings are being systematically undermined.

> If you lose confidence in the testimonies you will drift away from Bible truth.
> (*Testimonies for the Church*, Vol. 5, p. 98).

43   No Coherent Corpus of Belief

Welshman, Lord Roy Jenkins, is a man of great secular accomplishments. He was born on November 11, 1920, exactly two years after the signing of the Armistice which ended the First World War. The son of a coal miner who was awarded a trade union scholarship to Ruskin College, Oxford, and later became the member for Pontypool in the British House of Commons, Baron Jenkins' working-class background was no barrier to his own achievements.

Lord Jenkins graduated from Oxford University and himself was elected to the House of Commons as a Labour Party member in 1948, after having served in World War II helping to decode the Enigma ciphers. He held two of the three most senior cabinet offices in the British Parliament with distinction: Home Secretary and Chancellor of the Exchequer, the grandiose title for the Treasurer, in the Labour Government of Prime Minister Harold Wilson. He was groomed to be Harold Wilson's successor. When this did not eventuate he left the House of Commons and became President of the European Commission in 1977 and set in place the process of the European Monetary System which, after many years, led to the creation of the euro currency now used in many European nations.

Lord Jenkins later returned to the House of Commons, having co-founded the Social Democratic party of which he became leader. He was honored by his appointment as Chancellor (Chairman of the Board) of Oxford University and became President of the Royal College of Literature. In 2001 he was awarded the prestigious Wolfson History Prize for historical writing. Russell possesses a personally autographed copy of his autobiography, *A Life at the Centre*, which he dated 26:ix:91 (September 26, 1991). After his retirement from the House of Commons, Roy Jenkins was rewarded with a life peerage and as Baron Jenkins entered the British House of Lords.

In his most recent 912-page historical tome, *Churchill*, Lord Jenkins – writing about the political career of Sir Winston Churchill's father, Lord Randolf Churchill – described Lord Churchill's contribution when a Member of the House of Commons as a politician whose contributions were dominated by

> political attitudes [which] were dictated by opportunism and not by any coherent corpus of belief.
>
> (Lord Roy Jenkins, *Churchill*, Pan Macmillan Ltd, Oxford, 2001, p. 15).

Today within the Seventh-day Adventist Church we, too, have established a body of "faith" which possesses no coherent corpus of belief. Let politicians operate in this fashion. They, in many cases, know no better. But we are different! We are Seventh-day Adventists! God in His mighty love has provided us with the most perfect coherent corpus of belief. No body of Christians, even in the pure Christian Church of the first century of the Christian era, has possessed such a full, logical and unchallengable body of belief.

Destroy one pillar in this corpus and the entire belief structure collapses, for each challenge to truth leads to further logical deductions from the error which destroys yet other pillars and planks in this body of truth. We illustrate: when some theologians concluded that sanctified characters, obedience to God's laws even empowered by the Holy Spirit, were impossible, then Christ's example having been tempted

> in all points like as we are, yet without sin   (Hebrews 4:15)

was inevitably destroyed by declaring Christ as possessing a pre-fall human nature. This has eventually led to desecration of the holy Sabbath day for it is the Commandment of character perfection, for if Christ possessed a human nature different from our own, then He is not our example and in God's power we cannot obey His law.

> Remember the Sabbath day to keep it HOLY   (Exodus 20:8, emphasis added).

> No other institution which was committed to the Jews tended so fully to distinguish them from surrounding nations as did the Sabbath. God designed that its observance should designate them as His worshipers. It was to be a token of their separation from idolatry, and their connection with the true God. But in order to keep the Sabbath holy, men must themselves be holy. Through faith they must become partakers of the righteousness of Christ. When the command was given to Israel, "Remember the Sabbath day, to keep it holy," the Lord said also to them, "Ye shall be holy men unto Me." Ex. 20:8; 22:31. Only thus could the Sabbath distinguish Israel as the worshipers of God.   (*Desire of Ages*, p. 283).

Notice here that the Sabbath:
1. Distinguishes us from surrounding faiths;
2. Designates us as God's worshippers;
3. Is a token of our separation from idolatry;
4. Establishes our connection with the true God;
5. Can only be kept in holiness by holy men and women – those free from sin;
6. Produces partakers of Christ's righteousness.

The desecration of the Sabbath (see chapter entitled *The Seal of God*) has become entrenched in our church. Since the holiness of Sabbath-keeping is a pivotal element of character perfection, all other doctrines and qualities of character are destroyed when the holiness of the Sabbath day is defiled. The Sabbath is a transcript of Christ's character. When Sabbath sacredness is violated we cannot emulate Christ's character. We inevitably, as a consequence, forfeit our coherent corpus of belief.

Below we list salient consequences of defiling God's holy day. Each point raised corresponds to the five elements of true Sabbath-keeping cited above.

1. We now attempt to minimize the vast doctrinal gulf between us and other Christian faiths and have launched into the Satanic ploy of ecumenism;
2. Commonly we no longer deem it necessary to worship God in the beauty of holiness (1 Chronicles 16:29; 2 Chronicles 20:21; Psalm 29:2) and have launched into the blasphemous worship styles of the fallen Churches of Babylon.
3. Today we are a church immersed in idolatry.

> It is as easy to make an idol of false doctrines and theories as to fashion an idol of wood or stone. (*Great Controversy*, p. 583).

Further, the idolatry of every form of entertainment prevails in our church as does the idolatry of materialism.

4. Today many Seventh-day Adventists worship Satan rather than God for they worship a "god" who cannot empower victory over all sin. The only such impotent "god" is Satan.
5. We have ceased to be servants of God because we no longer believe in freedom from sin.

> But now being made free from sin, and become servants to God, ye have your fruit unto holiness, and the end everlasting life. (Romans 6:22).

6. The doctrine of righteousness by faith has been thoroughly emasculated as we have shown in our books, *Deceptions of the New Theology and Adventism Vindicated*.

It does not end there. The sealing message of Revelation chapter seven is seldom preached in our churches. Yet we are in the era when its pointed message was never more needed. This is a logical result of the premise that we cannot keep the commandments, for only "the servants of our God" (Revelation 7:3) receive the seal of the living God and we have just read above the characteristics of the servants of God. They are free from sin and possess holy characters.

> But now being made free from sin, and become servants to God, ye have your fruit unto holiness, and the end everlasting life. (Romans 6:22).

Further, to destroy the Sabbath we must destroy Genesis chapters 1 and 2, for the Sabbath is a memorial of creation. This book has amply documented this process which now appears to possess an unstoppable momentum.

We could illustrate this logical progression to doctrine after doctrine, all initiated by the acceptance of a single unscriptural premise – sin cannot be overcome in God's power until the Second Coming. God through Sister White magnificently spoke of this disgraceful process which is rapidly leaving our church with no coherent corpus of belief.

> Men fall into error by starting with false premises and then bringing everything to bear to prove the error true. In some cases the first principles have a measure of truth interwoven with the error; but it leads to no just action; and this is why men are misled. They desire to reign and become a power, and, in the effort to justify their principles, they adopt the methods of Satan.
> (*Testimonies for the Church*, Vol. 7, p. 181).

> But how do men fall into such error? By starting with false premises, and then bringing everything to bear to prove the error true. In some cases the first principles have a measure of truth interwoven with the error, but it does not lead to any just action, and this is why men are misled. In order to reign and become a power, they employ Satan's methods to justify their own principles. They exalt themselves as men of superior judgment, and they have stood as representatives of God. These are false gods. (*Testimonies to Ministers*, p. 364).

> The path of faith lies close beside the path of presumption. Satan is ever seeking to lead us into false paths. He sees that a misunderstanding of what constitutes faith will confuse and disappoint. He is pleased when he can persuade men and women to reason from false premises. (*Selected Messages*, Vol. 2, p. 345).

Accepting Satan's lying words presented to Eve, that disobedience to God's law is no impediment to eternal life, the adherents of the New Theology have developed a coherent corpus of disbelief which is now clear for all to see. By contrast to the Seventh-day Adventist coherent corpus of truth, the New Theology presents a corpus of doctrine which is an empty shell containing no bone, no muscle, with no tendon, no ligament, to unite the powerful doctrinal skeletal structure with the mighty muscle of active witness. The New Theology possesses: no heart to love our Savior by keeping His Commandments (John 14:15); no brain to discern His truth: no senses, no tongues to sing His praises and to taste the good things of the Lord; no ear to hear His Word; no eye to see the true glories of the Lord; no olfactory system to sense the sweet incense of heaven; no sense of touch to be consoled by the touch of the Master's hand; no lungs to breathe in the power of the Holy Spirit and the atmosphere of heaven. What remains of the incomparable, coherent corpus of Seventh-day Adventist belief is an empty shell of withered skin collapsing in upon itself – withered by the antiquity of its accumulation of the heresies long promoted by the fallen churches of Babylon.

We regret that we cannot set before God's professed people sanguine prognostications for our church as a whole, except to glory in God's revelation that the Seventh-day Adventist Church, refined by the shaking process and reduced to a mere remnant, will complete the task that God commissioned it to undertake – the spread of the pure gospel of the three angels to every corner of the earth.

Avondale College typifies many other Seventh-day Adventist tertiary institutions worldwide, in demonstrating this withered shell of belief. As Russell recently wrote,

> I can think of no tertiary institution in the South Pacific which is less fitted to train young people for God's service than Avondale College. It has rejected the S.D.A. faith and does its utmost to destroy that faith. Will the students find the sanctuary message there? No! Will they discover the Three Angels' Messages? No! Will they be motivated to seek Christian character perfection? No! Will they learn to worship God in the beauty of holiness? No! Will they learn to keep the Sabbath day holy? No! Will the students be fitted for translation at Avondale College? Of course not! They will be assiduously encouraged to believe they will sin until the Second Coming. Will the students learn appropriate entertainment standards? Most certainly not! Will the fallen human nature of Christ be taught? Unquestionably it will not! Will the Spirit of Prophecy be espoused in the manner which is appropriate? No! Will end-time prophecy be taught as set forth in [the Biblical books of] Daniel and Revelation and the Spirit of Prophecy? No! Would an Avondale College student be provided a proper concept of the Remnant? No! Would he possess an accurate knowledge that there is no mediatorial work available after the close of probation? No! Would such a student learn the proper and holy work of Christ through self-supporting ministry? Certainly not! Would the Avondale College undergraduate be taught the evil of the ecumenical movement? No! (*Remnant Herald*, No. 79, February 2003).

In presenting this list Russell was abstemious. He could have added many more established Bible and Spirit of Prophecy truths which would be unlikely to be uplifted by the majority of professors at Avondale College. These include the fact that the Sunday-keeping churches constitute end-time Babylon; the antichrist power is the papacy; the mark of the beast will, at the end time, constitute Sunday worship; the seal of the living God is manifested in true Sabbath-keeping; the promotion of true Seventh-day Adventist education standards as set forth in the book *Education* and other Spirit of Prophecy counsels; true principles of health in the personal life and our health institutions; the Spirit of Prophecy as an element in the lives of the remnant; the work of the Holy Spirit to empower victory over sin; the fact that God created the earth and all that is in it in six days about six thousand years ago; the need to present the Elijah message within our church; and there would not be agreement that sanctification along with justification constitute righteousness by faith.

Few Seventh-day Adventists appear to recognize the terrible carnage to our faith that the New Theology has wrought in our midst in the less-than-fifty years since the book *Questions on Doctrine* was published in 1957. How has this occurred? It has occurred because professors of our faith accepted one false premise – the premise that man will continue to sin until the Second Coming. The Bible and Spirit of Prophecy-based coherent corpus of belief had been breached and, as Sister White was inspired to write, error after error was brought

No Coherent Corpus of Belief

to bear in order to build up a structure of falsehood which has demolished the entire corpus of our faith.

Of course, Australia is not unique in this demolition. It is also found in our institutions worldwide – especially in North America, Europe and Asia – and is rapidly gathering momentum in Africa and South and Central America. We have failed to discern the lessons as clearly evident in the same collapse of the faith of God in the rabbinical schools. They understood nothing of the Messianic prophecies. They misunderstood Sabbath-keeping. The Biblical state of the dead and the work of angels were assiduously challenged. Acceptable prayer practices were abandoned. Pride replaced humility. Legalism substituted for God's grace. The letter of the law was separated from the spirit of the law. Christ's inestimable sacrifice possessed no value to them. Secular education replaced the education of the schools of the prophets. Simony became more persuasive in the election of the church leaders than the call of God. The use of the secular state to enforce its ecclesiastical will was regarded as a necessity. Unjust legal procedures were countenanced. The hope of the advent was replaced by the desire for the return of national temporal sovereignty. The accumulation of wealth replaced the laying up of treasure in heaven. The rules of men replaced Bible principles of conduct. God's house was desecrated by the commercial greed of His professed people. Evangelism for those outside the faith was all but dead. The Sanctuary services had lost their significance and the words of God's prophet of the First Advent were spurned. In summary, God's Jewish Church of that era possessed no coherent body of belief. It, too, was an empty, withered shell.

As a consequence,

> John was called to do a special work; he was to prepare the way of the Lord, to make straight His paths. The Lord did not send him to the school of the prophets and rabbis. He took him away from the assemblies of men to the desert, that he might learn of nature and nature's God. God did not desire him to have the mold of the priests and rulers. He was called to do a special work. The Lord gave him his message. Did he go to the priests and rulers and ask if he might proclaim this message?—No, God put him away from them that he might not be influenced by their spirit and teaching. He was the voice of one crying in the wilderness, "Prepare ye the way of the Lord, make straight in the desert a highway for our God. Every valley shall be exalted, and every mountain and hill shall be made low: and the crooked shall be made straight, and the rough places plain; and the glory of the Lord shall be revealed, and all flesh shall see it together: for the mouth of the Lord hath spoken it" (Isa. 40:3-5). This is the very message that must be given to our people; we are near the end of time, and the message is, Clear the King's highway; gather out the stones; raise up a standard for the people. The people must be awakened. It is no time now to cry peace and safety. We are exhorted to "cry aloud, spare not, lift up thy voice like a trumpet, and shew my people their transgression, and the house of Jacob their sins" (Isa. 5:1).
>
> (*Selected Messages*, Vol. 1, p. 410).

God's corpus of truth has ever formed a concatenation which is unbreakable. The removing of a single truth is all it takes to destroy the entire body of faith. Unless God's people stoutly resist any erosion of the faith they are doomed to depart from God's coherent corpus of belief.

Is it too late to muster ourselves to "awaken the people"? No, it is not! It is an urgent requirement of God that we do. The remnant will ever uplift the coherent corpus of belief. Praise God! They will ever seek to share it in the body of Christ's church and in the world while precious probationary time lasts.

44 The End Point

The various attempts to destroy the Seventh-day Adventist faith from within since the nineteenth century through the twentieth century to our day have all possessed a monotonous pattern, yet one which has proven effective in deceiving a complacent, non-studying laity and ministry.

The Spirit of Prophecy has, consistently, been the first target of these thrusts against the most comprehensive, challenging, sanctifying and urgent message ever entrusted to mankind. Of course the attacks, of necessity, have initially been subtle. Sister White's inspired counsels have been disparaged either in the midst of faint praise or by neglect.

There have been occasions when her plainest words have been destroyed in the midst of high praise. In 1962 when Russell was completing his medical training and Colin his doctorate at the University of Sydney, we invited our former Australasian Missionary College (now Avondale College) fellow student, Dr. Desmond Ford, to speak on the subject of the Spirit of Prophecy to a combined gathering of the Sydney University and the University of New South Wales Seventh-day Adventist Students' Societies. Russell had been President of the eighty-four strong member Sydney University Society in 1960 and Colin in 1961, 1962.

As students at Avondale College we had judged Desmond Ford to be the most academically brilliant, the most capable speaker and the most dedicated in the student body. When he returned to Australia after completing his Master's Degree at the Seventh-day Adventist Theological Seminary, then in Washington D.C., and having completed his doctorate in Rhetoric at the Michigan State University, we were confident that Dr. Ford would convincingly raise the flagging confidence that a few of the Seventh-day Adventist students attending these two universities were evidencing. Around one hundred students were in attendance.

We were more than satisfied with Dr. Ford's able presentation during the first three-quarters of that meeting. His praise of the positive impact of the writings of the Spirit of Prophecy upon his early days as a Seventh-day Adventist was both eloquent and helpful. It was no minor testimony.

But to our utter dismay, when nearing the conclusion of his presentation, Dr. Ford declared that Sister White sometimes included some mistakes in her inspired writings. By way of example he conjectured that the age of the earth was not six-thousand years, as Sister White declared no less than eighty-three times – forty-two times speaking of approximately six-thousand years at the time of her writing, and approximately four-thousand years at the time of the First Advent forty-one times. (See Dr. Gerhard Pfandl, of the Biblical Research

Institute of the General Conference, "Ellen G. White and Earth Science," *Journal of the Adventist Theological Society*, Vol. 14, No. 1, Spring 2003, p.187).

We were not only dismayed: we were stunned! In private conversation with Dr. Ford after the meeting, he emphasized that he was not suggesting millions of years: only eight – or ten – thousand years, because scientists had dated the glaciers that spread into the United States at about 5000 BC. Dr. Ford also commented that archaeological findings could not be accommodated by an earth which was a mere six-thousand years old.

By the dawn of the twenty-first century Dr. Ford had "advanced" from a nine thousand year-old earth to one of millions of years. By then he disputed the fact that the earth was created in six days and spiritualized the Biblical account of Creation. This matter is central to the current, all-out attack on the Spirit of Prophecy in the South Pacific Division, for, as we have already recorded, the Avondale College Church – including many of the College professors –conducted a campaign in 2001 and 2002, to have Dr. Ford return to our pulpits.

On two occasions over Sydney radio 2GB Dr. Ford referred to the book *Creation Reconsidered: Scientific, Biblical and Theological Perspectives*, Roseville, California: Association of Adventist Forums, 2000, edited by Dr James Earl Hayward. Dr Ford indicated that this book set forth material which is now considered normative Seventh-day Adventism in relationship to Genesis chapters 1 – 3.

Russell's son, Dr. Timothy Standish, who is a research scientist at the General Conference Geoscience Research Institute in California, has written a critique of this book. Timothy reminded the readers that the book is a collection of papers from a field conference held sixteen years previously. He pointed out that the book

> provides a historical perspective of liberal Adventists speaking at the time.

Timothy also suggested the book could have been better entitled "The Flood Reconsidered" or "Adventism Reconsidered" or "Science and the Bible Reconsidered."

Timothy wrote,

> Several chapters are dedicated to critiques of other Adventist scholars' attempts to reconcile the Biblical flood and a short chronology with the geological record. Strangely no chapter, not one, deals with evidence logically consistent with creation like biological complexity and the anthropic [the cosmological principle that theories of the origin of the universe are constrained by the necessity to allow individual human existence] principles in physics."

Timothy's critique also stated that

> the reader is left to assume that any literal interpretation of historical accounts given in the book of Genesis, especially those made by Adventist scholars who

take the Bible at its word, is questionable. While it is not stated explicitly, this seems to be the point of these chapters especially when Ross Bains' arrogant-sounding, dedicatory statement about 'collective organisational naivety' and 'inescapable conclusions' are allowed to color one's view of the book.

Those interested in the history of liberal Adventist thought about interpreting Genesis will find this book interesting. Other than this small group, it is hard to think of any general class of readers who would benefit from reading *Creation Reconsidered*.

For Dr. Ford to suggest that this book, edited by Dr. Hayward, is in any way normative Seventh-day Adventism is a distortion of fact. To do so publicly defamed our faith and called into serious question the authenticity of Scripture and the Spirit of Prophecy.

Dr. Desmond Ford was also interviewed by Dr. Gordon Moyes [a minister of the Uniting Church and now a member of the Upper House of the New South Wales Parliament] on August 3, 2002 over Sydney Radio Station 2GB. Here again he made some very significant statements concerning Creation. We quote a few of them.

> Even theistic evolution, whose numbers increase every day, I am not one, but I must say some of the finest Christians who have ever lived and now living were/are theistic evolutionists. Henry Drummond, who wrote *The Greatest Thing in the World* – theistic evolutionist. Benjamin Warfield, one of the greatest theologians of America – theistic evolutionist. The most respected pastor of Christendom, according to Billy Graham, John Stott, sees nothing inconsistent with the gospel and theistic evolution.

We do not know how anyone who is a theistic evolutionist could be regarded as among the 'finest Christians who have ever lived' since they specifically deny the plainest words of Scripture and thus do an enormous disservice to Christ, who ever uplifted the literal words of Genesis during His earthly stay and who inspired the prophet Moses to write the first book of the Bible.

Dr. Ford's evaluation here is a serious mistake. He also spiritualized away the first chapter of Scripture.

> Genesis one, there is a beautiful parable of what happens. In the beginning we are without form and void spiritually. Darkness upon our mind. We can't distinguish between light and darkness. And the Spirit of God works upon us. And the word of God speaks to us and we begin to separate good from evil. Then the early fruit comes up – repentance and sorrow for sin, faith in God. Then becomes life more abundant. Then we become lights in the dark world, being conformed to the image of Christ, who was love. Then we enter into rest, which is the union of the heart with God. As every dew-drop reflects the sun, every extended passage of Scripture reflects Christ, the Sun of Righteousness. The prophets pointed to Him.

Priests pointed to Him. Kings pointed to Him. The Temple pointed to Him. Every sacrifice pointed to Him.

It may be possible to draw lessons from Genesis chapter one, but they do not replace the historicity of that which is described under inspiration in Scripture. Once again Dr. Ford went back to the book which Dr. James Hayward edited:

> Here's a book written by Seventh-day Adventists, leading theologians and scientists. And on page 300 I read this: 'in wandering around the highways and byways of recent theology, I have not encountered one example of a serious, sustained theological argument confirming the creation of the world in six literal days a few thousand years ago.
>
> Adventists! Adventists! From Adventists came Ellen White – the great evangelical Christian. But she wrote in the nineteenth century and so she used Usher's chronology. And George McCready Price, a brave, generous, intelligent man, trusted Ellen White so much he perverted his science unknowingly. And that's where our creation research movement comes from – it was spawned by George McCready Price. But it's gone. Even the Adventists have thrown out that old approach.

This is a very serious statement, for clearly Dr. Ford is once more agreeing with the statement in the book *Creation Reconsidered*. The statement that the creation of the world in six literal days has no theological support indicated that Dr. Ford believed that God's plainest words written with His own finger in the Fourth Commandment are a downright falsehood. It is very serious to imply such a charge. It also destroys the Scriptural testimony that God cannot lie. (Titus 1:2).

Our belief in the six-day creation week about six-thousand years ago, was established in our faith on the basis of inspiration long before George McCready Price (1870-1963) was born. His work upheld that which God had previously established.

Furthermore, as we have seen from Russell's son, Timothy's, critique, it is not correct to say that the literal and true understanding of Genesis chapter 1 is **"gone. Even the Adventists have thrown out that old approach."** We have done no such thing, either as faithful Seventh-day Adventists or on a denomination-wide basis. Such inaccuracies defame the Seventh-day Adventist Church and we are sorry to have to report that these statements were made for the public to hear.

Surely it is time for Seventh-day Adventists to stand up mightily for the truth; and for the South Pacific Division leadership to state plainly that it will in no way, either overtly or covertly, lend support to the Avondale College initiative to have the pulpits of our church open to this sort of message from Dr. Ford. For all to see, we now know where the New Theology has led. It is time for us to come back to the old paths: those paths of truth and righteousness!

Dr. Desmond Ford's wife, Gillian, has authored a document entitled *Genesis 1: The Light That Challenges the Darkness*. The introduction was written by Dr. Ford.

In the Introduction, Dr. Ford spiritualized away the facts of Genesis 1 in yet another manner:

> For example Christ is set forth as the last Adam, and he, too, falls asleep on the sixth day of the week shouting "finished" with his dying breath. And this took place in a garden where he hung on a tree, which, henceforth would be both the tree of life and the tree of knowledge of good and evil. All this in order that His side might be opened so that he might have a bride – the church.
>
> He was placed in a tomb – the symbol of chaos and the abyss. Before his death, darkness reigned for three hours as the light of the world was gradually extinguished.
>
> Should we not follow the example of the apostles and use Genesis in this way rather than trying to meet the scientific exigency, which has only emerged after millenniums of human and church history?
>
> Never does the NT use the OT for scientific purposes. Wherever time and eternity meet, metaphor must be used as at both ends of the bible [sic]. The Bible never reveals supernaturally anything humans can themselves discover, just so, Christ, the Living Word, spoke only of the way of salvation.
>
> If Genesis were intended as science it would consist purely of equations. Written for oral use among the children of earth who would be illiterate through most of the coming millenniums, the inspired word speaks in a manner that all would be able to understand.
>
> As Christ took human symbols (Aramaic words) to express heavenly truth, so Moses, under inspiration, used contemporary idioms to tell WHO (not HOW or WHEN) CREATED THE UNIVERSE. – (Desmond Ford, parenthesis in original).

Dr. Ford's statement that "if Genesis were intended as science it would consist purely of equations" is most curious. We have read many science books and journals of high repute. We have yet to read a single one that consisted of equations alone. The esteemed oceanographer, Matthew Maury (1806-1873), born in Fredericksburg, Virginia, close to Hartland Institute, was a man of God. Maury's work on tides, winds, and the physical geography of the sea, dramatically cut times sailing boats took to reach their destinations and opened the way for the trans-Atlantic telegraphic cable to be laid. Critics in his day argued that the Bible was not meant to be a book of science and thus could not be used for scientific accuracy. His response was as telling as it was succinct:

> I have been blamed by men of science ... for quoting the Bible in confirmation of the doctrines of physical geography. The Bible, they say, was not written for scientific purposes, and is therefore of no authority in matters of science. I beg

pardon! The Bible is authority for everything it touches. What would you think of the historian who would refuse to consult the historical records of the Bible, because the Bible was not written for the purpose of history? The Bible is true and science is true, and therefore each if truly read, but proves the truth of the other.

(M. F. Maury, address given at the University of the South, Tennessee, November 30, 1860, cited in D. F. M. Corbin, *A Life of Matthew Fontaine Maury, USN & CSN*, Sampson and Lowe and Co., 1888, pp. 158, 159).

We note that Dr. Ford not only denied the literal account of Creation, confirmed in the clearest words written by God in the Ten Commandments, but that he cast doubt upon the book of Revelation when he referred to "both ends of the Bible."

Yet Avondale College Church desired to promote Dr. Ford as a safe preacher in our pulpits. (*Mapping the Past and Sketching the Future* – Consultation Document prepared by the Membership and Relational issues Committee appointed by the Avondale College Church Business Meeting on October 30, 2001 – edited draft of December 30, 2001). This tells us more about Avondale College Church than it does even about Dr. Ford. Dr. Ford clearly supported his wife's material. We quote just one section of her document recorded on pages 6, 7.

Consider this statement in the book, quoted approvingly, from the writings of a Catholic teaching brother:

> Genesis 1:1-2:4 provides us with a different kind of literature. By analyzing the Creation story in the light of literary forms and archaeological discoveries, Bible scholars have come to realize that this first chapter of Genesis is based upon an ancient myth. Unfortunately most modern readers consider "myth" to be the equivalent to "fairy tale" – a good story perhaps, but without truth. This understanding of myth, howsoever, is totally different from what the sacred writer and biblical scholar intend.
>
> A myth is a human way of exploring and dealing with a mystery. The people of Israel did not know how the world was made, but they were convinced that it was their God who made it. Without the advantage of telescopes and satellites, the sacred writer had to settle for a less scientific way of expressing his faith conviction that Yahweh was the Creator. Borrowing an old Babylonian myth, Enuma Elish, the Jewish author stripped the story of its specifically pagan elements and used what was left to express his belief. Under the form of sacred myth, he tells a beautiful story of Creation, dramatically expressing the truth of God's power, goodness, wisdom and love. Today's science and technology show us a different picture of the physical origins of our world. But the truth of the biblical account is as firm as ever: Yahweh made the heavens and the earth and all they contain. (Fr. Norman Langenbrunner, *How to Understand the Bible: Examining the Tools of today's Scripture Scholars*).

A Christian theologian or scientist, as well as the rest of us, ought to be able to pursue reasonable areas of knowledge with freedom. Why is it so difficult for a literalist to accept as his brother and sister, someone who believes like this? (Gillian Ford, *op. cit*).

It is an absolute destruction of Scripture, all of which was given by inspiration of God, to declare that Moses simply modified a Babylonian myth. Has Mrs. Ford forgotten that the Babylonians descended from Noah and that their ancestors well knew the true story of creation? It was they who distorted the truth to accord with their pagan concepts.

Surely it is time for Avondale College Church members to admit their serious error of judgment in promoting Dr. Ford's return to our pulpits. It is time for the South Pacific Division leadership to put a stop to this matter by publicly condemning the initiative of the Avondale College Church; by declaring the many errors of Dr. Ford's theology, including his destruction of Creation week, and – by extension – the Sabbath. If the Lord did not create the world in six days and rest the seventh, we have absolutely no basis for Sabbath-keeping. All who accept Dr. Ford's error will willingly align themselves with the mark of the beast. Dr. Ford unconvincingly denied this fact in a document he authored entitled *Questions on Doctrine*.

In that same document, he stated that

> The LITERAL VIEW is negated by several factors. (p.31).

The third of these factors stated:

> **The most obvious objection, however, is the fact that the whole universe is set forth as 'made in six days.'**

Yet nowhere does Genesis 1 mention "the whole universe." In the same document (p.32) – speaking of the fourth commandment – Dr. Ford stated that,

> the reference to days is based on human experience of the week, not the duration of the divine fiats.

The presentation of this evidence should not be construed as a personal vendetta against Dr. Ford, who was a fellow College student with us at Avondale in 1950. We will not help Dr. Ford return to truth and righteousness by muting our concern, nor would we help God's people by refraining from warning them of the errors abroad. He has spoken and written publicly. We reply, likewise, publicly.

The evidence of Dr. Ford's beliefs are documented for all to evaluate. There is a decided necessity for the South Pacific Division leadership to make its position clear in this matter. Unless this is done, a serious doubt will continue to remain as to where our leaders stand after more than two years of intermittent discussion on this matter with the Avondale College Church leaders.

While Dr. Ford voluntarily withdrew from Seventh-day Adventist Church membership when he returned to Australia after residing in the United States for a quarter of a century, he is still widely consulted by not a few pastors in our church. He was offered membership in the Avondale College Church in 2001, but declined it. His influence compels us to cite his current views on Creation.

The New Theology, now promoted in the highest eschelons of our church, is the most destructive of the numerous winds of doctrine blighting the Seventh-day Adventist Church, for it destroys every element of the faith and holy living. It is the most significant cause of the disunity of our church today. It is the most masterful of Satan's wily arts in his purpose to destroy God's faith and His Remnant Church.

God foresaw this apostasy.

> [11]And he gave some, apostles; and some, prophets; and some, evangelists; and some, pastors and teachers; [12]For the perfecting of the saints, for the work of the ministry, for the edifying of the body of Christ: [13]Till we all come in the unity of the faith, and of the knowledge of the Son of God, unto a perfect man, unto the measure of the stature of the fulness of Christ: [14]That we henceforth be no more children, tossed to and fro, and carried about with every wind of doctrine, by the sleight of men, and cunning craftiness, whereby they lie in wait to deceive; [15]But speaking the truth in love, may grow up into him in all things, which is the head, even Christ: [16]From whom the whole body fitly joined together and compacted by that which every joint supplieth, according to the effectual working in the measure of every part, maketh increase of the body unto the edifying of itself in love. (Ephesians 4:11-16).

In this time of unprecedented tempest within the Seventh-day Adventist Church, the New Theology offers a tattered and dilapidated umbrella for protection from the spiritual tornados tearing Christianity apart. That which God's people desperately require is not this "shelter" from the ferocious tempest assailing our church, but rather a glorious mansion of refuge erected on mighty foundations of the hewn rock of Scripture and the Spirit of Prophecy, foundations of which Christ is the Mighty Cornerstone.

We state this matter, not in a sententious spirit, but in a sense of deepest concern and profuse sorrow as we witness the daily destruction of our faith and our divinely-granted commission, and in tender love for our Savior and His precious children. The ineluctable result of this course, if left unchallenged, will be the demise of God's church on earth. Praise God for His very small remnant for,

> Except the LORD of hosts had left unto us a very small remnant, we should have been as Sodom, and we should have been like unto Gomorrah. (Isaiah 1:9).

The end point of the attack upon the Spirit of Prophecy in the South Pacific Division is most certainly not a defense of Sister White's credibility as a prophet, for the "defense" offered leads to a loss of confidence in her writings. It is not even the exposure of Sister White's alleged "mistakes." The end point is no less than the total destruction of the Seventh-day Adventist faith by a clique of Avondale College professors and supporters, promoted by South Pacific

Division leadership. In this they believe they are assisting our church. They, most decidedly, are not!

In the South Pacific Division we are currently fulfilling God-inspired prophecy.

> The very last deception of Satan will be to make of none effect the testimony of the Spirit of God. (*Selected Messages*, Vol. 2, p. 78).

> There will be a hatred kindled against the testimonies which is satanic. The workings of Satan will be to unsettle the faith of the churches in them, for this reason: Satan cannot have so clear a track to bring in his deceptions and bind up souls in his delusions if the warnings and reproofs and counsels of the Spirit of God are heeded. (*Selected Messages*, Vol. 1, p. 48).

> If you lose confidence in the testimonies you will drift away from Bible truth.
> (*Testimonies for the Church*, Vol. 5, p.98).

It is not only the veracity of the Spirit of Prophecy which is at stake but also the truthfulness of the Holy Scriptures.

A recent letter Russell wrote included, in part, his assessment of the attempted demolition of Bible doctrines through the influence of Avondale College.

> As a general rule, in our Division the pastors no longer preach the Three Angels' Messages. They no longer support the Sanctuary Message. They no longer believe that they serve a God who can empower purity of character. They ignore the clearest evidence of Scripture and the Spirit of Prophecy, that Christ possessed a fallen human nature. They no longer believe in a literal reading of Genesis chapters 1-11. They do not promote true Christian education. They no longer present the true health message. They no longer believe that the antichrist is the Papacy. Nor do they believe that the Sunday-keeping churches of Christendom constitute Babylon. They do not promote the Biblical concept that God's chosen church is to be a peculiar (unique) church, ever working for those of other churches but never uniting with them in evangelistic causes. They no longer promote the worship of God in the beauty of holiness. They no longer see the Seventh-day Adventist Church as the remnant church. They no longer keep the Sabbath holy, and many are not proclaiming the nearness of the close of probation and the earnest need to seek God's power to be fitted for Heaven. It also seems that they have largely adopted the Evangelical Protestant principles of prophetic interpretation, which are wide of the mark. They have lost all knowledge of God's entertainment standards. They are leading our youth, not heavenward, but downward to perdition. They have stultified our evangelistic work. They persecute the few who are faithful to the Biblical and Spirit of Prophecy principles of the faith, not fanatics, not hating God's church, but loving it supremely, so that they cry and sigh in sincere sorrow for the abominations done

therein. And need I add, that the Testimonies of the Spirit of God are made of no effect. Our poor people are now largely enveloped in a morass of deadly error. This, I am sorry to say, is the final agenda of this feverish activity in the month of February, 2004.

(Letter written by Russell Standish to Dr. Arthur Patrick dated February 16, 2004 – parenthesis in the original).

Here, unquestionably, is the end point of the present "defense" of Sister White.

45 Cities of Favor

God has ever possessed a precious church in which He deposited the treasures of salvation. His first church was the Patriarchal Church. Subsequently the favour of His truth passed to the Israelite Church and thence to the Apostolic Christian Church, the Protestant Reformation Church and finally to the Seventh-day Adventist Church. Since the establishment of the capital of Israel by King David in Jerusalem, this city has ever served as the continuing symbol of God's favored church. Today Jerusalem is the Seventh-day Adventist Church.

When God spoke of the implanting of the seal of the living God upon the foreheads of His end-time people, He referred to that church as Jerusalem.

> And the LORD said unto him, Go through the midst of the city, through the midst of Jerusalem, and set a mark upon the foreheads of the men that sigh and that cry for all the abominations that be done in the midst thereof. (Ezekiel 9:4).

Satan, too, has ever possessed a favored church. It was first established by Cain. When all members of Satan's antediluvian church were destroyed in the Noachian flood, Satan appointed Noah's great-grandson, Nimrod as the architect of his church in the city of Babylon.

> And the beginning of his [Nimrod's] kingdom was Babylon.
> (Genesis 10:10, margin).

Ever since the city of Babylon has received the favor of Satan. It passed through Medo-Persia, Greece, Rome and finally to the Papacy. Later the apostate Protestant Churches effectively united with Rome.

While God's treasured church and Satan's favored church have ever been at enmity, this enmity first came to serious military conflict in 605 BC when Nebuchadnezzar's Babylonian armies attacked Jerusalem. Daniel and his three companions, along with ten thousand others, were taken captive.

This defeat was a demoralizing set-back for Judah. Although the Babylonian army was more powerful than that of Judah's, they had expected success for they prayed to the God of heaven, claiming His sure promise:

> The LORD shall cause thine enemies that rise up against thee to be smitten before thy face: they shall come out against thee one way, and flee before thee seven ways. (Deuteronomy 28:7).

This divine promise was not conditional upon Judah possessing greater military might than its adversary. Yet, it appeared to Jerusalem, that God had broken His promise, for it was they who had fled "seven ways."

When the Babylonian army returned in 597 BC, the same prayers were offered and the same promise claimed. The result of this conflict was no better than that eight years earlier. More Jews were taken captive including the priestly-prophet, Ezekiel.

It was crisis time for Jerusalem, God's church. A re-examination of Scripture was mandatory. But such a course was not deemed profitable in the face of God, in the view of the church leaders, having twice "failed" to keep His promise.

God's promises are certain and He never resiles from these divine assurances. What Judah had ignored was the crucial element of condition associated with all Scriptural promises. Had the leaders of God's church re-studied the promise claimed they would have been challenged by the preamble to God's guarantee of the defeat of all military assailants.

> [1] And it shall come to pass, if thou shalt hearken diligently unto the voice of the LORD thy God, to observe and to do all his commandments which I command thee this day, that the LORD thy God will set thee on high above all nations of the earth: [2] And all these blessings shall come on thee, and overtake thee, if thou shalt hearken unto the voice of the LORD thy God. (Deuteronomy 28:1, 2).

Further, had they read on they would have discerned the reason for their successive defeats at the hand of Babylon.

> [15] But it shall come to pass, if thou wilt not hearken unto the voice of the LORD thy God, to observe to do all his commandments and his statutes which I command thee this day; that all these curses shall come upon thee, and overtake thee:... [25] The LORD shall cause thee to be smitten before thine enemies: thou shalt go out one way against them, and flee seven ways before them: and shalt be removed into all the kingdoms of the earth. (Deuteronomy 28:15, 25).

God, in His love for Jerusalem, had not left the city without warning, but the prophet who was chosen to present that warning, Jeremiah, was sentenced to death by the priests, his life only being saved by the state officials (the princes) and the older generation. (See Jeremiah 26:1-19). Admittedly, Jeremiah had not moderated his words when faithfully warning Jerusalem of its apostasy.

> [1] They say, If a man put away his wife, and she go from him, and become another man's, shall he return unto her again? shall not that land be greatly polluted? but thou hast played the harlot with many lovers; yet return again to me, saith the LORD. [2] Lift up thine eyes unto the high places, and see where thou hast not been lien with. In the ways hast thou sat for them, as the Arabian in the wilderness; and thou hast polluted the land with thy whoredoms and with thy wickedness. [3] Therefore the showers have been withholden, and there hath been no latter rain; and thou hadst a whore's forehead, thou refusedst to be ashamed. [4] Wilt thou not from this time cry unto me, My father, thou art the guide of my youth? [5] Will he reserve his anger for ever? will he keep it to the end? Behold, thou hast spoken and

> done evil things as thou couldest. ⁶The LORD said also unto me in the days of Josiah the king, Hast thou seen that which backsliding Israel hath done? she is gone up upon every high mountain and under every green tree, and there hath played the harlot. ⁷And I said after she had done all these things, Turn thou unto me. But she returned not. And her treacherous sister Judah saw it.
>
> (Jeremiah 3:1-7).

The church organization, consisting of the priests, was not of a mind to heed the words of a self-supporting worker in the person of the prophet Jeremiah, even in this time of fearful peril. Rather, it turned the apostate views of the contemporary fallen churches of Babylon in order to forestall an inevitable third Babylonian invasion. Repentance and reformation were far from their thinking.

The current theory in ecclesiastical circles of the idol-worshipping cults of the Middle East was the view that whoever served the more powerful god was victorious in any military conflict. Clearly, they reasoned, the Babylonian idol, Bel, was more powerful than the God of heaven.

In captivity in Babylon, the prophet Ezekiel was shown the steps taken to implement this new conviction. The holy temple in Jerusalem was converted into a pagan temple by church leaders. Ezekiel cited five vile pagan abominations, including idol worship and the twenty-five senior priests of the temple engaging in sun worship. These priests were almost certainly the High Priest and the leaders of each of the twenty-four courses of priests. We document these activities.

> ⁵Then said he unto me, Son of man, lift up thine eyes now the way toward the north. So I lifted up mine eyes the way toward the north, and behold northward at the gate of the altar this image of jealousy in the entry.... ¹⁰So I went in and saw; and behold every form of creeping things, and abominable beasts, and all the idols of the house of Israel, portrayed upon the wall round about. ¹¹And there stood before them seventy men of the ancients of the house of Israel, and in the midst of them stood Jaazaniah the son of Shaphan, with every man his censer in his hand; and a thick cloud of incense went up. ¹²Then said he unto me, Son of man, hast thou seen what the ancients of the house of Israel do in the dark, every man in the chambers of his imagery? for they say, The LORD seeth us not; the LORD hath forsaken the earth.... ¹⁴Then he brought me to the door of the gate of the LORD'S house which *was* toward the north; and, behold, there sat women weeping for Tammuz.... ¹⁶And he brought me into the inner court of the LORD'S house, and, behold, at the door of the temple of the LORD, between the porch and the altar, were about five and twenty men, with their backs toward the temple of the LORD, and their faces toward the east; and they worshipped the sun toward the east. (Ezekiel 8:5, 10-12, 14, 16).

Jerusalem's doom was sealed. So defiled had the religion of the city become that in 586 BC, almost two decades after Babylon's first attack, the entire city was destroyed and its inhabitants taken to the city of Babylon, after whose religious principles they had thirsted. They had rejected the pure faith of God.

If it had not been for a "very small remnant" whose descendants formed the nucleus of those who returned seventy years later to restore Jerusalem, the city would have disappeared from the world atlas.

Incomprehensively, God's modern-day Jerusalem, the Seventh-day Adventist Church, has ignored the pertinent lessons of God's church of the late seventh and early sixth centuries, BC. We, too, have absorbed the religion of Babylon into the precious faith of Jerusalem. (See our book, *The Road to Rome*).

The 1956 dialogue between Evangelical Protestants; Presbyterian minister, Dr. Donald Barnhouse and Baptist minister, Walter Martin, on the one hand, and General Conference leaders, on the other, ushered in an era of ecumenism, now prevalent for almost half a century in our beloved church. Unlike Jerusalem of old, this was not a course initiated in response to military attack or persecution. It was engendered by a desire to win the plaudits of Babylon. The current destruction of our faith is the result.

The history of the 1956 Evangelical-Seventh-day Adventist dialogue has already been charted in our book, *The Gathering Storm and the Storm Bursts*, (Hartland Publications, P.O. Box 1, Rapidan, Virginia, 22733, USA). The results of this zest for ecumenical recognition and approval has been no less dire to the faith of our church today than the acceptance of Babylonian precepts in Jerusalem of old. It has led us into Pentecostalism for we have sought their church-growth success and eschewed God's counsels on this issue. These counsels are to be found in books such as *Evangelism* and *Gospel Workers*.

In 1882 Sister White was shown the very situation in Jerusalem today. How closely it parallels Jerusalem in the days of Jeremiah. What Sister White wrote one hundred and twenty years ago so accurately describes the Seventh-day Adventist Church of the first decade of the twenty-first century, that had the manuscript been discovered today we would have concluded that it had been written in this century, not the nineteenth. Once more we ask, If Sister White was not inspired of God to present this information, who was the prophet from whom she plagiarized?

All statements set forth below may be found within the confines of just four pages from *Testimonies for the Church*, Vol. 5, pp. 209-212.

Notice the present-day condition of Jerusalem, our church. Yet, that which was revealed to God's servant twelve decades past describes God's church fully today. It is no longer prophecy. It is a tragic picture of contemporary history. Sister White's general description of today's Seventh-day Adventist Church follows. We place it in point form.

1. ...those who have had the greatest light and privileges have become contaminated by the prevailing iniquity. (p. 209).
2. ...contempt for them [divine precepts] increases. (p. 209).
3. ...the church ... members are doing after the manner of the world. (p. 210).

4. ...religion [is] despised in the very homes of those who have had great light. (p. 210).
5. ...pride, avarice, selfishness, and deceptions of almost every kind are in the church. (p. 210).
6. ...others try to throw a cloak over the existing evil. (p. 210).
7. ...the servants of Satan triumph, God is dishonored, the truth made of none effect. (p. 211).

The concerns of the genuine believers are also set forth:
1. Love for divine precepts increases. (p. 209).
2. Those who walk in the light will see signs of the approaching peril. (p. 209).
3. At the time when the danger and depression of the church are greatest, the little company who are standing in the light will be sighing and crying for the abominations that are done in the land...their prayers will rise in behalf of the church. (pp. 209, 210).
4. ...those who have a zeal for God's honor and a love for souls will not hold their peace to obtain favour of any. Their righteous souls are vexed day by day with the unholy works and conversation of the unrighteous. They are powerless to stop the rushing torrent of iniquity, and hence they are filled with grief and alarm. (p. 210).
5. they mourn before God to see religion despised. (p. 210).

The state of today's ministry and eldership was revealed to God's servant one hundred and twenty years ago.
1. The ancient men, those to whom God has given great light and who had stood as guardians of the spiritual interests of the people, had betrayed their trust. (p. 211).
2. They [the ministers and elders] had taken the position that ... times have changed. (p. 211).
3. [These] men ... will never again lift up their voice like a trumpet to show God's people their transgression and the house of Jacob their sins. (p. 211).
4. These dumb dogs that would not bark are the ones to feel the just vengeance of an offended God. (p. 211).
5. No superiority of rank, dignity, or worldly wisdom, no position in sacred office, will preserve men from sacrificing principle when left to their deceitful hearts. (p. 212).

Today, Babylon has all but destroyed Jerusalem and captured its erstwhile leaders and citizens. But Scripture is encouraging. It is Babylon which will be utterly annihilated and Jerusalem which will reign eternally. Instructive are the final references to these two favored cities in Scripture. The ultimate destiny of each is certain, Babylon is doomed and Jerusalem will be elevated as the capital of all of God's creation. Below are the final references to Babylon and Jerusalem in Scripture.

> And a mighty angel took up a stone like a great millstone, and cast it into the sea, saying, Thus with violence shall that great city Babylon be thrown down, and shall be found no more at all. (Revelation 18:21).
>
> ¹⁰And he carried me away in the spirit to a great and high mountain, and showed me that great city, the holy Jerusalem, descending out of heaven from God, ¹¹Having the glory of God: and her light was like unto a stone most precious, even like a jasper stone, clear as crystal; (Revelation 21:10, 11).

The present ascendancy of Babylon is no omen of its future status; nor is the present-day destruction of Jerusalem, held captive under the dogmas of Babylon, a sign of Jerusalem's future destiny. In her last reference to Babylon in *The Great Controversy* the servant of the Lord recorded the terrifying kismet of its doomed citizens:

> There are papist priests and prelates, who claimed to be Christ's ambassadors, yet employed the rack, the dungeon, and the stake to control the consciences of His people. There are the proud pontiffs who exalted themselves above God and presumed to change the law of the Most High. Those pretended fathers of the church have an account to render to God from which they would fain be excused. Too late they are made to see that the Omniscient One is jealous of His law and that He will in no wise clear the guilty. They learn now that Christ identifies His interest with that of His suffering people; and they feel the force of His own words: "Inasmuch as ye have done it unto one of the least of these My brethren, ye have done it unto Me." Matthew 25:40. (*Great Controversy*, p. 668).

In the same inspired book is recorded the final reference to Jerusalem:

> There is the New Jerusalem, the metropolis of the glorified new earth, "a crown of glory in the hand of the Lord, and a royal diadem in the hand of thy God." "Her light was like unto a stone most precious, even like a jasper stone, clear as crystal." "The nations of them which are saved shall walk in the light of it: and the kings of the earth do bring their glory and honor into it." Saith the Lord: "I will rejoice in Jerusalem, and joy in My people." "The tabernacle of God is with men, and He will dwell with them, and they shall be His people, and God Himself shall be with them, and be their God." Isaiah 62:3; Revelation 21:11, 24; Isaiah 65:19; Revelation 21:3.
>
> In the City of God "there shall be no night." None will need or desire repose. There will be no weariness in doing the will of God and offering praise to His name. We shall ever feel the freshness of the morning and shall ever be far from its close. "And they need no candle, neither light of the sun; for the Lord God giveth them light." Revelation 22:5. The light of the sun will be superseded by a radiance which is not painfully dazzling, yet which immeasurably surpasses the brightness of our noontide. The glory of God and the Lamb floods the Holy City with unfading light. The redeemed walk in the sunless glory of perpetual day. (*Ibid*, p. 676).

Oh Jerusalem! Jerusalem! the home of the redeemed – the glory of our God, the site of His throne, established eternally in glory. Does not each reader thirst for Jerusalem? This is the eternal reward of God's grace. This grace is unmerited and free, yet in order to receive it, it costs our all for it is bestowed by the Pearl of Great Price.

> The day of God's vengeance is just upon us. The seal of God will be placed upon the foreheads of those only who sigh and cry for the abominations done in the land. Those who link in sympathy with the world are eating and drinking with the drunken and will surely be destroyed with the workers of iniquity. "The eyes of the Lord are over the righteous, and His ears are open unto their prayers: but the face of the Lord is against them that do evil."
> (*Testimonies for the Church*, Vol. 5, p. 212).

> Courage, fortitude, faith, and implicit trust in God's power to save do not come in a moment. These heavenly graces are acquired by the experience of years. By a life of holy endeavor and firm adherence to the right the children of God were sealing their destiny. (*Ibid*, p. 213).

> Not one of us will ever receive the seal of God while our characters have one spot or stain upon them. It is left with us to remedy the defects in our characters, to cleanse the soul temple of every defilement. Then the latter rain will fall upon us as the early rain fell upon the disciples on the Day of Pentecost. (*Ibid*, p. 214).

> It is now that we must keep ourselves and our children unspotted from the world. It is now that we must wash our robes of character and make them white in the blood of the Lamb. It is now that we must overcome pride, passion, and spiritual slothfulness. It is now that we must awake and make determined effort for symmetry of character. "Today if ye will hear His voice, harden not your hearts."
> (*Ibid*, pp. 215, 216).

Those who are distrustful of self, who are humbling themselves before God and purifying their souls by obeying the truth these are receiving the heavenly mold and preparing for the seal of God in their foreheads. When the decree goes forth and the stamp is impressed, their character will remain pure and spotless for eternity.

Now is the time to prepare. The seal of God will never be placed upon the forehead of an impure man or woman. It will never be placed upon the forehead of the ambitious, world-loving man or woman. It will never be placed upon the forehead of men or women of false tongues or deceitful hearts. All who receive the seal must be without spot before God –candidates for heaven. Go forward, my brethren and sisters. I can only write briefly upon these points at this time, merely calling your attention to the necessity of preparation. Search the Scriptures for yourselves, that you may understand the fearful solemnity of the present hour.
(*Ibid*, p. 216).

46 The T-Junction

God's holy church, the church which in tender love He calls to be the one object of His supreme regard, the church to which He entrusted the depository of His holy law and the three angels' and loud cry messages, has traveled a road which now has entered a T-Junction. This is the junction of decision.

For most workers in the church organization the vital decision of the direction to turn appears to have been settled. This majority has taken the left-hand turn leading to a city called the Omega of Apostasy. Of this tragic fact there can be no valid denial, for we now see:

1. Under a guise of reformatory faith the organization has given "up the doctrines which stand as the pillars of our faith";
2. It has engaged in "a process of reorganization";
3. "The principles of truth that God in His wisdom has given to the remnant church [have been] discarded";
4. "Our religion [has been] changed";
5. "The fundamental principles that have sustained the work for the last [one hundred and sixty years have been] accounted as error";
6. "A new organization [has been] established";
7. "Books of a new order [continue to be] written" and published;
8. "A system of intellectual philosophy [has been] introduced";
9. "The Sabbath, of course, [is] lightly regarded";
10. "As also [is the] God who created it";
11. "Nothing [is] allowed to stand in the way of the new movement";
12. While "the leaders ... teach that virtue is better than vice, but God being removed, they [have] put their dependence on human power, which, without God, is worthless." (Compare *Selected Messages*, Vol. 1, pp. 204, 205).

It cannot be far distant that,

> storm and tempest [will] sweep away the structure. (*Ibid*, p. 205),

for surely the outpouring of the latter rain is near.

> Under the showers of the latter rain the inventions of man, the human machinery, will at times be swept away, the boundary of man's authority will be as broken reeds, and the Holy Spirit will speak through the living, human agent, with convincing power. No one then will watch to see if the sentences are well rounded off, if the grammar is faultless. The living water will flow in God's own channels. (*Ibid*, Vol. 2, pp. 58, 59).

God graciously has made full provision for an alternative road. Only if we are hard-nosed opponents of the truth of God need we take the left-hand turn at the T-Junction. For those of such a determined bent of mind we would warn of Sister White's vision.

> I cried to God to spare His people, some of whom were fainting and dying. Then I saw that the judgments of the Almighty were speedily coming, and I begged of the angel to speak in his language to the people. Said he, "All the thunders and lightnings of Mount Sinai would not move those who will not be moved by the plain truths of the Word of God, neither would an angel's message awake them.
>
> (*Early Writings*, p. 51).

We remind our fellow brethren in the ministry that while many Laodicean laypeople will fawn over them now and flatter their "understanding and loving" failure to rebuke sin and worldliness, another day is nigh at hand when these very souls, whom these ministers have destroyed, will display another attitude toward them. After the close of probation these flatterers will turn upon these ministers with a terrible ferocity and hate.

> The people turned upon their ministers with bitter hate and reproached them, saying, "You have not warned us. You told us that all the world was to be converted, and cried, Peace, peace, to quiet every fear that was aroused. You have not told us of this hour; and those who warned us of it you declared to be fanatics and evil men, who would ruin us." But I saw that the ministers did not escape the wrath of God. Their suffering was tenfold greater than that of their people.
>
> (*Early Writings*, p. 282).

In concluding this book we quote a letter written almost thirty years ago by Pastor James Winston Kent (1890-1983), in our judgment the greatest Seventh-day Adventist orator we have ever heard. He was successively President of the North New South Wales, Western Australian and South Australian Conferences and earlier a most successful evangelist. He was the evangelist who was used of the Holy Spirit to bring the Seventh-day Adventist truth to a young man in Christchurch, New Zealand in the 1920's. That young man, George Burnside, became the most successful evangelist in the South Pacific Division. Pastor Burnside told us that he only went to the theater to hear Pr. Kent one Sunday because he was bored with nothing else to do. Skeptical of Christianity and unimpressed with clerics whom he regarded as namby-pambies, he nevertheless decided to enter the theater in order to while away his Sunday afternoon.

Many adjectives could be used to describe Pastor Kent, but namby-pamby was decidedly not one of them. He was a man's man in every respect! Pastor Kent's subject was the Second Coming of Christ. So powerful and convincing was his presentation that the nineteen-year-old George Burnside was in a state of the terror of the lost at its conclusion. Pastor Burnside described his reaction to us. "I thought the Second Coming would rush in through the back door of the theater at any moment, and I was lost!"

Pastor Kent's letter certified that the evil consequences of the New Theology were well understood before 1975. He was eighty-five years of age when he wrote this letter. His passion for the old and true faith is evident. His oratorical skills were clearly expressed in this written response to the President of the Australasian Division, Pastor Robert Frame, President 1970-1976.

We include this letter for it is of great historical value. It demonstrates that Pastor J. W. Kent and his band of faithful pastors of that era perceptively saw the results of the course upon which our church had even by then chosen to follow. We see the same misrepresentation of the motives which continue to be leveled by leadership in order to besmirch the reputations of all ministers and laypeople standing in defense of truth and righteousness.

For his fidelity Pastor Kent, along with Past George Burnside (1908-1994), who was posthumously declared in the South Pacific *Record* to be the South Pacific Division's most successful evangelist, were in writing banned from the pulpits of the Greater Sydney Conference. A new generation of church administrators possesses no greater tolerance of preachers of truth today. But the Elijah message, God's pure call to truth and righteousness within His church, will be heard by every church member within the South Pacific Division. Our loving God will not afford a lesser opportunity to His professed people to receive the incomparable rewards of the full and pure acceptance of His sacrifice which He provides through the Three Angels' Messages to those outside the profession of His faith. Please read Pastor Kent's letter with due attention and care.

Dear Pastor Frame,

Inasmuch as I have no pleasure at all in writing this letter to you, but rather the reverse, I earnestly desire that you would remember that I hold you personally in the highest esteem and I am strictly loyal to your administration. But I feel that I have a duty that I must discharge, but I do it with the above sentiments possessing me wholly.

Your recent letter to Brother [John B] Keith [former President of both the Coral Sea Union Mission and the Trans-Australia Union Conference] and me amazed and perplexed me. Inter alia, you say: "Having said that, I must inform you brethren that the representative group with whom I discussed your letter, Brother Kent, expressed concern over the way these matters of which you wrote were drawn to your attention. They agreed unanimously that it is a dangerous departure from time-honoured organisational procedure to study a report from a self-appointed group which met without the knowledge and counsel of leadership." Further, we are warned against being a pressure group.

Whether your representative group intended it or not, we take that as an offensive judgment, so underserved by a humble request for enlightenment and help from our leaders. The guide lines left with you which were intended only for our gathering, contradict that judgment. I quote therefrom: "And further, we must remember that we are enquiring from men whom God has, through the vote of

The T-Junction

His church, entrusted with the safeguarding of the faith once delivered to the saints. Therefore our enquiries should be fraught with LOYAL COURTEOUS SINCERITY." (Emphasis this letter only).

Surely, that does not sound like a pressure group! As a matter of fact we had not the remotest intention of exerting any pressure. Not an impulse of such even rippled through our gathering.

Your letter also says that the representative group was concerned over the way the matters of which I wrote reached me. Brother Frame, I am not conscious of writing anything about these matters. What I did write were guide lines intended solely for our group contemplating a meeting of enquiry from our leaders, with justification for doing so. No pressure group was contemplated or intended. Just to know where we were tending as a church doctrinally. But the representative group judged differently. They read into these guide lines something that was not there. With due courtesy I would remind them that Scripture hath it: "He that answereth a matter before he heareth it, it is folly and shame unto him." Prov. 18:13. Had they agreed to hear us, then you would have had no need to write to us as you did. We were simply seeking information from within which is not available from without, and we were going to the right place in the right way in order to get it.

You well know, Brother Frame, that it is my invariable practice to go to leadership to solve problems, instead of discussing them down the line of gossip.

Another thing that stung me was that your advisers classify us an unlawful assembly. Your letter tells us that they "Expressed concern over the way these matters about which you wrote were drawn to your attention." I would to the dear Lord that this were really so; for I obtained my information from eye-catching displayed articles in the Signs of the Times, and from the Ministry. Like a trumpet blast of invasion on our doctrinal heritage, these articles aroused me from my retirement bed. I rubbed my ageing eyes in astonishment at what I read. I'll come back to this later.

In the next sentence, you write: "They" – your panel of advisers – "agreed unanimously that it is a dangerous departure from time-honoured organizational procedure to study a report from a self-appointed group which met without the knowledge and counsel of leadership." May I ask, Where is the law or directive that we have infringed? I know of none, and I used to be rather familiar with conference procedures and the Church's by-laws. God forbid that we should ever come to the time when erstwhile trusted ministers cannot come together to study the old sacred paths trodden by their once youthful feet without engendering suspicion from current leadership. Surely, Brother Frame, your Council is not afraid of its retired ministry to whom under God, they owe so much. "A self-appointed group which met without the knowledge and counsel of leadership" you write. In answer we would say, we met, it is true, but we acquainted you with our meeting which was convened to ask counsel of our leaders, and what did we get? Misunderstanding and offensive direction. I speak as a man, but nevertheless kindly. And further, we get this from your advisers: you infer our group is presumed to be composed of pressure people and of individuals with personal or doctrinal bias in attempting to gain their objectives.

Brother Frame, such a judgment as that imposes a real strain on goodwill and charity. It is so utterly wrong. We are not pressure people, and we had no intention of exerting any. No doctrinal bias save for the doctrine of God contained in the revelation of The Word, and emphasized by the Spirit of Prophecy and our church fathers. We are not agitators, neither are we schismatics nor heresy hunters. Just a body of troubled men standing by the old pillars of our faith, seeking from their leaders whether there is any change of what is written thereon. Thankful of heart as we met together that we are not under a Papal Flag, and neither in Russia where permission for such gatherings must be sought, only to be denied.

The brethren of your panel are concerned, also, about the personal campaign which they misread into our gathering. We are not interested in that at all. No personal campaign possesses us, or even comes into our thinking. We are concerned with Truth and its principles, not persons. We do not wish to enquire about Brother Ford. The Brethren introduced his name into this discussion. We did not. Our guide lines plainly told them that "we are not here to downgrade anyone". Personally, we love Brother Ford. But with apologies to Shakespeare, We do not love Ford the less, but Truth the more. We know of the important position he holds, and we pray that he may ever fill it with the approval of his God. Nevertheless, it is not the brand on a horse that makes him travel, but rather the stuff of which he is made. More to the point is the warning of the Servant of the Lord that many a star which we have admired for its brilliance will go out in utter darkness.

There is something else that perplexed me in your letter. Instead of going to you, as our leader, and your officers, together with other representative leaders to clarify our troubled thinking, which was our expressed request made to you, the leading Brethren advised us to go to the Biblical Research Committee. Now, if I mistake not this committee is the former New Light Committee with which in my day, I was quite familiar. This committee set up to take care of instruction given to us by the beloved Servant of the Lord was, as its name suggests, for those who had new or additional ideas on established doctrine. They were not to preach these ideas or disseminate them in any way among the Flock. They were to bring them to a committee composed of leadership and experienced ministers. The verdict of such a committee was final. To this every loyal Truth lover must agree. And rightly so. It was mandatory.

But, my dear Brother Frame, this does not apply to us. We are advancing no new theories. We are standing by the old Pillars of our Faith, which we have taught to hundreds, yes, thousands of converts. The Faith once delivered wholly possesses us. If it does not sound irritable, I would exclaim, What in the world are the Brethren thinking about when they tender us such advice? I ask with kindly concern. Those who are allowing a passing cloud of Futurism to obscure what is written into the Pillars of our Faith – these are the ones that need to do that. Had they done so, and had the Biblical Research Committee done its duty, then I would not be "burning the midnight oil" in order to write this letter to my beloved Leader tonight.

There is no doubt that Brother Ford has presented something entirely new to Adventist teaching in his articles in the Signs of the Times and the Ministry. As a result, the Editorial Department of the Ministry screened him in order to ascertain whether he was still a Fundamentalist, vide The Ministry, Oct 1974. The said department says also: "Doctor Ford is emphasising a new application of verses 24-27 of Dan. 9." In the light of what I have written above on the New Light Committee, why did not Brother Ford submit his new application to the Biblical Research Committee for examination and decision? I look for an answer to this from your panel of advisers. That is why we asked for a meeting with our leaders. This is part of our problem. There are other problems to which the representative leaders may have a satisfactory answer that would set our minds at rest. Historicism's teaching of the 70th week [of Daniel 9:24] and related doctrines, based on complete fulfilment at the time of the cross taught and supported by the Spirit of Prophecy and the founding Fathers of the Advent Faith, permits no variation whatsoever in its confrontation with Brethrenism's Futuristic teaching of the said 70th week. Is this still right?

Strange it is that those who are content with the light as it was from the beginning are requested to go with fettered hands before the New Light Committee, while those who are bringing in darkness are left at large.

The Panel may consider us an unauthorised assembly of pressure group men, divested of authority and leadership supervision, but our conviction is that we are humbly following the direction of the Lord through His Servant, when He says: "My message to you is: 'No longer consent to listen without protest to the perversion of truth'." 1.SM. p. 196.

In conclusion, permit me, Brother Frame, to assure you that I am wholly responsible for this letter, while extending to you my personal regards, loyalty to your leadership, and daily prayers for your divine guidance.

Sincerely yours,

J. W. Kent.

(Letter written by Pastor J. W. Kent to Pastor Robert Frame, President of the Australasian Division, dated May 7, 1975).

Here we see the departure from the faith in the South Pacific Division. The following year, on February 3, 4, 1976, sixteen men, led by Pastor J. W. Kent, took Dr. Ford before the Division Biblical Research Committee. Russell was in this group. It was a window of opportunity for the Division, but that moment passed. These elderly pastors demonstrated their unfailing fidelity to God's truth. But sadly the Committee released its judgment on the side of error:

> WHEREAS: The Biblical Research Institute has on two occasions, February 3, 1976, at Avondale College, and February 4, 1976, at the office of the Australasian Division, heard a plea of a number of senior ministers who have expressed their concern about the teaching of theology at Avondale College, particularly in the area of the Sanctuary, the Age of the Earth, and Inspiration, it now desires to present its findings to the administration of the Australasian Division as follows:
>
> 1. That the Theology Department at Avondale is committed to generally accepted, moderate Seventh-day Adventist doctrinal positions and that Dr. Desmond Ford ably demonstrated that such stances as he takes which appear to diverge from what some senior men hold as 'Present Truth' can be justified by reference to majority positions taken by current Seventh-day Adventist authors and scholars.
>
> 2. The senior ministers (as represented by their speakers) were somewhat unaware of the movements in Adventist thought and the style of doctrinal presentation in recent years, a fact which explains their reaction to some contemporary expositions.
>
> 3. That it expresses its sustained confidence in Avondale College and its Theological Faculty, but it is of the view that certain counsel should be appropriately tendered to the College administration:
>
>   a. That the Theological Department and the ministry in the field communicate actively on the exposition of Adventist doctrine in terms which can be understood by the Church generally.
>
>   b. That an even stronger and positive emphasis in the classroom on the fundamental truths of the Church be maintained.
>
>   c. That all College lecturers continue to be careful to emphasize the Bible as the inspired Word of God and the source of all truth and be ever mindful that the students they teach are working at undergraduate level.
>
> 4. That it draws attention to and reaffirms the guidelines already established that all material prepared by the ministry or by members of the Avondale College faculty which may be of a controversial nature theologically (other than material normally used within the College for regular instruction) should not be distributed unless approved by the Institute. (Notice of the action of the Australasian Division Biblical Research Institution on file at *The Remnant Herald* Office. All parenthesis in the original).

We record the names of the eleven faithful pastors and five laymen who stood for truth on that occasion.

1. Pastor Ormond Anderson, retired evangelist, departmental director, college Bible teacher and missionary to the Middle East.
2. Pastor Frank Basham, retired pastor and evangelist.
3. Pastor Frank Breaden, retired pastor and evangelist.
4. Pastor George Burnside, retired evangelist and former Australasian Division ministerial secretary.
5. Dr. John Clifford, Melbourne physician; secretary, Committee of Concerned Laymen.
6. Pastor Ronald Heggie, retired Mission president and church pastor.
7. Pastor Arthur Jacobson, retired pastor and Mission president.
8. Pastor Llewellyn Jones, retired evangelist and Conference Departmental director.
9. Pastor John Keith, retired Union Conference president and Union Mission president.
10. Pastor James Kent, retired Conference president and leading evangelist.
11. Pastor Arthur Knight, retired evangelist, youth leader and hospital chaplain.
12. Brother Raglan Marks, Cooranbong businessman.
13. Pastor Elwyn Martin, retired evangelist and missionary.
14. Brother Harold Reid, Melbourne engineer, chairman of the Committee of Concerned Laymen.
15. Dr. Russell Standish, Melbourne physician.
16. Brother Frederick Williams, retired Sydney businessman.

All eleven ordained pastors are now dead. Pastor O. K. Anderson (1905-2001) was the last to die and the only one to live into the twenty-first century. Russell was not ordained until almost five years later, on December 6, 1980. He, along with Dr. John Clifford and Brother Harold Reid are the only survivors of the group.

Sixteen of the twenty selected by the Division to hear the matter still survive. We list the names of those who represented the Australasian Division at the meetings.

1. Pastor Cyrus Adams, president, Tasmanian Conference.
2. Pastor Donald Bain, Australasian Division health director.
3. Pastor Clive Barritt, president, Victorian Conference.
4. *Pastor Clem Christian, president, South New Zealand Conference.
5. Dr. Desmond Ford, Chairman, Theology Dept., Avondale College.
6. Pastor Robert Frame, Australasian Division president.
7. Pastor Alfred Jorgensen, Australasian Division field secretary.
8. Pastor Claude Judd, president, Trans-Tasman Union Conference.
9. Dr. Eric Magnusson, president, Avondale College.
10. Pastor Rex Moe, president, Western Australian Conference.
11. *Pastor Laurence Naden, retired Australasian Division president.
12. *Pastor Keith Parmenter, Australasian Division secretary.
13. Pastor Robert Parr, editor, Australasian Signs of the Times.

14. Pastor Arthur Patrick, Theology Dept., Avondale College.
15. Dr. Alwyn Salom, pastor, Wahroonga Church.
16. Pastor Raymond Stanley, ministerial secretary, Australasian Division.
17. Pastor Athal Tolhurst, president, North New South Wales Conference.
18. Pastor Leonard Tolhurst, Theology Dept., Avondale College.
19. *Pastor Stewart Uttley, president, Trans-Australian Union Conference.
20. Dr. Norman Young, Theology Dept., Avondale College.

* Deceased

God has always had men who not only believed the truth but who also proclaimed it with boldness. Among these were two who have been mentioned previously: Pastor George Burnside and Pastor J. W. Kent. These men had read Dr. Ford's Ph.D. thesis submitted to the University of Manchester, England, and they had noted that what Dr. Ford had written was in direct contradiction to the Spirit of Prophecy on the matter of the man of sin. Thus they published a paper entitled, *Dr. D. Ford Verses E. G. White on the Vital Subject of the Man of Sin*. These men stated, "May God give every lover of the Advent Message grace to continually lift voice, pen, means and influence, in combating this enemy of truth."

In his thesis Dr. Ford had asserted that the anti-Christ would "appear only at the end of time." He also stated that the anti-Christ "belongs to the future and not to history." (Both of these quotations appeared in *Dr. D. Ford Versus E. G. White on the vital Subject of the Man of Sin*.) Clearly, Dr. Ford was in gross error, having succumbed to the Plymouth Brethren and Jesuit Futuristic interpretation of prophecy, and therefore, having discounted the inspiration-based, historicist interpretation of prophecy as confirmed by the Spirit of Prophecy. Dr. Ford also had clearly stated that the papal succession did not represent the power of anti-Christ.

For warning God's people concerning this matter, Pastors Kent and Burnside were banned from the pulpit. The ministers of the Greater Sydney Conference received the following letter:

> Considerable anguish has been caused in the Conference by the circulation of an anonymous document entitled, 'The Man of Sin.' Pastor J. W. Kent states that he and Pastor Burnside are responsible for the document. It has apparently been placed in the hands of some retired ministers and possibly some laymen at Cooranbong, who have assisted in its circulation. The document is unscholarly, unethical and seriously misrepresents Dr. Desmond Ford. The conclusions drawn in the document are totally invalid and the spirit of it certainly not good. We consider that while this document is in circulation, Pastors J. W. Kent and G. Burnside should not occupy the pulpit in our Conference churches, and we are therefore asking you not to list them for preaching appointments.
>
> (Letter written by Pastor Kenneth Bullock,
> President of the Greater Sydney Conference, to ministers,
> Great Sydney Conference, dated December 18, 1978).

No act could have more clearly demonstrated the dangers of the New Theology than the banning of an 86-year-old pastor, who had been one of the leading evangelists in the Australasian Division and three times Conference president; and another man in his seventies, who had been one of the most successful evangelists this denomination has known within the Australasian Division. So many people in Australia rose up and called these men blessed that it was inevitable that this action left good men and women aghast.

The Conference leadership was deluged with protests, and very shortly the president telephoned the two men concerned and suggested that the ban on their preaching had been lifted. However, Pastor Kent very properly stated that the ban had been placed in writing and distributed to the ministry of the Conference, and he believed that the only proper course for its lifting was to follow a similar procedure. This request was never implemented.

What we now see in the South Pacific Division are the dismal results of gross rejection of the faith. Russell presented one of the papers at that conference. Not surprisingly his paper defended the approximately six-thousand years history of this earth. He still possesses that paper. Unlike current conferences, these presentations were not concealed by those who made them. Other papers were presented by Pastor Basham and Dr. John Clifford (both on Righteousness by Faith), Pastor Burnside (the Sanctuary Message), and Pastor Breaden, (The Inerrancy of Scripture). Our book *The Gathering Storm and The Storm Bursts*, published in 1985 by Hartland Publications, remains the sole detailed history of the early days of the advent of the New Theology into our midst.

But praise God He will safely take His Seventh-day Adventist faithful believers to their heavenly home. His pure truth will be proclaimed with latter rain power and Christ's blood will assuredly atone for His faithful people.

In the meantime remember the words of God's servant.

> There [in heaven] all who have wrought with unselfish spirit will behold the fruit of their labors. The outworking of every right principle and noble deed will be seen. Something of this we see here. But how little of the result of the world's noblest work is in this life manifest to the doer! How many toil unselfishly and unweariedly for those who pass beyond their reach and knowledge!
>
> (*Education*, p. 305, 306).

In that group will be Sister White and all faithful witnesses to God's truth.

When despondency over the state of our beloved church threatens to overwhelm us, we turn our thoughts to Christ's parallel experience, of which Sister White wrote in our dear homeland, Australia, in Manuscript 31a, March 7, 1898:

> But those who had been entrusted with the oracles of God, that they might be faithful expositors of the Scriptures, rejected and denied the Teacher sent from heaven. Christ saw that their spirit and principles were entirely contrary to the Scriptures. He saw that the Word of God was misinterpreted and misapplied. He

saw how difficult it would be to instruct the people to read the Scriptures correctly, when their teachers read them in the light of their perverted judgment. What could He do to soften and subdue their hearts? This was the burden of His prayer. (*The Upward Look*, p. 80).

We are then comforted by the thought and assurance that He, today, still takes our burden as His burden and provides us with the joy of the blessed hope.

We pray with deep earnestness that the direct words of this book will cause each reader to turn right at the T-Junction and see what the prophet of the end time saw.

> I then beheld the beauty and loveliness of Jesus. His robe was whiter than the whitest white. No language can describe His glory and exalted loveliness. All, all who keep the commandments of God, will enter in through the gates into the city and have right to the tree of life and ever be in the presence of the lovely Jesus, whose countenance shines brighter than the sun at noonday.
>
> (*Early Writings*, p. 51).

May Christ's sweet blessings, His anodyne Spirit, and His saving grace rest in your hearts and may your walk be along the road to the city called the New Jerusalem.

INDEXES
1. Scriptural Index
2. Spirit of Prophecy Index
3. Index of Personalities
4. Books Authored By Colin and Russell Standish

Scriptural Index

Genesis
Chapter 1	364, 365, 367
Chapters 1, 2	116, 117 123, 356
Chapters 1-3	362
Chapters 1-11	129
1:1	118, 120, 310
1:1, 2	116, 117, 122
1:2	121
1:2 - 2:4	366
1:3	116, 117, 121
1:14-19	118
1:16	118
1:17	118
1:26	228
1:29, 30	126
2:7	120
2:7, 19, 21, 22	121
2:16, 17	99
2:19	120
2:21, 22	120
3:1-5	99
6:4	230
6:5, 6	231
7:6	231
7:8	299
7:11	232
8:13	232
10:10	371
11:10-17	232
11:12	232

Exodus
20:8	310, 355
20:10	310
20:9, 10	308
20:11	116, 126
20:13	305
22:31	355
23:19	321
31:16, 17	116
31:17	116, 120

Leviticus
7:26	127
11:10	328
14:6	127
16:29, 31	68
17:11	127
23:27, 32	68

Numbers
29:7	68

Deuteronomy
22:6, 7	127
28:1, 2	372
28:1, 7, 15, 25	335
28:7	371
28:15, 25	372

Joshua
6:21	345

2 Samuel
6:6	339
6:7	339

1 Kings
18:19	7
18:21	7
19:18	7

1 Chronicles
13:10	339
16:29	356

2 Chronicles
20:20	185, 198, 235
20:21	356

Nehemiah
13:15-17	308

Job
38:7	118
38:41	127

Psalms
22:1-8	61
29:2	356
33:6-9	121
34:7	280
35:19	171
50:11	127
63:4	171
66:18	282
91:1-7	281
113:5, 6	121
137:8, 9	346
147:9	127
148:5	121

Proverbs
18:13	381

Isaiah
1:5	313
1:9	54, 215, 302, 368
2:22	225
5:1	359
8:12, 13	302
8:13-15	303
8:16	303
8:19	102
8:20	102
9:1, 2	171
10:22	61
28:15-18	304
40:1-5	307
40:3-5	359
53:4	171
55:8	121
55:8, 9	330
56:10-12	244
59:14	283
62:3	376
65:19	376

Jeremiah
3:1	305
3:1-7	373
17:5	225
26:1-19	372
42:10, 13, 15	79
42:18	79
50:24	182
51:30	182
51:31, 32	182

Ezekiel
8:5, 10-12, 14, 16	373
9:4	371

Daniel
Chapter 7	65, 71, 290, 296
Chapter 8	67, 71, 290, 296
Chapter 12	290, 296
5:1-4, 30	182
7:9-14	64
7:14, 18, 27	64
7:25	63
8:13, 14	69
8:14	64, 65, 68, 69, 70
9:24-27	383
9:25	69
9:27	243

Nahum
3:7	335

Zephaniah
2:13	335

Scriptural Index

Malachi
4:1	43

Matthew
Chapter 7	93
Chapter 15	321
Chapter 24	290
4:12-16	171
6:26	127
7:16	93
7:20	101
8:16, 17	171
8:28	82
11:11	4
13:27, 28	228
14:26	321
15:38	321
19:16, 17	38
20:28	63
20:29	84
20:29, 30	83
20:30	84
20:33	85
20:34	85
24:15	67, 243
25:40	376
25:41-46	110
26:34	81
26:75	81
28:2	82

Mark
5:2	83
5:9	83
6:25	6
6:44	321
10:18	85
10:46, 47	83, 84
10:47, 48	84
14:30	81
14:68	81
15:34	61
16:5	82

Luke
3:11-14	37
7:28	4
8:27	83
8:30	83
9:14	321
10:25-28	37
12:24	127
12:46-48	318
16:13	91
16:31	336
18:8	93
18:35	84
18:35-38; 19:1	83
18:37	84
18:39	85
18:41	84
20:60	81
22:34	81
24:4	82
24:25	22
24:27	22

John
1:14	35
12:42, 43	246
13:38	81
14:15	281, 357
15:23-25	171
16:13	344
18:27	81
20:11, 12	82

Acts
7:22-24	172
17:28	185, 349
19:1-5	37
24:25	219

Romans
5:12	125
6:22	356
8:1	68
8:1 NIV	68

9:27	61	3:10	109
9:27-29	54, 219, 303		
9:30-33	304	**1 Timothy**	
13:11	262	4:1, 2	29
		4:1-5	318
1 Corinthians		4:6, 16	38
1:14, 15	101	6:1, 3-5	39
1:14-16	347, 302		
6:4	245	**2 Timothy**	
11:7, 8	80	3:1-5	29
11:8, 9	80	3:16	35, 39, 347
13:12 (NIV)	59	3:16, 17	36, 103
14:34	80	4:3, 4	28
15:33	349		
16:15	347	**Titus**	
16:17	347	1:12	349
		1:9	39
2 Corinthians		2:1, 7, 10	39
4:4	12		
4:7	12	**Hebrews**	
6:2	219	4:15	355
7:1	247	7:25	318
11:2	305	11:19	172
12:9	38		
		James	
Galatians		2:10	306
6:7	92		
		1 Peter	
Ephesians		2:6-8	304
4:11-18	368	2:9-12	305
4:14	93, 247	5:8	4
Colossians		**2 Peter**	
1:5, 6	344	1:16-21	307
1:23	344	1:19	70
		1:19-21	343
1 Thessalonians		3:9	286
4:17	335		
5:5	262	**1 John**	
5:21, 22 (NIV)	58	Chapter 2	290
		Chapter 4	290
2 Thessalonians		2:3-6	301
Chapter 2	290	3:2-9	301
2:13	247	3:6, 9	247

2 John

Chapter — 290

3 John

Chapter — 124

Jude

1:14, 15 — 85, 172
1:24 — 281, 309

Revelation

Book — 124
Chapter 11 — 296
Chapter 12 — 290, 296
Chapter 13 — 71, 261, 282, 283, 285, 290, 296, 298
Chapter 14 — 290
Chapter 17 — 71, 190, 191, 290
Chapter 18 — 290
Chapter 19 — 290
3:14-22 — 53
3:21 (RSV) — 52
5:6 — 63
7:1 — 285
7:1-3 — 280
7:2, 3 — 286, 310
12:9 — 305
12:14 — 308
12:17 — 305, 306
13:3 — 63, 63 261
13:5-7 — 63
13:11-18 — 261
13:15-17 — 282, 284, 292
13:17 — 283, 285
14:6-12 — 241
14:7 — 310
14:12 — 246, 248, 285
14:12 (RSV) — 52
17:4-6, 18 — 191, 192
18:21 — 376
19:10 — 306, 307
20:2 — 305
21:3 — 376
21:10, 11 — 376
21:11, 24 — 376
22:10 — 52
22:11 — 52, 248, 309

Spirit of Prophecy Index

Acts of the Apostles
83, 84	8
593	333

Broadside
Jan. 31, 1849	332

Child Guidance
528	89

Christ's Object Lessons
69	332
120	333

Colporteur Ministry
128	193
130	193

Confrontation
14	100

Counsels to Parents, Teachers & Students
66	229

Counsels to Writers and Editors
17	352
19	352
20	352
21	352

Desire of Ages
59, 60	350
101	337
221, 222	6, 8
283	310, 355
337	83
555, 556	53
711, 712	82
788, 789	82

Education
305, 306	387

Evangelism
257	316
362	115
444	84
510	357
553	84
616	244

Early Writings
38	286
39, 40	97
42	326
51	379, 388
55	66
64, 67	332
124, 125	92
184	233
251	66
282	246, 317, 379

Fundamentals of Christian Education
63	328
84, 85	138

Gospel Workers
302	40

Great Controversy
v	35, 124, 234
v, vi	35
vi	35, 36
vi, vii	36
vii	36, 104
ix	202

x-xii	74	676	376
xi	153		
xi, xii	153, 194	**Health Reformer**	
xii	46	July, 1867	322
45	9	Jan, 1871	322
50	157	Oct. 1, 1871	322
50 [1888]	157		
54	63	**Letters**	
65	144, 157	12, 1890	41
65 [1888]	157	4, 1896	233
65, 66	142	175, 1896	231
97, 119	44	98a, 1897	4
100	150	65 1898	231
100, 101	100, 146, 149	170, 1906	329
177	48		
249	103	**Life Sketches**	
266	63, 143	468, 469	168
272	158		
272 [1888]	140, 158	**Manuscripts**	
273	158	No. 29, 1886	223
273 [1888]	158	No. 25, 1890	140
286, 287	159	No. 31a, 1898	387
286, 287 [1888]	159	No. 66, 1899	244
287, 288	159		
287, 288 [1888]	159	**Ministry of Healing**	
306	160	107	84
306 [1888]	160	313	222
381	190	327	185, 223
381 [1888]	190	446	357
382	191		
382 [1888]	191, 192	**My Life Today**	
383	190	25	104
383 [1888]	190		
400	69	**Patriarchs and Prophets**	
439	143	44	120
489, 490	68	45	231
564	292	62	125, 127
571	298	112	121
578, 579 [1888]	261	117	75
579	63	366	307
583	356	492	347
606	349	705	340
644	231	706	340
668	376		

Prophets and Kings

531	181

Review and Herald

June 11, 1861	325
Dec. 26, 1882	327
Jan. 5, 1886	336, 338, 339, 341, 342
Oct. 16, 1900	346
Dec. 10, 1903	233
June 14, 1906	328
August 21, 1919	163
Feb 21, 1980	53

Selected Messages, Vol. 1

48	40, 369
50, 51	187
59-73	324
62	324
63	324
63, 64	325
64	325
68	332
74	324
122	186
196	383
197	91
204, 205	253, 378
205	311, 317, 378
410	359
416	104

Selected Messages, Vol. 2

36	357
58	318
58, 59	317, 378
78	369
288	228
345	357
371	302
416	48

Selected Messages, Vol. 3

89	166
90, 91	168
92	165
92, 93	166
93	168
112	182
433, 465	182
348, 349	5
435	154, 155
435, 436	155
436	74, 156
437	195
439	196
443	161
443, 444	195

SDA Bible Commentary
Vol. 1

1086	228
1089	231

Vol. 2

995	346

Vol. 4

1141, 1142	302

Vol. 5

1111	84
1139, 1140	330

Vol. 6

1115, 1116	330

Signs of the Times

April 14, 1881	346
Mar 2, 1882	328
Feb. 22, 1883	327
Mar. 21, 1906	104

Sketches from the Life of Paul

Book	183

Sons and Daughters of God

126	84
325	350

Special Testimonies in Education
229

Special Testimonies to Ministers and Workers - Series A
No. 7, 36-41   201

Special Testimonies to Ministers and Workers - Series B, No. 2
91

Spirit of Prophecy
Vol. 1
69	197
91	74
266	76

Vol. 4
Chapter 27	194
191	140
232, 233	193
233	192
380	262
381	263
382	268
382, 383	269
387, 388	269
405	260
407	279
407, 408	280
408	282

Spiritual Gifts
Vol. 1
70	233

Vol. 2
83	96
202	84

Vol. 3
34	231
64	197, 227
75	197, 228
96	74
301	75

Vol. 4a
120	231
128	223

Steps to Christ
112, 113	187

Story of Redemption
13, 14	119
19, 20	119
21	231
48	307
66	341
72	75
337	103

Testimonies to Ministers
114	316
135, 136	117
136	121, 128
364	357
472-475	161, 194

Testimonies for the Church
Vol. 1
116	331
131, 132	334
187	52
205	329
206, 207	329
207	331
259	78
321	214
426-433	179
429, 430	179
486	201
496, 497	357
713	331

Vol. 2			
96	330	456	215
392	220, 223	525	29
402	223	655, 656	39
462	350	675	343

Vol. 3		Vol. 6	
32	84	266	84
138, 139	231	355	89
280, 281	7	406-407	89
281	9	407	89, 90
		450	333

Vol. 4		Vol. 7	
178	84	137	201
355	84	181	357
435	328	203	350
653	229		

Vol. 5		Vol. 8	
	223	5	92
91	309, 342, 353, 369	26	333
98	374, 375	115, 116	333
209	375	258, 259	117, 120
209, 210	374	293	92
209-212	245, 374, 375	293, 294	92
210	213		
210, 211	245, 375	Vol. 9	
211	246, 377, 375	11-17	345
212	377	12	287
213	377	12, 13	278
214	248, 377	29	333
215, 216	377		
216	104	Upward Look	
264	102	80	388
292		101	80

Index of Personalities

A

Abbotsworth, E. F.	163
Abednego	371
Abraham	232, 307, 350
Adam	4, 99, 120, 125
Adams, Cyrus	385
Agassi, André	352
Ahab, King	243
Alcott, William	209, 220
Alexander V, Antipope	296
Alexander VI, Pope	151, 298
Anderson, Jacob	163, 170, 173, 174, 189
Anderson, Pr. O. K.	385
Anderson, Dr. R. A.	89, 198
Antiochus Epiphanes	243
Aratas	349
Archer, Dr. Gleason	84, 317
Arphaxad	232
Aschcroft, Attorney-General, John	283
Ashton, Dr. John	114

B

Babbage, Charles	216
Bacchiocchi, Dr. Samuele	141-143, 177
Bacon, Premier Jim	222
Bain, Pr. Donald	385
Bains, Ross	363
Ball, Dr. Bryan	46
Ballenger, Elder Albion	11, 329
Ballis, Dr. Harry	17, 26
Balzak, Prime Minister	270
Barnabas, missionary	350
Barnhouse, Dr. Donald	89, 374
Barritt, Pr. Clive	385
Basham, Pr. Frank	385, 387
Bates, Captain Joseph	96, 97

Bea, Cardinal Agostino	267
Bell, Francine	311
Benedict XIII, Antipope	147, 148, 296
Benson, Elder C. L.	163, 173, 175, 176, 177, 188
Bently, Tony	311
Birch, Dr. Alf	45
Birch, Professor L. G.	226
Bismark, Count Otto von	269, 270
Blair, Senator William	260
Bobby G	314
Bollman, Elder Calvin	163
Bottomley, Dr. Richard	113
Bovio	270
Bradford, Dr. Graeme	many references
Bradley, Ron	214
Brancas	150
Branson, Bruce	202
Branson, Dr. Roy	202
Branson, Elder William	201, 202
Breaden, Pr. Frank	139, 385, 387
Bridget, "St."	147
Brinsmead, Robert	11
Brown, Nathan	94, 352
Bruinsma, Dr. Reinder	288, 289, 293, 295, 298
Bull, Dr. Brian	127
Bullock, Pr. Kenneth	386
Burnett, Sir Macfarlane	197
Burnside, Pr. George	54, 139, 254, 379, 385, 386, 387
Bush Jnr., President George	137, 272, 273, 275, 276, 283, 284
Bush Snr., President George	266

C

Cain	371
Canright, Elder Dudley	11
Carter, Dr. Ron	124

Carver, Dr. Washington	217	Davison, Ellen	143
Cassells, Samuel	262	deBurgh, Professor Patrick	226
Caviness, Dr. Leon	163	deRosa, Dr. Peter	148, 149, 296, 297
Christian, Pr. Clem	385	Devine, Dr. Lester	18, 21, 94, 95, 97, 98
Churchill, Lord Randolf	354		
Churchill, Sir Winston	354	Dollinger, Dr. Johann	142
Clapham, Dr. Noel	26, 42	"Doug"	20, 130, 344
Clare, Dennis	311	Dower, Elder Reggie	211
Clarence the Clown	313	"Downton, Elder Jared"	20, 344
Clark, Dr. Harold	227	Drummond, Henry	363
Clark, General Mark	261	Dunlop, Dugald	130
Claude, Bishop	143	Dunlop, Dr. "Weary"	130
Cleopas	22		
Clifford, Dr. John	11, 385, 387	**E**	
Clinton, President Bill	268	Eastman, Elder William	196
Colonna, Cardinal Otto	128	Eber, the Patriarch	232
Colquhoun, Pr. Peter	254	Eddy, Mary Baker	202, 308, 344
Comstock, Darryl	45	Einstein, Dr. Albert	217
Conradi, Pr. Louis	11	Elijah, the Prophet	7, 307, 350
Constantine, Emperor	143	Elisha, the Prophet	307
Conybeare, William	184	Ely, Professor Richard	260
Cooke, Pr. Austin	17, 42	Enoch, the Patriarch	172, 307
Cornwell, Dr. John	269	Epimendes	349
Couperus, Dr. Molleurus	202	Esaias (see Isaiah)	
Cress, Elder James	34	Eugene IV, Pope	298
Crick, Dr. Francis	197, 229	Eva, Pr. Duncan	10
Crispus	347	Evans, Larry	114, 255
Curie, Madam Marie	218	Evans, Pr. Laurie	12, 19, 72-76
Curie, Pierre	218	Eve	99, 125, 357
Curvier, George	215	Ezekiel, the Prophet	67, 307, 372, 373
Cyrus, King	181, 182	Ezra, the Scribe	133
D		**F**	
Daniel, the Prophet	4, 22, 67, 69, 307, 371	Faraday, Michael	216
		Felix, Governor	219
Daniells, Elder Arthur	many references	Ferret, Rick	26
		Flemming, Sir Ambrose	217
D'Aubigne, Dr. Merle	130, 131, 138, 326	Fletcher, Dr. Charles	222
		Fletcher, Pr. William	11
David, King	307, 350, 371	Folkenburg, Elder Robert	302
Davidson, Dr. Richard	116, 117, 120, 122	Ford, Dr. Desmond	many references
		Ford, Gillian	365
Davis, President Jefferson	78	Frame, Pr. Robert	380-382, 385
Davis, Marian	165, 168, 195	French, Pr. Thomas	164

Index of Personalities

French, Pr. Wayne	311
Froome, Dr. Le Roy	26, 89, 198

G

Gadatas	182
Gaius	347
Gamaliel	8
Garne, Pr. Geoffrey	54
Gibbons, Edwin	148
Gillett, Ezra	138
Gladstone, Prime Minister William	270
Gobryas	182
Goldstein, Clifford	68
Goodwin, Dr. H. Thomas	124
Gorbachev, President Mikhail	267
Graham, Billy	363
Graham, Senator	275
Graham, Sylvester	209, 220
Grant, President Ulysses	264
Graybill, Dr. Ron	26, 30, 58, 100, 145-147, 149-152, 154, 344
Gregory VII, Pope	146, 268
Gregory XII, Pope	147, 149, 296
Gregory XIII, Pope	157
Greive, Pr. Robert	11
Gungadoo, Dr. Stenio	62
Guy, Dr. Fritz	26, 123

H

Hackett, Elder Willis	108
Hammill, Dr. Richard	53
Hankinson, Pr. Denis	207, 254, 255
Harker, Dr. Barry	18
Hartley, John	117
Hasel, Dr. Frank	128
Hayward, Dr. James	363, 364
Heft, Bishop	311
Heggie, Pr. Ronald	385
Heisler, Elder Robert	112
Henkel, M.	122
Henry IV, King	268
Henry, Pr. A. R.	189
Herod, King	5, 7
Herodias	5
Herodotus, Historian	181, 182
Herschel, Astronomer	160
Hitler, Chancellor Adolf	265, 282
Holbrook, Dr. Frank	25
Holmes, Elder C. E.	184
Hook, Dr. Milton	26
Hoover, President Herbert	264
Horrobin, Dr. David	224
House, Elder B. H.	164
Howell, Elder Warren	164, 170
Howson, J. S.	184
Hoyt, Dr. Fred	26
Hugon, Augusto	141
Huldah, the Prophet	307
Hull, Elder	179
Huss, John, the Reformer	26, 44, 58, 59, 94, 100, 103, 138, 145-152, 296
Hussein, President Sadam	137

I

Innocent III, Pope	151, 157
Isaiah, the Prophet	172, 307

J

Jackson, James	209, 220
Jacobson, Pr. Arthur	385
James, the Brother of Jesus	348
Janovius	147
"Jean"	20, 130, 344, 348
Jenkins, Lord Roy	354
Jeremiah, the Prophet	4, 79, 307, 350, 373
Jeremie, Metropolitan	302
Jerome	44
Job	279
John, the Apostle	8, 22, 41, 67, 82, 267, 270, 307, 348
John, the Baptist	4, 6, 7, 37, 171, 307, 336, 359
John, King	151
John XXIII, Antipope	146-151, 294, 295
John XXIII, Pope	261

John Paul II, Pope	268-270, 277, 291, 293, 3444, 345	Lister, Baron of Lyme Regis	217
Johnsson, Dr. William	18, 26	Lockyer, Colin	16
Jonah, the Prophet	335	Longacre, Elder Charles	164
Jones, Elder A. T.	24, 86-88	Loughborough, Elder J. N.	97, 324
Jones, Pr. Llewellyn	385	Luke, the Physician	82, 83
Jorgenson, Pr. Alfred	385	Luther, Martin	92, 103

M

Joule, James	187, 216		
Judd, Pr. Claude	385	McAdams, Dr. Don	23, 26, 27, 58, 138
Judson, Adroniram	159	McCartney, Paul	352
		McElhaney, Elder James	227

K

		McMahon, Dr. Don	203, 208, 212
Karlow, Dr. Edwin	115, 123, 125, 126, 128	Magi, the	349
		Magnusson, Dr. Eric	385
Keith, Pr. J. B.	380, 385	Malachi, the Prophet	307
Kellogg, Dr. J. H.	86-88, 91, 176, 204, 209, 329	Malichev, Colonel Uri	273
		Mann, Horace	221
Kelvin, Baron of Largs	217	Manners, Pr. Bruce	many references
Kent, Pr. J. W.	379, 380, 383, 385-387	Mansfield, Professor Bruce	296
Kern, Elder Milton	88, 164, 175, 227	Marconi, Marchese Gugielmo	218
Knight, Pr. Arthur	385	Mark, the Evangelist	81-83
Knight, Dr. George	26	Marks, Raglan	385
Knopper, Pr. Jan	94, 95, 97, 98, 154	Marsh, Dr. Frank	226, 227
Koch, Dr. Robert	222	Martin, Pr. Elwyn	385
Koranteng-Pipim, Dr. Samuel	25	Martin, Dr. Malachi	266, 267
Kubo, Dr. Sakae	26	Martin, Dr. Walter	89, 374
		Martin V, Pope	147

L

		Mary, Christ's mother	294
Lacantius	127	Matthew, the Apostle	82, 83
Lacey, Elder Herbert	39, 162, 164, 177, 178, 183	Maury, Matthew	365
		Maximillian, Archduke Emperor	264
Laden, Osama bin	271, 274	Maxwell, James	217
Land, Dr. Gary	15, 202	Medinger, Alan	109
Langenbrunner, Norman	366	Melady, Ambassador Thomas	260
Larson, Betty	32	Menander	349
Larson, Pr. Ralph	32	Mendel, Gregor	217
Lawson, Dr. Ron	26	Meshach	371
"Lazarus", the poor man	336	Meyers, Hilton	193
Lee, Elder	169	Milicius	146
Lee, Pr. Gordon	253	Miller, William	60, 325
Lefant, Jacques	138	Moe, Pr. Rex	385
Leo X, Pope	157	Molnar, Almedeo	141
Leo XIII, Pope	291, 293	Monroe, President James	264
Lewis, C. S.	127	Morgan, Dr. Douglas	208, 209

Index of Personalities

Morse, Samuel 216
Moses, the Prophet 4, 22, 97, 116, 124, 172, 307, 321, 336, 341, 350, 367
Moulds, Pr. Lennel 210
Moyes, Dr. Gordon 363
Muay, Matthew 216

N

Nachon 340
Naden, Pr. L. C. 211, 385
Nahum, the Prophet 307
Nathan, the Prophet 307
Nancarrow, James 131
Navarro-Vallis, Joaquin 277
Newman, Dr. Albert 143
Nichol, Elder F. D. 131, 184, 202
Nick, Dr. Kevin 124
Nimrod 232, 371
Nitocris, Queen 181
Nix, Dr. James 15, 40, 41, 202
Noah, the Prophet 4, 232, 307, 367
Nostradamus 277
Numbers, Dr. Ronald 26, 27, 132, 201-203, 209, 220, 221, 328, 331, 332

O

Oliver, Dr. Barry 18, 61, 243
Olivira, Pr. Enoch 210
Olson, Bro. 183
Olson, Dr. Robert 30, 154, 156, 344
Olson, Attorney William 284

P

Palmerston, Prime Mnister, the Third Viscount Henry 78
Parmenter, Pr. Keith 385
Parsons, D. A. 164
Parr, Pr. Robert 385
Pasteur, Louis 216
Patrick, Dr. Arthur many references
Paul, the Apostle 29, 38, 58, 60, 79, 80, 101, 327, 333, 335, 347-350
Paulien, Dr. Jon 15, 16, 18, 29
Paulsen, Dr. Jan 113, 115, 212
Pavlov, Petrovich 218
Paxton, Geoffrey 11
Peleg, the Patriarch 232
Pennington, Dr. David 205, 206
Pepi, the Penguin 313
Perez, Pr. Rafael 291
Peter, the Apostle 8, 81, 82, 267, 304, 343, 348, 350
Petersen, Pr. Paul 12, 15, 62-71
Pfandl, Dr. Gerhard 123, 361
Pfeiffer, Dr. Carl 224
Pierson, Elder Robert 10, 25, 51, 54, 129, 168
Pius V, Pope 157
Pius IX, Pope 47, 155
Polk, President James 264
Powell, General Colin 275, 276
Prescott, Elder W. W. 76, 86, 160, 164, 177, 182, 188-192
Price, Dr. George McCready 364
Puni, Pr. Erika 62

R

Ramik, Attorney Vincent 57
Rea, Elder Walter 25-27, 132
Read, Pr. W. E. 89, 198
Reagan, President Ronald 261, 268
Rees, Sir Martin 230
Reid, Harold 385
Riberra, Francisco 63
Richards Snr, Elder H. M. S. 76
Robertson, Lord George 273
Rodriguez, Dr. Angel 339
Roennfeldt, Dr. Ray many references
Roosevelt, President Franklin 264
Rudin, Rabbi 261
Russell, Charles 202, 308

S

Salah, the Patriarch 232
Salom, Dr. Alwyn 386
Salome 5
Samuel, the Prophet 350
Schwartz, Dr. Richard 202

Self, Caroline	32	Thompson, Dr. Alden	25, 27
Self, William	32	Thompson, George	165
Shadrach	371	Thompson, William (see Kelvin, Baron)	
Shakespeare, William	382	Timm, Alberto	210
Shea, Dr. Willliam	64, 69	Tolhurst, Pr. Athal	386
Shelby, Senator	275	Tolhurst, Pr. Leonard	386
Shem, the Patriarch	232	Townend, Pr. Calvyn	254
Shull, C. A.	164, 180	Trall, Russell	220
Sigismund, Emperor	147	Truman, President Harry	261
Skeodowska, Marja (see Curie, Madam)		Turner, Dr. Laurence	27
Smith, Dr. Adam	182		
Smith, Dr. Dunbar	3, 4	**U**	
Smith, Joseph	202, 308	"Uncle Sam"	260
Smith, Louis	184	Unruh, Elder T. E.	89
Smith, Elder Uriah	58, 75	Uttley, Pr. Stewart	386
"Smithurst, Dr. Harold"	20, 101, 162, 234, 324, 344-350	Uzzah	339, 340
Snyder, Elder Dave	45		
Sorenson, Christian	164, 165, 170, 177	**V**	
		Valentine, Dr. Gilbert	27
		Van Dolson, Dr. Leo	25
Spencer, Dr. Lee	124	Veltman, Dr. Fred	56
Spicer, Elder W.A.	169	Vlk, Cardinal	302
Stacey, Brenton	62	Voerman, Pr. Jan	150, 152
Standish, Pr. Colin	many references	Vogel, Pr. Ken	62
Standish, Darcy	90, 130		
Standish, Hilda	90, 130	**W**	
Standish, Attorney James	284	Waggoner, Elder Ellet	24, 91
Standish, Pr. Russell	many references	Wakenham, W. H.	165, 176
Standish, Samuel	30	Waldo, Peter	142, 143
Standish, Dr. Timothy	114, 362, 363	Waldoff, Bro	165, 173
Stankovic, Robert	16	Warfield, Benjamin	363
Stanley, Pr. Chester	255	Washington, President George	264
Stanley, Pr. Raymond	386	Watson, Dr. James	197, 229
Stephanus	347	Wenceslas, King	150
Stewart, Dr.	328, 329	Wesley, John	127
Stott, John	363	Westmoreland, General	274
Surburg, Raymond	122	White, Elder Arthur	55, 88, 131, 203, 329
Sylvester I, Pope	143		
		White, Sister Ellen	many references
T		White, Elder William	86, 141, 154, 160, 165, 194, 195, 196, 198
Tait, Asa	164		
Taylor, Elder Clifton	164, 166, 169, 170, 174, 175	Wilcox, Elder Francis	6, 165, 180, 189
		Wilcox, Elder Milton	165
Terreros, Dr. Marco	124-127	Wilkinson, Dr. Benjamin	143

Williams, Flora	165	**X**	
Williams, Frederick	385	Xenophone, the Historian	182
Williams, Roger	260		
Williams, Tony	311	**Y**	
Wilson, Prime Minister Harold	354	Yost, Dr. F. Donald	163
Wilson, Elder Neal	111, 336	Young, Dr. Norman	27, 243, 386
Wilson, Ambassador William	261	Younker, Dr. Randall	123
Wilson, President Woodrow	264		
Wirth, W. G.	165	**Z**	
Wolfgramme, Dr. Robert	27	Zacharias, the Priest	336
Wood, Elder Kenneth	53	Zbynek, Archbishop	150
Wright, Orville	218	Zechariah, the Prophet	67, 307
Wright, Wilbur	218	"Zeus"	312
Wycliffe, Reformer John	103, 151	Zwingli, Reformer Ulrich	103
Wylie, Dr. James	138, 140, 146-149		

BOOKS AUTHORED BY COLIN AND RUSSELL STANDISH

1979	**Adventism Vindicated**	

1979 **Adventism Vindicated**
A Biblical and Spirit of Prophecy rebuttal of the New Theology

1983 **The Sacrificial Priest**
[Adventism Unveiled]
An exposition of Christ's High Priestly Ministry.

1984 **Adventism Proclaimed**
The three angels' messages together with the loud cry message explained

1984 **Adventism Imperiled**
True Seventh-day Adventist education, containing relevant Spirit of Prophecy quotations.

1984 **God's Solution for Depression, Guilt and Mental Illness**
[Adventism Jeopardized]
[Family Crisis, God's Solution]
Biblical psychology and family life.

1985 **The Gathering Storm and the Storm Bursts**
[Adventism Challenged, Volumes I and II]
A detailed history of the entry of the New Theology concepts into our church – 1955-1985.

1988 **Keepers of the Faith**
An examination of the 'isms' entering our church throughout our college system.

1988 **Youth Do You Dare**
A call to young people to follow truth and righteousness, and to live morally upright lives. Liberally drawing on true incidents in the lives of young people.

1989 **Deceptions of the New Theology**
An exposition of the doctrinal errors promoted by the New Theology teachings.

1989 **Second Coming – Fervent Hope or Faded Dream**
A biblical examination of the doctrine of the Second Coming of Christ.

1990 **Antichrist is Here**
An historical and biblical evaluation of the Papacy

1992 **Perils of Time Setting**
Erroneous efforts to date various last-day events by use of a futurist interpretation of the seals of Revelation evaluated and discounted.

Books Authored by Colin and Russell Standish

1992   **The Sepulchres are Whited**
Evidence that within the Seventh-day Adventist church God's work has been seriously devaluated and diminished by administrative actions.

1992   **The Road to Rome**
The serious intrusion of Roman Catholic concepts and practices into the Seventh-day Adventist church.

1993   **Modern Bible Translations Unmasked**
A defense of the King James Version of Scripture, together with the pointing out of major defects in the great majority of modern translations.

1993   **Spiritism in the Seventh-day Adventist Church**
Adoption of subtle spiritualistic principles into the faith and practice of Seventh-day Adventists.

1994   **Evangelical Dilemma**
An examination of the major doctrinal errors of Evangelical Protestants

1994   **Organizational Structure and Apostasy**
[The Temple Cleansed]
In view of the dangers of the false denominational organizational structure, more akin to that of Rome than the Scriptures, the inspired counsels on this matter are presented.

1984   **Education for Excellence – the Christian Advantage**
[Adaptation of Adventism Imperiled]
The Christian philosophy of education.

1995   **The Embattled Church**
Spirit of Prophecy counsels set forth to illuminate the course of faithful Seventh-day Adventists when open apostasy and blasphemous worship services enter their local congregations.

1996   **The Mystery of Death**
A biblical presentation of the Seventh-day Adventist understanding of the state of the dead.

1996   **Swarming Independents**
The Bible and Spirit of Prophecy validation of self-supporting work with emphasis upon the facts that the majority of Scripture was written by self-supporting workers and that both John the Baptist and Christ were self-supporting workers; and further, that God has always designed that there would be denominational workers alongside self-supporting workers. This is illustrated in the Old Testament by the priests (denominational workers) and the prophets (self-supporting workers).

1997   **Tithes and Offerings – Trampling the Conscience**
A thorough Bible and Spirit of Prophecy examination of the use of the sacred tithes and offerings.

1998	**Liberty in the Balance**	

1998 **Liberty in the Balance**
An historical and biblical account of religious liberty. The historical examination chiefly centers upon the United Kingdom and the United States.

1998 **The Big Bang Exploded**
A refutation of the theory of evolution together with evidence in support of God's creative power.

1999 **Georgia Sits On Grandpa's Knee**
Stories for children based largely upon the experiences of Russell's three sons in the mission field. (Authored by Russell only).

1999 **The Pope's Letter and Sunday Laws**
A detailed examination of John Paul II's apostolic letter, "Dies Domini", along with a presentation of the three angels' message. A chart demonstrates that the little horn, the man of sin, the antichrist, the beasts of Revelation 13 and 17, Babylon and the whore are all symbolic of the papacy.

1999 **Holy Relics or Revelation**
An evaluation of Ron Wyatt's archaeological discoveries with emphasis on his claim to have discovered the ark of the covenant. This book includes an evaluation of this claimed discovery in relation to the sanctuary message and the new theology.

1999 **Winds of Doctrine**
A Biblical and Spirit of Prophecy analysis of many of the winds of doctrine rampaging through Seventh-day Adventism.

2000 **The Entertainment Syndrome**
The devastating effects of the use of entertainment by our church and the encouragement of worldly practices and competitive sport.

2001 **Two Beasts, Three Deadly Wounds and Fourteen Popes**
New source material, largely from Roman Catholic historians, confirming the fulfillment of Revelation chapter thirteen. The contribution of each of the fourteen popes who have sat on the papal throne since 1798 is detailed

2002 **Grandpa, You're Back!**
Further children's stories concerning Russell's experiences throughout his life (authored by Russell only).

2002 **The Lord's Day – Moral Decay, Evolution and the Threat to Liberty.**
A examination of the Sabbath in Scripture.

2002 **The Perils of Ecumenism**
The evil consequences of the ecumenical movement.

2003 **The Vision and God's Providences**
The history of Hartland Institute 1983-2003 (Authored by Colin only).

2003	**Gwanpa's and Nanny's Home**	

2003 **Gwanpa's and Nanny's Home**
Stories for children aged 3-7, as told through the eyes of Ella, Glenice and Russell's granddaughter. (Authored by Russell only).

2004 **The Rapture and the Antichrist.**
An examination of the Evangelical Protestant understanding of end-time events – Book I.

2004 **The Rapture, The End Times and The Millennium.**
A further examination of the Evangelical Protestant understanding of end-time events.

Note: Titles in square brackets indicate the former title of the book.
All the above books may be ordered from:

Remnant Herald
PO Box 175
KALORAMA
Victoria 3766
Australia

Phone: 03 - 97511932 (Australia)
         613- 97511932 (Overseas)

Fax: 03 - 97511648 (Australia)
         613 - 97511648 (Overseas)

Email: remnantherald@optusnet.com.au

OR

Hartland Publications
PO Box 1
Rapidan
Virginia 22733
USA

Phone: 540-6723566 (USA)
         1-540-6723566 (Overseas)

Fax: 540-6723568 (USA)
         1-540-6723568 (Overseas)

Email: flyons@hartland.edu

About the Authors

COLIN AND RUSSELL STANDISH were born in Newcastle, Australia, in 1933. They both obtained their teaching diplomas from Avondale College in 1951. They were appointed to one-teacher Seventh-day Adventist primary (elementary) schools in rural areas of New South Wales, each teaching for three years.

Both in 1958 completed a major in history and undertook an honors degree in psychology at Sydney University in the field of learning theory. Colin continued in this area, obtaining his Master of Arts degree with honors in 1961, and his Doctor of Philosophy in 1964. In 1967 he completed a Masters Degree in Education.

Russell graduated as a physician in 1964. Six years later he was admitted to the Royal College of Physicians (UK) by examination. He was elevated to the Fellowship of the Royal Colleges of Physicians in Edinburgh (1983) and Glasgow (1984).

In 1965, Colin was appointed Chairman of the Education Department at Avondale College. Subsequently he held the posts of Academic Dean at West Indies College (1970), President of West Indies College (1970-73), Chairman of the Department of Psychology, Columbia Union College (1974), President of Columbia Union College (1974-78), Dean of Weimar College (1978-83). He was invited to become the foundational president of Hartland Institute, which consists of a degree-issuing college, a wellness center, publishing house and a world mission division.

Russell as a Consultant Physician (Internist) has held the posts of Deputy Medical Superintendent of the Austin Hospital, University of Melbourne (1975-1978), President of the Bangkok Adventist Hospital (!979-1984), Medical Director at Enton Medical Centre, England (1984-1986), President of Penang Adventist Hospital (1986-1989), and Director of Health Services in the Southeast Asia Union (1989-1992). Since 1992 he has been speaker and editor for *Remnant Herald*.

Both Colin (1970) and Russell (1980) were ordained to the Seventh-day Adventist ministry. Both have been appointed delegates to General Conference Sessions – Colin in 1975 and Russell in 1980 and 1990. They have co-authored forty books.